Contents

In Search of Cinema

Writings on International Film Art

BERT CARDULLO

FOREWORD BY RICHARD GILMAN

McGill-Queen's University Press
Montreal & Kingston · London · Ithaca

© McGill-Queen's University Press 2004
ISBN 0-7735-2706-0 (cloth)
ISBN 0-7735-2707-9 (paper)

Legal deposit second quarter 2004
Bibliothèque nationale du Québec

Printed in Canada on acid-free paper

This book has been published with the help of a grant from the University
of Michigan.

National Library of Canada Cataloguing in Publication

Cardullo, Bert
    In search of cinema : writings on international film art /
    Bert Cardullo ; foreword by Richard Gilman.

    Includes bibliographical references and index.
    ISBN 0-7735-2706-0 (bnd)
    ISBN 0-7735-2707-9 (pbk)

    1. Motion pictures – Reviews.   2. Motion pictures – History.   I. Title.

    PN1995.C37 2004   791.43'09   C2003-906892-7

Typeset in 10½/13 Baskerville by True to Type

My thanks to the editors of the following magazines for permission
to reprint material originally contained in their pages:
The Hudson Review, Antioch Review, New Orleans Review, and
Literature/Film Quarterly.

Of Films, Critics, and Chronicity

RICHARD GILMAN

There are two kinds of film critics. The first kind works for the daily or weekly press, television, or radio and reviews mostly the mass production of Hollywood studios. The format of their reviews as well as the short deadlines under which they must operate largely accounts for the fleetingness of their work. These constraints explain why, short of a few personal impressions, such writers generally limit themselves to a synopsis of the film in question and a brief overview of the quality of its acting. They barely have time and space for an in-depth analysis of the main themes and characters, let alone of the artistic merits of a film's cinematography. Their work is essentially journalistic and is as much intended for mass consumption as are the movies these people write about. Such an endeavor can be deemed a part of the post-production process in which every commercial movie must now engage to be potentially successful. It aims at luring the largest possible number of viewers into the movie theatres and thus ends up being – paradoxically – uncritical. This category of film critics, of course, is that of reviewers, who are anything but critics. Ultimately, they are serving the interests of the Hollywood industry, whose merits are measured in monetary terms, more than they are serving those of their readers. Their work is therefore – to repeat – of the transient kind, as is the cinema with which it deals, or, to use Cardullo's term, both are "disposable."

Bert Cardullo belongs to the second category of critics: that of film chroniclers, of film essayists, who write for a more discriminating readership – not simply one of academic connoisseurs or film buffs, but a readership of men and women for whom the cinema isn't limited to excitement through sensation or special effects. For Bert Cardullo and his readers, cinema is not merely a form of entertainment like baseball or bowling, but also an art form *sui generis*, the principal mode of aesthetic expression of the twentieth and now the twenty-first century, which ranks as high as any of the fine arts – indeed, the French call it *le Septième Art* ("the Seventh Art"). As Cardullo himself declares in his introduction,

I write about cinema ... because I believe that it is the true *Gesamtkunstwerk* (or total work of art) and therefore has greater expressive capacity than any other art; because I agree with the pronouncement that, as the one technology that can be absolutely humanist in its outcome, which can embody all the technological impulses, cravings, and interests of our age in the employ, not of machinery, but of the human spirit, film was *the* art form of the twentieth century and continues to be in the twenty-first; and because I think that criticism of film, still the least appreciated of the arts, matters.

But Cardullo's criticism is not simply intellectual, as the films he writes about are often – wrongly – believed to be; his is a compassionate, heartfelt criticism that delves into the same, innermost human wellsprings as the films it sets out to examine, without ever falling into a cheap, sentimental, or patronizing posture.

Or a cynical one, for that matter. Indeed, as we begin the twenty-first century, it seems as if contemporary film criticism is distinguished from that of earlier decades by its cynicism about the state of the art of filmmaking. In these politically correct times, the act of criticism is marked more than anything else by the *hutzpah* of our know-it-all critics, who appear to hold criticism in higher regard than the art it purports to criticize. In such a climate, Bert Cardullo's writing on contemporary film is a welcome antidote. As the film chronicler of the prestigious quarterly *The Hudson Review* for the past fifteen years, Cardullo has displayed admirable taste and restraint in his choice of films for discussion. Unlike reviewers for daily newspapers and weekly periodicals, Cardullo is in a sense constrained by the limitations of his medium – he writes about only eight films per year. I firmly believe, however, that in criticism as in most art forms, limitations create opportunities for expression, and in the case of the film criticism of Bert Cardullo, this is certainly true. For he shows his steadfastness of purpose and strength of character in the films he chooses to write about. Cardullo rarely writes about mainstream movies that he dislikes, instead focusing on lesser-known independent and foreign films in order to bring them the greater attention he believes they deserve. By writing about these "smaller" films, and for the most part ignoring the machine-like output of Hollywood, Cardullo achieves the most laudable aims of multiculturalism without engaging in cultural politics.

Yet there is an unmistakable edge to Cardullo's work: the razor-sharp language of the critic-as-provocateur. He demands our attention, but unlike many provocateurs he supports his arguments about films with hard facts, placing each motion picture in a larger artistic and social context so that its outlines come into sharp relief and its substance becomes palpable. Whether we accept his arguments does not matter – his ideas challenge us to meet them, and the films they illumine, on a higher intellectual plane, making us better moviegoers in the process.

Bert Cardullo has collected in the present volume some of his finest work, work that is worthy of his illustrious predecessor at *The Hudson Review*, Vernon Young. Cardullo's chronicles explore the world of film from all possible angles, including the geographical one. Thus over the years, his pen has taken his readers to England, France, Canada, China, Italy, Spain, Norway, Sweden, Denmark, India, Russia, and, naturally, the United States. But it has also invited *The Hudson Review*'s subscribers to more "remote" regions of the globe, such as Mexico, Israel, Iran, Taiwan, Finland, Holland, Iceland, Lebanon, Cuba, Scotland, Ireland, New Zealand, Japan, Brazil, Belgium, Lapland, and Burkina Faso – all cinematic midgets in Hollywood terms. Cardullo's columns are always, and unmistakably, minutely documented. Being no stranger to some of the countries whose film production he writes about, Cardullo has a fine eye for detail, which makes his chronicles impeccably correct from a socio-geographical point of view. His writing is also crisp and clear, unhampered by cinematic, theoretical, or dogmatic jargon. In all respects, it is superb prose.

Among his many critical strategies, Cardullo frequently examines films in the context of film history in order to evaluate them not just as ideas or expressions of the moment, but within the larger framework of the history of cinema as well. See what he has to say, for example, about the relationship of such "faraway" pictures as *West Beirut* (1998) and *What Time Is It There?* (2001) to the French New Wave in general and to the films of François Truffaut in particular. Or look at his observation about the inverse relationship of such French pictures as *Late August, Early September* (1999) and *Autumn Tale* (1998), with their deployment of well-articulated thought as a form of action, to the American Western. Cardullo notes a different debt in the case of Neil LaBute's *Your Friends and Neighbors* (1998): the borrowing, in an American film, of the machinery of symmetrical plotting and the air of sexual ruthlessness from the late seventeenth-century British comedy of manners. He even identifies the Restoration play from which scenes are rehearsed during the movie: William Wycherley's *The Country Wife*. Each of Cardullo's review-essays thus not only suggests new and recent films for viewing, it also sends readers racing back to the classics section of their local video stores – or their public library – to become (re)acquainted with older works of cinematic art.

In writing about what used to be called foreign films, Cardullo often places his argument in the context of the native culture of the director or the cultural setting of the picture. His analysis of *The Circle* (2000), for instance, makes clear that without the following information (which he provides), much of this Iranian film would be puzzling if not incomprehensible:

Women in Iran are not allowed to smoke in public, and they may not ride in a car driven by a man to whom they are not related or otherwise travel unaccompanied by an adult male relative. They can't check into a hotel by themselves; do not have the right to divorce a man, and, if divorced by him, do not get custody of their children; and cannot receive an abortion without the consent of a father or husband. Moreover, women cannot move outdoors or enter certain buildings without putting on a *chador*, part of the "uniform" that covers up their hair, their bodies, even their faces. And they can't walk alone at night without it being assumed that they are soliciting sex. (Ironically, prostitution is one of the only ways in which an Iranian woman can make an independent living.)

Evidence of additional "cultural contextualizing" can be found in Cardullo's telling comment on four thematically related films from his own culture: *Bad Manners* (1997), *Very Bad Things* (1998), *Happiness* (1998), and *Your Friends and Neighbors*. He calls them products of "the age of hedonism" – of ego-gratification as well as egoism. And that ego-gratification comes primarily in the form of sex ... [Such] American movies about American moral shallowness or sensual debasement are endemic to ... the close of this, the American century." By contrast, Cardullo is quick to point out that one of the reasons the equally North American, but nonetheless Canadian, *The Sweet Hereafter* (1997) achieves success is its lack of egoistic American star-power. In its place, we find Ian Holm "complemented by a largely Canadian ensemble that has followed the thirty-eight-year-old Egoyan through his ever-growing career ... I can pay these actors no higher compliment than to say that each of them truly knows what the word 'ensemble' means: not only to work together on a film, ... but also to remain together over several films, so as to enhance one's own – and thus the pictures' – artistry."

Speaking of artistry, Cardullo never forgets to scrutinize the aesthetic quality of the particular movie he writes about, inasmuch as it supports this picture's thematic concerns, without ever encumbering his criticism with abstruse technicalities foreign to the non-specialists in his audience. In this respect, Cardullo's pen does film art as much justice as it does the reader's intelligence and taste. Witness the following descriptions of the cinematography or visual symbology in the aforementioned *Sweet Hereafter* and the Iranian *Taste of Cherry* (1997), respectively:

Snow in *The Sweet Hereafter* ... comes to symbolize ... its own paradox: that snow combines the ideas of ethereality and materiality, confinement and liberation, numbness and sensation, vista-vision and purblindness. These ideas are also contained in the narrative, so nature felicitously serves art in this instance, not the other way around.

Kiarostami clearly shot the picture in autumn to take advantage of the metaphysical significance of the season of dying. The hills outside Tehran are therefore parched, the grass dead ..., and everything Homayoun Payvar's camera shoots seems yellow-brown: the dirt mounds, dirt roads, ... the dusty air, even the occasional tree or bush. The sun has been here, but this is not a sunny place; the weather may not be cold but the subject is chilly enough.

Perhaps most striking about Cardullo's criticism is less his knowledge of cinematographic means than his understanding of arts other than the cinema – an understanding regularly revealed by his close analyses of the adaptation of novels to film. Not content to prefer novels merely because they are literature, Cardullo sees *The Sweet Hereafter* and *Affliction* (1998), for example, as improvements over their source material, sorting through each director's alterations in plot and narrative form to uncover his unique cinematic vision. This critic thereby unearths aspects of moviemaking that many critics miss: the scripting of films from pre-existent sources; the ways in which a film can express a narrative voice distinct from that of the original novel; and the numerous other thematic and visual as well as technical choices a writer-director makes in transferring a piece of fiction to the screen.

In undertaking his mission, Cardullo is doing more than merely explaining or analyzing movies: he is serving as a proponent for a type of filmmaking. While a lot of critics are content to champion particular pictures for inconsistent or inexplicable reasons, Cardullo has developed an aesthetic that he defends vigorously with each and every film chronicle. The catholicity of his taste shouldn't hide the fact that he does have particular ideas about how good films work, what good directors and designers do, and what the art of screen acting is all about. He recognizes that even the most realistic or naturalistic motion picture must selectively shape reality, and he searches for films that utilize camerawork, editing, space, color, and music to create a unique vision of the world – one that is free of the sentimentality and melodrama of most Hollywood movies. That original, independent vision may be marked by something so simple as the use of *temps mort*, or "dead time," to illustrate what goes unsaid after a dramatic moment (as in *The Straight Story* [1999]); or by the use of separate matching shots of each participant in a conversation, instead of a single shot of both characters, in order to affect our perception of these characters' relationship (as in *A Taste of Cherry*).

Cardullo's notions about good acting are flexible; he merely, and intelligently, requires that the performances fit the nature of the script and the film. Though he appreciates the use of non-professional actors in the Iranian cinema, for one, he is open-minded enough to champion the virtuoso performance of Nick Nolte in *Affliction*, despite his reservations about the larger body of Nolte's mostly forgettable work. And he recognizes the appropriate contribution of character actors like Richard Farnsworth (*The Straight Story*), Dylan Baker (*Happiness*), Stênio Garcia (*Me, You, Them* [2000]), and Stellan Skarsgård (*Aberdeen* [2000]) to their character-centered films. Throughout, Cardullo remains vehemently opposed to the type of Hollywood movie that sacrifices its thematic and aesthetic integrity to the blatant display of glamor and spectacle or that panders to the lowest common audience-denominator by putting mawkishness or melodrama before subtlety of idea and technique. Nonetheless, he acknowledges the important influence Hollywood exerts on foreign cultures, even if that "titanic" influence sometimes produces the musical score that mars *The Road Home* (2000). And he willingly recognizes the worthy, albeit rare, Hollywood film that surmounts the barriers inherent in the Hollywood system (as so sterlingly seen in his review of David Lynch's *Straight Story*).

Ultimately, he challenges us to re-examine the ways in which we view films. Whether he is asking us to work past our superficial satisfaction with the appearance of yet another movie by Pedro Almodóvar or forcing us to look beyond our initial gratitude for the seriousness of *Amer-*

ican Beauty (1999) and *The Virgin Suicides* (2000) in order to see their grave shortcomings, Cardullo is professing in the best sense of the word. A professor of theatre and drama when he is not writing film criticism (although he would say the two pursuits feed off each other), he strenuously advances his view of the cinema, always teaching yet always making discoveries of his own as he confronts the reader. By putting forth his argument with as much evidence as he can muster, he forces us to defend our views in the same way – that is, to be active, thinking, sensitive audience members.

At the same time, there is something about Cardullo's relaxed but stylish prose that suggests a café conversation over a cup of coffee and a cigarette. A heated conversation, to be sure, perhaps fueled by a bit too much caffeine and nicotine, but a friendly one in the end. It is a testament, I think, to his accepting and optimistic worldview that Cardullo professes his fondness for films of all cultures, of manifold political and social complexion, rather than exercising his considerable critical muscle on easy targets for denigration. Make no mistake: Bert Cardullo is an American citizen, but he is also a citizen of the world and thus what I would call a universal, not just a national (or worse, provincial), critic. His chronicles open up the world of cinema (which, believe it or not, isn't limited to Planet Hollywood) to his readers. They tend to make films that are not readily accessible more comprehensible, and thus more watchable, to what Europeans and Canadians regard as the self-centered American moviegoing audience. As such, Cardullo's review-essays are an opening onto the world at large.

Indeed, his understanding of international cinema is synonymous with an understanding of humanity in the broadest sense of the word. That, above all, is why I feel that Cardullo's critical mission deserves our utmost respect and most profound admiration, particularly in so relativistic, even nihilistic, an age as the current one. It is a pleasure to read his work and an honor to introduce it to his readers. They may conclude, as I have done, that the film criticism of Bert Cardullo will last as long as the films it immortalizes.

Will Cardullo himself last, however? That is, after fifteen years, will he continue to write the kind of film criticism we have come to expect from him? It should come as no surprise that several film critics – quite unlike their counterparts in music, art, or even drama – have abandoned their jobs in a loudly demonstrative way, washing their hands of the whole business of criticism in public. In the mid-1940s, for instance (prior to the eruption of Italian neorealism and the French New Wave, it must be said), the *New Yorker* writer Wolcott Gibbs spent nine months reviewing movies, then wrote a piece called "The Country of the Blind," which began, "The purpose of this essay is to explain, as clearly as I can and while certain memories are still green, why it seems to me that the cinema resists rational criticism almost as firmly as a six-day bicycle race, or perhaps love." Writing about banal American movies – something that Cardullo has never had to do – costing over a million dollars was "a small but fascinating literary comedy." According to Gibbs, such a writer is driven to debase his language by frequent recourse to "a very special vocabulary" ("luminous," "taut," "haunting," "lyric," "riveting," "compassionate," "intriguing," etc.), and is compelled to suggest the presence of elusive, if not non-existent, symbols.

Ten years later, in 1956, Harry Schein, the wealthy engineer who later created the Swedish Film Institute, signed off an eight-year stint as film critic of *Bonniers Litterära Magasin*, Sweden's pre-eminent cultural monthly, with an essay called "Trött på film" (which means both "tired of" and "tired by" films). He was fed up with movies and thought not only that had he said everything he had to say about the medium but that everything of interest had actually already been said when "the film industry was in its infancy and the discoveries were real." To Schein, what was "new in filmic development [was], in fact, the emergence of new generations of film critics rather than the rejuvenation of an artistic medium." Five years after Schein's piece, Jörn Donner, the future movie director and author of a book on Ingmar Bergman, resigned after only two years from his job as film critic for *Dagens Nyheter*, Sweden's leading liberal daily newspaper, and wrote an article dedicated to Schein called "Tired of/by Films II."

In Great Britain, Kenneth Tynan, who had been forced to give up his job as drama critic of *The Observer* upon becoming literary advisor to Laurence Olivier at the National Theatre, spent a couple of years as the paper's movie critic before himself writing an article titled "Tynan's Farewell" in the spring of 1966. His "valediction as a film critic" had three main points. First, a film was fixed long before a critic saw it, so it "cannot be modified by what he says," whereas a play "is still a living organism capable of change and alteration." Second, a critic "can sometimes unearth an audience for a minority movie [the kind Cardullo writes about almost exclusively] but he cannot compete with the vast organizing techniques that ensure a mass audience for a majority movie." Third, even if a critic wanted to influence big-budget pictures, what chance would he have? About as much chance, Tynan suggested, as asking General Motors to manufacture brooms instead of cars.

Gibbs, Schein (followed by Donner), and Tynan make valid points, and from time to time I am sure Cardullo shares their doubts. It is only the complacent hack in the tabloid press who is never touched by his own possible incapacity, irrelevance, or manipulability. But in time of doubt I myself always remember what John Simon once said about his belief in the importance of critics and about having his faith in his own judgment restored every spring when the movie industry revealed its tastes by way of the Academy Awards.

Simon also wrote with persuasive eloquence about the critic's role in the introduction to a 1981 collection of his reviews, *Reverse Angle*, the following portion of which sits framed above Bert Cardullo's desk:

What is film criticism all about? Praise for our product, says the industry. Recognition or, failing that, constructive suggestions, say the filmmakers. Reliable guidance, says the public. All of those things, say the reviewers, except, of course, praise only for good products. None of these things principally, say critics. Critics are after something harder and more elusive: pursuing their own reactions down to the rock bottom of their subjectivity and expressing them with the utmost artistry, so that what will always elude the test of objective truth will at least become a kind of art: the art of illumination, persuasion, and good thinking as well as good writing. The industry is not to be indulged, any more than the filmmaker is to be told how he should make movies: the one would be dishonest, the other presumptuous. The public, to be sure, is to be guided, but not in the simplistic way it hopes for.

It is not for the critic to do the reader's thinking for him; it is for the critic merely to do his own thinking for the reader's benefit. This may seem like a slight difference, but it is in fact tremendous.

Even as I write, Bert Cardullo continues "merely" to do his own thinking, to his readers' eternal benefit. And this is one reader who wouldn't want him to stop any time soon.

IN SEARCH OF CINEMA

First Principles

To my knowledge, Robert Warshow was the first American critic to write film chronicles, or quarterly considerations of new movies, as opposed to daily, weekly, or even monthly reviews. This put him, not on the front lines of criticism, but at a forward observation point – behind the front lines but ahead of the rear guard, which consists of the moviegoing public and would later include scholars and theorists from the academy. Warshow did not live long enough to make the film chronicle a mainstay of either the aptly named *Partisan Review*, for which he wrote, or other literary quarterlies, but even had he lived there might have been resistance to the idea of serious consideration of film in the pages of literary magazines. The evidence for this con-clusion is the number of quarterly critics since Warshow's death. I can think of only three: Charles Thomas Samuels, who wrote for *The Amer-ican Scholar* and, like Warshow, died before his fortieth birthday; Ver-non Young, who wrote for *The Hudson Review* from 1955 to 1986; and Gilberto Perez, the sometime film critic for *The Yale Review*. Even the monthlies have their reservations about film criticism. When I pro-posed a regular column to *The New Criterion* in 1986, its editor was incredulous: take the movies seriously, in the pages of this highbrow journal?

I succeeded Vernon Young at *The Hudson Review* in 1987, and a num-ber of the columns contained in this, my fourth collection of movie criticism, were first published by that illustrious journal, albeit in much abbreviated form. Why write for a quarterly rather than a daily news-paper or a weekly magazine? The reasons should be obvious: more space in which to express one's views and more time to decide just what those views are, both of which are conducive to thoughtful, detailed considerations of films deemed important in their own right, or for the insights these films offer about the development of a major director or into the state of the cinema as an art form. Charles Thomas Samuels once wrote that "most movie criticism is merely inept, without aesthetics, standards of judgment, or critical vocabulary. Between the effusions of the film buffs and the misunderstandings of newspaper reviewers, there is little to choose" (xvii). Samuels chose Stanley Kauffmann, John Simon, and Dwight Macdonald, the best "front line" critics of his day, the first two writing for weeklies and the third for a monthly. But as good as these three were (and, in the cases of Kauffmann and Simon, still are), they were unable to write at length about a film, let alone several films, unless they used two successive columns or published a long essay somewhere else – a practice pioneered by James Agee in the 1940s.

Nonetheless, their definition of the critic's functions coincided with Samuels': (1) to analyze the theme of a film and to judge the quality of its ideas, technical execution, and individual contributions (for example, acting and cinematography); (2) to relate the film to other works by the same filmmaker; and (3) to relate it to other directors' films and the history of cinema. Implicit in these functions is not only a belief in this relatively young form – 100 years old as of 1995 – as art but also a thorough knowledge of the art form. Just as critics of art and music approach their work with erudition and knowledge in their fields, so film critics must approach their work with a thorough background in film. Contemporary films, with their complexities of style, technique, and subject matter, yield far more readily to analysis if the critic has done his homework. The literary critic is better equipped to write about a complex novel like Thomas Mann's *Dr Faustus* after having read the earlier works of the novelist. Similarly, film critics are best able to review *Hour of the Wolf* (1968) if they understand its relationship to Bergman's earlier films *Through a Glass Darkly* (1962) and *Persona* (1966).

Moreover, contemporary films contain so many references to the other arts that it is no longer possible (if it ever was) to write about film without some knowledge of music, painting, literature, and theatre. For example, the *commedia dell'arte* tradition of the Italian theatre, with its stock figures and sometimes mimed as well as improvised action, influenced the final sequence of Antonioni's *Blow-Up* (1966). An interpretation of this film would therefore be incomplete without an understanding of this theatrical tradition. Film art such as *Blow-Up*, of course, does not preclude entertainment, but it can never be described merely in terms of its "entertainment value," and this is where film critics part company with film buffs and reviewers.

For me, film art, like any other, must entertain as well as interpret our lives, engage our emotions, respect the intricacies of our characters, and dramatize our present concerns while linking us to both the past and the future. Speaking of past, present, and future, little has been said about film as a medium for tragedy, or what must approximate genuine tragedy in the modern era, precisely because action in film is more of a journey *in the present* than a confrontation based on the past (the usual form of tragedy in drama); the one is filled with possibility or promise, the other with suspense or foreboding. By its very form, film reflects for spectators the belief that the world is a place in which man can leave the past behind and create his own future. I don't mean by this that there aren't tragic possibilities in film – see *Kadosh* (1999) and *Mina Tannenbaum* (1994), for example – just that they are formally different from the tragic inevitabilities we encounter in drama (except where film deliberately takes over the tragic form of drama, as in the faithful adaptation of a play); they are *possibilities* and for this reason do not attract the attention of critics relentlessly following the scent of tragedy as we know it in drama. Tragic characters in the cinema are more often makers of their own destinies in the present than they are victims of the past, and they make those destinies in present *space* as well as in the present tense.

I am attracted to the idea of space as a kind of character or commenter in cinema, and remark upon its use as often as possible in this collection for two reasons: (1) film can make space live, can endow it with meaning, in ways that painting and the theatre (let alone literature) cannot, simply because the camera can select what it wants the eye to see, show it from different angles, and return to it again and again; and (2) few filmmakers exploit this ability of the medium to the fullest, instead treating cinema more as the incarnation of literature, of verbal fictions, and as the fluid extension of plays over space and time, than as the medium of *moving pictures*.

This is not to say that I am an ardent enthusiast of abstract cinema, in which the depiction of people, places, and things is a pretext for the artist's exploration of the geometry of form and space. Abstract cinema has been with us at least since the work of Hans Richter, Viking Eggeling, and Walter Ruttmann in the early 1920s, but, unlike abstract art, it has never gained a wide audience, most likely because film, which can move and talk, seems inextricably bound up with the human form and the "thingness" of this world – with the representation of physical reality – in a way that painting or sculpture does not. We see on screen real people (be they professional actors or not) in real settings, and as a result we search for the common bond between ourselves and them; we seek to know them and their surroundings in order to have them, in their allure and complexity, tell us something about our own lives.

Cinematic *departures* from such traditional notions of character and empathy interest me because this sort of experimentation has been going on wholesale in literature for some time but seems to occur only sporadically in films. The reason again, clearly, is that, unlike literature, film embodies rather than evokes the human figure; and unlike theatre (where such experimentation has a long and continuing tradition), film most often photographs the real world along with the veristic behavior of its inhabitants, instead of attempting to re-fashion that world and reorder that behavior. Surrealistic and expressionistic films are, of course, the exceptions that prove this rule. I don't address any full-blown avant-garde works in *In Search of Cinema*, but I do investigate such experiments in narrative as *The Wind Will Carry Us* (1999) and *What Time Is It There?* (2001), a partial venture into the realm of the fantastic like *Ratcatcher* (1999), that self-reflexive meditation on the process of artistic creation by the title of *Mina Tannenbaum*, and at least one examination of the nature of cinematic illusion: *The Mirror* (1997). Insofar as spiritual or transcendental style in the cinema constitutes a species of abstraction, I examine it in no fewer than three films – *The Straight Story* (1999), *Rosetta* (1999), and *Europe '51* (1952) – and I intimate the existence of such a style in *Under the Sand* (2000) and *The Son's Room* (2001). And insofar as films about children constitute departures from traditional notions of (adult) character, I investigate such departures – made possible, moreover, by the cinema's visual-visceral as opposed to verbal-ratiocinative emphasis – in films as different as *The White Balloon* (1995), *The Children Are Watching Us* (1942), *The Apple* (1998), and *The Color of Paradise* (1999).

In my aesthetic, then, good film comes in many forms, but "goodness" in all those forms is defined, finally, by the skill with which the moviemakers use the resources of the medium to pursue complex, significant human goals. What are those resources that distinguish film from every other art?

1 Film's ability to duplicate the real world.
2 Film's inclusion of other art forms: photography, painting, and sculpture; music, theatre, and dance; fiction, poetry, and drama.

3 Film's ability to explore interiority. Film can go inside human beings
  in a way that a play, for example, cannot: through the voice, through
  the close-up, and through the capacity to display multiple states of
  consciousness (present awareness, memory, dream, and daydream).
  A novel could do this too, of course, but its words would not have the
  immediacy and effect of film, the arresting power of the image.
4 Film's ability, through cutting, to select or isolate factors in a work. It
  is in the nature of the cinematic medium to allow artists to arrange
  space and assign prominence.
5 Film's attributes of spectacle and motion – its ability to move anywhere and show anything.

As Pier Paolo Pasolini has maintained, the resourceful cinema is thus
far more suited to the transmission of myth than either poetry or prose,
because its images are larger than life at the same time as they can
replicate physical reality; because, like myths, dreams, and fairy tales,
film can shift emotional tones just as fluidly as it moves through time
and space; and because, even as myth exists both outside and inside history and arrives at universals through particulars, so does the cinema
transcend a national language of words by means of the international
language of images and transform the reality of those images into an
iconography of the human psyche.

Furthermore, to speak of the representation of human feelings as
opposed to mythic truths, I know of no more compelling way to evoke the
feeling of loneliness than to isolate the human figure within the frame,
silent yet silently speaking both to itself and to the camera that implaca-
bly photographs its presence. Such a scene could not be maintained for
long on the stage, where language is the primary means of communication and hence demands almost immediate utterance; in a painting or
still photograph, only one moment from such a scene could be frozen in
time; and in a novel or poem, words would mediate between us and the
loneliness of the character or narrator, between us and the company of
the lonely. Only on film can we have it both ways, can we have the long
silence that nonetheless speaks through glance, gesture, and spirit at the
same time as it titillates us with the knowledge that yes, in fact, the sound
of silence will eventually be broken by the voice of speech.

HISTORY OF FILM FOR CULTURED AUDIENCES

By the time the movies became a reality, at the end of the nineteenth
century, the intellectual community had clearly demarcated the

differences between highbrow and lowbrow art, between artworks seriously aimed at discerning audiences and those aimed at the unwashed
masses. In the United States, movies were popular entertainment similar in form and function to dime novels, circuses, and the music hall,
and thus not worth either experiencing or commenting upon as far as
intellectuals were concerned. Nevertheless, over the years, a few cultured individuals found in the movies something of human relevance
for the discerning mind.

Vachel Lindsay, an American poet, in 1915 wrote a book-length
study, *The Art of the Moving Picture*, in which he attempted to distinguish the properties of film from those of other arts and to synthesize
the properties of other arts within the one art of cinema. In the following year, Hugo Münsterberg, an eminent psychologist on the fac-
ulty of Harvard, explored the psychological relationship between the
film viewer and the screen image in his book *The Photoplay: A Psychological Study*. Writing at the very beginning of the history of the motion
picture, Münsterberg was aware of the way in which early films
recorded the activities of the world in front of the camera, thereby
performing an educational or instructional, descriptive function. But
he makes an excellent case for the position that the motion picture's
greatest strength lies in its ability to portray human emotions. "To picture emotions must be the central aim of the photoplay," writes Münsterberg (48). He also goes on to suggest that, as in some of the other
arts, the representation of the human heart and mind on film necessarily raises moral issues; for him film narrative presents the opportunity for making moral judgments, on the part of both the moviemaker
and the audience. The truth of the representation must be tested
against the truth of the viewer's own experience of the world. Though,
in one sense, these early books by a poet and a psychologist might be
classed as works of film theory rather than as evaluations of specific
films, they were both written by cultured individuals who were not primarily film scholars or critics. And both felt compelled to argue that,
despite continued neglect by the intellectual community, the cinema
deserved a place alongside the time-honored arts of literature, music,
and painting.

For the most part, Lindsay's and Münsterberg's rhetoric failed to
convince their peers – at least in America. In Europe, on the other
hand, intellectuals had been attracted to filmmaking from the birth of
the medium. (France, for example, had initiated the extensive filming
of classic plays and novels well before the First World War.) So it is not
surprising that all over Europe – in Paris, Berlin, Moscow – during the

1920s, intellectuals and artists talked and wrote about the movies as the equivalent of the other arts. Between the world wars in America, however, intellectuals scarcely noted the existence of the medium. There were, of course, some thoughtful reviews of specific films in major periodicals by critics more commonly given to writing about high-class literature. Edmund Wilson, Aldous Huxley, and Robert E. Sherwood were among the few who did not condescend when they occasionally wrote about the films of the 1920s and 1930s.

Other reviewers who wrote regularly about specific films from the 1930s through the 1950s, in magazines intended for a cultured readership, and who accepted the film as worthy of intellectual scrutiny included Harry Alan Potamkin, Otis Ferguson, and the aforementioned Robert Warshow and James Agee. These writers, though clearly identifiable under the title of "reviewers," also wrote what can be considered genuine criticism, since their perceptions about film included thoughtful references to contemporary ideas in psychology, sociology, politics, and aesthetics that would be understood by a cultured audience. They did not simply recount the plot of a film and say whether they liked it or not but went further in trying to relate their experiences of individual movies to the intellectual concerns of the day.

Robert Warshow, for example, in his 1954 essay titled "The Westerner," about the hero of Western movies, discusses not simply a number of films but also the American fascination with violence. He compares two movie incarnations of that fascination – the urban gangster and the cowboy gunfighter – in great detail, but always in the context of what was then, as now, a great concern in American culture. Just what is this fascination we have with the gun and the use of force to attain our ends? Thus Warshow's movie criticism goes beyond simply reviewing films or identifying the characteristics of a genre figure. He suggests that the educated observer of the time automatically abhorred the images of violence found in popular literature, television, and cinema but, by avoiding an examination of the problem of such violence, allowed the producers of these media free rein. "The celebration of acts of violence is left more and more to the irresponsible: on the higher cultural levels to writers like Céline, and lower down to Mickey Spillane or Horace McCoy, or to the comic books, television, and the movies" (152). Warshow makes an appeal, then, for closer scrutiny – and hence informed acceptance or rejection – by the critical commentator of the artifacts of the age.

Nevertheless, the American intellectual community as a whole did not make film one of its concerns until after World War II. In part

because of the pressure of returning veterans, some of whom had seen
non-Hollywood films while stationed abroad, and in part because of an
increase in experimental or avant-garde filmmaking by members of the
art community who were working in academic departments, film societies sprang up on college campuses all over the country. In addition
to providing inexpensive entertainment to students making do on the
G.I. Bill, the film societies introduced Americans to foreign films like
those from Italy, which attempted to treat postwar problems realisti-
cally, to present life as it was lived and not as it was dramatized or glam-
orized in the well-known, predictable genres of most Hollywood films.
The film societies also filled out their programs with silent movies from
all countries, thereby suggesting the existence of a body of work, a history of early cinema, whose value was sufficient to pass the test of time.
These silents had been preserved because they had enduring aesthetic
and moral value; they were worth viewing because they were still relevant. The experience of watching old movies not for their camp appeal
but for honest intellectual satisfaction invited more organization on
the part of film societies, and soon such random exposure to the classics of world cinema became codified into college courses.

By the late 1950s and early 1960s, a large number of college-edu-
cated Americans had come to realize that movies existed that were not
simply escapist entertainment, but which held possibilities for human
enrichment similar to the possibilities offered by the other, more traditional arts of drama, painting, and literature. The early films of Ingmar Bergman (e.g., *The Seventh Seal*, 1956) and Federico Fellini (e.g.,
La Strada, 1954) were the first to be reviewed and praised by highbrow
critics in prestigious journals. The first films of the French New Wave –
François Truffaut's *The Four Hundred Blows*, Jean-Luc Godard's *Breath-
less*, and Alain Resnais's *Hiroshima, Mon Amour* – won prizes at Cannes
in 1959. Anyone who claimed to be an intellectual, a cultured individual aware of the artistic trends in contemporary life, had to see these
pictures. They were the talk of the town and the campus. Hollywood
films were fit for the lowbrow, the average, run-of-the-mill person, but
these foreign films were deemed high-class art. A circuit of art-house
cinemas that featured such films appeared and distributed them all
over the country. Popcorn, candy, and soda pop were gradually abandoned for espresso and natural foods. People came not to forget their
cares but to think about the difficulties and problems of living in the
nuclear age.

And a lively and informed criticism of these movies began to appear
in print, not only in intellectual magazines like *The New Republic* and

The New Leader but also in hundreds of highly literate books by writers from a wide variety of disciplines, as the intellectual community sought to map out this new area of human study. In 1967 W.R. Robinson, a professor of English, titled his collection of essays – written by poets, novelists, screenwriters, and academics who were not primarily teachers of film – *Man and the Movies*. Covering a plethora of film subjects and personal views, these articles are connected by the notion that film matters deeply to anyone who is concerned with contemporary arts and ideas. In the early 1970s, moreover, several universities sponsored new journals devoted to a wide-ranging, well-practiced criticism, such as *Film Heritage* and *Literature/Film Quarterly*. During the late 1970s and into the 1980s, however – as film studies in the academic world became more specialized, "theoreticized," and thereby legitimized, evolving on many campuses into doctorate-granting departments – fewer writers from other disciplines felt comfortable about making the crossover into movie criticism. Yet the pluralistic, practical approach is still alive and well anywhere and any time generalists, however few in number, decide to analyze the movies.

WRITING ABOUT FILMS
ONE'S AUDIENCE HAS ALREADY SEEN

One of the distinguishing features of critical, as opposed to consumerist, writing about film is the assumption that the reader has seen the film or films under discussion. Even if it appears in a monthly magazine, such an article's primary function is not to guide people to see or not to see the film but rather to comment on a cinematic event that writer and readers have already shared. Presumably, then, the film chosen is one judged to have lasting value. Either it has been around for a while – a classic shown frequently in revival theatres or in film classes – or, if it is a new picture, the writer is hazarding a guess that it will be around in the future. There is the implicit assumption that the writer has seen the film several times, that his judgments and analysis are not vaguely recalled from a single viewing, and that the reader may verify the claims made by the writer by seeing the film again – that is, the reader may disagree with the writer, can return to see the film, and, if inclined to do so, may offer a rebuttal. In short, there is the assumption that the reader and the writer have a common body of experience and knowledge within which a serious critical discussion can take place.

For instance, what Robin Wood wrote about Alfred Hitchcock's *Psycho* (1960) in a 1965 book implied that this film would be seen again and again, not only because it was by Hitchcock but also because it is "one of the key works of our age. Its themes are not new – obvious forerunners include *Macbeth* and Conrad's *Heart of Darkness* – but the intensity and horror of their treatment place them in an age that has witnessed both the discoveries of Freud and the Nazi concentration camps" (113). Wood sees in the film a restatement of a modern cliché: all people have a dark and violent, unconscious part of their being. But he suggests that *Psycho* forces us to feel the reality of such a statement, not just to understand it. He says that the end of the film cannot

remove our sense of complicity. We have been led to accept Norman Bates as a potential extension of ourselves. That we all carry within us somewhere every human potentiality for good and evil, so that we all share in a common guilt, may be, intellectually, a truism; the greatness of *Psycho* lies in its ability, not merely to *tell* us this, but to make us experience it. (112)

It is clear that Wood is serious about this film and expects his readers to be also. And since *Psycho* is still a popular, regularly re-seen movie today, this analysis of the film written in the 1960s is still relevant reading for a richer understanding of its complexities.

I should also point out that writing serious, in-depth criticism about particular films suggests that these films are more difficult than others – that, in fact, they need interpretation. Like many works of modern literature, films that attract intellectual inquiry appear to hide their deeper meanings, to be puzzling to the casual viewer, who needs the guidance of a critic in order to discover the truths lying beneath the surface. In a certain sense, then, the films chosen for analysis are self-selecting: they make use of symbolism; they work by analogy and allegory. The easy pleasures of thrills, chills, and laughter provided by Hollywood genre films, evident even to a child, may not need a gloss, but films about existential characters lost in the maze of urban modernity, unable to find hope and comfort in traditional religious verities, frequently cry out for interpretation. And, as Randall Jarrell rhetorically put it in his essay "The Age of Criticism" (1952), "Critics exist simply to help us with works of art – isn't that true?" (199).

Ingmar Bergman's films, of course, have always struck most viewers as possessing deeper, hidden meanings that require interpretation, and critics have spent a lot of time unraveling the threads of his discourse. *The Seventh Seal* – a story set during the Middle Ages in the time of the plague, in which Death appears as a character – is difficult to understand unless one sees it as an allegory. Michael Pressler, in an article in *Literature/Film Quarterly*, describes such an allegorical interpretation of the actions of Block, the knight, and Jons, his squire, as they move through the landscape of the plague-inflicted world:

For Block, Death first appears on the beach – suddenly and fittingly – as an allegorical personification, standing slightly atilt, like a black post, a suitable opponent for a game of chess. For Jons, Death's appearance is characteristically material, arising from an unexpected encounter with the rotting corpse of a plague victim – a figure which the squire would of course find "most eloquent." Similarly, the knight's troubled matins are set against the squire's own brand of morning service, a bawdy song. The antithesis of the two characters, reflecting the early Christian debate between the soul and the body, develops in the course of the screenplay into a full-scale moral dialogue and provides it with its major structural motif. (98)

Curiously enough, once the intellectual community took up the complex, subtle, and sometimes arcane films of European and Asian filmmakers flooding our shores during the 1950s and 1960s, it also learned – through the writings of French *auteurist* critics – that some (I emphasize "some") Hollywood films might have deeper, hidden meanings, too, that John Ford movies, for instance, might be more than just good Westerns. Analysis of a character's movements, gestures, and activities, and of lighting schemes, graphic composition, and narrative strategies often resulted in the uncovering of underlying motifs in American films. In *On the Verge of Revolt: Women in American Films of the Fifties*, the writer Brandon French shows how such analysis of a tiny action, easily overlooked by the casual viewer, can illuminate the major theme of a film such as *Sunset Boulevard* (Billy Wilder, 1950).

In this picture a young, would-be screenwriter in Hollywood becomes involved with an aging actress from the days of silent film who is hoping to make a comeback. After the two grow to live off each other's fantasies, Joe tries desperately to shake off her influence. But he fails: living in her house, on her money, doing whatever she tells him, he has lost his self-respect. At a bizarre New Year's Eve party in the grand ballroom of the old mansion where Norma Desmond has secreted herself all these years, Joe is so humiliated that he breaks away from Norma and heads for the door. He's going to see Betty, a girl of his own age whom he has met earlier in the film. French writes, "[A]s Joe tries to leave the house a moment later, the golden watch chain Norma bought for him catches on the door handle, symbolically suggesting the umbilical dependence Joe has on Norma as her kept man and the guilt that makes leaving her impossible" (9). Critical interpretative skills of this kind – close reading of the filmic text, often learned first through literary study – can thus be applied to any work of film art, old or new, American or foreign.

The first principle, then, is that movies, like any other form of creative endeavor, can be evaluated on the basis of their craftsmanship as well as their artistry – that is, on how well the perceptual elements of sight and sound have been organized to relay the intended meaning. Is the form of a film – its pictorial effects, its sound qualities, its editing – recognizably superior? Is significant meaning or content created as much through the deployment of visual devices and sound effects as through dialogue and action? If so, the film will be considered more cinematic, less like a filmed play, and hence be placed on a higher artistic plane. The second principle that follows is that, if technical and thematic excellence are achieved in a work of art, then these should be attributed to an artist, not to a production system.

Indeed, it may have been this necessary corollary to artistic achievement that prevented intellectuals in America from granting movies artistic stature earlier. Film production in America seemed like an assembly-line system, with no single person responsible for a Hollywood film's integrity. If a playwright or novelist appears totally responsible for the work to which she puts her name, who "authors" a film? There were studio decisions that determined which scripts would be produced, who would direct the actors, and who would play the parts. And then there were the camera crew, the editors, the composers of the music, the special-effects technicians, the second-unit photographers, and so on, whose presence in the production of any film seemed to blur the issue of authorship.

Although certain directors like D.W. Griffith achieved legendary status for making their own unique films before World War I, it wasn't until the early 1960s that cinephiles wholeheartedly came to embrace the idea that the director was the "author" (French writers used the term *auteur*) of the film. At last the critic could feel comfortable about locating an artist responsible for the creativity of a film, just as there had always been an artist responsible for drama, literature, painting, and music. Not only did the acceptance of the director as the author of a film attract writers and thinkers from other fields to movie criticism, but the extensive research that followed led to the reevaluation of a number of movies that, upon first viewing, had been dismissed – justifiably or not – as mere products of the Hollywood genre machine.

FINAL THOUGHTS

In conclusion, I write about the cinema because I believe that it is the true *Gesamtkunstwerk* (or total work of art) and therefore has greater expressive capacity than any other art; because I agree with the pronouncement that, as the one technology that can be absolutely humanist in its outcome, which can embody all the technological impulses, cravings, and interests of our age in the employ, not of machinery, but of the human spirit, film was *the* art form of the twentieth century and continues to be in the twenty-first; and because I think that criticism of film, still the least appreciated of the arts, matters. All the more so in the case of the films about which I choose to write, since they are, in two senses, the most private instances of this most public of art forms: with the exception of a politically or culturally correct movie like *American Beauty* (1999), these works get very little publicity from the media, yet their subtle motions and quiet meanings demand scrutiny from serious critics, whose job it is to introduce these works of art not only to their contemporaries but also to future generations of filmgoers. Film critics bear a great responsibility to the art of cinema, then, both because they educate audiences and also because in a sense they help to shape the future of the art form. If they write thoughtful, intelligent, and stimulating criticism, they can widen the periphery of dialogue about film and thereby serve a catalysts for the work of current and prospective moviemakers.

I must confess that I do sometimes feel guilty for not reviewing Hollywood's latest "blockbuster" releases, since these are the movies most people talk about. Indeed, the question usually put to me by friends and readers alike is "Why *don't* you review these pictures?" I respond by saying that the mass media cover such works in depth (if that is the phrase), so there's no need for me to add my two cents several months after the fact. But what I really mean is that, for the most part, Hollywood films don't need or invite analysis and criticism; what they want is *publicity*, and they get plenty of it. Of course there are exceptions, and those exceptions get the attention of every serious critic. They remain exceptions, however: works of compelling vision and imaginative execution in an art form that, more than any other, is controlled by the forces of the marketplace.

Like it or not, and for a variety of reasons whose discussion is beyond the purview of this introduction, most serious films (do I need to add that by "serious" I do not necessarily mean "unfunny"?) come from abroad; much trash is made abroad, too, but we import very little of that since we make our own brand over here. When I see small gems like *Solas* (1999), *West Beirut* (1998), and *The Children of Heaven* (1997), the products of modest national cinemas – or similar achievements from the United States like *Your Friends and Neighbors* (1998) and *Happiness* (1998) – I think of the overall immodesty of the commercial American cinema and all the money it spends each year on large duds (artistic duds, that is, which more often than not turn out to be box-office successes). Our cinema has always functioned in this manner; that is why it properly calls itself "the industry," and that is why most of its products are disposable. This situation isn't going to change, but it's nice to dream, to be reminded by relatively small, faraway lands, as well as by the independent cinema of our own country, of the large possibilities – some would say responsibilities – inherent in film art.

A further word about the public nature of film, which simultaneously attracts and repels me. Film is the only art form using words that is almost immediately available, through subtitles, to all people throughout the world; and, just as photography before it made all faces equal – made every human being's face reproducible, not only the faces of those who could afford to engage portrait painters – film placed the world at every individual's disposal, not merely the disposal of the rich who could travel anywhere and see anything they wanted. The attraction of such qualities is obvious. What renders them repellent is that they make filmmaking both too easy and too lucrative: turn on the camera, no matter how bad or sketchy or compromised your script, and, presto, you have images suitable for mass consumption – and disposal. I am convinced that the ease with which filmic images can be produced and the profit in producing them are what lure so many inferior artists to this, the most popular of entertainment forms. I am equally convinced that the difficulty of creating film art in collaboration with such lesser talents, and under tremendous pressure from the marketplace, is what drives many genuine artists to pursue other aesthetic outlets.

Still, film art continues to be created, albeit in small amounts, and it is the aim of this book to chronicle that art's international vitality between the years 1995 and 2001: countries represented here include Iran, France, Canada, Italy, Norway, Brazil, Spain, Taiwan, Israel, the United States, China, Scotland, and Lebanon. My focus, in part 1 of *In Search of Cinema*, is on Iranian film as it favorably compares with films from France, Canada, Scotland, China, and Italy in its use of cinematic resources to explore manifold, meaningful human questions. Though I exclude American movies – particularly the products of classical Hollywood cinema – from part 1, it is worth noting that the classics of classical Hollywood cinema (such as *Psycho* and *Stagecoach* [1939], both treated in part 3) had to deal, like Iranian pictures, with their own form of censorship in the form of the Production Code. And it is precisely this moralistic-cum-commercial censorship that forced studio directors and screenwriters, like their opposite numbers in Iran today, to find subtle, imaginative ways in which to express ideas and emotions (especially of the subversive kind found in American *film noir*). This is hardly an argument for censorship, of the theocratic or the democratic kind. It is an argument for restraint in place of excess, or an economy of means over a surfeit of devices; for artistic ingenuity instead of technical mastery, or spiritual suggestiveness as opposed to material manifestation.

I'd like to re-emphasize that all my review-essays are extended social, historical, literary, comparative, *and* cinematic considerations of serious yet engaging art films – several of them adapted from fiction, like *The Sweet Hereafter* (1997) and *Affliction* (1998) – not mere capsule reviews of run-of-the-mill, lightly entertaining releases from Planet Hollywood or one of its colonial outposts. In addition to fifteen of these review-essays in parts 1 and 2 (the latter of which privileges the cinema of Europe, the Middle East, Asia, and the Americas over myopically American film), in part 3 *In Search of Cinema* contains such items as meditations on the careers of Ingmar Bergman and Woody Allen; a reconsideration of the relationship between film and theatre, as well as between fiction and film; and short "takes" on such movies as *Claire's Knee* (1970) and *The Organizer* (1963), in addition to *Psycho* and *Stagecoach*.

I offer this collection as evidence of my continuing relationship with cinematic art, by which I mean films with not only stylistic signature but also style wedded (inseparably) to substantial content as opposed to fashionable or popular subject matter. I realize that this statement sounds hopelessly clichéd, if not naïve, to many, but it bears repeating again and again in an era that has seen the death (and resurrection) of the author, the rise of identity politics together with the resultant fragmentation of the body politic, and the decline if not disappearance of educational as well as artistic standards. Moreover, as far as critical – not cinematic – style is concerned, I have tried, in the belletristic tradition of Western criticism, to make my prose jargon-free and therefore accessible to the common, educated reader.

My critical method, for its part, depends on organic connections and thematic considerations within the work of art itself – as well as *between* filmic works of art – not on a theoretical framework imposed on the art object from without. The only theory that resides in my interpretations is that the film's the thing, not the theory; that the director-screen-writer is king, not the critic; that art and the artist are meant to be served, not supplanted. I continue to suffer, then, from what could be called the aesthetic bias: the compulsion to treat cinematic works of art as *works of art*, as alternative worlds to our own that are at once coherent and mysterious, compelling and cathartic, humane and cruel – in a word, so complex as ultimately to be inviolable and irreplaceable. In this regard, *Saint Cinema* could just as easily be this book's title as *In Search of Cinema*. I dedicate it to Father Darin Robert: friend, confessor, and savior if not saint.

WORKS CITED

French, Brandon. *On the Verge of Revolt: Women in American Films of the Fifties.* New York: Ungar, 1978.

Jarrell, Randall. "The Age of Criticism." *Partisan Review* 19, no. 2 (March-April 1952): 185–201.

Lindsay, Vachel. *The Art of the Moving Picture.* New York: Macmillan, 1915, rev. 1922.

Münsterberg, Hugo. *The Photoplay: A Psychological Study.* New York: D. Appleton, 1916.

Pressler, Michael. "The Idea Fused in the Fact: Bergman and *The Seventh Seal.*" *Literature/Film Quarterly* 13, no. 2 (1985): 95–101.

Robinson, W.R., ed. *Man and the Movies.* Baton Rouge: Louisiana State University Press, 1967.

Samuels, Charles Thomas. *Mastering the Film and Other Essays.* Knoxville: The University of Tennessee Press, 1977.

Warshow, Robert. "The Westerner." In *The Immediate Experience.* 1962. New York: Atheneum, 1971.

Wood, Robin. *Hitchcock's Films.* Cranbury, N.J.: A.S. Barnes, 1965, rev. 1969.

PART ONE

Focus on Iranian Cinema

1

Writing About Iranian Cinema

For Americans who want to look beyond the reductive image of Iran presented by the American media, Iran's cinema offers an alternative that is fascinating, even astonishing, for its artistic sophistication and passionate humanism. At a time when Hollywood has put many national cinemas virtually out of business and Hollywood itself is dominated by flashy, special effects-laden fantasies, Iran's filmmakers continue to impress audiences worldwide with their distinctive formal ingenuity and unwavering dedication to real-life people and problems. In the past decade, Iranian films have won nearly 300 awards at international festivals, where directors such as Abbas Kiarostami and Mohsen Makhmalbaf are recognized as being among the cinema's most accomplished artists. Many critics now rank Iran as having the world's most important national cinema, with a significance that invites comparison to that of Italian neorealism in the late 1940s and the Czech renaissance of the mid-1960s. Iranian cinema's artistic importance has also given rise in the United States, for one country, to a resurgence of interest in, and the practice of, film criticism, even as the intellectual as well as emotional vibrancy of the French New Wave and the postwar Japanese renaissance did the same for American criticism from the 1950s through the 1960s.

It was the decade preceding the 1979 revolution (which inaugurated the Islamic Republic) that saw the quiet emergence of Iran's own New Wave. A group of artists and intellectuals denounced the existing escapist cinema and launched a movement to produce indigenous films of high cinematic quality and genuine social consciousness. The picture that heralded the new cinema was Dariush Mehrjui's *The Cow* (1969), a disturbing tale of poverty and mental breakdown in which the mysterious death of the only cow in a village drives its owner insane. Despite its poor box-office performance, *The Cow* achieved a critical success that paved the way for a modest annual supply of New Wave films and thus an alternative movie environment. This environment helped breed a generation of filmmakers who are now considered old masters of the Iranian cinema, though they are still in their fifties. Besides Mehrjui, Kiarostami (*Where Is the Friend's House?*, 1987), Bahram Beizai (*Bashu, the Little Stranger*, 1985), Amir Naderi (*The Runner*, 1984), Parviz Sayyad (*The Mission*, 1984), and Sohrab Shaheed Saless (*Still Life*, 1975) are among the filmmakers who started their careers during this period.

The New Wave filmmakers were hampered in their efforts by a harsh system of censorship that essentially kept them from dealing directly with the unpleasant realities of Iranian life. *The Cow*, for instance, originally was banned because of its uncompromising depiction of despair in an impoverished village, and was conditionally released only after it won the Grand Prize at the Venice Film Festival. The censorship code forced filmmakers to resort to symbolic communication in exploring sociopolitical issues or to make less complicated pictures about simple characters and ordinary situations. This helps to explain the metaphorical complexities of some movies and the amazing transparency of others, including the emergence of a peculiar genre of films featuring children as characters.

The Islamic Revolution of 1979 initially struck a near-fatal blow even to censorship-hampered cinema in Iran. More than 180 movie theatres fell victim to the wrath of fanatical arsonists who perceived movies as agents of moral corruption; film production came to a halt; many directors were indicted on charges such as "corrupting the public" and then purged; and nearly 2,200 previously exhibited domestic as well as foreign films were re-inspected, with just over 200 receiving new screening permits. Some of these pictures had to be cut extensively before they could return to the screen.

In an attempt to establish an Islamic, anti-imperialist cinema, the government next established a new set of highly restrictive censorship codes that brought film production under tight control. Most of these codes were aimed at the representation of female characters. Strict Islamic dress, for example, requires women to cover their hair in public and to wear loose-fitting outer garments to cloak the body's curves. In addition, women can be intimate only with members of their immediate family. Therefore, actors playing couples could not even touch each other's hands on screen unless they were married in real life. Such restrictions have forced many filmmakers to give up altogether the idea of making movies about adult male-female relationships.

Currently, film censorship is implemented in four stages: first, the script must be approved to ensure that its content is appropriate; second, the list of cast and crew must be submitted if the picture is to receive a production permit; third, the finished film is sent to the censorship board, which may approve it unconditionally, require changes, or ban it altogether; finally, the producers of the approved movie must apply for a screening permit. All these controls amount to a multi-layered system of censorship that not only decides to some extent the content of a film but also determines how, or even if, the marketplace will react to it. American or European films, for their part, are virtually impossible to import, since few of them would conform to Iranian rules, and the government itself is the sole importer of the limited number of motion pictures found appropriate for distribution.

Paradoxically or not, the kind and degree of censorship enforced in Iran have served to make many artists all that much more skilled, resourceful, and determined. Cinematically speaking, Iran today has the electricity of a place where art, ideas, and ideals still matter. The key to resolving the apparent contradiction between Iran's repressive image and the renaissance of Iranian cinema is to understand the relationship that developed between art, society, and the state after the Islamic Revolution. The popular nature of this revolution, together with factionalism within the republic itself, gave artists and the public an opportunity to engage the government in an extended process of protest, negotiation, cooperation, and defiance. Over twenty years after its revolution, Iran is still involved in a great debate over its identity and direction as a society, and the cinema plays a remarkably important role in that collective self-examination. Despite restrictions, Iranian films have been shining in international arenas as well as at home for more than ten years now. More importantly, the fact that each year about twenty new directors make their début pictures promises that Iran will remain a reservoir of new cinematic talent and fresh moviemaking for years to come.

One indication of Iran's vibrant film culture is that ten film magazines are published in Tehran. One, *Film International*, which appears two or three times a year, is written in English. Slickly produced, it offers detailed coverage and critical appraisal of Iran's film production, as well as Iranian views of world festivals and developments in international cinema (including the work of American independents like Jim

Jarmusch and Hal Hartley). Even more surprisingly, Iranian women filmmakers, previously barely a presence, have made their mark both domestically and internationally in the last twenty years or so. While they are still greatly outnumbered by their male counterparts, their voices are distinct – chief among them Rakhshan Bani-Etemad (*Nargess*, 1992; *The Blue Veil*, 1994) and Tahmineh Milani (*Children of Divorce*, 1990; *Two Women*, 1998).

Of all the filmmakers working in Iran today, Abbas Kiarostami is surely the most important. Simple narratives, the use of non-professional actors, and blurring the line between fiction and documentary are characteristic of Kiarostami's films, which are essentially feature-length lyric meditations that elegantly combine his interests in painting, poetry, and philosophy. Although he has been making movies since 1970, it was his 1987 picture, *Where Is the Friend's House?*, that first stunned audiences in the West. Nominally about a little boy trying to exchange notebooks with a schoolmate, this deceptively simple gem has the rigor of poetry and the resonance of allegory. Since this film, Kiarostami's star has only continued to rise. He received the 1997 Palme d'Or at Cannes for *A Taste of Cherry* (the first Iranian film ever accorded this honor), and in 1999 he was unequivocally voted the most important director of the 1990s by two international critics' polls. Kiarostami is today acknowledged as a new master of world cinema on a par with such directors as Robert Bresson, Ingmar Bergman, and Akira Kurosawa.

Kiarostami's cinema, with its bare-boned aesthetics, forms one pole of the Iranian cinema. The other is exemplified by the masterful works of Bahram Beizai. An accomplished playwright as well as a filmmaker, Beizai explores in his films a visual realm redolent with mythology. His collaborations with the actress Sussan Taslimi have produced a number of intensely poignant pictures, including *Bashu, the Little Stranger*. Made during the Iran-Iraq war and originally banned, *Bashu* tells of a poor farm wife who tries to coax a young war refugee out of his fear bordering on trauma. In the case of this film, together with others of his, Beizai has not experienced the same ease as others in navigating the many regulations of moviemaking in the Islamic Republic, and the release of his most recent picture has been delayed for over two years.

If Beizai and Kiarostami form the twin pillars of Iranian cinema, Mohsen Makhmalbaf represents its focal point since the advent of the Islamic Revolution. Makhmalbaf, who emerged from an underprivileged background and was at first strongly identified with the Islamic regime, is a self-taught filmmaker. At once stylistically graceful and thematically bold, his prolific body of work includes sixteen features (as well as six shorts), among them *Gabbeh* (1996), *The Peddler* (1987), *The Cyclist* (1989), and *Once Upon a Time, Cinema* (1992). His latest film, *Kandahar* (2001), was made before the current crisis in Afghanistan and portrays in personal or individual terms the desperate situation that exists in that country. Makhmalbaf's daughter, Samira, herself emerged as the youngest of a new generation of directors when at age eighteen she presented her first film, *The Apple* (1998) – scripted and edited by her father – at the Cannes Festival. In 2000, her second feature, *Blackboards*, was awarded the Jury Prize at the same festival.

Several other filmmakers of note began their careers as assistants to veteran directors, including the dual recipients of the Camera d'Or in 2000 at Cannes: Bahman Ghobadi for *A Time for Drunken Horses* and Hassan Yektapanah for *Djomeh*. Both had worked as assistants to Abbas Kiarostami. Another ex-assistant of Kiarostami is Jafar Panahi, whose movie *The Circle* was awarded the Grand Prize at the Venice Festival in 2000. In 1996, Panahi's *The White Balloon* – which Kiarostami scripted and which was itself the winner of the Camera d'Or at Cannes and Best Foreign Film from the New York Film Critics' Circle – became the first Iranian picture to gain broad art-house distribution in the United States. And in the last few years, more than a dozen Iranian films have found distribution in America to both critical and popular acclaim.

What, then, are Iranian films like? In some ways, of course, they are as different as the very diverse individuals making them. Yet there are common threads that link many of these movies. They often focus, for example, on ordinary people caught in harsh circumstances brought about by social, cultural, or natural forces. The devastation caused by an earthquake, the wounds and traumas caused by war, the hardships heaped on the poor, the prejudices faced by women – these are powerful subjects. And Iranian filmmakers manage to address them not with easy sloganeering or smooth sentimentality but with penetrating insight and a sure sense of storytelling basics as well as dramatic purpose. Iranian films' most singular quality, however, may be a feeling of compassion for those who suffer.

Formally as well as narratively, moreover, Iranian moviemakers have shown a genius for making virtues out of constraints. Since the films are cheaply made, they often have a surface simplicity that belies their subtle realism; budgetary limitations are perhaps one reason their directors have also become famous for investigating the boundary between documentary and fiction. That Western-style violence, obscenity, and sex are prohibited has meant not only that filmmakers practice skillfully indirect, sometimes allegorical storytelling, but also that they search for subjects that go beyond the formulaic or the genre-specific. The Iranian specialty of films about children, for instance, is also a specialty of films not necessarily made *for* children, and this type of picture allows both for a form of oblique social commentary and for the depiction of intimacy – each of which would be difficult, if not impossible, to achieve with adult characters. In the very best Iranian films, this combination of artful simplicity and skilled suggestiveness produces results that refine our notions both of the cinema's expressive possibilities and of its connections to the other arts. I treat no fewer than eight of these movies at length in the first part of *In Search of Cinema*; they are *The White Balloon, A Taste of Cherry, The Apple, The Mirror* (1997), *The Children of Heaven* (1997), *The Color of Paradise* (1999), *The Circle,* and *The Wind Will Carry Us* (1999).

2

A Girl and Two Women

On Panahi's *The White Balloon* (1995, Iran) and
Dugowson's *Mina Tannenbaum* (1994, France)

Most of the best films about children are about boys: *Shoeshine* (1946), *Germany, Year Zero* (1947), and *Bicycle Thieves* (1948), for instance. Moreover, most of the best films about children were made by Italian neorealists, or by directors following their example, such as Buñuel with *Los Olvidados* (1951) and Clément with *Forbidden Games* (1952). *The White Balloon* (1995), by contrast, is about a girl and comes to us from – of all places – Iran. The essential theme of the neorealist film was the conflict in the wake of World War II between the common man and the immense societal forces that were completely external to him, yet completely determined his existence. The most pitiful victims of such forces, because the most innocent, are children, and therefore it is no accident that important neorealist films featured them. Iranian films made in the wake of the 1979 Islamic Revolution often feature them, too; in addition to *The White Balloon*, Amir Naderi's *The Runner* from 1984 (which depicts the aspirations of a boy living on an abandoned ship) and Ebrahim Foruzesh's *The Jar* from 1992 (about attempts to repair a crack in the communal water jar at an impoverished desert school) deserve mention.

But Iranian movies have child protagonists partly for a different reason: to avoid the minefield of Islamic restrictions on the portrayal of adult male-female relationships. Actors portraying a married couple, for instance, cannot touch each other on screen unless they are also married in real life because it is a violation of Islam for unrelated men and woman to touch. And actresses, like all Iranian females over the age of nine, must cover all the hair and curves of the body, even in scenes depicting private moments at home where, in real life, every woman sheds her Islamic coverings. In addition, there can't be any extended close-up of an attractive actress, because such a shot might be construed as an exploitation of female beauty; indeed, Iranian actresses deemed too seductively beautiful are forbidden to appear on screen at all. With female children, of course, none of these restrictions are an issue.

What is an issue in the censorship-bound Iranian cinema, however, is sociopolitical criticism or moral-philosophical speculation, even in films featuring children, whom Iranian *auteurs*, like the Italian neorealists before them, use partly as emblems of innocence in a world under internal as well as external siege. Each film must be approved in screenplay-form as well as in the final cut by the Islamic government, which generously funds domestic cinema, severely restricts foreign imports (especially those that contain sex and gratuitous violence), and did not, until 1988, with the end of the Iran-Iraq war, allow Iranian films to appear at international festivals. Furthermore, casts and crews themselves are vetted for political and religious correctness. Still, just as Italian neorealist cinema treated pressing postwar problems such as unemployment, poverty, and social injustice by focusing on the stories of recognizable characters taken from daily life, Iranian films for their part manage to be cautiously or obliquely critical of government failures and social malaise in a nation whose ordinary (not necessarily extremist) people have been ravaged by politico-religious revolution, economic recession, war with Iraq, and international isolation precipitated by Iran's hostile dealings with the United States. I'm thinking particularly of Kianoush Ayari's black-and-white, taxi-thief film of 1993, *Abadani-Ha*, which took De Sica's *Bicycle Thieves* as its model, and of *Nargess* (1992), made by the woman director Rakhshan Bani-Etemad in a country not known for championing the freedom of women, artistic or otherwise. Now we get *The White Balloon*, whose title itself is an oblique criticism and which scores its delicately political points by making them in a movie about a pre-political child.

The White Balloon has a script by Abbas Kiarostami, the celebrated Iranian director of a trilogy presenting a documentary-style look at mountain life in northern Iran before and after the terrible earthquake of June 1990, which claimed 50,000 lives: *Where Is the Friend's House?* (1987), *And Life Goes On ...* (1992), and *Through the Olive Trees* (1994). The director of *The White Balloon* is the young Jafar Panahi, who was Kiarostami's assistant on the quietly lovely *Through the Olive Trees* and here makes his first feature. Surely Panahi knows his film's namesake of sorts, the Frenchman Albert Lamorisse's *Red Balloon* (1956), which, like *The White Balloon*, was a big hit at the Cannes Film Festival at the time of its release. At thirty-five minutes, Lamorisse's short is only about two-fifths the length of Panahi's movie and has no sociopolitical element, but it uses its red balloon in much the same way that *The White Balloon* uses a goldfish: as a symbol of shining dreams, of mysterious yearnings, and as a poignant reminder of the poverty of those who do not have or have lost them. In the case of *The Red Balloon*, the suggestion is that the adult world – which we never really see – is poverty-stricken: weighed down so much by its cares that it cannot float along life's surface or soar up into the skies, like the little boy who adopts the red balloon (or vice versa) as his constant companion. In the case of *The White Balloon*, there is this suggestion but there is also more, for the owner of the titular balloon is a homeless Afghan boy, a refugee from yet another war.

We see this boy at the start of Panahi's film, selling his balloons amidst a crowd in the marketplace, but we do not see him again until the end of *The White Balloon*. Attention quickly shifts from the balloon-seller to a seven-year-old girl named Razieh, whom we and her mother find on a street in Tehran holding one of the Afghan's balloons – a blue one. The action takes place in real time (marked by clocks in the film) over the ninety minutes before the Persian New Year, celebrated by the feast of Nowruz, arrives at 6:30 p.m. on March 21. After the revolution that deposed Shah Mohammad Reza Pahlavi, the Ayatollah Ruhollah Khomeini, in an attempt to elevate the importance of religious holidays, discouraged observance of this pre-Islamic New Year's festival. But Shiite Islam's gloomy commemorations of martyrdom couldn't vanquish Nowruz; despite harassment, Iranians have clung to their joyous spring holiday, which takes place on the vernal equinox. So right away, *The White Balloon* sets an indirectly critical tone in what will turn out to be an almost entirely secular portrayal of Iranian daily life. Apart from an early scene in which a character passes a Huseinia-Shiite prayer place, whence voices rise and fall in their blessing of the prophet Mohammed, the film contains no reference to Islam.

Razieh's mother has been hurrying to finish the shopping for Nowruz when we come upon her, and when she gets home to the family's apartment, she hurries to finish the cleaning as well as the cooking in time for the arrival of her in-laws to celebrate the New Year. For this Persian feast, Iranians clean house, bathe carefully, and don new clothes – symbolic rituals through which they slough any lingering ills from the old year. The table is then decorated with a mirror, a candle, and white foods, for light, fire, and white are all representative of God in Zoroastrianism, the ancient Persian religion. In an echo of the ceremonial nourishment gathered by Jews every spring for their Passover table, Persians in addition assemble seven foods whose names begin with the letter "s," like *sabzi* – green herbs that symbolize nature's springtime rebirth. There will be gifts to exchange, and there must also be a bowl containing a goldfish, with the goldfish representing both the mystery and joy of life. (By tradition, Nowruz celebrants gather around a bowl containing a single goldfish and carefully observe its movements; the instant the fish is motionless, the new year begins.) It is the humanely comic quest of Razieh for such a fish that propels the action of *The White Balloon.* Her mother keeps small goldfish in a courtyard pool, which she sells to neighbors in order to help her family make ends meet (a few of which fish a neighborhood boy "borrows" for the New Year's celebration, only to exchange them for cash at the marketplace), but these aren't good enough for Razieh. She covets a marvelously plump, white-specked one that she has seen "dancing" in the window of the local pet shop.

Its cost is 100 tomans but Razieh's mother resists the girl's nagging pleas for money, since the family's budget is very tight and the woman of the house can't even afford new shoes for her son, Ali (the Nowruz equivalent of not being able to provide the major item on a Christmas list). Razieh tearfully persists, however, and with the aid of her brother – who gets his sister's blue balloon as a reward for his help – she finally persuades her mother to give her the family's last 500-toman note. And off the little girl goes with her money, a fishbowl, and the injunction that she return with 400 tomans in change. She leaves behind a harried mother who has to contend not only with her daughter's relentless entreaties but also with her husband's distracting demands. He has been an unseen but almost ominous presence throughout the scene in the apartment: complaining from the bathroom about the lack of hot water, scolding if not punching his son for failing to buy him shampoo, screaming for a towel. Like many economically struggling Tehranians, this meter reader has a second job, which translates into little leisure time and even less patience. It also translates into a great deal of secrecy about the source of his additional income, which is never revealed on account of its shamefulness or illicitness in so prohibitively moralistic a society.

None of this yet concerns Razieh, which of course is part of the point of childhood – at least early childhood, for the preteen Ali and Afghan balloon-seller seem acutely aware of the exigency of their economic sit-

Aida Mohammad-Khani as Razieh and Mohsen Kalifi as Ali in *The White Balloon.*

uations. So does the elderly snake charmer who tricks the passing Razieh into parting with her banknote before a forbidding all-male audience in an almost sunless vacant lot. He reluctantly gives it back to her in the end, but not before eliciting her tears together with her awareness of just how tenuous or provisional money – especially paper money – is. And that awareness is further brought home to her when she arrives at the pet shop to discover not only that the price of her goldfish has been raised to 200 tomans but also that she has somehow lost her mother's 500-toman note along the way. A kindly old woman helps Razieh to retrace her steps, and they locate the bill at the bottom of a sidewalk grating. The little girl needs assistance to retrieve it but the old woman cannot help, and neither can the petshop owner, a neighboring tailor, or a soldier on leave.

What emerges from Razieh's contacts with these Tehranians is something more important than the resolution of her dilemma, however – at least from a critical point of view if not that of Razieh herself. And this is socioeconomic context. The elderly tailor, for example, has little time or sympathy for the girl's plight, since he is busy arguing with a disgruntled young customer of the post-revolutionary generation who threatens to use the new political system against this oldtimer. The

friendly soldier whom Razieh encounters on the street amid the sound
of sirens is a lonely conscript from the provinces (not a Shiite zealot)
who says he misses his own little sisters and who reveals that he can't go
home for the New Year because he cannot afford the bus fare. Moreover, not only is this man not a Tehranian after all, but neither are
many of the other characters we meet in *The White Balloon,* who speak
Farsi with Turkish, Polish, and thick regional accents. The filmmakers'
point, I think, is to emphasize these characters' existential isolation
rather than Islamic communion in the Iranian capital.

Certainly this is the case for the balloon-seller, who naturally speaks
Farsi with an Afghan accent and who, when he happens upon Razieh's
street scene, immediately gets into a fight with her brother. Ali has
been sent by his mother to find his sister but realizes they must recover
the 500 tomans – and buy the goldfish – before returning home.
Therefore he seizes the balloon-seller's pole, to which is attached a
lone white balloon, with the intention of sticking it down the grate and
somehow pulling up the banknote. The fight begins because the
Afghan assumes that Ali is a thief until Razieh explains the situation,
after which he gladly lends both Iranian children a hand. They decide
that they need something sticky to attach to one end of the pole, so, as
rain begins to fall, Ali grabs some gum from a blind man hawking his
wares on the street; all three youngsters chew it; then Ali sticks the
Afghan's piece on the end of the pole, puts the pole down the grate,
and at last pulls up the piece of paper money to his sister's delight.
These two go off to purchase the goldfish, which the petshop owner
graciously lets Razieh have for the allotted 100 tomans, while the
Afghan boy poignantly remains behind sitting atop the grate and holding his single, unsold white balloon. The camera stays on him as several
figures reappear, including the snake charmer, the elderly tailor's dissatisfied client, and Razieh herself, passing through the frame with her
goldfish in its bowl and her brother in tow, but without so much as a
word or glance of acknowledgment directed toward the Afghan. A
clock can be heard ticking, and we see a title announcing the start of
the new year (1374, not 1996). As the balloon-seller finally gets up to
go, the frame freezes on his image and *The White Balloon* ends, its formal symmetry as well as temporal ineluctability having been sufficiently
disturbed by this boy's haunting presence.

The shooting of this final scene is representative of Panahi's shooting
style throughout. The film was photographed almost entirely in tight
frames that mimic a child's-eye view of the world; the images are
unpanoramic, with the focal point always on what is close and immediate.

Thus does Panahi create the ardent intensity of childhood in a sometimes oblivious adult world – an intensity that is only increased by his habit of filming in long takes and cutting less for visual variety than to isolate Razieh even further in her own little world. The look or quality of Farzad Jowdat's cinematography is such that, despite its colors, what we remember of Razieh's unspectacular Tehran is the proximate, geometrically patterned background provided by its weathered mud bricks. If *The Red Balloon* was photographed (by Edmond Séchan) in an old quarter of Paris in soft hues of blue and gray against which the bright red balloon shines, *The White Balloon* is shot in central Tehran in drab hues of olive and brown against which nothing shines – particularly a pale white balloon – or into which everything is absorbed, like a white-specked goldfish already encased in glass and not even as plump as it had appeared to be.

Panahi's point is not that Razieh feels any less joy than Lamorisse's little boy at the granting of her wish but that the lives of those around her – other children as well as adults – are pervaded by a quiet desperation born of financial worry, social isolation, and political uneasiness. The bursting of the little boy's red balloon at the end of Lamorisse's film may signify his inevitable entry into the earthbound world of adulthood, but the buying of the goldfish at the end of *The White Balloon* may ironically signify something more threatening: the idea that not only every Iranian female over the age of nine lives her life in a fishbowl, but that in a sense so too does every other inhabitant of Iran, especially a resident alien like the Afghan boy. The goldfish, then, may be a symbol of the mystery and joy of life for Persians celebrating Nowruz, but in the context of this film, it becomes a symbol of the restrictiveness and subjugation of Iranian humanity as well.

The kerchiefed little girl who plays Razieh, Aida Mohammad-Khani – with her pudgy face, frequently peevish stubbornness, and only occasional gap-toothed smile – may not be any Shirley Temple in look or manner, but then this is no Shirley Temple movie. Mohammad-Khani is not a programmed doll with dimples and curls (nor, unlike America's sweetheart, is she surrounded by a stock-and-stale cast), but a spontaneous human being whose unconstrained want her society will soon mechanically seek to stifle, lest it be transformed into a desire for sexual freedom. Her homely naturalness in a film that could easily have exploited another little girl's affected cuteness – from the point of view of Iranian censors, precisely because she is a little girl and not a young woman – seems to me not only aesthetically smart but also commercially refreshing. Western cinema, by contrast, has historically had no qualms about exploiting the cuteness, beauty, charm, seductiveness, or sensuality of any female in any movie. This subject is addressed both implicitly and explicitly by the first film of the French writer-director Martine Dugowson, *Mina Tannenbaum* (1994).

The style of this movie reminds some critics of the work of François Truffaut: several characters, one of them choric, address the camera from time to time, and at the end of the film the crew appears on screen as it abandons the set; the camera irises out on a character at least thrice, splits the screen at least once, and employs no fewer than two stop-action shots; scenes from a character's life are replayed in a way that she would have preferred, while other scenes are altogether fantasized, such as the one in which the titular figure meets her younger self; a character's private thoughts on the soundtrack counterpoint her actual conversation with another person on screen; and Mina's first as well as second sightings of a handsome young man are shown in reverential slow motion. But *Mina Tannenbaum*'s subject should remind viewers of Truffaut as well, for one of his chief subjects was women (the other, children), about whom he had complex feelings.

To him, women were warm, attractive, malleable objects of romance, in an old-style, balcony-serenade way; they were also – and sometimes simultaneously – repellent, destructive, absolutist killer-castrators of men in the most steely eyed, post-Freudian manner. Here, as evidence, are a few of Truffaut's titles: *The Bride Wore Black* (1968), *Mississippi Mermaid* ("siren" in French; 1969), *The Man Who Loved Women* (1977), and *The Woman Next Door* (1981). In each of these films women are seen from a man's point of view, or through the "male gaze," as Laura Mulvey would have it. Martine Dugowson naturally sees women, and men, from a female's point of view – from a reverse angle, as it were – but she knows something about the pervasive effect of the male gaze in cinema as in life, and she shows it. She also reminds us of the magnetic power of the cinematic eye – or, better, she disrupts that power – through the stylistic devices enumerated above.

Mina Tannenbaum is the story of the twenty-five-year friendship between Mina Tannenbaum and Ethel Bénégui as they grow from children in the 1960s to adults in the 1990s. Both girls are Jewish, and both are born on the same day in 1958 in a Parisian hospital. They meet in a ballet class when they are ten years old, at which age each has already been subjected to the male gaze: boys have called Mina "four eyes" on account of the glasses she must wear (one addresses the camera as he does so, which is Dugowson's cleverly amusing way of placing herself, as a woman filmmaker, under masculine scrutiny), and boys have shunned the overweight Ethel at a bar mitzvah party during which they dance with every girl except her. Each of these scenes ends with the overexposure of the image to such an extent that the screen turns almost completely to white, which is an audacious attempt simultaneously to suggest the blinding nature of the male gaze and the self-negating effect it can have on the female psyche. The ballet class ends with Ethel's theft of a drawing from Mina's knapsack, then her return of it a few days later as the two girls sit on a park bench and strike up what will become a fast friendship.

Mina's drawing is a copy of a painting by Thomas Gainsborough of two girls (either the Linley sisters or his own daughters), and it is no accident either that the girls are viewed through a man's eyes in this work or that Mina is copying it. In her career to come as a painter, she will support herself less through sales of her own art – which a dealer criticizes for being "too big," that is, for being drawn on too large (too masculine?) a scale – than by copying the paintings of great male artists like Auguste Renoir either for wide public consumption or for narrow technical study by lesser male artists. She identifies so much with Renoir's point of view as she copies him that she imagines herself as the woman in his famous painting *Dance at Bougival* (1883), dancing with the man of her dreams. One reason Mina is such a good imitator is that, perhaps unconsciously, she has assimilated both her art teacher's and her art dealer's mostly negative opinions of her original work, unrequitedly falling in love with the latter in the process as well as attracting some sexist sexual interest from the former. The teacher tells Mina, "When you can paint for eight hours and not think of yourself, maybe you'll paint something with feeling." This sounds like good advice, since it appears to argue for a denial of self, of self-absorption or narcissistic subjectivity, in favor of devotion to the art object. However, a total denial of self, of one's thoughts and emotions, for the sake of one's painting is to deny life or feeling to the pictures as well. Thus the instructor's advice comes to seem more like an exhortation to Mina to deny her female self and serve instead a male conception of art, which is to say merely to become a copyist or imitator of artwork fervently produced by men. Ironically, the artist Serge, the last man with whom Mina will live, paints in her shadow until he begins passing off her unique style and colors as his own.

If I appear to be concentrating more on Mina Tannenbaum than Ethel Bénégui in this review, that is because the film does so both by announcing its primary subject through its title (and through that singular title also avoiding the suggestion that it is one more female "buddy picture") and then by making Mina's character carry the dramatic weight of the narrative. The lives of these two female figures parallel each other somewhat, but they also diverge, and the more they do so the more Mina's tale advances in importance while Ethel's recedes. Even as they hint of divergence, the parallels between the women are

instructive yet witty, compelling yet modulated. Their mothers, for
instance: Mina's, a concentration camp survivor, severely forbids her
daughter's young German acquaintances to enter their home in the
Paris of the 1970s, while Ethel's mother, even on her deathbed, comically continues to plague her daughter about finding a Jewish husband.

But, thankfully, the film in no way paints Mina and Ethel as either
targets of anti-Semitism or illustrations of Jewish intellectual superiority. To wit: in Ethel's fantasy of herself as a Jewish Brigitte Bardot, it is
Mina in disguise as a rabbi who attempts to rape her! The stern Mina
will grow into an intense, "rabbinical" artist, even if she does shed her
brainy glasses along the way, whereas the scatterbrained Ethel will
become a svelte and flirty journalist. Nonetheless, that does not keep
them from reading the same material: for example, Stendhal's *The Red
and the Black* (1830), whose setting in the France of 1830 – where the
tension in the relationships among the aristocracy, the bourgeoisie, the
working people, the monarchy, and the clergy would erupt in revolution – is drolly intended by Dugowson to clash with the setting in which
Mina and Ethel read the book. They do so in the France of 1974, after
a circular camera movement used to indicate not only the passage of
time but also the true nature of the 1968 student "revolution." The
girls' clothing is fabulously garish in the way only seventies' fashion can
be, and their serious reading is sandwiched between their real interest
at the time, which is the fruitless if not trivial pursuit of romance.

As Mina and Ethel begin to achieve success with men, each also
tellingly begins to fantasize that she is a movie star. The star with whom
Mina identifies is Bette Davis, whose screen image in such films as *The
Little Foxes* (1941) and *All About Eve* (1950) – as a willful, liberated
woman who managed to remain spitefully independent in a world
dominated by men – we see depicted in two clips. The star with whom
Ethel identifies, by contrast, is Rita Hayworth, whom we twice see
singing "Put the Blame on Mame, Boys" in *Gilda* (1946), the film that
more than any other confirmed her position in the 1940s as the erotic
queen or "Love Goddess" of Hollywood. According to male-gaze theory, Davis is a "disturbing," "guilty" woman who must be voyeuristically
investigated and then punished or saved, whereas Hayworth is an icon
of pleasure whose beauty men desire fetishistically to ravish. Over the
years, Ethel transforms herself into such an erotic object through
make-up, fasting, hair-coloring, and perhaps even cosmetic surgery on
her "Jewish" nose, and she uses her looks not only to get ahead in the
high-pressure (if lightweight) world of arts journalism but also to compete with Mina for men. (Ironically, she must impersonate her friend
in order to get an interview with the contemporary artist Degas, whose

Elsa Zylberstein as Ethel Bénégui and Romane Bohringer as Mina Tannenbaum in *Mina Tannenbaum.*

celebrated, nineteenth-century namesake, as we know, especially liked
to train his painterly male gaze on ballet danseuses like the young Mina
and Ethel.)

When we see her toward the end, Ethel is living with and perhaps
married to Gérard, the last in a series of Christian boyfriends for this
Jewish woman. She has had a child by him whom she has named Mina,
yet she can't seem to find time anymore for her friend of the same
name, who lives without a man. Mina has continued to paint but, due to
facial disfigurement caused by a car accident, she now attracts only
indifference or hostility from men. Masculine eyes no longer search her
out, and a movie poster featuring Michael Caine's eyes, gazing down at
her from the wall of her apartment, seems ironically to remind Mina of
her newfound undesirability. After Ethel cancels a lunch date with her
in order to go skiing with Gérard – and does so by impersonally leaving
a message on her answering machine – Mina blacks out a picture she
has been painting, swallows a handful of sleeping pills, then crawls into
the fetal position to die on the floor of her studio-cum-living space.

After her funeral and the news that, as a result of Mina's death, her
paintings have become hot items for the first time, we are left with an
epigraph from Kafka's "Investigations of a Dog." In it a dog, like the

more famous "hunger artist" of Kafka's story written a few months before (in the same year, 1922, with publication coming in 1924 as the titular tale of *A Hunger Artist,* a collection that included three other stories), resolved as one of his "scientific experiments" to "fast completely as long as [he] could stand it, and at the same time avoid all sight of food, all temptation." If "A Hunger Artist" is conventionally interpreted as an allegory of the artist's role in a modern society increasingly devoid of spiritual hunger or an inner life, then *Mina Tannenbaum* can be interpreted as a film about the female artist's role in such a society – except that, through Kafka's epigraph, she tragicomically metamorphoses into a bitch who, despite her yearnings to the contrary, exists solely for man's companionate consumption in a world so remote from God that the only hunger is for goods and services, the only art is the kind you can sell, and the only life is that of the flesh.

I trust that I haven't made *Mina Tannenbaum* seem like a dour piece of textbook feminism or victim-art, for it is no such didactic thing. The film has wit, style, and above all intelligence, and it treats its male characters just as fairly as its female ones. Part of the movie's quality, as one might guess, derives from the performances of its two leading roles – the adult version of those roles, that is, since two sets of children play Mina and Ethel, first at the age of five and then at ten. Romane Bohringer, who in 1992 had the title role in *The Accompanist* (directed by Truffaut-protégé Claude Miller) as well as the female lead in *Savage Nights*, is Mina Tannenbaum, and she is extraordinary in her ability to suggest the frequently unspoken depths of her character's agony and isolation. Elsa Zylberstein, as Ethel Bénégui, is equally good but quite the opposite of Bohringer in her ability to play the extroverted character of Ethel where she lives: on the surface. I'm not sure which approach to acting is harder to carry out: the more internal and implicative kind or the more external and expressive one. Perhaps the question doesn't really matter, since the acting style should fit the character one is playing – something often forgotten in the theatre but well remembered here by Mmes Bohringer and Zylberstein and the woman who directed them. By analogy, the cinematic style should fit the story one is filming, and Dominique Chapuis's cool, crisp color photography does so by creating just the right soberly contemplative mood to juxtapose against the jaunty spirit of Martine Barraqué and Dominique Gallieni's accomplished, dualistic editing. All of them women and all the better, as each works with her fellow artists toward a common good.

3

Blood and Cherries, Snow and Dust

On Egoyan's *The Sweet Hereafter* (1997, Canada) and Kiarostami's *A Taste of Cherry* (1997, Iran)

Since the passing of my beloved father six months ago, as well as my own brush with the Grim Reaper several years past, the subject of death has been much on my mind: death as the end of earthly life and the beginning of an afterlife, if only in the memories of the living; death as a wish in the old and infirm, as a terror to the young and healthy; natural death versus unnaturally prolonged life, death by disaster or suicide; the ritualistic ghoulishness of Christian burial in contrast to the cosmic cleanness of cremation; death as the ultimate confirmation either of life's meaninglessness or of its mean-ing*ful*ness. Obviously, there's nothing new in these oppositions, nor do I claim to have answers where others have only been able to put forward questions. But I have been living with death, and I have at least pondered the questions surrounding it as they are posed by two recent films: *The Sweet Hereafter* (1997) and *A Taste of Cherry* (1997).

The first of these is based on Russell Banks's 1991 novel of the same title, whose deathless epigraph (not cited in the movie) suits this dark, contemplative picture just as well as it does the hauntingly lyrical *Taste of Cherry*:

By homely gift and hindered Words
The human heart is told
Of Nothing –

"Nothing" is the force
That renovates the World –
    Emily Dickinson (#1563)[1]

The Canadian Atom Egoyan, who was born in Cairo but brought up in Armenia (and later Canada), both adapted and directed *The Sweet Hereafter*. Yet there is little in Egoyan's previous films, all written exclusively by him – *Next of Kin* (1984), *Family Viewing* (1988), *Speaking Parts* (1989), *The Adjuster* (1991), *Calendar* (1993), and *Exotica* (1994) – that could have presaged the humane richness of this new picture. His earlier work, often suffused with a black humor that's completely absent here, is less accessible than *The Sweet Hereafter* because of its aesthetic preening and postmodern affectlessness.

One quality all of Egoyan's films have in common, however, including this recent one, is a fragmented narrative that must be pieced together backward, either through flashback or by means of delayed, incomplete, and sometimes conflicting exposition, in a game of detective. So it's easy to understand what initially attracted him to Banks's novel, which is narrated retrospectively by four different characters, three of whom receive a chapter each and one who gets two chapters. In so splintering his narrative, Banks's intent is not, like Kurosawa's in *Rashomon* (1950), to demonstrate the relativity-cum-subjectivity of truth, since the stories of his narrators do not essentially contradict one another. This multiple first-person narrative does *isolate* each of the storytellers, however, and the destruction or fragmentation of small-town community is indeed one of the book's themes.

Egoyan sporadically employs a first-person narrative technique, voice-over, in his film of *The Sweet Hereafter*, but his real narrator, the camera, is omniscient, as it is in virtually all fiction features. So the director-screenwriter was faced with the problem of finding a cinematic equivalent for the sense of loneness shared by the characters in the novel, and he found it in two ways. First, he and his editor, Susan Shipton, frequently cut between or among faces in any one scene rather than holding the camera steady in medium-to-full shot on several characters together. And second, Egoyan makes a big-city outsider the main character, which has the effect of divorcing us somewhat from the townspeople even as they become very much alienated from one

1 *The Poems of Emily Dickinson*, Vol. 3, ed. Thomas H. Johnson (Cambridge: Harvard University Press, 1955), 1077. The year of this poem's composition is 1883.

another. In Banks's novel, it is Dolores Driscoll who could be called the main character, for she has two chapters to herself – significantly, the first and the last. Egoyan's shift of narrative focus to the outsider, Mitchell Stephens, does not make his film unfaithful to its literary source; this adaptation alters the voice and tone of the book without sacrificing its substance, which is to say that the movie turns a deeply felt but sometimes overemotional (and consequently flaccid), sometimes overliteral (and consequently flat) moral tale into an evocative, compassionate mystery on the subjects of children, community, and catastrophe. No small part of this mystery is Stephens himself, which is one of the reasons Egoyan foregrounds him at the expense of the transparent Dolores.

Another reason is that, as part liability lawyer, part ambulance chaser, Stephens is the only one in the novel who makes contact with the other first-person narrators – Billy Ansell and Nicole Burnell – in addition to Dolores, as well as with the non-narrating Walkers and Ottos. So, from the point of view of sheer plot or action – and remember that, while the novelist may see events through the medium of other people's minds, the filmmaker permits us to see other people's minds through the medium of events – he's the natural character around whom to center the film as he tries to solicit clients for a class-action negligence suit against the town of Sam Dent or the province of British Columbia. (The novel was set in the Adirondacks of upstate New York; Egoyan possibly placed the story in Canada to gain financing in his adopted country.) "There are no accidents," Stephens confidently declares from the start, in the movie as well as the book;[2] *someone*, namely someone with "deep pockets," had to be blamed for the "tragedy" that has befallen this half-barren, half-beautiful, once-unified mountain community.

On a snowbound, icy morning on the outskirts of town, you see, the local school bus had skidded off the side of a hill and plunged into a semi-frozen lake, killing fourteen of the twenty-two children aboard. Among the survivors were the bus driver, Dolores Driscoll, and the articulate, teenaged beauty queen Nicole Burnell, who will be wheelchair-bound for the rest of her life – her life having precipitously moved from the dizzying gaiety of a Ferris wheel (near which we first see her at an amusement park) to the vicious circularity of a wheel on a bus to the depressing monotony of a wheel on a chair. Among the

---

2 Russell Banks, *The Sweet Hereafter* (New York: HarperCollins, 1991), 91. Hereafter cited by page number.

dead were the widowed Billy Ansell's twins, Jessica and Mason; Risa and Wendell Walker's learning-disabled son, Sean; and Hartley and Wanda Otto's adopted Indian boy, Bear. In the aftermath of such a calamity, how does life go on? How do the parents cope? To whom do they turn for solace? Not to an ambulance-chasing attorney, the sparse population of this remote region at first seems to agree – and Mitchell Stephens is only one of a number of legal vultures who have swooped down on Sam Dent to prey on the eight families who lost children in the "accident." But Stephens doesn't view himself as a greedy bird of prey. He's already a huge professional success, and he is not without humane impulse, for he knows that even large financial recompense is small recompense for the loss of a child. "Let me represent your anger," Stephens exhorts one prospective litigant in the film, and through such representation he means to purge these bereaved parents of their anger if not their sadness, to direct their rage at some target. At least then, he argues, a vehicular catastrophe like this – the result, he has to believe, of faulty manufacturing or faulty (road or bus) maintenance, not of reckless driving on the part of the impecunious Dolores – will be less likely to occur in the future.

Stephens is driven by more than his own humanity, however: he's haunted by the twentysomething daughter that he (along with his wife, from whom he is divorced) has lost to heroin. He can deal with such a loss only through the surrogacy of this lawsuit, and it's a loss that torments him even more each time this taunting, frightening, itinerant young woman calls him collect from somewhere with a demand for money. Stephens' motives are never made explicit in the movie, but, paradoxically, they are simultaneously overexplained and underexplained in the novel:

... I don't need a shrink to tell me what motivates me. A shrink would probably tell me it's because I myself have lost a child and now identify with ... [t]he victims. Listen, identify with the victims and you become one yourself. Victims make lousy litigators. Simply, I do it because I'm pissed off, and that's what you get when you mix conviction with rage. ... Besides, the people of Sam Dent are not unique. We've all lost our children. ... Just look at them, for God's sake – violent on the streets, comatose in the malls, narcotized in front of the TV. In my lifetime something terrible happened that took our children away from us. I don't know if it was ... the sexual colonization of kids by industry, or drugs, or TV, or divorce, or what the hell it was; ... but the children are gone, that I know. (98–9)

We get none of this verbiage in the film, either through voice-over or dialogue. Instead, Egoyan's *Sweet Hereafter* begins by visually stating the picture's first theme, the parental love of children, with an overhead traveling shot of three sleeping people, exquisitely photographed in warm amber tones complemented by a woodgrain setting: the young Mitchell Stephens and his young wife Klara, with their infant daughter, Zoe, between them. Next we cut to Stephens in Sam Dent, trapped inside a car wash in a metaphorical equivalent of the children's entrapment in the sinking school bus; here, at Billy Ansell's garage (where the school bus was always serviced), he receives the first of several cellular phone calls from the nasty, drug-addicted Zoe and, after crawling out of his immobilized, inundated luxury car, here he gets his first look at the muddled, crumpled school bus retrieved from the bottom of the lake.

But immediately before Stephens' sighting of the bus, Egoyan intercuts a brief interlude at an amusement park in which we get our initial hint of the incestuous relationship between Nicole Burnell and her father, Sam. Thus the director-screenwriter has subtly suggested, mostly through images, what Banks laboriously literalizes in words: not only the connection between Stephens' estrangement from his once-beloved Zoe and Sam Dent's loss of its precious children, as well as this lawyer's habitual placing of his professional life ahead of his familial one, but also the buttoned-down rage he will use in the service of his clients – at this moment expressed toward his daughter over the telephone. Moreover, by means of the juxtaposed scene between Nicole and *her* father, Egoyan has shown the diametrical opposite of the extreme hatred Zoe has come to have for her father, and that he reflexively reciprocates: the excessive love that Sam Burnell has exhibited toward his daughter and that, for a time, she involuntarily returns.

As described above, the past exists on two levels in Egoyan's *Sweet Hereafter*: before the bus disaster on 6 December 1995 (27 January 1990 in the novel), and in its painful aftermath, commencing with Mitchell Stephens' arrival in Sam Dent. Present time in the film takes place in flash-forward, on 29 November 1997, inside an airplane carrying Stephens away from Sam Dent for the last time, to a big American city where he will rendezvous with the now AIDS-infected Zoe. (And where he will run into Dolores Driscoll at the airport, far enough away from home that she could get another bus-driving job, but obviously so closely identified with the mishap in Stephens' mind that her mysterious appearance here startles him – perhaps into the understanding that, even as he cannot shed parental responsibility for Zoe, he, like Dolores, will never be able to escape moral accountability for his part in the "death" of Sam Dent.) There is no such present in Banks's book: there, the present is solely the narrative one from which each solitary narrator relates his or her tale. Egoyan invents this airplane scene and the character of the young woman sitting next to Stephens – a scene to which he returns five times – in order to give the lawyer someone to whom he can confide the dreadful story of his daughter's degradation – a story not yet finished, and which he not only is powerless to stop but also cannot help assisting with his paternal dollars.

Coincidentally, this quietly concerned young woman, called Allison O'Donald, was a friend of Zoe's at school and is herself the daughter of an attorney – Stephens' former partner, in fact. Clearly, Allison is meant to represent the kind of person Zoe's father wishes his daughter had become: polite, well spoken, well groomed, and apparently accomplished. She doesn't say much during the flight because she need not, indeed should not. Her mere visage, combined with Stephens' own, says enough, particularly considering that we first encounter it shortly after the opening scenes depicting in turn the infant Zoe alongside her parents, the young adult Zoe on the phone to her father, and the teenaged Nicole Burnell being ogled by her father. Allison is another "ingredient" added to the narrative's mix of children, in other words, and a welcome one, for she provides a counterweight to Banks's unalleviated chronicle of desolation. The fact that Stephens remembers neither Allison's father nor her (if he ever met her) is noteworthy, for it suggests the extent to which he has denied himself affective investment in the lives of others as a way of coping with – or, worse, as a way of extending – the emotional bankruptcy of his relationship with his own wife and daughter.

Furthermore, that Stephens treats the personal as if it were the professional, or that he has systematically substituted the ice of the latter for the warmth of the former, is clear from a story he tells Allison about his Zoe's accidental brush with death as a child. While on vacation with her parents one summer on the Outer Banks of North Carolina, the napping little girl had been bitten by a black widow spider, with the result that her face, arms, and legs became swollen out of all proportion. Rushing her by car to an emergency room forty miles inland, in Elizabeth City, Stephens had to be prepared to perform an emergency tracheotomy with a Swiss Army knife if Zoe's throat closed up and stopped her breathing. He was prepared but never had to cut his daughter's windpipe: she was still breathing when they arrived at the hospital, where a doctor administered the antidote, Zoe's swelling receded, and she was back to normal in a few hours.

In Egoyan's *Sweet Hereafter*, Stephens tells this story without editorial comment, and we see images from it, so that *we* have to make the connection between his controlled role in his daughter's rescue and his equally controlled role in the proposed lawsuit on behalf of some of Sam Dent's aggrieved parents; so that *we* must perceive Stephens both as a controlling, even deadening or knifelike, force in Zoe's life and as a dominating, even divisive or cutting, force in the life of Sam Dent's inhabitants. Here, by contrast, is Russell Banks again to explain it all to you, in the person of Stephens himself – at least to spell out the first half of the above equation to such an extent that one feels robbed of the impulse to conjure up the second half:

I can't tell you why I connect that terrifying drive to Elizabeth City over two decades ago to this case in Sam Dent now, where children actually died ... but there is a powerful equivalence. With my knife in my hand and my child lying in my lap, smiling up at me, trusting me utterly, with her face swelling like a painted balloon, progressively distorting her features into grotesque versions of themselves, I felt the same clearheaded power that I felt during those first days in Sam Dent, when the suit was taking off. I felt no ambivalence, did no second guessing, had no mistrusted motives – ...

Now in my dreams of her, ... Zoe is still that child in my lap, trusting me utterly – even though I am the man who secretly held in his hand the knife that he had decided to use to cut into her throat, and thus I am in no way the man she sees smiling down at her ... (124–5)

Nicole Burnell comes to view Stephens not as a smiling knife-wielder but as a pied piper to the town of Sam Dent. Indeed, in one early scene, Egoyan has Nicole read Robert Browning's "The Pied Piper of Hamelin" (1842) to Billy Ansell's twins, whom she babysat before the bus accident. Then he threads verses from this "child's story," as Browning subtitled it, through the rest of the film; they continue to be spoken by Nicole, in these instances in voice-over, and they are always associated with either the legal activities of Mitchell Stephens or the incestuous acts of Sam Burnell, or, in *The Sweet Hereafter*'s climax, both at the same time. The use of this poem is Egoyan's invention – it appears nowhere in the novel – and it is meant to be a lyrical rendition of Nicole's feelings and ultimately her motives. In other words, it is yet another metaphorical substitute for Banks's lit-

Ian Holm as Mitchell Stephens and Sarah Polley as Nicole
Burnell in *The Sweet Hereafter*.

eralism, here expressed by Nicole in her role as the narrator of the
book's penultimate chapter:

... I hated my parents ... for all that had gone before – Daddy for what he knew
and had done, and Mom for what she didn't know and hadn't done – but I also
hated them for this new thing, this awful lawsuit. The lawsuit was wrong. Purely
wrong; but also it was making Billy Ansell sadder than life had already done on
its own, and that seemed stupid and cruel; and now it looked like half the people in town were doing it too, making everyone around them crazy with pain,
... so they didn't have to face their own pain and get over it.

Why couldn't they see that? Why couldn't they just stand up like good people and say to Mr. Stephens, "No, forget the lawsuit ... It's too harmful to too
many people. Goodbye, Mr. Stephens. Take your law practice back to [the big]
City, where people *like* to sue each other." (197)

Now Browning's pied piper leads the children of Hamelin to their
disappearance, not in a lake or river, but in a mountainside, where

A wondrous portal opened wide,
As if a cavern was suddenly hollowed;
And the Piper advanced and the children followed,
And when all were in to the very last,
The door in the mountain-side shut fast.

Did I say, all? No! One was lame,
   And could not dance the whole of the way; ...[3]

The piper steals these children because Hamelin's mayor and council-
men broke their promise to pay him a thousand guilders for ridding
the town of its numerous rats, all of which

Followed the piper for their lives.
From street to street he piped advancing,
And step for step they followed dancing,
Until they came to the river Weser,
   Wherein all plunged and perished! (338)

"The Pied Piper of Hamelin" doesn't appear to be a gloss on *The
Sweet Hereafter* for the obvious reason that Dolores Driscoll does not
intentionally lead fourteen of Sam Dent's children to their deaths in an
icy lake. But the poem is a gloss if one regards it, more or less, as a
reversal of the film, or the film's events as a reversal of the poem's. To
wit, the fourteen children of *The Sweet Hereafter* are "stolen away" before
the "pied piper," Mitchell Stephens, arrives (even as his own child has
long since been lost to another pied piper: addictive drugs); Stephens
is to be paid for "piping out" the "rat" that caused Dolores's bus to skid
off the mountain pass, so that no such calamity can ever rob the town
of its children again; and the grieving parents of Sam Dent – all of
them except Billy Ansell, who refuses to join any lawsuit – break their
promise, not by refusing to pay Stephens (as the government of
Hamelin did the pied piper), but by engaging him and other attorneys
for the purpose of *seeking* monetary damages. This is Billy Ansell's view,
in any case, and it becomes Nicole Burnell's: that the town has broken
its *communal* promise and thus become divided against itself to such a
degree that it cannot properly mourn its dead children, who for this
reason are condemned to die again and again in their parents' hearts
and minds. This is particularly true in Billy's case, as he witnessed the
accident in the novel as well as the film, in perhaps the worst of all possible ways: from the truck in which he followed the bus every morning,
waving to his two kids, who sat in the rear bus seat just so they could
wave back. Helpless to do anything except summon aid that would
arrive too late, Billy afterward did the next best thing, to his mind: he

---

3 *The Poetical Works of Robert Browning* (London: Oxford University Press,
   1905; rpt. 1957), 339. Hereafter cited by page number.

broke off his adulterous but unloving affair with the unhappily married and similarly grief-stricken Risa Walker.

The crippled Nicole figures in Browning's poem as the lame child left behind – somewhat like the trailing Billy Ansell – when "the door in the mountain-side shut fast." In "The Pied Piper of Hamelin," this child is powerless, however, either to join its young friends or to do anything about their disappearance:

> 'It's dull in our town since my playmates left!
> 'I can't forget that I'm bereft
> ...
> 'The music stopped and I stood still,
> 'And found myself outside the hill,
> 'Left alone against my will,
> ...' (339)

Nicole is not so powerless, nor is Sam Burnell innocent of having broken a father's promise by "stealing away" his daughter with his own kind of piping – in Egoyan's film associated with his interest in rockabilly music (composed by Mychael Danna, who also provided the sometimes eerie or insistent incidental score), which he uses to seduce the aspiring songster in Nicole.

In *The Sweet Hereafter*'s climax, Nicole has her revenge against her grasping, guilt-ridden father and the searching, sublimating Stephens by giving eyewitness testimony, in a pre-trial deposition, that Dolores Driscoll was speeding along at seventy-two miles per hour when the school bus careened off the road. Nicole is lying but her lie, in her view, is a malignant means to a benign end: the killing of the lawsuit, for now there is no one with "deep pockets" to sue for malfeasance. (At fifty-five miles per hour or so Dolores was not speeding, but, characteristically for this picture, the cause of the accident is otherwise left unspecified or unverifiable; in the novel, Dolores positivistically states that she hit her brakes when she thought she saw a dog up ahead, and that as a result the bus skidded off the icy road into a large sinkhole.) After Nicole tells her lie at the courthouse, the camera cuts between a tearful, chastened Sam Burnell and a shocked, defeated Mitchell Stephens as, for the last time, Nicole recites in voice-over from "The Pied Piper of Hamelin." Egoyan even gives her a verse, not found in Browning's poem, in which the piper questions the selfish, self-satisfied mayor as to why he lied, as if to underscore at once Nicole's own selfless and self-protective reasons for doing so.

The filmmaker also gives Nicole the concluding lines of the movie – lines that belong to Dolores Driscoll in the novel – which she speaks in voice-over as well: "All of us ... who survived the accident, and the children who did not – it was as if we were the citizens of a wholly different town now, as if we were a town of solitaries living in a sweet hereafter ..." (254). The bitter aftermath of the accident is sweet for Nicole only in the sense that her father no longer attempts to sexually abuse his physically disabled daughter, so what can she be talking about here? Well, she's talking about a kind of living death that is sweet or blissful in the sense that she and the other survivors are, by virtue of their near-miraculous survival, forever oblivious to the normal stresses and strains, the sourness and the sorriness, of everyday life. Nicole doesn't spell this out for us, which makes our deciphering of it all the more pleasurable – particularly since we must also decipher *The Sweet Hereafter*'s complementary and equally enigmatic final images. In them, the babysitter Nicole kisses Billy Ansell's kids goodnight in the past, in her imagination, or in the sweet afterlife, and then she walks out of their nearly darkened room to a window from which she appears to witness a new dawn or a sudden flash of light, subsequent to which the screen fades to black. By contrast, Banks predictably dispels all mystery from the book's ending: his Dolores continues the narration quoted above with the observation that, "even if we weren't dead, in an important way which no longer puzzled or frightened me and which I therefore no longer resisted, we were as good as dead ... Our [lives] ... were gone forever but still calling mournfully back to us" (254, 256).

Dolores is also permitted by Banks to voice a sentiment in her final chapter that Egoyan's film *shows* us throughout and that even the novel has already made implicit by virtue of its very structure: that "[a] town needs its children, just as much and in the same ways as a family does. It comes undone without them, turns a community into a windblown scattering of isolated individuals" (236–7). *The Sweet Hereafter*, then, is not about children but about how the loss of children – of their love – can lead to the dissolution of family and community. Thus is the child ironically made guardian to the man. A subject so infused with grief could easily become mawkish, but Egoyan avoids sentimentality by de-emphasizing Dolores Driscoll's featured role in the novel as the feeling victimizer unfeelingly victimized and by putting in her place the contained, directed Mitchell Stephens, litigator.

He's played by Ian Holm, or I should say that, within his compact range, Holm resonantly plays every note on the equally compressed scale of his character's personality. This trenchant actor is complemented by a largely Canadian ensemble that has followed Egoyan through his ever-growing career, including Bruce Greenwood as Billy Ansell, Gabrielle Rose as Dolores Driscoll, Arsinée Khanjian (the director's wife) as Wanda Otto, and Sarah Polley as Nicole Burnell. I can pay these actors no higher compliment than to say that each of them truly knows what the word "ensemble" means: not only to work together on a film, in mutual artistic support, but also to remain together over several films, so as to enhance one's own – and thus the pictures' – artistry. This is how the world's best theatre companies work, but, with few exceptions – the most notable being the cinema of Ingmar Bergman – it is not how movies are produced.

Bergman's cinematographer of choice was Sven Nykvist, and Egoyan's now appears to be Paul Sarossy, who shot *Speaking Parts, The Adjuster,* and *Exotica* prior to *The Sweet Hereafter.* Along with the production designer, Philip Barker, Sarossy captures in his images here not only the wet-wool feeling of wintry living but also the languid look of winter light, which includes the look of snow under that light. Snow in *The Sweet Hereafter* has colors other than solid or glistening white, as you might expect, and on account of its various shades this snow comes to symbolize something other than mere purity. Namely, its own paradox: that snow combines the ideas of ethereality and materiality, confinement and liberation, numbness and sensation, vista-vision and purblindness. These ideas are also contained in the narrative, so nature felicitously serves art in this instance, not the other way around (as in the cinema of spectacle).

Nature serves art in most of the Iranian films I know, as well, for the last thing one could call *The Runner* (1984), *The Jar* (1992), *Nargess* (1992), or *Abadani-Ha* (1993) is spectacular. One recent exception to this rule is Mohsen Makhmalbaf's *Gabbeh* (1996), whose story is the merest excuse for a rhapsody of natural textures: of the titular carpets, of vast plains, rock formations, clouds, and even of the streams in which the nomadic tribesmen of southeast Iran dip their colorful dyes. A sense of place is crucial, to be sure, in the films of Abbas Kiarostami, who, along with Makhmalbaf, Bahram Beizai, Amir Naderi, and Dariush Mehrjui, is the most esteemed of contemporary Iranian directors. The village of Koker in northwestern Iran, for example – particularly an undulating hillside there – unites the pictures in Kiarostami's loose trilogy around the devastating earthquake of 1990, *Where Is the Friend's House?* (1987), *And Life Goes On ...* (1992), and *Through the Olive Trees* (1994). But "place" here has nothing to do with groundless spectacle and everything to do with aesthetic grounding, with the visual communication of feeling and idea.

Perhaps the fifty-eight-year-old Kiarostami's concern with place derives from his work as a documentarian. He was the head, both in the pre-revolutionary days of the shah and the post-revolutionary era of the Shiite Muslim ayatollah, of the filmmaking section of the Center for the Intellectual Development of Children and Young Adults. (Kiarostami held this post from 1979 until 1988, when rightist hard-liners dislodged him.) There he made such documentaries about school children as *Case No. 1, Case No. 2* (1979), *Regular or Irregular* (1981), *First Graders* (1985), and *Homework* (1989). In all of these films, non-fictional location, rather than fictional narrative or even the "true story," comprises the motivating foundation for everything that we see and hear – as in documentaries generally, which aptly take their name from the French word for travelogue, or the chronicling of a place together with its people.

Even the first of Kiarostami's fiction films, a short titled *Bread and Alley* (1970) – which came in the wake of Mehrjui's *The Cow* (1969), the initiator of the New Wave of Iranian cinema – reveals this director's predilection for place. Its story, about a boy and minatory dog, is anec-dotally slight, but the way in which the camera observes and negotiates the labyrinthine alleyways of central Tehran is visually telling. Like *Bread and Alley*, as well as the previously cited documentaries, Kiarostami's first fiction feature, *The Traveler* (1974), also features a child in addition to a cityscape (which begins as a landscape). In this case, that child is a provincial boy who is on a desperate quest to reach Tehran in time to see a soccer match.

Numerous Iranian movies have such child protagonists, just as did the Italian neorealist cinema that Kiarostami claims as the greatest influence on his work;[4] indeed, Kiarostami wrote the script for Jafar Panahi's *White Balloon* (1995), described in the previous chapter and featuring a seven-year-old girl. No, Iranian filmmakers are not obsessed with children for their own sake (as, one could argue, François Truffaut was); as noted earlier, they are trying to avoid the minefield of Islamic restrictions on the portrayal of adult male-female relationships. Kiarostami's latest picture, *A Taste of Cherry*, does not feature a child, however, and it was almost blocked from export by the Iranian author-ities because of its adult subject, suicide. (Four of his movies have been banned within Iran, but only one is now deemed unfit for showing any-where in the world: *Case No. 1, Case No. 2*, an anti-authoritarian docu-mentary about classroom discipline.) Islamic law not only prohibits

---

4 Interview with Abbas Kiarostami, *Sight and Sound* 7, no. 1 (Jan. 1997): 24.

suicide, it also forbids even discussion of this topic. Yet somehow *A Taste of Cherry*, which Kiarostami wrote, directed, *and* edited, made it to the 1997 Cannes Film Festival, where it became the first film from Iran to be awarded the Palme d'Or – an event that, in its significance for the Moslem world, recalls Kurosawa's Grand Prix at Venice in 1951 for *Rashomon*, which first brought Asian art cinema to the attention of international audiences.

Although its subject is suicide, *A Taste of Cherry* has a theme in common with both *And Life Goes On ...* and *Through the Olive Trees*: the struggle of life against death, or death against life. And Kiarostami's most recent work, like all of his previous films, documentaries and fictional ones alike, acknowledges the means of its own creation. If *Homework* shows the director, his crew, and their equipment in addition to the school children being interviewed, *Through the Olive Trees* features an actor who plays Kiarostami as he shoots a scene, again and again, from the already-released *And Life Goes On ...* – a proposal scene between a man and a woman, both non-professionals, whose romantic involvement had in reality begun when they were recruited more or less to play themselves in the earlier picture. If *Regular or Irregular* puts Kiarostami on the soundtrack, commenting about the content as well as the form of the images in this short film about orderly versus disorderly children, the quasi-documentary *Close-Up* (1990) puts the actual persons involved in a real-life fraud – the duping of a wealthy family by a poor man impersonating the famous director Mohsen Makhmalbaf – in a cinematic reconstruction of the story.

Some commentators see Kiarostami's acknowledgment of the artifice of filmmaking, together with his blurring of the line between documentary and fiction, as nothing more than an obsessive directorial conceit that is didactic, manipulative, and by now – after over half a century of literary as well as cinematic homage to Brecht's theory of distanciation – otiose. I see this director's cinematic self-reference, however, as something more, and more profound: as his way of questioning, in so repressive a society as Iran's, the truth not merely of the government's pronouncements and propaganda but also of his own fictions and documentaries, of the very act of creating or chronicling, reshaping or recording. And nowhere is Kiarostami's self-doubting authorship more appropriate than in *A Taste of Cherry*, for this movie is concerned with individual self-doubt, self-ridicule, self-loathing, or just plain self-weariness so powerful that it would lead to self-annihilation.

Homayoun Ershadi, as Mr Badii, in his vehicle in
A Taste of Cherry.

Mr Badii, a middle-aged man with dark eyes, bruise-colored lips, a
powerful forehead, and magnificent nostrils, drives slowly around the
hilly outskirts of northeastern Tehran in his white Range Rover, searching for someone to assist him in his plan to commit suicide. He will pay
good money – 200,000 tomans – if someone of his choosing will return
the next morning to a prearranged spot in these hills – a hole by the
side of the road – and either pull him out if he is still alive or shovel
dirt onto his body if he is dead. (Compare his plan with that of the central figures in Vyacheslav Krishtofovich's *A Friend of the Deceased* [1997]
and Warren Beatty's *Bulworth* [1998] to have a hit man knock them off
– a device borrowed from Aki Kaurismäki's 1990 film *I Hired A Contract
Killer.*) Mr Badii, it becomes clear, is going to swallow a bottle of sleeping pills, lie down in that hole, and await the result. Though he wants
to commit the ultimate act of self-isolation, he also wants to be buried
– or not buried, he explains, if he is unconscious but not dead – a social
nicety that paradoxically will require his participation in one final
human relationship.

Robert Bresson's *The Devil, Probably* (1977) involves a similar
premise, but Bresson uses it to bemoan the corrupt and corrupting
state of the modern world, which the pure Catholic soul can gracefully
escape through suicide (another paradox, since Catholicism, like

Islam, proscribes the killing of oneself). In both *The Devil, Probably* and *A Taste of Cherry* the figure of the accomplice is a device used to give dramatic form to a moral-philosophical argument; in Kiarostami's picture, however, Bresson's argument is, if not reversed – with a damaged and damaging soul opposed by a good world – then certainly complicated. Indeed, Mr Badii never quite tells us why he wants to commit suicide or what his problem with existence is, beyond briefly alluding once to unhappiness, once to tiredness, and once to a propensity for hurting other people. It takes over twenty minutes of *A Taste of Cherry*, in fact, before we learn either Mr Badii's name or that he wants to kill himself.

We first see him in profile, in close-up, soberly driving past a crowd of unemployed laborers who are waiting for any kind of work and who offer their services. But Mr Badii shakes his head and moves on until he overhears a young man in a telephone booth complaining about a shortage of money. He offers this fellow a lift and financial help, but the latter refuses, as does another man who collects plastic bags and bottles from the countryside, then sells them back in the city. Still we do not know Mr Badii's name or his reason for soliciting these men, and as the film pauses to roll its minimal credits, we continue to hear the sounds of the searching Range Rover. There is no music, and there will be none until the coda or epilogue.

What we do know, at this point, is the nature of the place in which *A Taste of Cherry* transpires. Kiarostami clearly shot the picture in autumn to take advantage of the metaphorical significance of the season of dying. The hills outside Tehran are parched, the grass dead or sunburned, and everything the cinematographer Homayoun Payvar's camera shoots seems yellow-brown: the dirt mounds, dirt roads, ditches, the dusty air, even the occasional tree or bush. The sun has been here, but this is not a sunny place; the weather may not be cold but the subject is chilly enough; the sky is mostly overcast, the atmosphere polluted, the light flat, and the evening shadows long. We seem to be in an underdeveloped industrial wasteland – the opposite of the garishly colored, overdeveloped one in Antonioni's *Red Desert* (1964) – that features piled-up pipes, a sporadic derrick or water tower, rock piles, abandoned cars, forlorn phone lines, and halted building construction. The only moving vehicles we see besides Mr Badii's Range Rover are a few tractors and dump trucks, which appear to move dirt from one excavation site to another in a travesty of purposeful human activity. The only color we can detect in the landscape besides yellow-brown is gray-green; the only sound we hear, apart from that of human voices and motorized vehicles, is the momentary chirping of a few birds.

This is a place, you would think – at best inchoate and haphazard, at worst desolate and colorless – that might drive anyone to commit suicide, or at least to drive here in order to do it, but Mr Badii is the only man we observe who has a death wish. And he is the main character among a cast of characters made up almost exclusively of men, most of them displaced persons or menial laborers in contrast with the well-heeled Badii. There are few women in *A Taste of Cherry* – actually only one, among the extras – almost certainly because of the Islamic restrictions on their use in motion pictures. But it's tempting to speculate, from a Western point of view, that Mr Badii's loss of direction in life may have something to do with the absence of the female principle from his world, not to speak of the absence of the offspring of male-female unions: children.

Moreover, as Mr Badii's Range Rover negotiates yet another curve or passes through one more hollow in the terrain, we get the feeling that he is going in circles, and thus that the parabolic loop of his automobile is meant not only to parody the linear or progressive genre of the road movie but also to suggest the parabolic nature of this otherwise realistic tale. For geometric parabolas and narrative parables have this in common: they both derive from the ancient Greek word meaning to compare, or literally "to place beside," the plane curve of a parabola being less important than the locus of points equidistant from a fixed point on that parabola, even as the simple arc of events in a parable is less significant than the moral or spiritual lesson illustrated by that arc.

That arc really begins with the first man who accepts a ride in Mr Badii's Range Rover, in the front seat of which most of *A Taste of Cherry* will take place, most of it in medium, shot-reverse-shot between Badii and each of his interlocutors. Such a shooting style, separating the characters in their own frames, is entirely appropriate to the theme of the film, for Mr Badii has already made the decision to separate himself from this world, and – in an echo of one of the themes from Kiarostami's screenplay for *The White Balloon* – the three men he propositions are, each in his own way, isolated or estranged from Iranian society. That first one is a shy young Kurdish conscript, on the way back to his military barracks at five o'clock in the afternoon; a farmer back home, he seems to know almost no one in Tehran and shows no sign of having acclimated himself to army life. Yet it is to this man that the protagonist first reveals his name and his underlying purpose. And it is with this soldier's entrance into *A Taste of Cherry* that we get our initial look at Mr Badii's Range Rover from the outside, in the first of several bird's-eye view shots that establish the expansiveness of Tehran's hill country at the same time as they diminish the size of all those who would traverse it. But despite the fact that 200,000 tomans equal six months of a soldier's pay – and that Mr Badii is willing to pay in advance (with the rest of the money to be left for the taking in his vehicle or at his side) – the Kurd refuses to participate in Mr Badii's suicide plan. Scared and confused, he runs away when the Range Rover stops at the would-be grave site.

Undeterred, Mr Badii drives on, watching the world or eyeing the countryside from one remove: through the screen or protective barrier of his windshield. After he stops at an empty, idle cement plant, he again looks at the world through a screen, in this case the windows of the plant's watchtower, and we watch Mr Badii in medium long shot through another kind of screen, which identifies us with him even when the camera is not literally identifying us with his point of view. Here, with the same ulterior motive as before, he offers a ride to the lone security guard at the plant – an Afghan who, for much of their conversation, stands off-camera in a kitchenette cooking his supper – but is politely refused. The man says that he must not leave his post and that, though he'd like the momentary diversion and company that Mr Badii offers, he's grown accustomed to the loneliness of his job.

The watchman does have a friend visiting, however: another Afghan, a student at an Islamic seminary who came to Iran because of Afghanistan's war with the former Soviet Union and who admits to feeling at loose ends in his adopted country. This seminarian, this solider of Allah, if you will, does agree to take a drive with Mr Badii, and thus becomes the second individual to be propositioned. But he, too, refuses to play any role in Mr Badii's suicide plan, although he does not run away from the grave site that he's shown, as did the military conscript. Instead, the seminarian quotes from the Koran the standard Islamic injunctions against suicide, one of which is that killing yourself is still killing, and killing is wrong. He is doubtless sincere but undoubtedly ineffective, for Mr Badii does not end his quest to find an accomplice in self-murder.

He finds that person in Mr Bagheri, an older man and a Turk, who works as a taxidermist at a natural history museum. Such a workplace also appears in Bresson's *Une femme douce* (1969), where the female protagonist commits suicide as well. In this film the young woman complains that "we're all – men and animals – composed of the same matter, the same raw material," and later we have this truism visually confirmed when she herself visits the museum of natural history. She would transcend, you see, a universe in which all is matter and where even human beings, like animals, often seem to behave in a preconditioned manner – preconditioned to accumulate wealth and possessions, to glorify the self, even to respond to art in a particular way. Perhaps the seemingly affluent Mr Badii feels the same way, if the humble Mr Bagheri does not. In any event, the latter finds the former, not vice versa as in the previous two cases: the taxidermist suddenly materializes, alone, in the Range Rover alongside a road, to which vehicle Mr Badii returns after morbidly examining yet another excavation site (where a large hole covered with a metal grate is being filled with dirt). And one can reasonably conclude therefrom that the Turk has asked for, as opposed to being offered, a ride, or, indeed, that he has been heaven-sent for a higher purpose.

Unlike the Kurdish soldier and the Afghan seminarian, this Turkish taxidermist is ruminative and talkative: he tells a joke, relates a story, even sings a song. Furthermore, Mr Bagheri almost immediately agrees to do what Mr Badii asks, because he needs the money to help his sickly child; but then he tries to talk the Iranian out of suicide by talking up the joys of life and nature. He admits that he tried to commit suicide in 1960 by hanging himself from a mulberry tree, but in the process of climbing the tree to secure a rope, he decided to taste one of the mulberries. The succulent taste of that berry altered his view, reclaiming his life for him. Later the taxidermist asks what for him is a rhetorical question, but for which Mr Badii has long since had the unorthodox answer. "You want to give up the taste of cherries?" Mr Bagheri inquires, and it is the mark of Kiarostami's subtlety that this question gives the picture its title. For it comes, not out of nowhere but, still, some time after the story that gives it its full meaning, and almost as an aside. Yet Kiarostami showcases the singular object of this question in his title, which is a metaphorical way of "privileging" not only the pleasurable dailiness of daily life but also the pleasurable potency of the chance remark, the spontaneous gesture, the anti-climactic action, or the random encounter that may come out of such life. (For similar titles and thematic preoccupations, see such films as *A Hen in the Wind* [1948], *The Flavor of Green Tea over Rice* [1952], and *Twilight in Tokyo* [1957] by the Japanese director Yasujiro Ozu.) As a declaration and not a question, moreover, the title *A Taste of Cherry* is a way of saying that this movie is a metaphorical taste of cherry for its audience, even as life was such a cherry for Mr Badii that he tasted and found wanting.

Mr Bagheri thinks that the Iranian's mind is his problem, not the world itself, that Mr Badii must change his outlook on the world – his screen on it, if you will – if the world is to change its look for him. The taxidermist illustrates his argument by analogy, with a joke that reveals his tactile or sensual placement of himself in the world:

A fellow goes to his doctor and says, "Everything's wrong with me, but I don't know what disease I have. I touch my head, and it hurts. I touch my chest, and it hurts. I touch my leg, and it hurts. What's the problem?" The doctor examines him and says, "Your finger's broken."

But Mr Badii neither laughs at nor otherwise acknowledges the folk wisdom in Mr Bagheri's little story. In a film dominated by questions– mostly Mr Badii's own probing interrogation of the suitability as well as agreeability of his passengers to the moribund task at hand – the would-be suicide has no more to ask and nothing more to say. Like the soldier and the seminarian before him, Mr Bagheri himself hasn't been asking many questions; he has been volubly responding to Mr Badii's queries, as if it were his and, to a lesser extent, the other two men's thoughts and feelings that *A Taste of Cherry* wished to elicit more than anything else. That Mr Bagheri in addition tells stories to reveal his analysis of Mr Badii's problem and neither the Kurd nor the Afghan even attempts such a metaphorical analysis are subtle indications that, as members of a lower social class, all three lack the moral authority to question their superior. Such a lack of inquisitional authority, of course, partly explains why we don't discover Mr Badii's reasons for wanting to end his life.

As twilight approaches, and right after Mr Bagheri has told yet another story – this time in song – about the virtue of friendship, Mr Badii drops the taxidermist off at the natural history museum, where his accomplice optimistically avows that, at 6 a.m. the following morning, he will pull a living Mr Badii out of his makeshift grave. We see Mr Bagheri at work here – or rather we see Mr Badii see him through the windows of a museum shop – showing students how to stuff and mount a quail, just as, not long before, we had seen Mr Badii perform a roughly analogous act of "immortalization" by agreeing to take the picture of a young couple along the side of a road. In the subsequent interlude – worthy of Antonioni at his best in the coda of *L'eclisse* (1962), with his camera inhabiting an *a priori* world – we see Mr Badii outside his car, and for once he is neither looking at the world through a screen nor looking down at earth in which he would be covered up. He looks up to see a jet stream, turns to observe some children playing, then watches a man just sitting on a bench. Next he himself sits down on a hillside and looks out at Tehran in the distance as the sun languorously goes down and the moon majestically comes up.

After *A Taste of Cherry*'s first cross-fade, we next find ourselves looking at Mr Badii for the duration of a long nighttime take through the picture window of his Tehran apartment, as he paces back and forth seemingly in mental agony. A taxi honks its horn from the street, the lights in the apartment go out, and Mr Badii leaves to be driven to his designated grave in the hills as a thunder storm approaches. We observe that hole in the earth in *temps mort* before he gets there, then we watch him in another long take as he sits near the grave, walks down into it, and finally lies on his back. The last time we see Mr Badii, he is looking up at the camera from his supine position in the ground. As the moon retreats behind the clouds and rain begins to fall, the screen fades to black on his face and remains black for quite some time, though we know that *A Taste of Cherry* has not ended because we continue to hear rain and thunder (but no music) and even see flashes of lightning.

Finally morning comes, but there's been a cinematographic change: the image we see, of the place where Mr Badii had lain down to die, is presented in that grainy texture filmmakers use to give us the idea we are looking at a TV screen or at something that is being video-taped for eventual television airing, with the landscape transformed into the fertile green of spring. Then we see a film crew on the hill-side, in the midst of their work shooting a group of soldiers who march in the background; we pick out the actor who plays Mr Badii, lighting a cigarette as he walks around out-of-character amidst the cameras and microphone booms, and we even observe Kiarostami himself shouting that "the shoot is over." An instrumental version of the Dixieland tune "St James Infirmary" – a mainstay of the New Orleans jazz funeral – subsequently begins to play on the soundtrack as the conscripts rest by the roadside, the crew prepares to return to Tehran, and, in the very last shot, Mr Badii's Range Rover drives off into the distance.

Did Mr Badii die of the overdose of sleeping pills? Did he even take the pills, since we don't see him do so? Did Mr Bagheri arrive to either bury or resuscitate Mr Badii? We do not know, or rather Kiarostami does not tell us. His character is in search of an author, and that author is the movie audience, with whom Mr Badii has been identified because, to repeat, his looking at life through screens or barriers mimics the very experience of watching a film. In this open ending in which the questions are left hanging, *we* must make the life-and-death decision, and whatever we decide, based on our sifting of all the visual and aural evidence, will be a measure of our own sensibility – not Kiarostami's or Mr Badii's.

Kiarostami has said that "The filmmaker can only raise questions, and it is the audience who should seek the answer, who should have the opportunity for reflection to find questions in their own mind to complete the unfinished part of a work. So there are as many different versions of the same film as there are members of a given audience."[5] In the last sentence above, I would put the emphasis on the various "members of a given audience." For I believe, as I implied earlier, that one of this author-director's missions is to empower that audience – particularly an Iranian one, to free it to think and decide for itself, especially about taboo subjects like suicide. Kiarostami is no reader-response theorist, aesthetic relativist, or cinematic subjectivist: he's a species of existential philosopher trapped or paralyzed inside an autocratic theocracy, an Ingmar Bergman of the Islamic world, if you will, whose camera would represent reality at the same time as it exposes the means of its representation.

Included in that representation is the work of non-actors, whom Kiarostami prefers to use both because they are less theatrical or self-dramatizing – and therefore more realistic – than professionals, and because they are more manipulable or moldable, and hence less resistant to this *auteur*'s formalistic designs. To wit, the chief (non)actors in *A Taste of Cherry* – Homayoun Ershadi (Mr Badii), an architect in real life who also plays the leading role in Dariush Mehrjui's *The Pear Tree* (1998); Abdolhossein Bagheri (Mr Bagheri); Safir Ali Moradi (the Kurdish soldier); and Mir Hossein Nouri (the Afghan seminarian) – did not work with each other in the scenes in which we see them. Although most of the picture takes place in the front seat of Mr Badii's Range Rover, as he drives and converses with one passenger after another, the two segments of each sequence – the driver's contribution to the dia-

5 Kiarostami interview, p. 24.

logue, on the one hand, and the passenger's, on the other – were filmed separately.

According to the press kit, in each case the sequence was shot with Kiarostami himself (his presence unseen and his voice unheard) doing the driving and initiating the conversation, while the other man, on camera, responded. Subsequently, this footage was intercut with shots of Mr Badii at the wheel, asking the same questions and making the same remarks in Kiarostami's place. Serendipitously, such a method calls for a shot-reverse-shot editing style that, as I've already indicated, is thematically apt here. But one has to conclude that Kiarostami's prime reason for using this (invisible) split-screen device, like Godard and Bresson before him, was to guard against acting in the conventional sense – acting, that is, that inadvertently calls attention to its own devices, causes actors to fall out of tune with the world around the shot, and by its very self-exhibitive roundedness, fullness, or variegation would lend a self-importance to this film's characters that they themselves do not possess.

As different as *A Taste of Cherry* is from *The Sweet Hereafter* – not only in acting style, directorial signature, and titular import but also in physical as well as spiritual ambiance – in Mitchell Stephens and Mr Badii these two films share protagonists who, for all the dissimilarity of their dramatic objectives, are alike in the mystery or tacitness of their motives. Moreover, both individuals are from a social class that is significantly higher than that of each potential client or possible accomplice they encounter. And, even as Stephens is a big-city sophisticate who journeys to the small, provincial town of Sam Dent, so too is Mr Badii a Tehranian who drives to the isolated hill country outside Iran's capital, where he solicits a series of simple men expatriated from Kurdistan, Afghanistan, or Turkey. Mr Badii promises money to someone who will help him die, while Stephens offers legal assistance – with the ultimate promise of money – to families whose children have been killed. Mr Badii finds men who are already displaced, discarded, or disconnected, yet not disconsolate; Mr Stephens, for his part, finds people who once were just the opposite of discordant or disunited, but he leaves them in a state of disarray and dissociation. The latter fails in his litigious mission, in other words, and the community of Sam Dent would have failed even had the lawsuit of its bereaved parents succeeded. Mr Badii may or may not succeed in his desire to be dead and buried, and our (in)decision to let him live or die will say as much about the community of which we would be a part as it will about our own divided sensibilities.

4

Mirror Images, or Children of Paradise

On Makhmalbaf's *The Apple* (1998, Iran) and Panahi's *The Mirror* (1997, Iran)

The cinema of the Islamic theocracy of Iran is chiefly known today for two qualities: its children's films (by which I mean movies about the young but not necessarily for them) and its self-reflexivity (by which I mean the posing of deep questions about fiction, reality, and filmmaking). It's common knowledge by now that children are often used as artistic subjects in Iran because directors there can deal with them openly and honestly – i.e., without sex, violence, philosophy, and politics, and therefore without running into the problem of censorship. Among the best pictures from the mid-eighties to the mid-nineties were Amir Naderi's *The Runner* (1984), Abbas Kiarostami's *Where Is the Friend's House?* (1987), Ebrahim Foruzesh's *The Jar* (1992), and Jafar Panahi's *The White Balloon* (1995). This is not to say that these pictures are devoid of philosophy and politics, even socio-clerical criticism, only that such grown-up themes are often cloaked in the metaphorical raiment of children's stories, which themselves frequently blur the line between documentary and fiction. Children do the same, of course, but, again, the purpose of such blurring here is less mimetic than metaphorical: to investigate, in so repressive an autocracy as the ayatollah's, the truth and nature not merely of the government's pronouncements but also of cinematic art, of the very act of aesthetic creation or reportorial chronicling on film.

The Apple (1998) was the first of two Iranian children's films to come my way in the spring of 1999, before the summer crackdown on student demonstrators in the streets of Tehran – which nearly spelled trouble for the (already limited) artistic freedom of the country's moviemakers as well. Only eighty-five minutes in length, this picture was made by Samira Makhmalbaf, the daughter of Mohsen Makhmalbaf, who was the scenarist as well as editor of the movie. Like Kiarostami's *Close-Up* (1990), *The Apple* metafictionally features the actual members of the family whose disturbingly true story is at its center. They are the Naderis: sixty-five-year-old Ghorbanali, the father; Soghra, his blind wife; and their twelve-year-old twin daughters, Zahra and Massoumeh. These girls were virtually imprisoned by their father in their Tehran home, away from sunlight, for all of their first twelve years, which means that they cannot speak their native Farsi (although they can make sounds), they walk in an ungainly manner, do not bathe, and possess the ironic gestural tic of a literally wagging tongue. As you might guess, Zahra and Massoumeh have never attended school and know no children other than each other.

One thinks immediately in this context of Truffaut's *Wild Child* (1969) and Herzog's *Mystery of Kaspar Hauser* (1975), except that in *The Apple* there is no real mystery behind the twins' confinement. Their father, a religious man who makes his living by offering up prayers for others, reveals that he has kept his daughters locked up because their blind mother could not look after them, and he was afraid he might be dishonored if they were to come into physical contact with any of the neighborhood boys. The film begins when residents of this neighborhood in Tehran (known as Valiasr) petition the local government to intervene on Zahra and Massoumeh's behalf. Or, more precisely, *The Apple* begins with a beautiful image of poetic clarity (an image repeated at least twice): the arm of one of the girls stretches out as far as it can, through the bars of the gate that restricts her and into the cinematographic frame, to pour water from a cup onto a scruffy, potted, flowering plant. Water, naturally, is what Zahra and Massoumeh require, figuratively as well as literally, if *they* are to grow, for they are not (or need not be), as their father benightedly believes, flowers who will automatically wilt in the sun of men's gazes.

Water is what the twins get when, as a result of the complaint against Ghorbanali Naderi, they are removed from his home by child-welfare authorities for a good scrubbing in addition to a short haircut. Zahra and Massoumeh are returned to their father after he promises not to keep them locked up anymore, but Ghorbanali immediately breaks his promise by secreting the girls once again inside the Naderis' sparse, dimly lit home with their sightless mother. Instead of a front door, this townhouse of sorts has a front gate that looks out onto a small courtyard that itself is gated, and we watch the father methodically unlocking and locking these gates as he comes and goes for work, food, and ice. Mind you, Ghorbanali is not overtly cruel or hateful toward his daughters, just obtusely, suffocatingly protective; and they, for their part, are anything but hostile toward him and their mother. Indeed, Zahra and Massoumeh do not seem unhappy, for they know no alternative to the life they are living.

They do, however, seem unconsciously attracted to sounds or images of growth and renewal: a baby crying across the alley; the plant inside their courtyard, whose flowers they attempt to replicate by splattering muddy handprints on a wall; a boy selling ice cream on the street; a woman washing clothes on her balcony next door. When the twins are finally freed from their domestic dungeon by Azizeh Mohamadi, a social worker (who, like the Naderi family, plays herself) dispatched to hold Ghorbanali to his promise, the first action they pleasurably take is to look into a mirror given to them by Mrs Mohamadi, followed by their amused splashing of water onto their visages in that mirror. Literally and figuratively, the girls are seeing or identifying themselves for the very first time, which naturally is a prerequisite for their cognitive development. But the mirror is also a sly reminder here of the nature of filmic illusion, a clever reference to the (distortive?) mirror held up to nature – especially in a film whose performers reenact events from their own lives, or, as it were, mirror their private images and existences for all to see.

The result of Mrs Mohamadi's visit to the Naderis is a reversal: not only does she set Zahra and Massoumeh free, she also locks their parents inside their own house, even as they did their children, and gives the uncomprehending girls the key. Next the social worker borrows a hacksaw from a neighbor and hands it to Ghorbanali with the warning that, if he doesn't saw through all the bars of the gate to his home, she will return to take his daughters away from him permanently. Meanwhile, as their humbled father saws and their enraged mother complains, Zahra and Massoumeh go out, after some homebound hesitation, to meet the world in the form of other children. Most important among them is a boy with a long fishing pole, at the end of whose line is attached an apple. He dangles it from the window of an apartment building, the twins try but fail to grab it, then the boy shows them where they can buy their own apples, which they do with money cadged from their now compliant father.

Clearly the apple is meant to recall the Biblical temptation of Adam in the Garden of Eden. The difference, however, is that a boy is doing the tempting, not the female Eve, which means – aptly in as patriarchal

Massoumeh Naderi and Zahra Naderi bubble with mischief in *The Apple*.

a society as Iran's – that a male is responsible for the girls' symbolic introduction to knowledge or consciousness, just as a male was responsible for their cloistering. And with such an introduction to "sin" comes the suggestion that the world holds perils as well as pleasures, exasperations as well as ecstasies, for Zahra and Massoumeh Naderi, while their cave at least offered the sameness of ironclad, perdurable security. So *The Apple* is no simple fable about the blessed civilizing of primitives; rather, it is a complex metaphor both for the inhumane repression of women in a theocratic state *and* for the merciful removal of those same women not simply from the pervasive precariousness of male-dominated or malevolent existence but also (through such concealing clothing as the *chador*) from the incessant glare of the male gaze.

The metaphor extends itself when, after purchasing some apples, the twins meet two uniformed schoolgirls on a playground. Massoumeh innocently smacks an apple against one girl's face, then hands her the fruit. Baffled but beguiled by this attempt at communication, the girl kisses Massoumeh, who, interpreting the kiss as a reward for her aggression and not for the apple, strikes her new friend again. (This is neither the first nor the last of *The Apple*'s divinely comic moments.) After this incident, all four girls lie down on some rocks (yes, rocks) and eat the apples. Here, of course, it is one female who is "tempting" another, and here, also, temptation is associated both with pleasure (the kiss, the apple) and pain (the smack, the rocks), as it was for Adam and has been for everyone else ever since.

As the girls leave the playground after eating their fruit, the talk – at least for the two who can talk – turns to watches and the telling of time, an appropriate subject given the symbolic import of apple-eating together with literal departure from the world of play. For time is a human construct primarily connected with the workaday world, which is the one Zahra and Massoumeh will eventually enter now that they have gained consciousness as well as liberation of the self, and which is where (at an open-air market) they find watches for sale. The twins want one, even though they may not know its function yet, and it is to their father they turn again for the money. They find him at home, dutifully watched by Mrs Mohamadi as he continues to saw through the bars of his house-gate. And, with the social worker's permission, Zahra and Massoumeh free Ghorbanali from *his* prison by unlocking the gate with his key.

The last time we see this man, he is on his way to the watchmaker's booth at the marketplace, escorted by his daughters and their two new friends. His wife remains behind, alone and bewildered, faceless beneath her *chador* as well as blind. Aptly if unwittingly, Soghra looks into her daughters' mirror, even as they had playfully put the same mirror up to their father's face. Then she walks through the open gates out into the street, calling for her girls but instead running into the apple – dangled by the same boy from the same apartment window. He teases Soghra with it but at last she is able to grab the fruit, at which point the frame freezes and *The Apple* ends. By now an otherwise meaningless cliché, the frozen frame here takes on poignant meaning, for it suggests that, frozen in space and time, the twins' mother can neither taste the fruit of knowledge nor escape the glare of light, neither retreat to the safety of her grotto nor advance to the call of the wild.

Beyond the use of this frozen frame, *The Apple*'s cinematography, by Ebrahim Ghafori and Mohamed Ahmadi, calls attention to itself by being of two distinct kinds: grainy, documentary-like, even blurred color footage, mostly for scenes at the child-welfare office, and smooth, devised, even warm images of muted browns and yellows tinged with turquoise for all other scenes, particularly those at the Naderi home. The turquoise naturally suggests the water – the fluid attention or liquid sustenance – that flowering plants, and blossoming girls, require to survive. But perhaps more interesting in this split between cinematographic styles is the suggestion of the turquoise-tinged scenes – compounded by the remoteness or distance of the camera during the documentary-like footage – that, however misguidedly raised by their parents, Zahra and Massoumeh still have and need those parents' love, even when these youngsters are finally left to their own devices in the streets, parks, and squares of Tehran. In other words, there is no slick, black-and-white opposition in *The Apple* between "good" authorities and "bad" fathers. Indeed, one could argue that Ghorbanali is the extreme, patriarchal product of the very system that now castigates his parental behavior. And when he laments to a neighbor "how hard it is to put back the pieces of a broken mirror," this father more than implies that his familial mirror has been shattered as much by the (state-run) media's distorted, sensationalized coverage of his daughters' privation as by that privation itself.

But has that familial mirror ultimately been shattered, or has it instead merely been turned around to reflect the outside world as much as the interior one of the Naderi home? That is the question, and it isn't easy to answer, for we cannot know what has become of the Naderi family, particularly of Zahra and Massoumeh, since *The Apple* was made. Certainly one can only wish them the growth and success enjoyed by the Iranian cinema itself ever since it emerged from the stultifying shadow of the imams and into the beaming light of the world screen – a growth and success apparently premised on the use of non-actors like the Naderis. Yet, if Iran is the home of today's one great national cinema, as a number of commentators have argued, how has it been able to achieve this status without the use of almost any professional actors?

Because, as Vernon Young argued years ago, "Film criticism can usually afford to disregard actors in a film's total effect, unless they are grossly bad or overwhelmimgly good." Film criticism can so proceed because, in general in the cinema, theatrical performance, the acting of the words, is not the thing; more so than acting onstage, acting on film is part of a larger picture that depends for effect on its cinematographic rendering – on how it is photographed and edited and even scored. (Although, paradoxically, a number of movies that depend on non-actors, like *The Apple* and the other Iranian film I shall discuss, use little or no music to buttress their performances.) And that larger picture includes the *faces* of actors, from which, without benefit of words, the camera can elicit character in a way that the stage obviously cannot (hence one of the beauties of silent film).

For an example of what I mean, watch the "performances" of Zahra and Massoumeh Naderi as themselves: they don't speak any words, but they move us by the pathetic beauty of their sweetly smiling presences, by the simple framing of that clumsy, youthful beauty as it shuffles through the Tehranian cityscape of Samira and Mohsen Makhmalbaf's narrative. Like the rest of the "cast," the twins are neither overwhelm-

ingly good nor grossly bad because they aren't really acting, they're
being, and judgment of how good they are at being themselves is out of
the question; each is allowing the camera to penetrate into the essence
of her reality rather than presenting to that camera a reality framed by
words. Perhaps the example of their father would be even better: in
spite of his role as his daughters' jailer, despite his whining defense of
his behavior toward them, and despite his sudden sheepishness in the
face of the social worker's easy imperiousness, Ghorbanali appears to
the camera-eye as a kindly, well-meaning if injudicious man. Which is
exactly what he is.

What's true of the acting in *The Apple* is equally true of Mina Mohammad-Khani's performance in Jafar Panahi's *The Mirror* (1997). Indeed,
Mina bears a striking resemblance to, and may be the slightly younger
sister of, Aida Mohammad-Khani, the kerchiefed little girl who had the
leading role in the same director's *White Balloon* (1995). Rendered, like
The White Balloon, in an approximation of real time, *The Mirror* concerns the efforts of a small girl, Mina, to make her way home through
the busy streets of Tehran. When her pregnant mother fails to pick her
up after school (first grade, in Mina's case), she begins her journey –
scowling, kerchiefed, and with one arm in sling, as we see her for the
first time on the curb at the end of a lengthy, initial establishing shot
in which the camera crosses and recrosses a crowded thoroughfare, as
if it itself were searching for this girl. Despite lots of hustle and bustle
to and fro, however – including a ride on a motorbike, a telephone call
home, an encounter with her teacher, and several navigations of her
own across the same dangerous roadway (once by hanging onto the
arm of a blind man) – Mina makes little progress. Moreover, her willy-
nilly odyssey is sporadically mirrored or echoed, here and throughout
the film, by the radio broadcast all over the city of a tumultuous soccer
match between Iran and South Korea in which the teams frequently
exchange the lead. Finally, the worried girl hops on a bus that she
hopes will drop her off close to the apartment building where she lives,
but that proves after ten to fifteen minutes to be heading in the wrong
direction.

During this time aboard the bus, unpatronized as a child alone and
isolated at the back in the women's section, Mina overhears the dis-
contented, even bitter, conversations of a number of Iranian females.
An old widow complains about the cruelty and ingratitude of her children toward her ever since the death of their father; a group of young
women discuss a husband who cheats on his wife; a palm reader consoles a mother that her only child, a daughter, will be better than any

son could have been; and some older women talk about an upcoming wedding between a badly matched couple. Through all of this the camera remains mostly in medium close-up on Mina or adopts her eye-level when it cuts to the women around her, and what we begin to see is a little girl whose feistiness, doggedness, and uninhibitedness are already being translated into the hard, critical demeanor of a middle-aged woman. Furthermore, when someone on the bus finally smiles – from the men's section in front – it is not at Mina, as we are initially led to believe, but at a pretty woman sitting next to her. Thus begins an adult flirtation that, in the context of this picture, will go nowhere. When Mina herself has contact with the opposite sex, it is in the form of a boy, but this moment remains completely unsentimentalized. He is a street musician, and, after he plays a tune from the men's section in front, someone silently gives the girl a coin to give to him, which she unceremoniously does (and nothing more) as the bus continues on its way.

But it doesn't do so for long, for it has reached the end of the line without a sign of Mina's stop. When the almost tearful child complains to the driver that she needs to get to Republic Square, he informs her that she must take a bus going in the opposite direction. Although Mina does so, *The Mirror* now takes a surprising turn at this, the halfway point or so of its ninety-five minutes. Miss Mohammad-Khani removes her sling, declares, "I'm not acting anymore," and climbs off the bus. After all efforts to change her mind fail, the child then walks off the "set" and starts to find her way home. Still miked for sound, however, Mina is followed by the cameras of the film crew (some of whom we occasionally glimpse), who say they want to see what they can salvage from their work-in-progress.

Yet Mina the actress's journey home proves to be just as willy-nilly as that of Mina the character. She asks for directions, first to Parliament Square, then to Victory Avenue; she telephones home to no avail; Mina runs into the old widow from the bus, who says she is not a professional actress but was just playing herself; and this little girl takes several taxis through the teeming streets of Tehran, in one of which she listens to a heated conversation between the cabbie and another passenger about women's rights, working women, and the responsibilities of mothers and wives. Eventually, the lost child finds her way to the toy shop of the man who recruited her for the film, gives him back her body microphone despite his protests, and disappears into the large passageway of the apartment building where she lives – after reiterating to a crew member that she no longer wants to be in the movie. At about this time we also hear the last of the radio broadcast of the national soccer game, which Iran wins over South Korea by a score of six to two, after which *The Mirror* cuts abruptly to black.

Just as abruptly, *The Mirror* had shifted midway from an engrossing exercise in slice-of-life realism, à la *The White Balloon* (a reference to which we see relatively early in the latest picture, as a leisurely balloon-seller crosses the anxious Mina's path), to a mock documentary in the style of *cinéma vérité*. We know that the second part of the film is "mock," not real, because Panahi – *The Mirror*'s screenwriter and editor as well as director – has said he was toying with this idea all along, but did not commit to it until the first little girl he had cast actually did refuse to continue in her role and had to be replaced with Mina Mohammad-Khani. (The first girl appears only in the finished picture's lengthy opening shot.) At first one is tempted to feel betrayed by this conceit, yet what saves the movie from being an extended, somewhat cruel prank on its audience is the "mirroring" of its two segments. To wit, part 2 essentially continues the narrative of part 1 on a different level, for both parts are about a small child who is trying to find her way home through heavy traffic in a heavily populated city.

Still, part 2 is shot in a radically different cinematic style from part 1, even as *The Apple*'s cinematography was made up of two disparate types. Part 1 is a fluid, controlled stretch of film that has been carefully crafted to simulate the randomness and spontaneity of everyday urban life. By contrast, part 2 – though possibly just as precisely planned as the first segment – fakes the appearance of off-the-cuff, on-the-fly moviemaking through jittery, handheld camerawork that sometimes seems to be farther off course than the little child it is attempting to follow, as she either totally eludes the lens's range or is completely hidden by passing vehicles; through a soundtrack that fades in and out, as if the microphone were malfunctioning; and through Farzad Jowdat's color cinematography, which moves from being merely sun-suffused in part 1 to being sun-bleached or overexposed and even out of focus in part 2.

So *The Mirror* has its fun with us, but it keeps its promises, too, not only to examine the nature of cinematic illusion but also to suggest that the invention of plots to make reality palatable or spectacular is a flight from the richness of real life. In this *The Mirror*, like *The Apple*, approaches pure or ideal neorealism as described by the screenwriter Cesare Zavattini in his ringing manifesto "Some Ideas on the Cinema" (1952):

The artist's task is to make people reflect on ... real things, exactly as they are. ... No fable for a starving man, because that is less effective and less moral. ...

No other medium of expression has the cinema's innate capacity for showing things as they happen day by day – in their longest and truest duration. ... The time has come to tell the audience that they are the true protagonists of life. Otherwise the frequent habit of identifying oneself with fictional characters will become very dangerous. The world is composed of millions of people thinking of myths.

Zavattini seems here to be calling for the making of documentaries, but he is really calling for a type of film in which the story is absolutely minimal and in which "the actor as a person fictitiously lending his own flesh to another has no more right to exist than the 'story.' In neorealism, as I intend it, everyone must be his own actor." By this definition, as Zavattini knew, none of the best-known films of Italian neorealism – *Open City* (1945), *Paisan* (1946), *Bicycle Thieves* (1948), or even *Umberto D.* (1951) – qualifies as neorealistic. But when he wrote in "Some Ideas on the Cinema" that "We have not yet reached the center of neorealism, which today is an army ready to start," little could this Italian artist have known that such an army would ultimately come out of undemocratic Iran – though he may have realized that its citizen-soldiers would consist chiefly of children in all their assiduous playfulness.

5

Angels beyond America

On Majidi's *The Children of Heaven* (1997, Iran) and Zonca's *The Dreamlife of Angels* (1998, France)

I give you two films, one from France and the other from Iran, that share ironic – and not so ironic – titles on ostensibly similar subjects; natural or naturalistic acting of the highest order, arrived at through different means; and the depiction of working-class experience more from an emotional angle than a sociopolitical one – in countries so different, moreover, that one cannot imagine the story of the French picture transposed to Iran, or vice versa. To be sure, neither movie's narrative element is fresh, and their themes are more or less familiar in any cinematic purview of contemporary society, Near Eastern or Western. Yet both *The Children of Heaven* (1997) and *The Dreamlife of Angels* (1998) are absorbing and affecting in ways that the putatively profound *American Beauty* (1999) and the purportedly ingenious *Illuminata* (1999) are not.

I've deliberately named two American films here because I'm frequently asked why I don't write about such glossy releases from my own country. I don't because I have no interest in gloss, especially when it is accompanied by gas, as in the case of both these pictures. The cynically titled *American Beauty* proffers a heavy dose of facile metaphysics about the dehumanizing limits placed on the human spirit in the anesthetic atmosphere of urban-suburban America – an old story by now, better told in numerous other places. (In Italy, for one, where Antonioni dissected the numbingly modernistic E.U.R. district of Rome in *L'eclisse* [1962].) The pretentiously titled *Illuminata* is yet another lightweight backstage drama in which what happens on the boards is mirrored by what takes place off them – except that this movie, not content merely to be fictitious fun like its English cousin *Shakespeare in Love* (1998), pretends to explore the age-old theme of illusion versus reality. But *Illuminata* is really about actor-director John Turturro's turgid love affair with himself, his wife (who co-stars), and acting. As such it is one more participant, like *American Beauty*, in our long-running national orgy of sex, violence, consumption, and narcissism – an orgy that painfully testifies to the fact that we have become, if we have not always been, a nation of emotional cripples, spiritual paupers, and moral delinquents.

Americans may act like children, then, but rarely are children the subjects of serious American films. Not so in Iran, the reasons for which I've made abundantly clear in the previous chapters as well as in columns in *The Hudson Review* (those of Autumn 1996, Summer 1999, and Winter 2000). *The Children of Heaven*, the first Iranian film ever nominated for an Academy Award (won, alas, by the mawkish *Life Is Beautiful* [1997]), was written and directed by Majid Majidi. It was his third film after *Baduk* (1992), about fatherless children sold into slavery, and *The Father* (1995), which centers on the troubled relationship between an adolescent boy and his stepfather.

In *The Children of Heaven* the object of its hero's quest seems pedestrian: a pair of shoes. For the sad-eyed, nine-year-old Ali Mandegar (Amir Farrokh Hashemian) has lost the recently mended shoes of his younger sister Zahra (Bahare Sediqi), and the children are afraid to tell their father (Amir Naji) about the loss because their impoverished family cannot afford to buy a new pair. Residents of Tehran's run-down southern section, the Mandegars consist of five members: a new baby in addition to Ali and Zahra, and, along with their dad, a mother (Fereshteh Sarabandi), who is disabled by a serious back condition that may require surgery. The father, Karim, has no trade to speak of, though he does occasional work as a handyman and gardener; he is not lazy or irresponsible, just devoted to Allah, whom he serves, without pay, in various capacities at the local mosque. (Perhaps it is in this sense that his youngsters may be regarded, without irony, as "children of heaven.") And Islam, like Christianity in the West, seems to serve Near Eastern capitalism by keeping the Karims of the region – plus the homeless beggars one social rung lower – in their place as gouging shopkeepers and uncharitable landlords (representatives of which groups we observe in *The Children of Heaven*) profit off them.

In such a relatively underdeveloped country as Iran, what you wear on your feet says as much about your economic or social status as would the car you drive in the Great Satan of America. Therefore it's not by chance that, despite its relative brevity at eighty-eight minutes, *The*

Children of Heaven opens with a long, stationary take of Zahra's shoes being fastidiously repaired by a pair of hands; we hear off-camera noise during this scene, but we see no human faces – neither the shoe-maker's nor Ali's – until the shoes are ready. Never has owning a pair of serviceable shoes seemed so important as in this film, and the camera continues to linger on individual pairs of shoes as they are piled up outside mosques as well as displayed in shoe stores and television advertisements, then as they are deployed in soccer games and gym classes. Indeed, this movie does for shoes what De Sica's *Bicycle Thieves* (1948) did for bikes: make us see them less as podiatric ornament or accessory, vehicular recreation or diversion, than as absolutely necessary to human transportation, particularly in urban quarters. So much so that, at one point, Ali's own shoe nearly takes on a life of its own as it floats down a drainage ditch, just out of reach of the frantic Zahra who would retrieve it; at another point, Zahra's shoes come back to life, as it were, on the feet of a classmate whose blind, street-hawking father managed to find them where Ali dropped them.

Politically unaware though the proletarian Mandegars may be, this family will nonetheless experience the loss of a pair of shoes as a bitter financial setback, which the grave Ali and his adoring sister both know. Zahra is willing to believe, however, that her determined brother might somehow recover the shoes, so she reluctantly, if not fretfully, goes along with his plan to hide their predicament from their parents by sharing Ali's beat-up sneakers (his only pair of shoes). Although they are at least a size too big, Zahra wears them to her half day of school in the morning, then races to exchange them with Ali at a prearranged meeting place so that her brother can wear them to his half day of school in the afternoon – running as fast as he can to get there, yet sometimes showing up late and being confronted by the scowling principal. This system works, but Ali knows that it cannot work for long without detection, so he begs his way into a grueling, four-kilometer race for third- and fourth-graders (for which, though otherwise eligible, he has been late to sign up), third prize in which is a new pair of shoes.

All the boy's running to school has prepared him well for this race – too well, it turns out, as he finds it impossible to finish anywhere but first, despite the ironic use of normally formulaic slow-motion photography to reduce his speed. And first place is not good enough, for it nets Ali only a trophy and a medal. His feet bruised and bloody, his eyes teary, and his worn sneakers now in tatters, the heroically good-willed Ali must return home to face his disappointed sister. As the two children glumly sit by the courtyard pool outside their family's apartment, with Ali's feet soaking in the water, surrounded by goldfish – to Iranians, symbols of the mystery and joy of life – *The Children of Heaven* ends. We know, however, that the picture's real ending will not be unhappy, for, as we see in a cross-cut shot, Karim Mandegar is on his way home by bicycle with food for his family and new shoes for Zahra (a surprise gift, since he never learned that Ali had lost his sister's old pair). The father has purchased all of these goods with money earned from his handyman-cum-gardener work – assisted by Ali, who must also forego playing soccer with his friends to help his mother out with domestic chores – in the cloistered suburb that is Tehran's wealthiest (and snootiest).

Yet we never actually see Karim arrive home with the shoes, to his children's surprise and salvation, which is one way of ensuring a happy ending but avoiding its patness. The real purpose of Majidi's ending, though, is to get us to focus on what has led up to it, on the conditions of life in Iran that have created the need for such a *humanus ex machina*. Those conditions are often photographed by Parviz Malek in tight, unpanoramic frames (even during the four-kilometer race) that, as in *The White Balloon* (1995), mimic a child's-eye view of the world and isolate Ali and Zahra even further in their own little world.

Tellingly, the look or quality of the images in *The Children of Heaven* is such that what we remember of these siblings' unspectacular, drably colored Tehran (as opposed to the lush greenery of the sequence shot in the moneyed section of town) is the proximate, geometrically patterned background provided by its weathered mud bricks and walled-in alleys. Contrast this straitened environment with the prettified and expansive one of any American movie about kids, and you'll get some idea of the difference between the two cinemas' respective treatment of children. Given that such children are mirrors of their parents and their immediate society, given in particular that child characters in both American and Iranian films have to some degree been devised to please domestic (adult) audiences, I'll take the sober decorum of Zahra and Ali over the wised-up precocity of, say, the young Tatum O'Neal and the younger still Macauley Culkin. That decorum is best illustrated in *The Children of Heaven* by a scene that would be unimaginable in a mainstream American movie, because it sports no silly sentiment and is only tangentially related to the picture's already slender plot: at his parents' request, Ali matter-of-factly takes a gift of some soup to an elderly, shut-in couple who live nearby, and they in turn express their no-tears gratitude to him with a gift of a handful of – nuts.

Speaking of such professional child actors as O'Neal and Culkin, in contrast with such non-actors as Amir Farrokh Hashemian and Bahare Sediqi, how has Iran been able to achieve the status of today's one great national cinema without the use of almost any professional actors? For the same reasons that the Italian neorealists and Soviet formalists, who both employed their share of amateur actors, were able to achieve international artistic status in the 1940s and 1920s, respectively. Because film actors do not have to sustain a performance over continuous time, as stage actors must; because a cinematic scene can be repeated again and again until the performer gets it right and the camera captures the (repeatable) moment forever; because cutters can edit an actress into and out of a scene as required, and composers can score a movie so as to add emotional ballast to the weaker performances (although, paradoxically, a number of films that depend on non-actors, like *The Children of Heaven* as well as *The Apple* (1998) and *The Mirror* (1997), use little or no music); because words are less important than pictures on screen, and a photogenic face – one, that is, that reveals underlying character in the same way that a star's image exudes archetypal personality – is at least as important as acting ability; and finally, in the case of children, because they are naturals at unselfconscious play as well as at playing or being themselves, which the cinema simply calls upon them to do before a rolling camera. For an example of what I mean, watch the "performances" of Hashemian and Sediqi in the very last scene of *The Children of Heaven*: they don't speak any words, but they move us by their nascent humanity and the juxtaposition of their pathetic beauty with the happy obliviousness of goldfish swimming in a courtyard pool.

In its minimalist approach to acting, so complementarily slender a fiction as *The Children of Heaven* is the polar opposite of *The Dreamlife of Angels*, the Frenchman Érick Zonca's first feature film after three shorts. Zonca studied acting in New York as well as Paris, and he has stated that his experience as an actor helped him in his work with his two female leads, Élodie Bouchez and Natacha Régnier, whom he even required to live together during the making of the movie. The result is the creation of two working-class characters whose existence we cannot doubt, in the way that we can doubt the existence of a working-class character played, say, by Michelle Pfeiffer – try her Frankie in *Frankie and Johnny* (1991) – with her film face and star's life. (Indeed, Bouchez's character and *The Dreamlife of Angels* as a whole were inspired by an actual young woman.)

Both Bouchez and Régnier have appeared in other pictures (the former in André Téchiné's *Wild Reeds* [1994], for instance, the latter in Pascal Bonitzer's *Encore* [1996]), but each has a real face: Bouchez that of a younger, hipper, darker Giulietta Masina come to life; Régnier that of the bitter, angry, and vulnerable Barbara Stanwyck in her youth, yet with no attempt at prettification. And each woman has so identified with her character, has put together so full a portrait out of the increments of that character's working and dream lives, that Zonca's film need be concerned with little more than displaying these fictionalized figures in all the richness of their rawness. For such "character actors," he has appositely written (with Roger Bohbot) a character drama that consists less of a plot than a string of events, less even of these external happenings than of internal flickerings in the two women as they dynamically interact with each other and the earn-and-spend world around them. (Plot may have been the soul of drama for Aristotle, but it could only be so in an ancient world where public, civic action had more significance than private, individual being.)

The Dreamlife of Angels is about Isabelle Tostin (Bouchez) and Marie Thomas (Régnier), two twentyish Frenchwomen adrift among the Gauls, living strictly in the moment and living hand-to-mouth or working only when they must. Isa is a scruffy yet serene opportunist who has literally drifted from her southeastern hometown of Valence to the northern city of Lille, where we catch up with her on the street, toting a rucksack, as she tries to raise pocket money by hustling religious pictures to passersby. Unsuccessful at this enterprise and having had to break into a building in order to find a warm place to sleep for the night, Isa takes a job the next day on a sewing machine in an assembly line to earn some cash. Although she is soon fired for gross inefficiency, she meets another seamstress at this garment factory, Marie, a brooding, angry, bitter loner of a local girl who has much the same alienation from routine labor and a routine life. The latter quits her sweatshop job as well (which she's held for only two weeks as compared to Isa's two days), but not before cautiously agreeing to permit her toothy, rough-featured new acquaintance to stay at a place where she is apartment-sitting for a woman and her daughter who were gravely injured in an automobile accident.

Opposites Isa and Marie certainly are, in look as well as outlook and manner, the one an innate if simple-minded philosopher, the other a fierce if inchoate intelligence; they seem to share only an affection for idle cigarette smoking that is as great as their disaffection with utilitarian work. Yet they come together for a time as roommates if not completely as human beings. Their budding friendship may promise relief from obscure emotional pain – endured by Marie as the daughter of what she calls a victimized mother, by Isa as a child of divorce – but neither woman finds that relief in the other. Yes, they apply for some degrading jobs together and, yes, they pal around with two bouncers at a rock club who are also bikers. Isa and Marie's relationship, however, remains static, stagnant, or standoffish, no matter how hard the former tries to penetrate the latter's sullen, dead-eyed carapace. So each pursues genuine intimacy with another even though they both continue to occupy the same dwelling.

Isa begins by reading the diaries of Sandrine Val, the teenager who normally lives in the apartment but who is comatose in the hospital. (The girl's mother has by now died of her injuries.) Against Marie's strenuous advice, Isa is drawn to this girl, visits her often, and even assumes the role of Sandrine's guardian, seeming to share the minor ups and major downs of her prostrate fate. Though Sandrine is quite unconscious and never awakens from her coma, Isa has a sense, because of the diaries, of connection with her – a connection that the slightly older woman obviously wants and needs. The irony of such intimacy is clear but not overdone, in part because the overtone suggested is that the inert girl has achieved a dreamlike state that Isa almost envies: to be in the world but safe from, or untarnished by, it. So the title of the film may refer to Sandrine instead of being merely a tongue-in-cheek reference to Isa and Marie, who are obviously not angelic and whose dreamlife we plainly do not see.

Yet Marie accuses Isa of being a dreamer; Isa says she hopes Marie finds the life she dreams of; and the last word in the movie's title is "angels," not "angel." I'm reminded here, and perhaps Zonca was also, of a Bergman picture whose title is the opposite of *The Dreamlife of Angels: From the Life of the Marionettes* (1980), the case history – replete with dream sequences! – of a successful businessman going through a marriage crisis who ravishes and then murders a prostitute. Isa and Marie are living marionettes, too, if by that word one means that they are the deterministic products of their heredity and environment. But they are more, for each is burdened with buried discontents or yearnings that are these women's greatest virtue, that separate them from the rest of undifferentiated humanity, and that make them unwitting messengers of the spirit in this ungodly age of high technology.

One of Marie's yearnings has to do with men, even though she tells Isa, "I don't get stuck on guys; they get on my nerves." Well, she's the one who has sex with Charly, the hefty bouncer-cum-biker (played with incongruous tenderness by Patrick Mercado); Isa, for her part, does not go to bed with his slimmer partner, Fredo (Jo Prestia), nor with any other man in the film. Marie wants love more than sex, however, and she doesn't want it from Charly, though he would give it to her. After some initial resistance, even overt hostility, from her end, she thinks she's found her romantic soulmate in Chriss (Grégoire Colin), a swarthy, wealthy young man who owns a string of clubs, including the one where Charly and Fredo work. Despite Isa's insistent warnings, Marie proceeds to let down her guard and respond warmly to Chriss's skilled seducings, which include a weekend by the sea, an afternoon in an expensive hotel, and a possible job working at his Blue Club. But for this fellow their furious carnality is no more than that (a point underlined by Yannick Kergoat's fragmented, depersonalized editing of the couple's sex scenes) and, ultimately, he drops Marie for a prettier, more polished young woman.

The result is dire: on the verge of losing her apartment (which is under renovation at this point and will soon be taken over by Mrs Val's brother) and by now almost completely estranged from Isa, Marie intentionally slips from the ledge of her bedroom window and falls two stories to her death in the schoolyard below – the joyous sounds of whose playing children have recurred like musical counterpoint, or a gently wafting breeze, throughout *The Dreamlife of Angels*. Having just returned from a visit to the slightly improved Sandrine (still unconscious but now out of intensive care, and with her eyes open) and herself preparing to vacate the dwelling, Isa must be the one to find the body of the woman she continues to call her friend. For it is she who is the primary bearer of Zonca's moving, soulful vision of our shared responsibility for one another's lives. Indeed, horribly, Isa is in the apartment writing a goodbye note when Marie – who she thought was asleep, and who may know that Isa is there – jumps.

The very last sequence of this picture finds the surviving member of this "couple" in an overhead shot on her first day of employment at another factory, this time clothed in a white laboratory coat and assembling computer chips amidst a high-tech, antiseptic atmosphere. After her new boss compliments Isa with the portentous words, "You work as if you've done this all your life," the camera moves from a medium close-up of her face to the same shot of another working woman and then of several more in succession, until the image finally fades to black. The suggestion, of course, is not only that all of them will be doing this labor for the rest of their lives but also that each woman in the process will become undistinguishable from the others. We may infer, then, that Isa has been defeated or has gotten "adjusted" like her co-workers; we may hope against hope, however, that she continues to resist being turned into grist for the job mill; and surely we are allowed to suspect that human beings such as these were not put on earth to drizzle away their lives in the service of machines, to become living marionettes of the workaday kind.

The protest against such dehumanization or automatization has been a steady – and, alas, ineffective – note in the Western world ever since Marx sounded his warning against industrial alienation. In films René Clair and Charlie Chaplin repeated it in *À Nous la Liberté* (1931) and *Modern Times* (1936) respectively; and there are hints, early as well as late in *The Dreamlife of Angels*, of the flat, millstone-ground, pedestrian horror that one finds in German expressionist plays such as Georg Kaiser's *Gas, I* (1918) and Ernst Toller's *The Machine Wreckers* (1922). The triumph of Zonca's film, though, is that it surpasses the demand for mere novelty. It is so strongly felt, and so directly built on those strong feelings, that we do not care if we have seen other treatments of the subject, on screen or elsewhere. All that matters is the passionate concern, the utter conviction, and the consummate artistry of Zonca's protest.

Yet it is Isa and Marie's protest as well as their creator's, and this is what distinguishes *The Dreamlife of Angels* from Ermanno Olmi's neorealist-influenced *Il Posto* (1961), despite the fact that their final sequences are similar in form and content. In the Italian movie, the rage against the machine is only the director-screenwriter's, not in addition that of his male and female characters, both of whom accept the condition of their lives completely: the herd treatment, the rote work, and the enforced politeness, all in return for the sated snuggling into a lifelong cubbyhole. Missing from Olmi's picture, too, is an intimacy with the lives of women, since he focuses on his twenty-year-old male character and treats the female only as she exists in relationship to him, not from her own or another woman's perspective. *The Dreamlife of Angels* has that intimacy – enhanced by Agnès Godard's shooting of a noticeable portion of the picture in medium close-up to offset its suitably desaturated, almost hardhearted, color – which it shares with several other French-language films of the past thirty years.

I'm thinking not only of the work of such women directors as Agnès Varda and the Belgian Chantal Akerman (say, of the former's haunting *Vagabonde* [1985] and the latter's disquieting *Jeanne Dielman, 23 Quai du Commerce, 1080 Bruxelles* [1975]), but also of Alain Tanner's *La Salamandre* (1971), the sobering account of a young woman's struggle against drowning in the humdrum sea of *Swiss* prosperity. (Obviously,

I do not accept the silly – as well as sexist – argument of many feminists that men cannot portray the female experience truthfully, which is to say sensitively and complexly.) Another such intimate or personal film has come from Belgium: the Dardennes brothers' *Rosetta* (1999), about one proletarian woman's angry search for a job that she can live with. *Rosetta* won the Palme d'Or at Cannes in 1999, even as *The Dreamlife of Angels* received the Best Actresses award at the same festival in 1998 for the performances of Élodie Bouchez and Natacha Régnier.

Zonca's intimacy with, or impassioned caring about, Marie and Isa is so great, incidentally, that it needs no Pavlovian reinforcement from an actual musical score. There is no such score in *The Dreamlife of Angels*, although the movie's title might have led one to believe that its action would be accompanied by angelic choruses, just as the American title of *Il Posto* (which means *The Job*), *The Sound of Trumpets*, misleadingly prepared viewers for a blast or two from Gabriel's horn. We don't hear any trumpets in Olmi's film, especially not at the end, where the final sound is the chilling slickety-whir, slickety-whir of a mimeograph machine. And we don't hear any music in Zonca's picture – except for the occasional cacophony blaring from a rock club – until the closing credits, when a female voice sings a plaintive yet driving lyric of romantic abandon followed by post-haste abandonment.

This dearth of music is yet another quality that *The Dreamlife of Angels* shares with *The Children of Heaven*, although the two films in the end could not be more different: the one concerned with the adult, atomistic anomie peculiar to the post-industrial, democratic West, the other preoccupied by the childlike, unifying faith endemic to all the world's children but perhaps easier to maintain into adulthood in the underdeveloped, undemocratic nations of the Near East. It's true that Isabelle Tostin also gives off an impression of (earthly) grace and of absolute confidence in life, but Érick Zonca's point is precisely that these are qualities that can be maintained in the long run only apart from the materialistic, positivistic mainstream. I don't find it accidental, for example, that we come upon Isa, at the start of *The Dreamlife of Angels*, in flirtatious commerce with that consumer mainstream as she unapologetically hawks religious pictures – the money from whose sale, she glibly lies, will go to benefit sick children. Nor do I think it adventitious that the voices of innocent schoolkids in this movie are juxtaposed, like an aural leitmotif, against the apartmental activities of Isa and Marie.

In contrast to Zonca's two characters, for whom God appears to be a non-entity, Karim Mandegar of *The Children of Heaven* is so consecrated to Allah that no (unpaid) task is too menial for him to perform at the local mosque, including the cutting up of a huge block of sugar into tiny cubes for the tea service that accompanies the mosque's "mourning ceremony"; from Karim's point of view, Allah will ultimately reward him and especially his family for the many services he humbly renders unto his maker. I'm certainly not putting forth an argument here for the return to, or institution in, the West of autocracy-cum-theocracy. I would like to posit, however, that all our mundane political, economic, and social progress has cost us something, and that something may be the regular, blissful contemplation, in supernal art as in diurnal existence, of the dream or ideal life enjoyed by angels – or by their human counterparts, cherubic children and saintly adults. Movies such as *American Beauty* and *Illuminata* (not to speak of Kevin Smith's jejune *Dogma* [1999], in which actual angels appear for all the wrong reasons) are the embarrassing artistic price we pay for such secular progress. Those like *The Dreamlife of Angels* and, say, Wim Wenders' *Wings of Desire* (1987; *Heaven over Berlin* is the literal translation of the German title) are the rare aesthetic wonders that confirm me, for one, in my atavistic retrogression.

6

The Children Are Watching Us

On De Sica's *The Children Are Watching Us*
(1943, Italy) and
Majidi's *The Color of Paradise* (1999, Iran)

I described in the introduction the ease of cinema's mythmaking. Where children are concerned, two myths predominate on film: that of the original innocence of children, an innocence that only becomes sullied by contact with the society of grown-ups, and that of the child-as-father-to-the-man, of childhood as a prelude to the main event of adulthood. Among films of the first kind, Benoît-Lévy's *La Maternelle* (1932), Duvivier's *Poil de Carotte* (1932), Daquin's *Portrait of Innocence* (1941), Buñuel's *Los Olvidados* (1951), Grede's *Hugo and Josephine* (1967), and Nair's *Salaam Bombay!* (1988) deserve special mention. Among films of the second kind, Hallström's *My Life as a Dog* (1985) and August's *Pelle the Conqueror* (1988) were almost simultaneously joined by Ouédraogo's *Yaaba* (1987) and Gaup's *Pathfinder* (1988), two works whose mythic quality stands out all the more for its association with a "primitive" society (Burkina Faso in the former instance, Lapland in the latter) – that is, one unencumbered by the baggage of modern history and uncluttered by the artifacts of modern culture.

For the record, before 1900 the Lumière brothers had made the first films about children: one documenting the feeding of a baby (*Baby's Lunch*, 1895), and another showing some juvenile shenanigans with a garden hose (*The Sprinkler Sprinkled*, 1895). Soon thereafter virtually every film culture grasped the new possibilities of capturing children's cuteness and mischief and pathos. Of course the theatre had long used child actors, but theatrical techniques and circumstances make it more difficult to deal with them. It is much easier to use children in movies for the same reasons why it is possible to use non-professional actors, as outlined in the previous chapter.

In the vein of juvenile performance – with professional child actors as well as non-professionals, which is to say "non-actors" or "real" children (the Lumières themselves used both kinds) – no film culture has done better than France. Think only, most recently, of Jacques Doillon's *Ponette* (1996) and of *It All Starts Today* (1999), a film by the redoubtable Bertrand Tavernier about pre-school children living amidst Zolaesque conditions in contemporary northern France. The only possible exception to the rule of the French is Italy, which gave us Tornatore's *Cinema Paradiso* in 1988 and Amelio's *Stolen Children* in 1992 and, long before these movies, such neorealist masterpieces as Rossellini's *Germany, Year Zero* (1947) and De Sica's *Shoeshine* (1946) as well as his *Bicycle Thieves* (1948). Because neorealism replaced the traditional cinematic emphasis on the psychological complexities of the exceptional or unique individual with a desire to investigate everyday human beings in their social, economic, and political context, non-professional child actors in particular, and non-professional performers in general, were (and are) more directable in this style than any other (with the possible exception of Soviet formalism). For here they did not have to create an internalized or psychologized character in the Stanislavskian sense, a process that requires a considerable amount of training; the players in such a picture had only extemporaneously to respond to the stimuli of their immediate environment rather than studiously motivate their every thought or action deep from within.

De Sica himself used a child protagonist for the first time, not in *Shoeshine*, but in his first truly serious film, *The Children Are Watching Us* (1943).[1] Recently released on videotape, it was based on Cesare Giulio Viola's 1928 novel, *Pricò*, and scripted by the author, De Sica, and Cesare Zavattini, formerly a journalist, critic, and humorist. Zavattini thus became an acknowledged member of the De Sica team for the first time, and he was to prove himself, as De Sica's scenarist of choice, the most lyrical and imaginative screenwriter in the history of cinema. Zavattini's touch is immediately apparent in the extraordinary melan-

---

1 Despite his historical as well as artistic importance, De Sica curiously was never the subject of a single critical book in English until the year 2000, when the University of Toronto Press published a collection of essays titled *Vittorio De Sica: Contemporary Perspectives*, edited by Howard Curle and Stephen Snyder. Coincidentally, *The Children Are Watching Us* is now available on videotape from Home Vision for $29.95.

choly with which the story unfolds; there is an intensity of feeling throughout the picture far beyond any of the cozy sentiments displayed in De Sica's prior movies, either as an actor or a director. And it was this unrelieved emotion that made *The Children Are Watching Us* such a radical departure for a film made during the last years of the Fascist regime. Like the fatalism of Visconti's *Obsession* (1942), that masterly harbinger of Italian neorealism made around the same time, the frank, undiluted bleakness of this story was nearly unprecedented on the Italian screen. (De Sica did not even sweeten the bitter pill by casting lovable star personalities like himself in the adult parts; the best-known member of the cast was Isa Pola as the adulterous mother, an actress then considered a has-been who never really quite was.)

In 1942, when *Obsession* and *The Children Are Watching Us* were either being made or released, the idea of the cinema was being transformed in Italy. Influenced by French cinematic realism and prevailing Italian literary trends, Visconti shot *Obsession* on location in the region of Romagna; the plot (based on James M. Cain's novel *The Postman Always Rings Twice* [1934]) and atmosphere were seamy as well as steamy, and they did not adhere to the resolved structures or polished tones of conventional Italian movies. Visconti's film was previewed in the spring of 1943 and quickly censored, not to be appreciated until after the war. Around the same time, Gianni Franciolini's *Headlights in the Fog* (1941) was portraying infidelity among truck drivers and seamstresses, while Alessandro Blasetti's *Four Steps in the Clouds* (1942) – co-scripted by Zavattini and starring De Sica's wife, Giuditta Rissone – was being praised for its return to realism in a warm-hearted story of peasant life shot in natural settings. De Sica, too, was dissatisfied with the general state of the Italian cinema, and, after the relative success of such formulaic films of his as *Red Roses* (1940), *Maddalena, Zero for Conduct* (1941), *Teresa Venerdì* (1941), and *A Garibaldian in the Convent* (1942), he felt it was time for a new challenge. Like Zavattini, who had by now achieved a measure of screenwriting success, De Sica wanted to do some serious work that could express his ideas about human problems and human values.

The title of his new film had already been the heading of one of Zavattini's famous newspaper columns, and the subject matter of the story would be deemed scandalous when it reached the screen. *The Children Are Watching Us* examines the impact on a young boy's life of his mother's extramarital affair with a family friend. The five-year-old Pricò becomes painfully aware of the rift in his family life, and his sense of loss is made even more acute when his father sends him away from

The child (Luciano De Ambrosis) torn between his father (Adriano Rimoldi) and his mother (Isa Pola) in *The Children Are Watching Us*.

Rome to live – first in the country with his unreceptive paternal grandmother, then at a Jesuit boarding school. His mother's love affair leads finally to the suicide of Pricò's ego-shattered father, and, at the end of the film, when his mother (draped in mourning dress) comes to the school to reclaim her child, Pricò rejects her. The last time we see him, he has turned his back on his remaining parent and is walking away by himself, a small, agonized figure dwarfed by the huge, impersonal lobby of the school. The cause of the marital rift leading to the wife's infidelity is never revealed, the concern of De Sica and his screenwriters being purely with the effect of the rupture on the little boy. And it is this concentration on a child's view of the world – here the world of the petit bourgeois family almost apart from the economic and political forces that combine to influence its workings (a world similarly explored, *sans* children, in *Obsession*) – that gives a basically banal, even melodramatic tale a profounder aspect. Except for René Clément's *Forbidden Games* (1952), there has never been such an implacable view of the antagonism and desolation that separate the lives of adults and children.

The Children Are Watching Us owes much to the remarkable performance of the boy, Luciano De Ambrosis, himself orphaned just before work on the picture began, and whose previous acting experience was limited to a walk-on in a Pirandello play. De Sica's uncanny directorial rapport with his five-year-old protagonist would, of course, later prove vital in the making of *Shoeshine* and *Bicycle Thieves*, which share with *The Children Are Watching Us* the theme of childhood innocence in confrontation with adult realities (although, in *Bicycle Thieves*, the child is less victim of than father to the man). Arguably, De Sica would become the most eloquent director of children the screen has ever known, with the possible exception only of François Truffaut in such films as *The Four Hundred Blows* (1959), *The Wild Child* (1969), and *Small Change* (1976). And *The Children Are Watching Us* gave the first evidence of that extraordinary dual perspective that De Sica conveyed in his films about children. At the same time, he subtly managed both to simulate a child's vantage point on the baffling adult sorrows that surround him and to establish an authorial detachment – expressed in the spare neutrality of his *mise en scène*, even the physical distance he so often maintains between the camera and his subject – a detachment that somehow makes the predicament of his characters doubly moving. This "detachment" was chief among the grand illusions of the neorealist movement to come, and one fostered by the frequent use of non-professional actors photographed in actual locations as opposed to the simulated confines of a movie studio.

As in his subsequent neorealistic films, De Sica's cinematographer (Giuseppe Caracciolo) is not called upon in *The Children Are Watching Us* to exhibit striking angles or exhilarating movement: the compositions rarely startle us by their ingenuity; the use of the camera is clear-eyed rather than ingenious. *What* De Sica focuses on at a given point is more significant than the way in which he focuses his attention. The way is never neglected, it simply is not exploited; for it is to De Sica's purpose to move in tandem with un-elliptical life as closely as he dares without vitiating motion-picture technique altogether. To subordinate the essentially cinematic as he does is itself a technique of ineffable skill, and to efface his signature as a director from the style of a film argues a modest purity of aim that is refreshing.

De Sica tried out such a detached or reserved *mise en scène* for the first time in *The Children Are Watching Us*, whose simplicity of composition and subdued editing style markedly contrast with the formulaic, studio-dictated cinematic style of his previous four films. The tone of De Sica's fifth picture also strongly differs from that of *Red Roses, Maddalena, Zero for Conduct, Teresa Venerdì,* and even the otherwise dramatic period piece *A Garibaldian in the Convent,* for there is no comedy in *The*

Children Are Watching Us, what relief we get from Pricò's suffering comes only in the form of his own heightened or mature perception and sensitivity – indeed, his name is a shortened form of the Italian word for precocious. Not only is there no comedy in the movie, there is a tragic ending that signaled a change in De Sica's artistic vision. The alienation evident at the start of *The Children Are Watching Us* does not disappear; on the contrary, the gap in communication between the mother and her child widens. The discordant ending of this film, moreover, in which Pricò returns alone down a long corridor to his tiny dormitory room, is one of the most powerful in all of De Sica's work – challenged only by the final scene of *Shoeshine*, where a boy slips to his death from a bridge in an attempt to escape attack by the best friend who has turned on him. The ending of *The Children Are Watching Us* thus contrasts markedly with the comic endings of this director's first four movies, where the strife and confusion of the fictional world are replaced by happy harmony and romantic union.

The Children Are Watching Us, then, proved to be a key work, thematically as well as stylistically, in De Sica's directing career: it cemented his collaborative artistic relationship with Cesare Zavattini, and it marked the beginning of his breakthrough as a filmmaker of more than provincial stature. In its thematic attempt to reveal the underside of Italy's moral life, shared with *Obsession*, this film was indicative of a rising new vision in Italian cinema. In exhibiting semi-documentary qualities by being shot partially on location at the beaches of Alassio and by using non-professional actors in some roles, *The Children Are Watching Us* was, again along with *Obsession* as well as the aforementioned pictures by Blasetti and Franciolini, a precursor of the neorealism that would issue forth after the liberation of occupied Rome.

De Sica's fifth film was not a financial success, however, and its negative reception was in part engineered by those who saw it as an impudent criticism of Italian morality. The unfavorable reaction to *The Children Are Watching Us* was also influenced, of course, by the strictures of the past: during the era of Mussolini's regime (which began in 1922 and more or less ended in 1943) and "white telephone" movies (trivial romantic comedies set in blatantly artificial studio surroundings), an insidious censorship had made it almost impossible for artists to deal with – and for audiences to appreciate – the moral, social, and spiritual components of actual, everyday life. This is one of the senses in which neorealism's roots were political, for the movement reacted ideologically not only to Fascist militarism, totalitarianism, and racism but also to the control and censorship of prewar Italian cinema.

Censorship is an issue in the contemporary Iranian cinema as well, which is the reason that numerous Iranian movies made in the wake of the 1979 Islamic Revolution feature child protagonists.[2] Majid Majidi's *The Children of Heaven* (1997), for one example, was concerned with an impoverished urban family whose young son and daughter learn the value of shoes when they lose the girl's only pair, only to find them on the feet of a child who is worse off than they are. The father of that child is a blind peddler, and blindness, figurative as well as literal, happens to be the subject of Majidi's fourth picture, *The Color of Paradise* (1999; formerly titled *The Color of God* or *The Color of Heaven*, depending on the translation), as this writer-director continues to explore the lives of people marginalized by a society whose uniformly strict codes of behavior are otherwise intended to ensure Islamic communion. (Majidi's fifth film, titled *Rain* [2002], is a love story between a young Iranian Turk and an Afghan refugee-cum-migrant worker that had to be filmed in secrecy because of its "shocking" subject matter.)

Blindness as a subject is hardly new to the cinema or the theatre before it. This is not surprising given the visual aspect of both art forms and the consequent irony that their audiences are having an experience denied to the blind themselves. From *Oedipus Rex* (430 B.C.) through *King Lear* (1605) to Maeterlinck's *The Blind* (1891) and even Leonard Gershe's *Butterflies Are Free* (1969), blindness has been more

---

2 The newly released documentary *Friendly Persuasion* (2000, dir. Jamsheed Akrami) explores contemporary Iranian cinema through the eyes of twelve of its participants, including the directors Abbas Kiarostami, Majid Majidi, Mohsen Makhmalbaf, Tahmineh Milani, and Rakhshan Bani-Etemad. Interviews with these men and women are interwoven with clips from their films, as *Friendly Persuasion* presents an intellectual as well as philosophical look at the history and present-day realities (e.g., government injunction against the importation of American pictures) of moviemaking in Iran. All those interviewed agree that Iranian cinema has achieved such artistic heights over the last twenty years or so partly due, paradoxically, to the restrictions and limitations placed upon it, particularly in its depiction of sex and violence. As Mohsen Makhmalbaf succinctly put the matter, "The difference between Iranian cinema and the dominant cinema in the rest of the world is the difference between a local dish and a hamburger. The entire world is eating hamburgers nowadays." Majidi's latest "local dish," *The Color of Paradise*, is available from Columbia TriStar Home Video at $29.95 for DVD and $98.95 for videotape.

than a subject, however – it has been one of the most potent of dramatic metaphors. That metaphor has been less potent on film, which has usually been content merely to present blind characters as people of serene temperament and superior virtue. I'm thinking of the beautiful flower-seller in Chaplin's *City Lights* (1931) and the hermit in James Whale's *Bride of Frankenstein* (1935), whose blank eyes see past the unattractive exterior of the little tramp and the hideous monster, respectively, to find the essential goodness underneath.

Or consider, on the one hand, the vulnerable and innocent yet brave Audrey Hepburn confronting a psychotic Alan Arkin along with his murderous henchmen in *Wait Until Dark* (1967), and, on the other, John Malkovich's transformation in *Places in the Heart* (1984) from the cranky, even bitter isolation of a blind World War I veteran to the devoted participation of a grateful tenant or boarder in the defense of his adopted farm family against the onslaught of economic depression. Rather more subtle – namely, less maudlin or less melodramatic – is the relationship between the honorable rabbi who is going blind in Woody Allen's *Crimes and Misdemeanors* (1989) and the moral blindness of the ophthalmologist who rejects this cleric's counsel. The same is true of the relationship between the blind orphan girl and the pastor who takes her into his family and raises her in Jean Delannoy's *La Symphonie Pastorale* (1946). It may indeed be easier for the cinema to present blind *children* as people of serene temperament and superior virtue, since such a presentation corroborates the myth of children's original innocence. In *La Symphonie Pastorale*, that innocence is underlined by the omnipresent motif of snow in the Swiss mountain village where the story takes place – a snow whose natural purity will inevitably become sullied, just as the blind girl's goodness is tarnished by her contact with the minister and his son.

Nature is also at work in *The Color of Paradise*, which mainly takes place in a rural setting – where it's cheaper to film, to be sure, but where there is also less interference (I'm told) from Iranian censors. The picture opens in Tehran, the capital in which eight-year-old Mohammad attends a boys-only boarding school for the blind. But *The Color of Paradise* begins only after the words "To the Glory of God" appear on a black screen and the screen remains black for a few minutes, while we hear the voices of boys and their teacher as radio music plays in the background. Thus does Majid Majidi begin his film in a minor key, as it were, giving us the aural experience of a blind person before substituting a visual one for all those who can see. Still, the soundtrack remains important throughout this movie – as it should in this stirring example of the cinema of blindness – with its alternating chorus of woodpeckers, wind, birds, insects, rain, footfalls, and rushing streams. *The Color of Paradise* is also an explicit example of religious cinema, as its epigraph and title more than suggest. And those who are not as religious as Majidi will find some of its moments contrived, manipulative, or lachrymose – but never sanctimonious.

When the action gets under way, the school term is ending for a three-month summer break and, as they finish packing, the boys are being picked up by their parents. Gradually, the students all depart except for Mohammad, who remains alone sitting on a bench outside in the school garden, waiting (through two dissolves indicating the passage of time) for his delinquent father. Fearful that the latter does not love him because he's blind and that his parent therefore will never appear, Mohammad movingly laments his having been born without sight, as his sympathetic teacher tries to comfort him before returning to his office. A small, infinitely sad presence, his wary yet open face expressing both his loneliness and his heightened sensitivity to sound, smell, and touch, the boy later gets distracted by the faint sound of a fledgling among some fallen leaves. So exquisitely attuned to the natural world is Mohammad that he not only locates the baby bird amid the leaves, he is also able arduously to climb a tree, find the fledgling's vacated nest, and put the tiny creature back where it belongs. Pleased with what he has accomplished, the youngster taps the baby's beak with his hand as its mother hovers suspiciously nearby.

Sheer sentimentality, you say? Integral metaphor, I aver. For Mohammad's father, Hashem, who has finally arrived, has been secretly watching his son during the boy's perilous descent from the tree instead of offering him assistance. And soon it becomes clear why: even as Mohammad yearns to be returned to the nest of his own family, his father would like to get rid of him. Widowed for five years with two young daughters plus an elderly mother to support far away in the northern highlands of Iran, Hashem pleads hardship and begs school officials to keep his son over the summer – indeed, permanently. But they refuse and reprimand him for trying to shirk his responsibilities as a father. So he reluctantly takes Mohammad back to the family's woodland home near the Caspian Sea, where Hashem does some farming but derives most of his (small) income from his job in a charcoal factory. Amidst a colorful, earthly paradise of fields filled with wildflowers, lush forests, and green hills, Hashem then symbolically proceeds to blacken himself as well as everyone else around him.

Mohammad does get a short reprieve, however – italicized by one or

Salimeh Feizi as the grandmother and Mohsen Ramezani as Mohammad in
The Color of Paradise.

two idyllic, slow-motion shots – as he is reunited with his beloved and
devout grandmother together with his two caring sisters, Hanyeh and
Bahareh; as he unites with nature in his attempts to "catch the wind,"
read the pebbles in a riverbed as if they were inscribed in Braille,
understand the language of birds, and "see" the colors of the rainbow;
and as he begins to attend the local grade school, which has not yet
begun its summer recess and where he is the best reader even though
he is blind. But Hashem forbids Mohammad to continue at the school,
possibly hoping to keep his son's existence a secret. We had a hint why
in Tehran when the father sold two of his family's Persian rugs in order
to buy some women's jewelry (ogling it first through a showcase window that excludes Mohammad's image and mirrors his own – which
will later fatefully crack when he accidentally drops his shaving mirror).
Then we learn that Hashem wants to remarry – this time into a prominent family with an attractive daughter (whose first fiancé has died)

and a sizable dowry. And the father sees his blind son as a shameful encumbrance, whereas his daughters and their grandmother will only be of service to his new wife.

Hashem's idea of a compromise – over his mother's fierce objections – is to leave Mohammad in the care of a blind, avuncular carpenter, who promises to train the boy as his apprentice, and who lives far enough away (in an isolated cabin in the woods) to require boarding a bus to visit him. Given Mohammad's belief that he has been abandoned even by those, like his grandmother, who love him, he takes solace in the thought that an invisible God loves the blind more than anyone else, because they *sense* His presence without needing or demanding to see Him. Given her belief that Mohammad (also the name of the founder of the Moslem religion) is a gift from God, Hashem's mother is appalled at her son's treatment of *his* son, fears for the father's soul, and decides to leave his house. We are equally appalled at this man's behavior, but let me emphasize that he is no grasping, concupiscent villain. Not unsympathetic, the hardworking Hashem is a struggling, insecure, truly desperate man who believes himself to be the victim of a cruel deity and who appears to be in a constant state of guilt, anxiety, or anguish (a state that creates a few comic moments during his rushed, cross-cut visits with his fiancée and her relatives).

Hashem's harried state is exacerbated by his mother's sudden departure, but he manages to drag her home in a driving rain and thus "save face." Still, the ominous appearance during the old woman's abbreviated trip of a little fish squirming in receding water – together with the recurrent sound, on track and in Hashem's tortured mind, of an eerie, minatory, bestial voice – tells us that this father's unnatural behavior toward his male offspring will have dire consequences for their family. Mohammad's grandmother may have been returned to the literal warmth of her home, but Hashem's lack of warmth toward his only son kills her. And nature itself seems activated by her death, as a screen-filling mist envelops Mohammad, who, miles away, has awakened at the moment of his grandmother's passing and gone outdoors. The family of Hashem's fiancée correctly regards that passing as a bad omen and cancels her imminent wedding, to which the distraught Hashem responds by going to retrieve what he has blindly viewed only as an obstacle to his re-marriage: his son.

Though Mohammad's "educated hands" seemed destined to do more than build cabinets by touch, the boy had resigned himself to his workman's fate – particularly under the tutelage of the blind carpenter, a confidant to whom he could finally bare his disconsolate soul. But, after turning back twice, Hashem finally reclaims his son and begins the long journey home. During that journey, we once again encounter an ill omen in nature: in this instance, a turtle trapped on its back beneath a big rock. Shortly thereafter, the wooden bridge across which Hashem is leading Mohammad, sitting atop a horse, collapses and the animal plunges into dangerous rapids along with the boy. Having already reached safe ground, his father hesitates for some time before attempting a rescue, more or less repeating the behavior of the two previous instances. (At the school for the blind in Tehran, as Hashem stood idly by, Mohammad could have fallen to his death from the tree housing the bird's nest; and at the charcoal factory in Iran's northern highlands, this father let his son wander outdoors without supervision, to the point of almost tumbling down a ravine before being rescued by two other workers.)

Hashem fails to rescue Mohammad, however, and himself nearly drowns in the treacherous current. After disappearing under water, the father finally emerges again, bruised and unconscious, on a beach. Slowly he awakens to wild geese passing overhead, only to see his son's body lying farther down the shore. In the last of this film's discreetly deployed high-angle or God's-eye-view shots, amidst mud and clouds and crying birds, Hashem tearfully goes to the boy and tries to revive him. Then the camera cranes down from behind the father to find itself on one of Mohammad's hands, which simultaneously moves as it is illuminated by what can only be called a heavenly light. Was the boy merely unconscious, like his father, and is he now waking up? Was he dead and has he been brought back to life by a benevolent deity pleased at Hashem's change of heart (and convinced that he has tested his Islamic namesake as much as He dares)? Is Mohammad in fact dead and does the heavenly light signify that he is now in God's hands, and his grandmother's blissful company, in the afterlife? We cannot know, because *The Color of Paradise* ends on this ambiguous note of – let us call it – tragic hope.

Majidi has been accused of resorting to melodramatics reminiscent of D.W. Griffith's *Way Down East* (1920) in this finale, and if the term melo-dramatics is thus hyphenated and taken literally, the charge is true. For Alireza Kohandairi's music here and elsewhere in *The Color of Paradise* is so sappy, so overemotional, in its calculated attempt to achieve a sympathetic audience-response, that it almost reduces the film to the bathetic level of nineteenth-century theatrical melodrama (where Griffith himself began as an actor). Except that there are no villains in this picture, the acting is not histrionic, and Mohammad Davoodi's color cinematography is subdued or restrained where it could easily have made a lush spectacle of northern Iran's natural wonders. (Moreover, there is no such pedestrian, "illustrative" musical score in Majidi's *Children of Heaven* or most of the Iranian movies I've seen that were made in the wake of the 1979 Islamic Revolution, including *The White Balloon* [1995] and *The Apple* [1998].) There *is* sentiment, and the only question is whether that sentiment gets transmogrified into sentimentality.

Aside from the music, it doesn't really. Even the camera's pinpointing of such a natural omen as the squirming fish works, despite the fact that Majidi has the grandmother save the fish by moving it to deeper water. For even as she performs this benevolent act, she accidentally drops (and loses) the sacred brooch that Mohammad had given her upon his return from Tehran. Majidi is obviously a true believer, and true believers see God's hand at work in the most mundane or incidental of human matters. As I observed earlier, whether we believe along with him is another matter. We need not do so, though, in order to appreciate this delicate, simple little film, for, unlike most religious art, *The Color of Paradise* doesn't propagandize for one simplistic view of God over another. It looks up, not sideways, and nowhere is this clearer than in its ending, where we cannot know which hand of God is at work, the sinister left or the salutary right. God remains invisible and inscrutable, but to be blind to His ubiquitousness and omnipotence, as Hashem learns, is the greatest of sins.

The mustachioed Hashem is played by a professional, Hossein Majub, who knows how to handle the complexities of such a man and therefore turns him into anything but a monochromatic character – which is what he quickly would have become in the hands of a less sensitive actor. Hashem's son is seemingly effortlessly acted by the charismatic, even beatific Mohsen Ramezani, a non-professional whom Majidi found at a school for the blind in Tehran. (Similarly, the major female roles are divided between a gently seasoned veteran and two naturally spontaneous non-actors: Salmeh Feizi as the grandmother; Elham Sharim as Hanyeh and Farahnaz Safari as her sister, Bahareh.) Ramezani grew up in the Iranian desert, with no concept of the sea, of birds, of the forest, which helps to account for his wondrous response to the verdancy and vibrance of nature in *The Color of Paradise*. What also helps to account for Ramezani's performance is the fact that he himself is from a poor family consisting of his widowed mother and four additional brothers – a family on which the blind boy believes (he has said) he is a financial burden.

Majid Majidi was sixteen when his own father died, creating a financial hardship for *his* surviving mother and her four other sons. As the
second-oldest, Majidi and his elder brother had to work and take care
of the whole family, and this writer-director's experiences in doing so
may have made him especially attuned to the plight of the disadvan-
taged or troubled children he depicts in his films. These children, like
Pricò of *The Children Are Watching Us*, are awakened, if not damaged or
destroyed, by their exposure to the world of adults. In *The Color of Paradise*, this world, like that of De Sica's 1943 movie, consists of a paternal grandmother, a boarding school, and a parent who would sacrifice
its child for the sake of a romantic union. But the difference between
the Italian film and the Iranian one is a matter of perspective.

To wit: it is as though De Sica's camera, in *The Children Are Watching
Us* as in the subsequent *Shoeshine* and *Umberto D.* (1952), were a passive
or removed witness to tragedy rather than the active force in the shaping of a fictional story. Majidi's lens, by contrast, is not afraid to move
in close or to shoot from on high – that is, to be aggressive in its, and
thus our, take on Mohammad's tale. Majidi would say that he has his
god, Mohammed, on his side or up above him – indeed, he shows as
well as says this in *The Color of Paradise* just as he did in *The Children of
Heaven*. De Sica, for his part, was nothing if not a critic of Catholicism
in his neorealist pictures, particularly *Bicycle Thieves* and *Miracle in
Milan* (1951). And, despite the fact that his secular humanism is sometimes buttressed by heart-tugging music, it ultimately leaves his characters – if not his audience – out in the cold. Sometimes in the end those
characters have each other, but "another" never seems to be enough;
other, worldly people, after all, are not the same as otherworldliness of
the divinely transcendent kind.

7

Women and Children First

On Panahi's *The Circle* (1997, Iran) and Ramsay's *The Ratcatcher* (1999, Scotland)

Now Iranian cinema is becoming known for its depiction of women as well as children, as two recent titles attest: *The Day I Became a Woman* (2001), directed by Marzieh Meshkini, and Jafar Panahi's third picture, *The Circle* (2000), from a screenplay by Kambozia Partovi[1] and Panahi, after two films by him that featured little girls (*The White Balloon* in

---

1 Initially banned in its own country by the government, *The Circle* was subsequently granted a limited release in Iran after winning the Golden Lion, or grand prize, at the 2000 Venice Film Festival. As for the forty-one-year-old Panahi himself, he was detained in April 2001 for over ten hours by immigration officials at JFK airport in New York, in nightmarish circumstances resembling those found in his latest movie. Attempting to change planes en route from a film festival in Hong Kong to one in Buenos Aires, Panahi was chained to a wooden bench in a makeshift holding cell because he refused to be fingerprinted and photographed by U.S. immigration, in accordance with State Department regulations requiring that Iranian citizens (i.e., potential terrorists) be subjected to extra scrutiny when they arrive, even if they're on American soil only for a few hours in order to change planes. During his jailing, Panahi was joined by a boy from Sri Lanka, a woman from India, and residents of Mexico, Peru, Pakistan, and Bangladesh. Ironically, while the director was in chains, *The Circle* was being screened in New York to applause and acclaim – and a Freedom of Expression Award from the National Board of Review, which Panahi has since returned in protest.

1995 and *The Mirror* in 1997). This development shouldn't really surprise, since women and children are alike in still being marginal citizens of Iran, even as they were everywhere else in the world (and continue to be in places like China) as late as the mid-twentieth century.

Women in Iran, for example, are not allowed to smoke in public, and they may not ride in a car driven by a man to whom they are not related or otherwise travel unaccompanied by an adult male relative. They can't check into a hotel by themselves; do not have the right to divorce a man, and, if divorced by him, do not get custody of their children; and cannot receive an abortion without the consent of a father or husband. Moreover, women cannot move outdoors or enter certain buildings without putting on a *chador*, part of the "uniform" that covers up their hair, their bodies, even their faces. And they can't walk alone at night without it being assumed that they are soliciting sex. (Ironically, prostitution is one of the only ways in which an Iranian woman can make an independent living.) Figuratively speaking, then, all of Iran is a prison for women – a point that Panahi underscores by making several of the women in *The Circle* literal prisoners who have recently been released, only to find that they are no less confined on the outside.

The film begins evocatively with the sound of a female voice, in the dark. Then we hear the moans and screams of a woman giving birth, or continuing the life cycle/circle, but her cries could just as well be for her own fate in Iranian society. When her newborn girl cries out – as cry she should over the life without value or autonomy that awaits her – the black screen finally turns to blinding white as a nurse announces the birth to the baby's maternal grandmother. Her reaction passes from denial to chagrin without ever stopping at joy, as she complains to the nurse, "The ultrasound said it was going to be a boy. Now my daughter's husband and her in-laws will insist on a divorce." We hear the mother's name – Solmoz Gholami – in this opening scene, and we shall hear it again in the final one, but we never see her, her invisibility itself becoming a metaphor for the negligible status of women in Iran. As for the grandmother, her scene of distress is a thematic prelude, in a single long take, to what follows, and as she leaves the hospital, the camera leaves her to focus on a group of three younger women huddled around a pay phone on a gritty, congested Tehran street peopled almost exclusively by men.

The camera may appear to be distracted here, but in fact it is initiating a daisy-chain dramatic structure that will eventually come full circle, and which can be found in a motion picture as old as Marcel

Nargess Mamizadeh as Nargess, in the foreground, early in *The Circle*.

Ophüls's *La Ronde* (1950, from the 1897 play by Arthur Schnitzler) and as recent as Richard Linklater's *Slacker* (1991). Rather than merely making clever use of a storytelling device, this incidentally yet seamlessly connected structure organically reinforces the film's thesis that gender discrimination is a force circumscribing the lives of all Iranian women. For it is as if the camera could randomly select and follow *any* of the other women we see on the streets and wind up more or less in the same desperate, heart-rending place. The vicious circle of social oppression thus encloses everyone – at least all females – in its unforgiving, unyielding perimeter (which may be extended for men, but remains confining for them as well in so authoritarian a society). And Panahi's camera (with cinematography by Bahram Badakhshani) reflects that encirclement or entrapment, for its frequently handheld shots – which simulate or capture the frightened, furtive nature of existence for these perpetually wary women – diminish in number with each succeeding episode. What this suggests, of course, is the ever-increasing immobilization of a life without options.

For reasons that emerge only gradually and obliquely, the three women found by the camera are in state of agitation and even panic.

Especially when police are in the area, they hide behind parked cars, dart into alleyways, hastily throw *chadors* over their heads and shoulders. The three of them seem to be in flight, though from what specific threat and toward what exact refuge is initially a mystery. We discover before long that they, like other women they will encounter in their peregrinations, have spent time in prison; yet these three are only on furlough for a group outing, have nonetheless decided not to return, and hence must be even more cautious in public than they would normally be. Why each of them, or any female in *The Circle* for that matter, was incarcerated, we never learn – not for the sake of arty ambiguity or teasing effect, but to assign political blame: to the nation of Iran as unthinking persecutor of women whose essential crime, whatever specific law they may have broken, is their gender.

One of the three women in the second sequence, Pari ("Fairy" in Farsi), gets rearrested by police (only to appear in the last third of the film). The other two are eighteen-year-old Nargess ("Daffodil"), who is marked by a livid bruise under her left eye, and the older Arezou ("Wish"), whose defining activity seems to be desperately seeking a safe place to smoke. She finds it this time with a man to whom she also sells her body so that she can buy Nargess a bus ticket home to her native village in western Iran. The younger woman naïvely thinks she sees her rural paradise depicted in the reproduction of a van Gogh painting she discovers while wandering through the marketplace, and Nargess wants her friend (who cannot return to her husband and son after two years in jail) to join her there. But the wiser Arezou declines the offer by saying, "I couldn't handle seeing that your paradise might not exist."

Nargess herself never finds out if it does, for she has neither the proper papers to travel (student identification, for example) nor a man to escort her – in this case, the twenty-year-old fiancé back home for whom this teenager poignantly buys a shirt at a shop in the bus terminal. And her ultimate frustration as well as separation or isolation is visually foreshadowed in the scene where she waits for Arezou to return from her sexual assignation. Terrified because she has already seen Pari rounded up and taken away, Nargess stands all alone at the bottom of a busy courtyard looking upward to the place where her friend has just disappeared. Males surround her – some uniformed, the rest civilians, several of them casually abusive – the setting is pen-like, and a carefully chosen close-up of Nargess's face not only reveals her anxiety but also seems of itself to close her off from her environment. This country girl may have benefitted for a while from the big-sisterly solicitude of Arezou, but one of *The Circle*'s points is that women in trouble in Iran can in the end do very little to help one another. Arezou can't put Nargess on a bus that will take her home, and Nargess cannot save her fellow traveler Pari, who has been remanded to the custody of her father. Nargess manages to trace Pari to this man's front door, only to be rebuffed and sent away.

Four months pregnant by her lover, who was also imprisoned and then executed for political reasons, Pari must leave the shelter of her father's house when her two brothers suddenly arrive by motor scooter and threaten her with violence. Once on the street, her goal is to obtain an abortion, and to this end she seeks help from two former fellow prisoners. The first is Monir, whom Pari finds working as the cashier at a Tehran movie theatre. Her reunion with Monir, in the cramped confines of the cinema's box office, is warm and loving, but this friend can do little more than lend a sympathetic ear to Pari. (Among Monir's problems: a husband with another wife in addition to her.) Moreover, their get-together has a slightly sinister overcast, for we glimpse it in a long take exclusively through the iron grill of the ticket booth, which makes the two women appear to be in jail. And not by accident, each time a patron purchases a ticket, he or she completely obscures or erases the images of Pari and Monir.

Pari makes her way next to a hospital, where she looks up Elham, now a nurse married to a prominent doctor who knows nothing of her past (and who divorced his first wife simply on the ground that she was "no good"). Pari hopes that Elham will get her husband or another physician to perform the illegal abortion – for, after all, which male relative of hers would grant such permission in this Kafkaesque world? But the risk is too great for this former inmate, who decides to look out only for herself and gives her friend the brush-off. Not permitted to either smoke or chew tobacco in this environment, and unable even to eat the food that Elham has guiltily provided, the depressed but otherwise strong-willed Pari can only sit in the hospital waiting room for the longest time, listening at one point to a woman mourn her dead child and at another to an ambulance attendant announcing that his stretcher bears a female suicide. (Panahi got the idea for *The Circle*, he said in the *New York Times* [15 April 2001, section 2, p. 13, column 1], from a newspaper report about a woman who killed herself after murdering her two daughters.)

With nowhere to go and beset by nausea, Pari wanders the city by night, encountering first a military policeman who makes her dial a number at a pay phone, then ask for a married woman who turns out to be his mistress. Next she meets a woman named Nayereh, who is in the process of abandoning her young daughter on the street, in the hope that the child (all dolled up for the occasion) will be adopted by a rich family that can at least insulate her from the sexism and misogyny of Iranian society. The mother succeeds on this, her third attempt to give up her daughter, and, in a visual reference to his *White Balloon* – which, like *The Mirror*, featured a brave, outspoken, and determined little girl not yet mechanically stifled by the Islamic patriarchy – Panahi shows the girl being comforted by a balloon-seller before being taken away by the police.

All the while this writer-director (who also edited *The Circle*) ironically counterpoints the scene of child abandonment, replete with unlit cigarettes hanging from Nayereh's and Pari's mouths, with a merry wedding celebration taking place at a hotel in the background. And even as Panahi's film declines to pass judgment on Pari or any of its other female characters (at the same time that it refuses to condescend to them by assuming their total innocence or goodness), Pari herself does not condemn Nayereh, although she does briefly try to dissuade her from taking such an extremely rejective action before moving on.

Predictably, the camera leaves Pari at this point to remain with Nayereh, who promptly accepts an automobile ride with the second man to come along, ostensibly for the purpose of prostituting herself. He turns out to be an undercover cop, but he seems to sense that she's no professional and lets her go when he finds a hardcore streetwalker called Mojhan, who has been detained at a roadblock (while her "john" has typically been set free). Mojhan wears bright red lipstick along with a leopard print headscarf, chews gum, and, with a sneer and a shrug, accepts her fate (being locked up regularly) as the price she has to pay if she is to make some kind of living for herself in as repressive a state as Iran. As she awaits transport to jail beneath cloudy skies, this young woman quizzically watches a limousine pass with the newlyweds from the previously glimpsed wedding party. Then, once inside the barred police van together with a male prisoner and four officers, Mojhan – seen now only in profile, in long takes that isolate her from the men – steals a smoke in a small or ephemeral, but nevertheless heroic, declaration of her existential freedom.

The ephemerality of this prostitute's gesture is brought home by a harsh cut to the dark, dungeon-like cell in which she is placed. Outside it rains and thunders. Inside Mojhan finds herself in a circle that includes or envelops the six other women who have been the subject of Jafar Panahi's camera: Nargess, Arezou, Pari, Monir, Elham, and Nayereh, all of them arrested in the course of the single day spanned by this film. In a 360-degree pan, that camera literally encircles these women at this point, while a guard talking on the telephone reveals that the elusive Solmoz Gholami – the mother of the baby girl born in the opening scene – has been transferred from this cell to yet another. Then the jailer closes the small window into which he has been peering – the only window into or out of what amounts to the seven women's cage. This aperture is tellingly mounted atop the heaviest of steel doors, and when it closes, so too does *The Circle.*

As for the role of men in this movie, let me say that, for the most part, they are not depicted as melodramatic villains. The jailer in the final scene, for instance, is photographed in such a way – through the small window in the cell door, either looking down at the imprisoned women or being looked down upon by them as he sits at his desk – that he is either reduced in size and thus diminished in stature, or his face is made to appear ensnared by the very frame of the opening through which he gazes. The implication, of course, is that he and other Iranian men are as dehumanized by their treatment of women (if only spiritually or figuratively) as the women themselves are. Life in Iran for your average male is hardly a picnic, after all; and, one can argue, the restrictiveness even of men in this intolerant society has led to their further subjugation of women, in keeping with the theory that the powerless themselves will oppress those they perceive as lying beneath them.

So, despite its political implications, *The Circle* is not a work of propaganda in which shrinking victims are pitted against boldfaced victimizers. Panahi's method is investigative rather than didactic, which is the reason that his circular metaphor can encompass societies other than his native one – any society, in fact, where abortion, prostitution, poverty, domestic violence, and child abandonment have become uncomfortable, even taboo subjects. Had Panahi merely wished to create a finger-pointing work of propaganda, he certainly could have done so: not only by altering his script so as to focus less on the lot of women themselves than on the opposition between men and women, but also by adding a stirringly emotional musical score (there is no score whatsoever) and getting Badakhshani to employ a less subtle or subdued color scheme in the cinematography.

He could also have engaged a cast of monochromatic professional actors – the kind that profess in only one dimension – but Panahi wisely chose to blend professionals and non-professionals into an integral, spontaneous, sentient whole. The three principal actresses – Mariam Parvin Almani as Arezou, Nargess Mamizadeh as Nargess, and Fereshteh Sadr Orafai as Pari – give remarkably layered performances, particularly when you consider that, by Iranian standards of propriety, their faces are all they have to work with. In addition, given *The Circle*'s

length of an hour and a half as well as its episodic nature, neither of
these three (let alone any of the other players) gets more than fifteen
or twenty minutes of screen time.

If the last place one might have looked for a film about women is
Iran, the last place one would think to find a movie about children –
perhaps anyone, for that matter – is Scotland. Yes, it's true that Scotland is not as remote as Iran; still, the representation of this country in
the cinema has more or less been limited over the last few decades – at
least for those of us living outside the United Kingdom – to the charm-
ingly whimsical comedy of Bill Forsyth in such pictures as *That Sinking
Feeling* (1979), *Gregory's Girl* (1981), and *Comfort and Joy* (1984).[2] And
although the depiction of British society generally in the cinema is certainly not limited to the Oxbridge-Thatcherite view of the world (witness the films of veterans like Ken Loach and Mike Leigh, as well as of
relative newcomers such as Gary Oldman [*Nil by Mouth*, 1997] and Tim
Roth [*The War Zone*, 1999]), this is the view, through yuppie eyes in the
British-Museum tradition of Alexander Korda, that gets the most international publicity. I'm thinking of movies like *Four Weddings and a
Funeral* (1994; the highest grossing film ever made and financed in
Great Britain), *Sense and Sensibility* (1995), *Jane Eyre* (1996), and *Emma*
(1996) – all of them, not by chance, concerned with young women in
search of rich husbands.

Well, the status quo changed temporarily with the export from Scotland of Danny Boyle's *Trainspotting* (1996), the second biggest box-
office success in British film history, unlike any other such homegrown
movie with a plebeian-as-protagonist from *Room at the Top* (1958) to *Riff
Raff* (1991). And the plebeians in this case were twenty-something
heroin addicts whose desire for chemically induced oblivion is made
comprehensible (as well as marketable when combined with sex and
rock-and-roll) by the sordid, disaffecting environment in which they

---

2 Here's a sampling of relatively recent, noteworthy Scottish films and
   directors that most American cinephiles – through no fault of their own –
   have never heard of: *Play Me Something, Silent Scream, Tickets to the Zoo, Blue
   Black Permanent, As an Eilean, Work, Rest and Play,* and *Venus Peter;* Timothy
   Neat, Mike Alexander, Bill Douglas (with whose *Childhood Trilogy,* a grim
   autobiographical account of growing up in a harsh Scottish mining town
   in the 1940s, Lynne Ramsay's *Ratcatcher* [my subject in the second half of
   this chapter] has a good deal in common), Murray Grigor, Peter Capaldi,
   Brian Crumlish, Charles Gormley, Douglas Aubrey, Allan Robertson, and
   Ian Sellar.

live – Leith, a working-class area of housing projects on Edinburgh's old dockside – and the capitalist-colonialist oppression they suffer.

With *Ratcatcher* (1999), a first feature written and directed by thirty-two-year-old Lynne Ramsay after two promising shorts, we're in a poverty-stricken neighborhood of Glasgow and the main character is a twelve-year-old boy – i.e., someone in danger of ultimately turning to drugs not only as a proletarian escape from alienation and depression but also as a release from the dark vale of late childhood. Ramsay's protagonist brings to mind, in addition to Mark Renton from *Trainspotting*, such youngsters as Elambert from Benoît-Levy's *La Maternelle* (1932), Edmund of Rossellini's *Germany, Year Zero* (1947), Antoine Doinel of Truffaut's *Four Hundred Blows* (1959), Bresson's *Mouchette* (1966), Briton Alan Clarke's *Christine* (1987), and the Dardenne brothers' *Rosetta* (1999). So *Ratcatcher*'s lineage is long, distinguished, and pan-European.

The movie takes place in the summer of 1979 on a grotesquely run-down Glasgow public housing estate, a dismal place made even more depressing by a garbage strike that has left mountains of stinking, uncollected, vermin-infested trash in the streets. In this sorry corner of the universe, the rats outnumber the populace – they eat better as well, and have the advantage over humans of being able to scurry from one habitat to another whenever they want. The estate is gradually being emptied of humans by the city council in preparation for demolition, but only some of its largely unemployed inhabitants are being shunted from the center of the city to new estates on the rural outskirts of Glasgow. As for the rest ... windows are boarded up, decay is rampant, and the empty apartments offer boundless opportunities for youthful vandalism, viciousness, and predation.

The garbage strike isn't merely a glib metaphor for an economically as well as emotionally pestilent environment, however. Also to be seen in the Sex Pistols documentary called *The Filth and the Fury* (2000), it is a feature of one of the critical moments in recent British history: the national public employees' strike of 1978–79 that became known as "The Winter of Discontent," when public transport, commercial trucking, and garbage collection all came to a halt. (In some places, the dead even went unburied.) This strike killed off the postwar liberal political consensus in England and led directly to the election of conservative Prime Minister Margaret Thatcher. So if the characters in *Ratcatcher* have a rough life in 1979, it's nothing compared to what lies ahead in the near future.

The film opens with the slow-motion image of a pre-adolescent boy, one Ryan Quinn, wrapping himself in a shower curtain as if it could protect him from the toxic world outside his dank council flat. Five minutes later, Ryan is dead – drowned in the brackish, stagnant canal across the street, a stinking hole that's as close as this down-at-the-heels neighborhood comes to a playground. The curtain, in retrospect, seems like the boy's shroud, and young James Gillespie is responsible for placing him in it. For, as they scuffle in what appears to be just fun, James accidentally-on-purpose drowns his best friend in the dark brown water. And that drowning is prefigured not only by the terribly beautiful image of the shower curtain but also by a dead-time shot of the stairway to Ryan's apartment, right after he has gone outside, as well as by the very next shot: of Ryan on the street as seen from his living room window, though his mother has just left to meet her ex-husband and no one else is home.

These images tell us immediately that we are in the hands, not of a mere kitchen-sink realist, but of a *poetic* verist (and former photographer) who is as concerned to evoke as to document, to show as to tell, to transcend as to descend. Moreover, Lynne Ramsay begins her film in a minor key, obliquely, rather than with her main character. She calls it *Ratcatcher* in an ironic reference to Robert Browning's "Pied Piper of Hamelin" (1842), who, because the mayor broke a promise to pay him a thousand guilders for ridding the town of its numerous rats, leads the children of Hamelin to their disappearance in a mountainside (as opposed to a canal or lake, like the one in this film and in Egoyan's *The Sweet Hereafter* [1997], which, in its dialogue as well as its action, makes direct and unironic reference to Browning's poem). And, unlike your average commercial moviemaker, Ramsay does not make the gradual yet suspenseful exposure of James Gillespie's homicide the subject of her film. Instead she takes us on an episodic journey into the small, circumscribed world of which he is a part. Throughout *Ratcatcher* James will be haunted by the drowning of Ryan Quinn, but his remorse is remote and nonverbal and therefore goes unnoticed by his family, which is concerned with simply surviving in this squalid atmosphere. The boy's guilt thus becomes one more item buried amidst the pile of woes that accumulate around the Gillespies and their neighbors like the mounds of uncollected rubbish that clog these tenants' roadways, sidewalks, and yards.

Nominal head of the Gillespie "clan," James's father is a genial drunk in his thirties more interested in televised soccer than his kids. For the most part not actively cruel, he is emotionally elsewhere, and his vacant, smoke-filled days seem to be a rehearsal for the broken-

William Eadie as James in *The Ratcatcher*.

toothed, sunken-chested wreck he will become in middle age. Ma Gillespie, for her part, is a decent woman trapped in a world she can't control or direct; rebuffing Da's drink-induced attentions and ignoring his flirtations with the occasional barfly, she consoles herself by listening to popular music from the 1960s and wearily tries to do right by her children (which, in these circumstances, means routinely combing the lice out of their hair). James has a snitch of a younger sister and a sneering older one, and along with their parents these three dream of getting out of their bleak surroundings – of getting one of those new council houses in what amounts, for them, to the suburbs.

To this end James takes a double-decker bus to the end of the line, where he stumbles upon a vision of his salvation: a public housing development under construction, beneath brilliant sunshine and next to a golden field of waving grain. He adopts one of the half-finished houses as his own, sitting down in an actual bathtub (unlike the galvanized, portable one the Gillespies must use) that is covered with plastic, urinating in a toilet despite the fact that the water has not yet been turned on, rolling around in the seemingly endless acres of wheat. The sometimes handheld camera struggles to keep up with James, portentously going overhead or performing a 360-degree pan in search of him; but it finally settles on an idyllic shot of the vast wheat field, as seen and savored by James through the paneless window of his adopted home. This shot is an expansion of a famous image from Terrence Malick's *Days of Heaven* (1978), which was made by a man who, somewhat like Ramsay, believes in the primacy of powerful imagery over narrative detail or psycho-sociological probing. But the wheat-field-through-the-window also recalls Andrew Wyeth's *Christina's World* (1948) – without Christina.

Stunted lives are the subject of *Ratcatcher*'s hellish canvas, and it is to that canvas James must return. (Indeed, the next time he returns to the construction site, the door to his adopted dwelling is locked and rain pours down, as we look through the picture window at James trudging home through the fields of grain.) Although his family has applied for a new home, their chance of getting one isn't good, for the council inspectors who visit their flat (to assess the Gillespies' suitability) are taken aback by its untidiness as well as by the nearly anomic state of its occupants. Meanwhile, the thin-faced, frail-shouldered, dark-eyed James idles away his days in the company of two friends, his clownishly large, or milk-pitcher, ears doing nothing to offset the gravity of a demeanor made more grave by the memory of Ryan's death.

The first of his friends – and these are the ones we'd expect him to have in this milieu – is the younger Kenny, a sprightly, optimistic, somewhat daft or retarded boy who was the only witness to Ryan's drowning (telling James what he saw but no one else), and who himself almost drowns in death canal. (Oddly enough, Kenny is rescued by James's father, who has to be roused from a drunken stupor in order to perform his "heroic" deed.) This boy is a collector of animals, including rats, and dreams of one day owning the biggest zoo in the world. His crackpot obsession gives him a beatific glow and seems to insulate or extricate him from the dreary confines of a neighborhood that weighs down those with better mental balance. Metaphorically to illustrate this point, Ramsay has Kenny shackle his pet mouse named Snowball to a basket and, with the help of a red helium balloon, gleefully launch the rodent "awa' off tae ra moon." This thoughtless act of cruelty is then comically undercut when, in a fantasy or dream sequence originating with James – whose envy of the animal's "escape" is palpable – the mouse arrives on a lunar surface populated with thousands of other, happy little white mice. On the soundtrack, we hear a selection from the German composer Carl Orff's *Musica Poetica* or *Music for Children* (1950–54), the same music used in the treehouse sequence of *Badlands* (1973), Malick's film about a mindlessly murderous nineteen-year-old garbage collector and his fourteen-year-old accomplice-cum-girlfriend.

James's other friend, Margaret Anne, is also a fourteen-year-old, but one so lovelorn and unhappy that, desperate for attention, she lets the local bullies use her as a sperm depository. When these toughs goad James into joining in the exploitation of Margaret Anne, he simply lies on top of her semi-clad body. Himself fully clothed, James finds comfort, not arousal, in Margaret Anne's Madonna-like embrace. This is a bewitching moment – photographed from a slight distance, overhead, rather than up close at bed-level (like the shots of the gang-bangers) – for it is filled with intimations of happiness and warmth that are scarcely evident elsewhere in *Ratcatcher*. Earlier, sitting on a stone wall above the polluted canal with the myopic, bespectacled Margaret Anne (whose myopia is itself a metaphor for the other characters' limited perspective, and is mimicked by Ramsay's camera, which is frequently so close to the action as to deny us *visual* perspective), James had been mesmerized by the visceral image of an angry red scrape on her knee. "Do you want to touch it?" she asks, and he places a tentative hand over the wound, which suggests Margaret Anne's masochistic sexuality as well as James's sense of being rubbed raw by life.

Later, these two cleanse each other's literal as well as figurative wounds by taking a bath together at her place (where Margaret Anne's mother seems never to be at home). Ramsay creates an island of tenderness here between tiny James and rangy Margaret Anne that makes everything that has come before almost disappear, that restores to these orphans of the storm some measure of the innocence stolen from them each day by their environment. Afterward, they sit in front of the television set wrapped in towels while eating sandwiches, like the most contented married couple in the world. They even sleep together, twice, and James professes his love for Margaret Anne, but if they have sex we don't see it – nor do we need to. (His touching idea of affection is to pull her ripped nylon stocking over her bare toe.) For *Ratcatcher* is less a coming-of-age than a coming-to-ruin story, and James Gillespie is drowning at the end of the film, even as Margaret Anne continues to drown herself in the purported affections of so many neighborhood ruffians.

We see James floundering beneath the murky canal water right after he has left Margaret Anne's bed, in one of three stunning juxtapositions that conflate love and death in this film (whose editor was Lucia Zucchetti). Then Ramsay cuts to a Magritte-like scene in which the Gillespies, including a trailing James, carry their furniture through sunlit fields to their heavenly new council home. *Ratcatcher*'s final image, however, is of James again, still submerged – or submerging himself out of a combination of guilt, fear, despair, and disgust – beneath the waters of death canal. If he isn't literally drowning, he is figuratively doing so in the here and now. And in a movie like this, with at least one other fantasy sequence (the one tracking the mouse-to-the-moon, though the shot of the wheat-field-through-the-window might qualify as well), the scene of the Gillespie family's happy journey from inner city to outermost country may be James's dying or futile wish for a life less brutal and bemired.

Ramsay isn't being coyly ambiguous in so ending *Ratcatcher*, she is combining, with some degree of consistency, the gritty tough-minded-ness of Ken Loach with the lyrical whimsy of Bill Forsyth. As someone who herself grew up in similar Glaswegian surroundings, Ramsay wants to be true to them in the social-realist or political protest tradition that (at least in Britain) can be traced back to the plays, films, and novels of all those "angry young men" from the late fifties and early sixties. At the same time, unlike most of these artists, she wants, through the creation of sometimes strangely insinuating images that go beyond realism (the literal meaning of "sur-realism," by the way), to give *Ratcatcher* a kind of cumulative poetic impact that somehow compensates for its threadbare and dispiriting story.

For us *moviegoers*, you might be muttering to yourself, but not for the wretched of the Glasgow slums. To which I would respond, "Yes and no." For it's clear that a number of these striking, hypnotic images orig-inate in James Gillespie's perfervid imagination – as put there by Lynne Ramsay (where they are more than once played out in dreamlike slow-motion). Which may be her way of saying that, in art as in life, it's mind over matter – something often forgotten by realists and naturalists who give far too much conceptual power to the unreconstructed material world. Ramsay got out of Glasgow's muck and, in a sense, so did James Gillespie: I saw him, or his movie, in Chicago.

He was helped there by everyone associated with *Ratcatcher*, including the composer Rachel Portman and the cinematographer Alwin Kuchler. Portman's plaintive score for piano and harp is one of her best, partly because it's so spare or incidental – unlike her lush, nudgy music for such comparatively big-budget pictures as *Chocolat* (2000), *The Legend of Bagger Vance* (2000), *The Cider House Rules* (1999), and *Beloved* (1998). Kuchler shot Ramsay's twenty-minute film *Gas Man* in 1997 (which, like her autobiographical short

Small Deaths [1995] and *Ratcatcher* itself, centers on the lives of children), then achieved some prominence as the director of photography for *One Day in September* (1999), the documentary about the 1972 Munich Olympics that won the Academy Award in 2000. Here Kuchler's palette consists mainly of cool blues, mildew greens, and mud browns: in other words, glumness picturized, then intensified by the frequently claustrophobic, myopic camera, which presses in from eye level, or by an oppressive, hyperopic one that weighs down from high above. But his lens gets its own redemption from *Ratcatcher*'s physical wretchedness when it photographs Snowball's trip to the moon or paints James's version of a field of dreams. (Kuchler also shot Ramsay's next film, *Morvern Callar* [2001]. It was adapted from Alan Warner's 1995 novel about a low-paid supermarket worker in an out-of-the-way Scottish port who covers up her boyfriend's suicide, sells his unpublished novel under her own name, then repairs to a sub-Club Med resort for fun and games.)

Kuchler and Portman are professionals, like the adults in *Ratcatcher*'s cast, particularly Tommy Flanagan as Da Gillespie and Mandy Matthews as Ma. The film's children are all non-professionals, however, and one wonders to what extent they themselves are products of Glasgow's mean streets. If their (subtitled) Glaswegian dialect is any indicator, here they were born and bred. (Certainly no one can accuse Ramsay of having cast these kids for their cuteness of speech *or* appearance.) Yet the real question may be, to what extent has their work in *Ratcatcher* helped to release them from their pernicious living conditions? Unlike the young hero of the ridiculously overpraised, paint-by-numbers tearjerker *Billy Elliot* (2000) – whose coal miners themselves must contend with the Thatcher-ordered suppression of their 1984 strike – James Gillespie is leading a life that's unlikely to take him much farther down the lane, let alone over the rainbow. But what about William Eadie, the boy who plays this difficult part so well, who renders James's emotional complexity with such delicacy? (The role is not easy precisely because James has so much to hide – something trained actors, not untrained ones and particularly not untrained children, are good at doing.)

Where are Eadie, Leanne Mullen (Margaret Anne), John Miller (Kenny), and the other children in the cast headed? What will they do now? To what extent will they or the young inhabitants of Glasgow's tenement houses benefit from this filmic record of their deplorable existence? These are naturally questions that one could ask about the non-professional, as well as professional, actresses in *The Circle*, given the pervasive constriction of women's lives in Iran. And, finally, these questions about life outside the frame are as interesting as those about the art within it. Put another way: art is short, life is long, or art exists for life's sake.

8

Carry Me Home

On Zhang Yimou's *The Road Home* (2000, China),
Kiarostami's *The Wind Will Carry Us* (1999, Iran),
and Rossellini's *Europe '51* (1952, Italy)

A chapter that treats two films by Zhang Yimou and Abbas Kiarostami, respectively, seems particularly apt in light of Zhang's revelation in a recent interview that he greatly admires Kiarostami's artistry, including the latter's ability to transcend social and political strictures. Zhang himself is the most prominent member of the first generation of China's filmmakers since the pre-Communist era – the so-called Fifth Generation – to make movies that do not automatically toe a socialist-realist line, that do not spew out Party propaganda as a matter of course. These directors, graduates of China's only film school, the Beijing Film Academy, began work in the mid-1980s and have produced a spate of notable features. Moreover, for several of these Zhang served as either the cinematographer or the leading actor: Chen Kaige's *Yellow Earth* (1984) and *The Big Parade* (1985), Zhang Junzhao's *The One and the Eight* (1984), Tian Zhuangzhuang's *The Horse Thief* (1987) and *Li Lianying* (1990), Li Shaohong's *Bloody Dawn* (1990), and Zhou Xiaowen's *Black Mountain Road* (1991).

But Zhang's work as a director, although it conveys an ecstatic awareness of the natural world similar to that of Kiarostami (with whom he shares an interest in photography), is less austere, less oblique, and more emotionally direct than that of the Iranian master. Zhang's initial directorial effort, *Red Sorghum* (1987), was fortunate enough to be a beneficiary of China's first open door policy since the launching of the Cultural Revolution in 1966, achieving international distribution (and with it the Golden Bear Award at the 1988 Berlin Film Festival) as well as wide release in its native land. His second and third films to be shown outside China, *Ju Dou* (1990) and *Raise the Red Lantern* (1991), which were produced by the Japanese and Taiwanese respectively, were originally forbidden release to the Chinese public – in part because each was nominated for an Oscar as best foreign language movie and each was the winner of a prize at a major Western film festival. What surer sign that these works espouse bourgeois liberal values, to be seen in their flouting of sexual norms that define the institution of marriage, their harrowing portrait of the systematic oppression of women, and their allegorical implication that young Chinese should rebel against the brutal, autocratic rule of impotent old men? (In *Red Sorghum*, by contrast, a man recalls his grandparents' bucolic love affair during the 1920s, then their heroic display of peasant vitality as, side by side, they fight against the invading Japanese in 1937.)

Zhang got himself into trouble with *To Live* (1994) as well: this picture was banned in its country of origin because of its purportedly negative portrayal of historical events as they affect a single family over the turbulent decades from the Communist Civil War to the "Great Leap Forward" to the Cultural Revolution. Furthermore, Zhang was forced to write an apology for wanting to promote *To Live* at the Cannes Festival. So, in *Not One Less* (1999) and *The Road Home* (2000), he abandoned the historical epic for a subject less fraught with political overtones, and one that he had first explored in *The Story of Qiu Ju* (1992): the heroic obstinacy of peasant women who, against overwhelming odds and with almost comical determination, succeed in bending the world (one that juxtaposes the countryside with the big city) to their own will. (We see the obverse of this theme in Zhang's *Shanghai Triad* [1995], a gangster movie where the country girl is corrupted by her life in the pre-revolutionary, mob-ruled city of Shanghai, as well as by a cruelly domineering patriarch of the kind found in *Ju Dou* and *Raise the Red Lantern*.) Though they were not made consecutively, these three films form a loose trilogy on the theme of sheer stubbornness, celebrating human beings' excessive, literal-minded devotion to principles that, at first glance, seem to be trivial or absurd.

In *The Story of Qiu Ju* (based on a novel called *The Wan Family's Lawsuit*), the seven-months-pregnant heroine demands satisfaction from bureaucrats at several levels after her husband is kicked in the groin during a quarrel with the political chief of their village. The wife's wearying journeys back and forth from village to various towns to a bustling modern city, and her unwearying patience with recalcitrant officials in cold offices or dusty anterooms, are, by any rational standard, far out of proportion to the substance of her complaint. And

before this film is at the halfway point, its heroine has us chuckling at
her terrier grip on the trouser-leg of Communist authority, more concerned about her husband's cause than he is. Yet her refusal to accept
a reasonable standard – pushing the demand for satisfaction to the
point of monomania (particularly on the part of a woman living in a
nation where female infanticide is practiced, even more in the countryside than in urban areas) – is, in Zhang Yimou's cinematic universe,
an ethical as well as a political imperative.

This imperative, however, can also turn into an impulse that proceeds from selfishness, suspicion, and disrespect for authority, as well
as sheer ignorance about the workings of the modern world. Thus
when she is first hired, the substitute teacher in *Not One Less* – a thir-
teen-year-old girl no bigger or smarter than her unruly pupils – is told
that she will forfeit her cash bonus if any of the children drop out of
school. When one girl is recruited by an elite training program for ath-
letes, a great source of pride to the village, the teacher is furious. She
tries to hide the girl, then chases after the car that has come to take
her away. When another student, the class clown, is forced by his debt-
ridden family's poverty to seek work in the city – where instead he
ends up begging and stealing to survive – his teacher struggles to earn
enough money to pay her own expenses as she goes after him. Both
too thickheaded to grasp the inevitability of failure *and* worried more
about her bonus than her missing pupil, this adolescent must bribe
children to help her search for the delinquent boy, whom she does
succeed in finding.

Everyone in *Not One Less*, then, thinks of himself or herself first,
demanding a cash reward for any effort put forward. And, in this sense,
the film seemed to express Zhang's concern over the dehumanizing
impact of capitalist practices on Communist China, or to portray the
conflict between his country's socialist humanism and the competitive-
ness-verging-on-exploitation of the market economy it had imported.
Not by chance, *Not One Less* was reportedly the first Zhang Yimou picture to please Chinese government censors, although in the West many
derided its critique of capitalism as socialist nostalgia bordering on propaganda. *The Road Home* (with a screenplay by Bao Shi, adapted from
his novel *Remembrance*) shares concerns similar to those Zhang
expressed in *Not One Less*, though it is less strident, and more sentimental, in conveying them.

The Road Home revisits the era of the "Great Leap Forward" (beginning in 1958 and followed by the Great Proletarian Cultural Revolution in 1965, when Zhang himself was just fourteen yet had his urban

education interrupted for life, work, and "re-education" on a farm) via
a framing, and parallel, story in the present of the late 1990s. The film
begins in that present with a successful businessman in his late thirties,
named Luo Yusheng, returning by sport-utility vehicle from the city
where he lives (East Gate) to his native village of Sanhetun in northern
China. His father, Luo Changyu, has died, and Yusheng (an only child)
is going home for the funeral as well as to comfort his grief-stricken
mother, Zhao Di. She is weaving the funeral cloth to cover her husband's coffin, and she insists, as age-old custom dictates, that his coffin
be carried by hand – not transported by truck – from the hospital
where the old man died to the village where he lived. Thus will he
never forget the road home – the very same road Di had chased him
down, during their courtship, so long ago.

But such a custom will be difficult to obey, for in this instance it
requires around thirty-five men working in shifts over a two-day period
in the middle of a harsh winter. And there are not enough such men –
young ones – to be found in Sanhetun, which, with their newfound
economic freedom, they, like Yusheng, have departed to work in the
rapidly expanding urban areas of China. Contemporary China, it
seems, has no time or inclination for this funeral custom or others like
it. More importantly, Zhao Di's intransigence over the matter of her
dead husband's transport is less an instance of an ill-tempered old
woman's incessant nagging than of an elderly lady's noble reassertion
of spiritual values that have been allowed to deteriorate in the decades
between her marriage and her widowhood.

Even her son tries to convince Di that a traditional funeral procession would be impractical, if not impossible, these days. And Yusheng's
point of view is understandable given this urban professional's long
absence from his rural home together with the fact that he has been
too busy working in an office to experience romance or find a mate of
his own. While the matter of the deceased Luo Changyu's transportation is being mooted by his family and village officials, *The Road Home*
moves back in time, to 1958, to its major subject: the meeting, wooing,
and ultimate marrying of Luo Changyu and Zhao Di. This story, of
course, was originally told by Di but is remembered here by Yusheng
(whom we occasionally hear in first-person voice-over, narrating the
transitions between sequences or episodes from the past).

Reversing the Hollywood convention that looks back at the faded
past from the vivid present, *The Road Home* takes us from a dreary,
bluish gray modernity, drained of contrast and beauty and photographed mostly from static viewpoints, into a bygone era radiating with

lush, textured color and filmed with sweeping camera movements. (The cinematographer was Hou Yong.) Ironically, the present, with its desaturated photography, grief, funeral arrangements, and blizzards, is more alienating and less immediate than the past, which is suffused with the warmth of young love and marked by a cascade of lovely seasonal images from the natural world. And while the grim burial preparations are presented with bleak, documentary-like detachment, the blooming love affair between twenty-year-old Luo Changyu and eighteen-year-old Zhao Di is characterized by subjective points of view or camera placements that position the spectator as a participant in the romance.

But Zhang is not romanticizing the past merely for the sake of such romanticization: you can find that in James Cameron's 1997 movie *Titanic* (more on which later). Zhang frames *The Road Home* in such a way as to articulate his, and presumably many of his countrymen's, nostalgia for a *socialist* past characterized by rustic innocence, pastoral romance, and collective altruism – in distinct contrast with the world-weariness, isolation or atomization, and self-interest of life in the commerce-driven, job-oriented city centers of today's China. It certainly is no accident that Yusheng's father was the village *teacher*, and that the older man journeyed from the city to out-of-the-way Sanhetun to pursue his humanistic vocation. Yusheng, by contrast, although educated to be a teacher and eventually to take his father's place, left Sanhetun for the city and its promise of ample economic opportunity (even as the teenaged teacher in *Not One Less* tries to turn her position itself into an economic opportunity). The son's own "road home" leads back to a Sanhetun whose old schoolhouse is now badly in need of repair, if not complete restoration, and whose few children have no one (or no man) left to teach them.

That schoolhouse, naturally, becomes the centerpiece of Yusheng's flashback, for it is being built (in a communal effort by the men of the village) in preparation for the arrival of the new teacher, Luo Changyu, a handsome young man who immediately catches the eye of beautiful young Zhao Di. Falling absolutely in love at absolute first sight, the youthful Di pursues her man with an unbound determination equaled only by the same kind her older self exhibits, in the present, in pursuit of the customary funeral cortège for her late husband. Di's romantic persistence is noteworthy not only because of the differences in status, background, and education (she was and remains illiterate) between her and Luo Changyu. That persistence is also remarkable because she is breaking with the cultural tradition of arranged marriages and

Zhang Ziyi, as young Zhao Di, and Zheng Hao, as
young Luo Changyu, share a romantic moment in
The Road Home.

attempting – against her blind, widowed mother's better judgment – to
choose her own mate (having already rejected several "approved" marriage proposals from men she did not love). As Luo Yusheng reveals in
voice-over, "This was a first for our village: the freedom of falling in
love" – a personal freedom that links Zhao Di to an aspect of the modern of which Zhang Yimou ostensibly approves.

That Zhang knows that, in the West, the issue of arranged or forbidden marriages was treated much earlier than in China – in life if not in
art – is evidenced by something we see on the walls of the elderly Zhao
Di's home: two posters advertising the Chinese release of Cameron's
Titanic. This American movie obviously represents the kind of
overblown, omnivorous spectacle that Zhang stubbornly opposes. Yet
there is also a curious and unmistakable affinity between *The Road
Home* and *Titanic,* each of which is built around the image of an old
woman reminiscing (through the instrument of her son in the Chinese
picture) about the great, convention-defying love of her youth – a love
that future generations will contemplate with wonder and longing.
Aside from the outline of their plots, however, these two films share

another affinity: their musical soundtracks. San Bao's over-orches-trated, relentlessly schmaltzy score shamelessly imitates James Horner's quieter theme music for *Titanic* and nudges *The Road Home* toward an emotional grandiosity that its delicate carriage cannot bear. Cameron's picture was the kind of big-budget production that could use such music, but Zhang's film is smaller, in the best sense of the word, and therefore calls for a far less intrusive, sentiment-indicating score.

To wit: the road home leads to a tiny, de-populated village in a remote area of northern China, not to a titanic vessel crossing the Atlantic Ocean with a passenger list of international proportions. Yet in the story of this small Chinese village, universal themes will be recog-nized: a child's responsibility to its parents (Yusheng's coming home to bury his father and honor his mother; Zhao Di's inheriting of her mother's sense of tradition at the same time as she goes against it in arranging her own marriage), the veneration (often unaccompanied by substantial remuneration) that societies feel for education and edu-cators, and the idea of pure, perfect, and spontaneous as well as never-ending love. *Idea* it is in *The Road Home,* for the emotions felt by Di and Changyu are the kind more often dreamt about than experienced in reality. Romantic fable though it may be, this film's approach to romance is chaste, indeed: there are no embraces, nor is there any kiss-ing or touching, let alone nudity and fornication. Di and Changyu's love resides solely in their eyes, their hearts, their minds, their manner. And, of course, it rests in the actions they must take to realize that love.

Di takes the first step, undertaking to prepare a delicious dish each day for Changyu's mid-day meal as he works along with the other men of Sanhetun to complete the construction of the new schoolhouse. The trouble is, all the village girls are preparing dishes for the communal table at which the men share lunch, and it is difficult (if not impossi-ble) for Di to see who takes her offering, given that the young women must remain at a distance while the workers eat. This scene, repeated several times, is carefully composed so that, as the men approach the table, one sees only their torsos and arms, which are covered in cloth-ing whose dark colors blend together to make these workers look like a herd. Simultaneously, the sounds of the men's shuffling footsteps, mixed with the rattling of dishes, drown out any individual voices. Thus does Zhang visualize and articulate the communal or cooperative nature of this rural society – not to speak of the ethos behind Com-munism itself. At the same time, he poignantly shows one woman's strenuous effort to assert her individuality by finding, on her own, the man with whom she will spend the rest of *his* life – literally, in the sense that she outlives him, and figuratively, in the sense that, individual though she may be, life without marriage in this patriarchal society is unthinkable to an uneducated Di prepared only for work in the home.

Some of that work involves weaving at a loom, which Di also does while the villagers build the schoolhouse in which Changyu will spend his entire career as a primary-school teacher. She lovingly weaves the traditional, lucky red (as well as Communist red) banner to be wound around the building's rafters, and we know by the way Di is photographed at the loom – through the weft of the fabric she's weaving – that Zhang is suggesting a union between man and machine (epitomized by the word "handicraft") that is anything but alienating. The fact that, in the present of 1998, she weaves her husband's funeral cloth at the same loom – but only after it has undergone extensive repair or restoration – is a comment not only about enduring love, craftsmanship, and folkways but also about the *passing* of all three in a postmodern world preoccupied with the new, the fast, and the convenient.

Indeed, there's nothing new, fast, or convenient about the way in which Di and Changyu formally meet for the first time. According to the village code, this teacher must visit each home for a meal, and after a month in Sanhetun he arrives at Di's house for lunch – during which her mother does most of the talking. Before this meeting, Di had unabashedly gone out of her way to cross paths with her beau-to-be: by drawing water from the old well that overlooks the schoolhouse from atop a hill, rather than from a newer one closer to her home; by waiting along the side of the road for Changyu and his students to pass after school lets out; and even by standing outside his classroom, if not to be seen by him, then at least to hear the sound of his mellifluous voice instructing the boys of Sanhetun village. At lunch Di and Changyu barely speak to each other, but their mutual admiration-cum-affection is clear from their smiles, their demeanors, and their plan to have additional meals together.

Just as this couple's romance is beginning, however, Changyu is called back to the city because of ominous-sounding but never-specified "political trouble." All of China was in a state of political upheaval at this time – 1958 – as a result of the "Great Leap Forward," which was designed not only to revolutionize agricultural production by a mass mobilization of the countryside into "people's communes." (Ironically, given *The Road Home*'s nostalgia for what we might call familial socialism, these communes would disrupt family living and loosen traditional family ties by freeing women from household chores and child care for the supposedly more edifying labor of the fields.) The "Great Leap Forward" was also intended to expand industry by *mechanizing* agriculture, another irony given *The Road Home*'s seeming championing of bucolic primitivism.

But the "Great Leap Forward" itself is not Zhang's subject or, in any event, not a convenient one, so he reduces his film's potential political content to a background element. Changyu may be "broken" by Communist Party officials when they interrogate him in the city, but Zhang is more interested here in symbolically portraying Di's broken heart at her chosen man's sudden departure and delayed return. She races across the countryside in an effort to catch up with Changyu's horse-drawn cart, say one last goodbye, and give him the mushroom dumplings she has made especially for him. But Di stumbles along the way, losing sight of the cart as it trundles down the road, almost losing the treasured hair clip Changyu recently gave her, and inadvertently breaking the china bowl from which he had previously eaten. It is Di's mother who pays an itinerant craftsman to painstakingly put this keepsake's pieces back together with metal staples – a process we watch as Hou Yong's camera naturally remains on the workman's hands. This repair process signifies not only the gradual mending of a daughter's heart, but also one mother's *change* of heart as she now resolves to unite behind Di in her energetic quest to win Changyu's hand in marriage.

Of course we know in advance that, whatever the delays and frustrations, this matter is going to be resolved in the girl's favor. Still, for good measure, Bao Shi and Zhang throw in two "moments of final suspense," one visualized and the other narrated. Against her mother's vigorous objections, Di decides to go by foot to the city to find Changyu when he doesn't come back after a month, as planned. But the winter weather literally stops her in her tracks, and we watch it do so, as she faints along the road – and comes close to dying before the chance passing by of the village mayor. He returns Di to the care of her mother, who gets a doctor to tend to her daughter's high fever, then gets the returned Changyu to sit with his dormant sweetheart until the fever passes.

After it does, these two are reunited in a manner completely appropriate to the tenor of *The Road Home* thus far: Di races through the snow to the schoolhouse, where she can hear Changyu and his pupils reciting verses in celebration of the imminent arrival of spring. When she arrives at the school, half the village (it seems) is already there, waiting outside to greet Di and tell Changyu that she has come. But instead of seeing this couple's physical or bodily reunion, we hear their son, Yusheng, reveal in voice-over that his mother and father were kept apart for another *two years* beyond this point, because the lovesick Changyu had illegally returned to Sanhetun from the city before his interrogation was completed.

The coda of the film, back in the stark, black-and-white present, takes up the issue of Changyu's funeral again, as Yusheng submits to his mother's wish for a traditional procession. He then rounds up from surrounding villages the thirty-five or so able-bodied men needed to carry his father's coffin (many of them Changyu's former students), offering to pay them a total of 5,000 yuan (around $600) for their collective effort. But they refuse the money at the same time as they accept the work, which Zhang shows us with his gift for elision as well as simple yet precise framing. In a deeply moving sequence, Zhao Di and her son walk arm in arm in the wintry weather toward a camera that is frequently in close, as Changyu's coffin trails behind them and itself is trailed by four to five vehicles (which transport the relief-pallbearers as well as provide light by night). Along the side of the long road home traversed by this caravan, people stand here and there, shouting out to Mr Luo according to custom that he is headed in the right direction.

He is buried next to the old well that benignly looks down on his school – the same place where Di will later be buried. Ever true to her love, she remains behind in Sanhetun with him, declining to move to the city with Yusheng at his invitation (though this mother expresses concern about the fact that her son is nearly forty and still single). Equally true to Changyu's vocation, Di will weave a new red banner for his soon-to-be-renovated schoolhouse – a renovation that will be funded by a donation of no less than 5,000 yuan from Yusheng. Before he leaves his native village, this businessman even consents to teach an impromptu gathering of children for one day, in his late father's memory, in the one-room school that Yusheng himself must once have attended. The elderly Di, accompanied by a host of villagers, listens to the recitation from outside, even as she often did in the past when her husband was leading the class. With this image, one could argue, *The Road Home* should have ended. Sentiment risks emphasis, however, when Zhang cross-fades to a color reprise of the youthful, exuberant Di running across the countryside to the strains of San Bao's florid theme music, only to be frozen in her tracks by a vertically craning camera as the film comes to a close.

Zhang may have tacked on this last glimpse of a young and smiling Zhao Di because she is played by the irresistibly attractive Zhang Ziyi, in her film début. (She was subsequently cast as Jen, the young tigress, in Ang Lee's popular *Crouching Tiger, Hidden Dragon* [2000].) The camera's proximity to and interest in – nay, near mesmerization by – the presence of Ziyi are such that it is hard to ignore her likeness to Zhang's previous leading lady and lost love, the redoubtable Gong Li. Indeed, the camera lingers on Ziyi's pretty face (not to speak of her lithe body), revealing an infatuation with her that is matched only by the young Di's with Changyu, in what could be called a marriage of the male and female gazes. But Ziyi's prettiness doesn't need discovering or emphasis: it is immediately there, whereas her tenderness, pride, persistence, and heartache must arrive as the narrative progresses. They do not do so sufficiently, in part because Ziyi lacks the conviction (possessed by Gong Li) for the suffering of love, in part because the transparency or superficiality of her performance is made all the more manifest by Zhang's repeatedly bringing her face into loving close-up on the wide, CinemaScopic screen.

Unburdened by such lavish attention, Zheng Hao, as the young Luo Changyu, by contrast strikes exactly the right chords of reticence, probity, dedication, and susceptibility. It is easy to believe that the man playing his son in the present, Sun Honglei, *is* his son, because he exhibits similar qualities even if they are buried beneath the harried or preoccupied veneer of a city-dweller. It is not so easy to believe that Zhao Yuelin, as Zhao Di in the present, is the young Di-become-an-elderly-woman. This is because Yuelin's tearful yet stubborn character-ization – again, unimpeded by the embrace of close-ups – is utterly true, marked by deep imaginative conviction as well as the conviction of this actress's own age and experience. Zhao Yuelin may convince us that her love for Changyu has survived four decades, but Zhang Zhongxi, in the small role of the itinerant pottery-mender, evokes the artisanal essence of numberless centuries.

Such an essence is similarly evoked by Abbas Kiarostami in *The Wind Will Carry Us* (1999), which is set in a mountain town in Iranian Kur-distan – Siah Dareh (about 450 miles from Tehran) – that is almost entirely excluded from the benefits of modern technology. For in this Iranian film, as in *The Road Home*, a city man in his late thirties or early forties must travel to so remote a place in order to re-establish contact with the deep currents of his country's being. And, like Yusheng, Behzad Dourani (the actor's as well as the character's name, which is also the case for the other characters in this film, as Kiarostami char-acteristically tries to blur the line between documentary and fiction) is drawn to this village by a death – or an impending one.

Called "the engineer," Behzad is more like a documentary filmmaker or director, coming from Tehran by Land Rover with his two- to three-man crew (whom we never see) to film an ancient mourning ceremony. During this ceremony, women cut their faces to express sympathy for a bereaved person – that person here being the elderly son of a dying woman said to be about 100 years old, one Mrs Malek (herself never seen). But the engineer, like Yusheng, seems to have had a death in his own family as well, for he remonstrates at one point by cellular phone with his parents in Tehran about a funeral at which he should be present, yet which he will have to miss (on account of his work) except for the seventh day of mourning.

Unlike *The Road Home*, however, *The Wind Will Carry Us* concentrates more on texture, on "atmosphere" and landscape, than on drama or narrative. And in this sense it is consistent with Kiarostami's previous pictures, just as it is in its inclusion of a child. The child in *The Wind Will Carry Us*, Farzad Sohrabi, serves as the engineer's guide and contact in Siah Dareh. But this boy is not the film's focus, as children are in many Iranian movies. Behzad is at the picture's center, though Farzad is used as a kind of shadow protagonist to reveal the engineer's state of mind and emotion in this village that seems so foreign to him. And the village of Siah Dareh makes up the rest of the circle at whose midpoint Behzad stands. For place in *The Wind Will Carry Us* is connected, as in *The Road Home*, with custom or tradition, the passage of time in one place (as opposed to one's passing of time through literal movement from place to place, or figurative movement from one activity to another), and the rootedness of agrarian life in the country in contrast to the rootlessness of mechanized existence in big cities.

But place in the Iranian film takes on a role far greater than the one it enjoys in the Chinese picture, because *The Wind Will Carry Us* takes place almost entirely outdoors. Kiarostami has said that he is no longer interested in filming in interiors with artificial light – partly because of limitations on intimate subject matter in Iranian movies – and exteriors, of course, provide a natural source of light in the sun. Thus not only does Kiarostami show us emblematic natural images; for the first time in his cinema he has his characters refer to them. In the opening sequence, for example, the Land Rover is snaking through wide, rolling hills in extreme long shot, but we hear the voices of the strangers from Tehran – the engineer and his crew – as if they were up close. They are discussing the landmark that will help them to reach their destination: "a single tree" along "the winding road."

This open, umber landscape will be complemented, however, by a complex, labyrinthine village-scape. (The key visual tone of *The Wind Will Carry Us*, in Mahmoud Kalari's camera, is umber, and appropri-

The schoolboy Farzad Sohrabi in *The Wind Will Carry Us*.

ately so given that the well-known use of this yellowish-to-reddish-brown earth as a permanent pigment, either in its raw or burnt state, underlines the "permanence," longevity, even antiquity of Siah Dareh.) For Siah Dareh is constructed across the fold of two hills, or is set pueblo-style in a mountainside, so that its roofs are pathways turning into archways and are connected to the streets below by steep stairs. Painted white with flashes of color (mainly blue), the village is thus a perfectly designed set for a camera intent on remaining in the open air. There, through the use of "dead time," long takes, and even circular camera movements, that camera not only emphasizes the deliberate pace of life for these Iranian Kurds, but it also evokes the "empty" time involved in waiting for someone to die.

Indeed, at three points Kiarostami wryly nudges those who are unsympathetic to the deliberate pace his work shares with that of such filmmakers as Yasujiro Ozu, Satyajit Ray, and Michelangelo Antonioni. In the first instance, early in *The Wind Will Carry Us*, the engineer drops or discards a little apple, and, for no dramatic or narrative reason, the camera follows this apple as it rolls. In the second instance, much later in this two-hour film, the engineer comes across a large turtle in his path, and, for no particular reason – perhaps just irked by *its* pace – he kicks it on its back. He walks ahead and gets into his Land Rover, while the turtle – to which the camera cuts back – struggles to its feet, then keeps on turtling. Shortly thereafter, Behzad bemusedly observes the third of this trio of moving fruits and animals: a beetle that must summon all its strength to move a rock.

Aside from inquiring about Mrs Malek's declining health (or lack thereof), the engineer, like the turtle, does not have much to do in Siah Dareh. (His film crew, for its part, sleeps much of the time.) Willingly or unwillingly, he has to live in the unhurried way the people of the village do, and they are mostly children, the elderly, and women, since the men are almost always working in the fields. In fact, the opening line of *The Wind Will Carry Us*, as Behzad and his colleagues are driving through the countryside in search of Siah Dareh, is, "We're heading nowhere ... going nowhere." So he is, in a sense, as he spins his wheels in anticipation of Mrs Malek's death.

While Behzad is waiting, his one occupation, so to speak, is answering his cellular phone, on which he receives calls from his Tehran-based producer. Her name is Mrs Godzari, and she calls around six times during the film to get updates on Mrs Malek's condition as well as the morale of her documentary team. Each time Mrs Godzari telephones, the engineer has to dash, panting, to his vehicle and race up the hills to higher ground (where he can get adequate reception) in what becomes, literally, a running joke about many people's increasing dependence on modern, if faulty, technology. Higher ground in this case is an old graveyard, where a man called Youssef is digging a ditch for the purpose of "telecommunications." We never see him (nor do we catch a glimpse of Mrs Godzari, for that matter) – we merely hear his half of the conversation during the four or five times he and Behzad talk. Thus, although Youssef's voice and views on life offer certain clues as to his character (at one point he tellingly declares to the engineer that "a man without love cannot live"), viewers are left to speculate about his actions and appearance. That is, we are asked to fill in the off-screen space with our own imaginations.

Kiarostami remarked a few years ago that he was in favor of such a

half-created cinema, an unfinished cinema that attains completion through the creative spirit of the audience. Whenever I get the opportunity, I like to provide for film the advantage of literature. The usual way in film is to show something. But my aim is to create a cinema to see how much we can do without actually showing it.[1]

---

1 This remark comes from a speech titled "An Unfinished Cinema," which Kiarostami delivered in Paris in 1995 for the Centenary of Cinema.

The "usual way in film" is to supply pyrotechnic overload, be it of sex, violence, or velocity. Kiarostami's way is to react strongly against the contemporary cinema's giddy infatuation with showing everything, and his adverse reaction will impact the engineer's documentary objective as well. For to see is not necessarily to understand, and the demand for everything to be seen, like the ancient mourning ritual practiced by the women of Siah Dareh, may simply be the other side of censorship's coin.

Youssef the ditchdigger's own invisibility, moreover, is implicitly connected to the partial darkness that cloaks his fiancée. One day Behzad sees this girl leaving the hilltop cemetery, and she turns out, as well, to be the sixteen-year-old daughter of a woman from whom he seeks to buy fresh milk. When the engineer goes to her house, this mother directs him to a dark stable in the cellar where her cow is kept. Descending into the gloomy space, his body gradually blocks out the light, leaving the screen totally black for several seconds. When he (and we) can see again, the daughter, who declines to show her face or give her name, is preparing to milk the family cow by the dim light of a hurricane lamp. (Like her "Romeo," this Juliet also works underground in a tomb of sorts.) To pass the time while he waits, Behzad chats with the teenager, then recites the poem "The Wind Will Carry Us," by Forough Farrokhzad (1932–67). All of this – the cow-milking juxtaposed against the poetry recitation – takes place in one lengthy shot. At the end of it – after Behzad finishes reciting the poem and the girl finishes the milking – he takes his pail, pays (only to have the money returned), and leaves.

His citing of Farrokhzad, furthermore, introduces yet another powerful off-screen presence into the picture. Not only is she one of Iran's leading modern poets, but she was also one of the first to deal explicitly with sex, as well as with women's problems, in so repressive and patriarchal a society. Born into a middle-class Tehran family, coming of age in the wake of the CIA-organized coup in 1953 that brought down the regime of nationalist Mohammad Mossadeq, and dying in an automobile accident at the age of only thirty-three, Farrokhzad led her life and created her poetry in the face of a great deal of official disapproval, even covert hostility. (That life included a divorce that caused her to lose custody of her only child according to Iranian law, and her work consisted of at least one documentary film, titled *The House Is Black* [1962], about a Tabriz leper colony.) She held, according to one biographer, a "popular, secular intellectual's view" of Iranian society, and Kiarostami himself has said that "her generous, sensual philosophy had always seemed close to that of [the celebrated twelfth-century Persian poet and mathematician,] Omar Khayyám." (His *Rubáiyát*, written in praise of the pleasures of earthly life, is quoted by a doctor later in the film.)

In her poem "The Wind Will Carry Us" (as translated by David Martin), Farrokhzad writes of the "terror of desolation" she feels in the night. The wind, gathering in the darkness, suggests to her an "alien happiness / I am addicted to my own hopelessness." The wind is growing, "the moon is red restless and uneasy," the clouds "like crowds of mourners / await to break in rain." Outside the window, "an unknown / something fears for me and you." She begs her lover to entrust his hands to her hands, his lips "to the caresses of my loving lips ... / the wind will carry us with it / the wind will carry us ..." And, indeed, people who are sweltering in the heat (like Iranian women in their black *chadors*), people who have been driven underground – along with love, beauty, and poetry – into the darkness and dust, in a society dominated by censorship, need the wind with its fresh, cooling air.

At the same time, the wind sweeps away what's dead or desiccated, as in "Ode to the West Wind." Here Shelley writes that its current will "Drive my dead thoughts over the universe, / Like withered leaves, to quicken a new birth." That birth may be connected with the seasonal force of renewal in nature, the "unextinguished" political hope that burns continually over the "unawakened Earth," or the very passion of artistic creativity itself. And those "dead thoughts" may be related to the power that produces self-sacrifice, even self-destruction, in individual lives. Where the engineer is concerned, "dead thoughts" is the operative phrase, for he comes to Siah Dareh looking for death (Mrs Malek's). There is in fact something insensitive, distasteful, and downright opportunistic about the nature of his business in the village, for, self-interestedly, Behzad awaits a death so that he can go to work. In other words, he is taking advantage of or exploiting the local people and their customs in the furtherance of his own career.

Moreover, the engineer goes about his work in a devious manner, lying to the villagers about his reason for being in Siah Dareh. His relations with Farzad come to an end after he angrily scolds this schoolboy for replying *honestly* to some questions about Mrs Malek's health asked by Behzad's colleagues. "I can't lie," Farzad tells Behzad. So, although this self-absorbed, romantically unattached member of the Iranian intelligentsia slowly discovers, and is even swallowed up by, the life of the village, he appears fundamentally dead inside and seems never to let the vitality of Siah Dareh "contaminate" him. It surely is no accident

that, instead of rushing to save the ditchdigger after the deep hole he
is digging caves in and nearly buries him alive, Behzad goes off to
gather other people in the village to do the rescuing in his place. Nor
is it by chance that, subsequent to Mrs Malek's death at dawn one day
(at the end of a two-week wait), the engineer cannot resist the temptation to take a few still-life photos of women as they begin to keen. For
he has given up his project of actually filming the elderly woman's
mourning ritual in part because his film crew has abandoned him.
(Similarly, Kiarostami himself was abandoned by all of his crew in the
making of *The Wind Will Carry Us*, save for a sound person and an assistant cameraman.)

The last thing the engineer does continues a pattern of behavior
underlined by his photographing of the keening women. He takes an
ancient human bone unearthed by the ditchdigger early in the picture,
given to Behzad, and prominently placed by him atop the dashboard
of his Land Rover, and tosses it into a stream. The camera remains on
the bone as it is carried along (to the accompaniment of brooding or
pensive music on the soundtrack, the first and last in the film), until it
finally passes out of the frame. Then there is an abrupt cut to black and
The Wind Will Carry Us ends. The implication is not only the obvious
one, that life goes on or is materially renewed, but also that the spiritual deadness in the solitary engineer, as symbolized by the ancient
bone, has left untouched or untarnished the vibrant currents of Siah
Dareh's communal (if theocratically constricted) existence. Or, conversely, that this human bone, this piece of lifeless death, has acquired
from the stream a new ability to move and participate in the flow of life,
even as Behzad may have acquired the same ability from his contact
with this rural village.

Certainly such an acquisition is suggested by Behzad's reciting of the
poem "The Wind Will Carry Us" to the teenaged milkmaid, as it is by his
final abandoning of the project to film Mrs Malek's mourning ceremony. That acquisition is also suggested by the engineer's encounter
with the ancient woman's (as well as the ditchdigger's) doctor, whose
"specialty" is "the whole body" and who takes Behzad on a nature-wor-
shipping motorcycle ride through the countryside. Along the way, the
doctor quotes the following lines from Khayyám's *Rubáiyát* (a work
banned in Iran as heretical and the citing of which has caused problems
for *The Wind Will Carry Us* with religious censors in its country of origin):

Some for Glories of This World; and some
Sigh for the Prophet's paradise to come;

Ah, take the Cash, and let the Credit go,
Nor heed the rumble of a distant Drum!

Comparable to the taxidermist in Kiarostami's *Taste of Cherry* (1997), who tries to talk that picture's protagonist out of suicide by talking up the joys of life and nature, the doctor calls on the engineer, through Khayyám's poetry, to live for today and to savor natural beauty. This is sound advice for a character that is impatient with a woman who takes "too long" to die, and it is advice he indirectly receives from two other characters. One is Farzad's teacher, a crippled man on crutches who is the only person to discuss the mourning ritual with Behzad, yet who ultimately comes down on the side of the living by declaring, "You may be interested in it [the ritual]. I'm not interested." (Another reason the teacher may not be interested is that, out of economic necessity, his mother once went so far as to cut and scar her face not only when her husband's boss had a bereavement but also when the boss's *cousin* subsequently lost a loved one.) The second character is the placid hostess of the little inn where the engineer and his crew are staying; she is pregnant with her tenth child, which she delivers (off-screen) during *The Wind Will Carry Us*. Startled at the size of this woman's family, Behzad can only respond by saying, "May God preserve you." But, of course, it's Behzad himself who needs preserving, deliverance, or saving.

Through him, Kiarostami has shifted the emphasis of *A Taste of Cherry* away from an enigmatic protagonist's personal dilemma to wider issues of life and death, of how to live and what to do (long) before one dies – issues present in two of Kiarostami's films made in the wake of the 1990 earthquake, *And Life Goes On ...* (1992) and *Through the Olive Trees* (1994). Also present in *The Wind Will Carry Us* is a concern with women's issues not familiar to me from this director's previous work. Indeed, apart from the invocation of the proto-feminist Forough Farrokhzad, there is a lively debate at one point in the film about women's roles versus men's in Iranian society. The first part of this debate occurs between the engineer and a feisty middle-aged woman who runs the local café (and who refuses to let Behzad photograph her), the second between this hardworking woman and her shiftless husband. All by herself, she nearly offsets the females in this film whose literal invisibility calls upon us to imagine them, as well as to contemplate their figurative invisibility in Iranian culture generally. (One of this picture's serio-comic leitmotifs, if you will, is the recurring image of an anonymous woman walking past the engineer, carrying an immense load of hay or firewood that almost totally obscures her person.)

All of these women, all of these people (save for the engineer and the voice of the off-screen ditchdigger, which belongs to assistant director Bahman Ghobadi), are played by non-professionals, actual residents of Siah Dareh. The obvious advantage of Kiarostami's using local people is that they don't have to learn how to be at home in a new environment: this *is* their home, and they are therefore completely at home in it. Another, not so obvious advantage is that, in a film that is less wrenching drama than (at least for the villagers) daily ritual, the performers must give themselves over to the ritual of dailiness more than they must dominate it, must act naturally more than they must supernaturally act. And this the untrained inhabitants of Siah Dareh are supremely qualified to do. They are aided in their work, of course, by the movie camera, whose framing mechanism and quiet movement have a way of conferring grandeur on the simplest, most unassuming of human lives.

Obviously, these villagers were also aided by Abbas Kiarostami, who has worked with non-professionals in the past and has developed his skills with them to the point where he can lead them, without artifice, to put themselves on film. One way in which he does this is by not having these actors memorize their lines, as he himself has pointed out:

On-the-spot creation of dialogue has been necessary because it's the only way I could work with people who are not professional actors, and some of the moments you see in my movies have surprised me. ... I don't give dialogue to the actors, but once you explain the scene to them, they just start talking, beyond what I would have imagined.[2]

As for the one professional in the cast, Behzad Dourani, he gently, almost casually embodies the series of ambiguities and even contradictions in the character of the engineer – or is it the filmmaker? For the citified Kiarostami, to a greater extent than his counterpart Zhang in China, clearly has mixed feelings about his own role as a preoccupied, if not self-absorbed, male artist-intellectual in so culturally, economically, and feministically underdeveloped a nation as Iran. What neither director has mixed feelings about is his country or, better, his country's people. Fundamental to both is a love for the customs, relationships, formalities, patterns, and reserves of his fellow citizens – a love for being Iranian, or for being Chinese. As I write these words, I think of a film by the Hungarian director Karoly Makk, itself called *Love* (1971).

2 Interview, *Film Comment* 36, no. 4 (July–August 2000).

Basically a political picture about the stubbornness of individual feeling, more than individual thought, in a society (like Iran's and China's
today) not designed to accommodate either, its seemingly mawkish
title – as well as its general subject matter – captures the essence of both
The Road Home and *The Wind Will Carry Us*. I'd love to see all three of
them again.

I did get the chance to see Roberto Rossellini's *Europe '51* (1952)
again recently, now that it has finally been released on videocassette.
And I think it would be appropriate briefly to discuss this underrated
film in conjunction with *The Wind Will Carry Us* in particular, since they
have several points of intersection. The first is the crossroads known as
death: a man waits for one in Kiarostami's picture, only to get side-
tracked, as it were, whereas a woman is taken unawares by death in
Europe '51, only to find her spiritual center as a result. The second
point of intersection is children, for a lively child is the engineer's
usher into the timeless or unchanging world of Siah Dareh, while the
death of a child incites the psychological transformation along with the
moral quest of the heroine in Rossellini's film.

The final point of intersection for these two films more or less sub-
sumes the second one: the cinematic style known as neorealism. But,
unlike some of the best neorealist films from Italy and Iran, neither *The
Wind Will Carry Us* nor *Europe '51* has a child as its main character or
the lot of children as its chief subject. Nor, unlike the Italian Vittorio
De Sica's *Shoeshine* (1946) or the Iranian Samira Makhmalbaf's *The
Apple* (1998), is either of these pictures neorealistic in content. For in
them Kiarostami and Rossellini do not treat, except tangentially, social,
political, and economic problems – like long-term unemployment,
grinding poverty, and gender discrimination – as they affect common
people in the wake of devastating worldwide war or tumultuous religious revolution.

What *The Wind Will Carry Us* and *Europe '51* both adopt, however, is
a neorealistic *style*. Essentially, this means that their cinematography
does not exhibit striking angles, exhilarating movement, or clever cutting. The composition of shots does not startle us through its ingenuity; instead, the *mise en scène* in each case is clear-eyed rather than ingenious, detached or reserved rather than flashy. *What* Kiarostami and
Rossellini focus on at any given point is more significant than the way
in which each director focuses his (and our) attention. Yet, to speak
now only of *Europe '51*, reviewers at the time of its release (to be succeeded by like-minded critics today) passed judgment on the film's subject without taking into consideration the ("styleless") style that gives it

its meaning and aesthetic value. Even as they wrongly accused De Sica in the same year – 1952 – of making a social melodrama with *Umberto D.*, they charged Rossellini with indulging in a confused, indeed reactionary, political ideology – moreover, of doing so in an "obvious, slow-moving story."

In *Europe '51*, a young, rich, and frivolous American lady living in Rome loses her only son, who commits suicide one evening when his mother is so preoccupied with her social life that she sends the boy to bed rather than be forced to pay attention to him. The poor woman's moral shock is so violent that it plunges her into a crisis of conscience that, on the advice of a cousin of hers who is a Communist intellectual, she initially tries to resolve by dedicating herself to humanitarian causes. But, little by little, she gets the feeling that this is only an immediate or preliminary stage beyond which she must pass if she is to achieve a mystical magnanimity all her own, one that transcends the boundaries of politics and even of social or religious morality. Accordingly, she looks after a sick prostitute until the latter dies, then aids in the escape of a young criminal from the police. This last initiative causes a small scandal and, with the complicity of an entire family alarmed by her behavior, the woman's husband, who understands her less and less, decides to have her committed to a sanitarium.

From the perspective of its action, Rossellini's script, in truth, is not devoid of naïveté and even of incoherence – or at any rate pretentiousness. We can see the particulars that the writer-director has borrowed from Simone Weil's life, without in fact being able to recapture the strength of her thinking. But such reservations don't hold up before the whole of a film that one must understand and judge on the basis of its *mise en scène*. What, for a salient instance, would Dostoyevsky's *The Idiot* be worth if it were to be reduced to a summary of its action? Because, like Kiarostami, Rossellini is a genuine director, the essence of his film does not consist in the elaboration of its plot: that essence is supplied by the very transparency of its style.

The *auteur* of *Germany, Year Zero* (in which a boy also kills himself) seems profoundly haunted in a personal way by the death of children, even more by the horror of their suicide. And it is around his heroine's authentic spiritual experience of such a suicide that *Europe '51* is organized. The eminently modern theme of lay sainthood then naturally emerged, but its more or less skillful development in the script matters very little. What counts is that each sequence is a kind of meditation or filmic song on this fundamental theme as revealed by the *mise en scène*, whose aim is not to demonstrate but to show or to reveal. Moreover, how could anyone resist the moving spiritual presence of Ingrid Bergman? Beyond this actress, how could the viewer remain insensitive to the intensity of a *mise en scène* in which the universe seems to be organized along spiritual lines of force, to the point that it sets them off as manifestly as the iron filings in a magnetic field? Seldom has the presence of the spiritual in human beings and in the world been expressed with such dazzling clarity.

Granted, Rossellini's neorealism here seems very different from, even contradictory to, De Sica's. Indeed, it seems more like the "transcendental style" of Robert Bresson in such a picture as *Diary of a Country Priest*, itself made in 1951. I think it wise, however, to reconcile Rossellini's and De Sica's neorealism as two poles of the same aesthetic school. Whereas De Sica investigates reality with ever more expansive curiosity in his neorealist films, Rossellini by contrast seems to strip it down further each time, to stylize that reality with a painful but nonetheless unrelenting rigor. In short, he appears to return to a neoclassicism of dramatic expression in *mise en scène* as well as in acting.

But, on closer examination, one discovers that this neoclassicism stems from a common neorealistic revolution. For Rossellini, as for De Sica (and later for Kiarostami), the aim is to reject the categories of acting and dramatic expression in order to force reality to reveal its significance solely through appearances. Rossellini does not make his actors *act* – be they professionals or non-professionals – he doesn't make them express this or that feeling; he compels them only to *be* a certain way before the camera. In such a *mise en scène*, the respective places of the characters, their movements on the set, their *ways* of moving, and their gestures have much more importance than the feelings they show on their faces, or even the words they say. Besides, what "feelings" could Ingrid Bergman "express"? Her drama lies far beyond any psychological nomenclature, and her face outlines only a certain property of suffering, as it did in Rossellini's earlier *Stromboli* (1949) and his subsequent *Voyage to Italy* (1953).

Europe '51 gives ample indication that such a human presence as Bergman's, in such a cinematographic *mise en scène*, calls for the most sophisticated stylization possible. A film like this is the opposite of a realistic one "drawn from life": it is the equivalent of austere and terse writing, which is so stripped of ornament that it sometimes verges on the ascetic. At this point, neorealism returns full circle to neoclassical abstraction and its generalizing quality. Hence this apparent paradox: the best version of *Europe '51* is not the dubbed Italian version, but the English one, which employs the greatest possible number of original voices among the major characters. At the far reaches of this realism, the accuracy of exterior social reality becomes unimportant. The children in the streets of Rossellini's Rome can therefore speak English without our even realizing the implausibility of such an occurrence. This is reality through style, or transcendence through secularity, and thus – like Kiarostami's combining of a daring artistic vision with a reverential view of dailiness – it is a reworking of the conventions of art.

PART TWO

Europe, the Americas, and Beyond

9

The Happiness of
Your Friends and Neighbors

On LaBute's *Your Friends and Neighbors* (1998, USA) and Solondz's *Happiness* (1998, USA)

Christopher Lasch once called our era the age of narcissism, but several recent films seem to be proposing that it is really the age of hedonism: of ego gratification as well as egoism. And that ego gratification comes primarily in the form of sex: the getting of it, the mastering of it, the getting rid of it or him or her. American movies about American morals have been plentiful from the beginning, but American movies about American moral shallowness or sensual debasement are endemic to – in any case, are proliferating at – the close of this, the American century. In recent months we've had *Bad Manners* (1997), *Very Bad Things* (1998), *Happiness* (1998), and *Your Friends and Neighbors* (1998), not to speak of the documentary *Unmade Beds* (1998) and the film adaptation of David Rabe's 1995 play, *Hurlyburly* (1999). (Rabe's work is recapitulated as well by the 1999 plays *This is Our Youth* and *Closer*, by the American Kenneth Lonergan and the Englishman Patrick Marber respectively, in what appears to be a late bid by the stage to match the sexual explicitness that mainstream cinema has enjoyed since Bertolucci's *Last Tango in Paris* [1972].)

"It's always about fucking," a character from Neil LaBute's *Your Friends and Neighbors* pithily explains, and all of the above works, to a greater or lesser degree, from a blackly comic angle to an icily clinical one, are critiques of the sheer value we place on sexual intercourse. The utopian rhetoric of the sexual revolution (a revolution for women more than for men, it must be recalled), combined with the commodification of sex to sell everything under the sun, has guaranteed, these motion pictures wittingly reveal, that millions of American are conditioned to expect erotic salvation on demand and become bitterly disappointed when their lust is not satisfied. Like an infant bawling for his toy, with pleasure as his sole standard, his instinctive need, these adults are crying for sex, with pleasure as their prime standard, their revolutionary right.

A different kind of sexual revolution occurred in England in the latter half of the seventeenth century, during the Restoration, when the upper class rejected the strict Puritanism of Cromwell's Commonwealth (where incest and adultery were capital crimes, as was fornication on the second offense) in favor of a carnal permissiveness that bordered on libertinism. In interviews, Neil LaBute has professed his admiration for the brittle, satirical style of Restoration comedy, although there is still some dispute over just what is being satirized: the Machiavellian licentiousness of aristocratic rakes or the increasingly philistine hypocrisy of the repressive society against which they were reacting. The same dispute cannot be said to exist about LaBute's first attempt at creating a contemporary American version of the constricted world of Restoration comedy, *In the Company of Men* (1997), which concerned the figurative revenge that two young men wreak on women in general by wooing a young woman individually and abandoning her together. Their vindictive prank is spoiled, however, by the inception of deep feeling in the woman, feeling that ensures our sympathy for her and that marks the two men off as objects of ridicule.

No feeling except sexual desire erupts in LaBute's second feature, *Your Friends and Neighbors,* but that desire occurs in a yuppie vacuum as opposed to a hippie rebellion, and therefore is doubtless the target of this screenwriter-director's satire. In addition to the same symmetrical plotting and the same air of sexual ruthlessness as the British comedy of manners, *Your Friends and Neighbors* even contains a scene in which Jerry, a theatre professor, lectures to a class on the subject of Restoration actresses and prostitution; moreover, there are two other scenes in which the same Jerry and one of his female students rehearse extracts from a well-known Restoration comedy, William Wycherley's *The Country Wife* (1675). It is in the first of these rehearsal scenes that Jerry utters what can be considered this picture's signature lines, "These characters want to fuck. It's always about fucking," even as Chad regularly intoned the mantra "Let's hurt somebody" in *In the Company of Men.*

The highly structured narrative of *Your Friends and Neighbors* unfolds with the neatness of a blueprint or a mathematical equation, which is one of the ways in which LaBute objectifies or dehumanizes his oversexed characters. Another way in which he does so is by *never* having these characters refer to each other by name, even though their first names (to which I refer for the sake of convenience) are listed in the credits. Then, as if to add insult to injury, LaBute has one of his male characters ask an acquaintance (by telephone) the following unanswered question about a female: "These pair of tits have a name, don't they?" Not only do we not know their names, we don't even know where our "friends and neighbors" live; the movie occurs in the bedrooms, bars, restaurants, art galleries, supermarkets, bookstores, and gyms of some unspecified American city, from which LaBute provides not a single exterior shot to help us get our bearings or gain some perspective. These people live in their own world, the filmmaker thereby implies, one that is just as constrained as the aristocratic circle of Caroline England from 1649 to 1685. In that world six people (two couples and two singles) advance through various combinations or permutations, as well as through the same circumscribed set of places, until they arrive pretty much back where they started: in a state of emotional frigidity or aridness that is only accentuated by the musical accompaniment of Apocalyptica as it performs the songs of Metallica.

Let's begin with Terri and Jerry, who are falling out as a couple (unmarried) on account of his inability to perform in the bedroom: she complains that he talks too much during intercourse, even during the rear entry kind (preferred by her), which only interferes with the unadulterated act of fucking. As Terri, an advertising copywriter for tampons, flatly puts it, "Fucking is fucking. It's not a time for sharing." Barry has similar problems with his wife, Mary, who also prefers not to face her partner during sex: "spooning" is her style, but leads to premature ejaculation for him. Barry's dysfunction may be related more to his penchant for masturbation, however, than to his mate's preference for "side saddle" intercourse. "Nobody gives me more pleasure than I give myself," he confesses to an acquaintance at work. "I'm my best lay." So his friend Jerry secretly tries to lay Mary but can't perform with her, either. Terri, for her part, abandons the quartet of Jerry-Terri-Barry-Mary – a quartet underscored on the soundtrack by two musical quartets from Dvořák and Schubert, and prefigured on screen by that early cinematic product of the American sexual revolution, *Bob and Carol and Ted and Alice* (1969) – to begin a lesbian affair with Cheri, whom she meets at an art gallery where the latter works as a curatorial assistant. "Love's a disease," these two women later both declare "but it's curable," adds Cheri as she begins to touch and kiss her new sexual partner.

Cheri meets every member of the "quartet" individually, in addition to the other single, Cary, when each visits the art gallery, and each meeting is shown in the same continuous medium to full shot, with the same framing, with similar conversation, and with the same artwork of hard-angled human bodies, or body parts, in the background. This, of course, reduces all six characters to the same common visual denominator, just as their two-syllable names ending in the same vowel sound reduce them almost to a single verbal designation. But these repetitious, even ritualistic, scenes in the art gallery do something more, for they suggest, contrary to what many of us would like to believe about the therapeutic powers of aesthetic experience, that art – particularly the fragmented, decontextualized kind found in this gallery (and in this movie?) – has done nothing to alleviate or ameliorate these characters' spiritual anomie, and especially not that of Cary. A medical doctor, he brings a detached, clinical approach to his work that matches the laboratory-controlled coolness he brings to the bedroom.

A sneeringly arrogant, vengefully misogynistic, repellently exploitative, brutally manipulative stud, Cary not only propositions Cheri (in the art gallery) and Terri (in a bookstore), however unsuccessfully in both cases, he also impregnates Mary. He ends *Your Friends and Neighbors* naked in bed with Barry's wife, dispassionately caressing her breast and asking, "How does that feel?" Appropriately, this unreconstructed, unrequited sexual predator opens the film as well, gymnastically practicing the moves of intercourse (not masturbating) at the same time as a tape recorder plays pillow talk "moves" that he has previously recorded. We hear the real Cary talking after sex, however, when he viciously berates one of his dates for staining his expensive linen sheets with her menstrual blood, then nonchalantly insults another partner by telling her to use, not *his* towels when she goes to the bathroom, but instead the ones specially designated for her – which she is instructed to throw onto the floor when done. Upon being asked by Jerry and Barry in a steam room to describe the best sex he has ever had, this malevolent monster proves his dedication above all to sexual gratification on his own terms, with anyone of his choosing, when he recounts with genuine delectation the revenge gang rape of a male high school classmate who had reported him and his friends for cheating.

Although Cary is certainly the worst, or most misanthropic, of this picture's characters, he has the competitive company of the other two men and the three women, who give as good as they get. This is particularly true of Terri, whom we see in her last scene in bed, her eyes masked as she tries to sleep, while Cheri uncharacteristically begs in vain for some kind of response from her "lover" (with whom she now lives) other than a sexually carnivorous one. Here Terri ignores not only Cheri but also Jerry, whose desperate telephone call after another episode of impotency, in this instance with one of his undergraduate students, goes unanswered. As for Barry, the final time we encounter him he is alone in bed, trying to have phone sex, but discovering to his dismay that he is now impotent even with himself. He obviously does not know about Jerry's own impotency, for Barry finally left Mary, or she finally left him, after Jerry lied that his best sexual experience ever was with her. Even the canny Terri believes this of Jerry, and left *him* to become a sexual opportunist of the lesbian kind.

Barry is photographed in his last scene (the film's penultimate one) from the overhead position, and LaBute's cinematographer, Nancy Schreiber, places her camera at just such a high, humanly diminishing angle for all the scenes of (aborted) sex. The quality of Schreiber's color imagery is such that, looking back, you remember it as color, unlike Tony Hettinger's stark, almost sterile cinematography for *In the Company of Men*, which in retrospect seemed to have been black and white. But still, this is color less by DeLuxe than by DeDuct, a flat type of color that gives the eye neither rest nor relief anywhere – that is, except in a few of the bedroom scenes, which are ironically lit in warm ochre-and-red tones to suggest loving intimacy where there is only lustful indulgence.

The editing of *Your Friends and Neighbors* also differs from that of *In the Company of Men*, yet the same man, Joel Plotch, cut both pictures. In fact there was little editing in LaBute's first film: scene after scene was placed before us, usually as a carefully apportioned full shot of two people, and got played in one extended take. The idea was that we as spectators were voyeuristically intruding – as opposed to having the director "intrude" for us through intercutting – on the lives of two male characters who themselves were intruding on the life of a third, female figure. In *Your Friends and Neighbors*, LaBute uses more intercutting from person to person within a scene and less crystallizing of a scene in one uninterrupted shot. And this intercutting is apposite not only because its visual isolation underlines each character's emotional disconnection or spiritual alienation, but also because such editing emphasizes the idea that LaBute is treating each of these people (or each is treating him- or herself) like a separate, interchangeable integer in his set of grand cinematic calculations, to be added now here and now there, if never to seek the incalculable solace of tender, yet permanent, equation.

Not only is there more editing in *Your Friends and Neighbors* than could be found in *In the Company of Men*, there is more camera movement – though, again, there was virtually none in LaBute's first movie. Here the camera will once in a while begin with a tight close-up and then pull back to a cooler distance; or, conversely, the camera will track slowly in on a character, getting as close as it can, say, to Cary as he recollects with relish his anal rape of the high school boy effetely named Timothy. Naturally, one is made very aware of such movement because it occurs so rarely. And such "moving" moments, or "momentous" movements, make us aware as well of LaBute's authorial presence behind the camera, a presence that is simultaneously fascinated and repelled by the characters it has created and that shows it.

The actors make no such narrative, or metacinematic, comment on their characters in this film, despite their irredeemable depravity, self-styled misery, or callous remoteness. Aaron Eckhart, who was the nastier of the two males in *In the Company of Men*, is softer and sadder here as Barry, proving that his success in the earlier picture was the success of a skilled performer, not of a man merely playing himself. The nastier role, of Cary, this time goes to Jason Patric (who co-produced *Your Friends and Neighbors*), and he makes almost too much of it, as in the hospital scene where LaBute has him dropkick a plastic, anatomically correct fetus during his coffee break, then abruptly devour what's left of his donut. Ben Stiller is his usual aggressively urban self as Jerry, a self that, in its paradoxical impotence or inefficacy, he has also displayed in such recent, subversively bawdy comedies as *Flirting with Disaster* (1996) and *There's Something about Mary* (1998).

Mary in *Your Friends and Neighbors* is played by Amy Brenneman, who bravely makes the least interesting of the film's three women just that – uninteresting – where many an actress would wrongly try to make this weepy character more, or more engaging, than she is. The two "interesting" women's roles are filled by Nastassja Kinski, as Cheri, and Catherine Keener, as Terri. Kinski makes a comeback of sorts here as a lipstick lesbian, and she is refreshing: supple, suggestive, and natural rather than brittle, obvious, and repressed, as we might have expected. Keener, for her part, is uniformly excellent in the pivotal female role – *thematically* pivotal because, like Cary's, Terri's sexual voraciousness knows no bounds, or at least does not observe the bounds of gender. This young woman was last seen by me in *Walking and Talking* (1996) and *Living in Oblivion* (1995), where she showed a quality that serves her well in *Your Friends and Neighbors*: the ability to treat candid subject matter with almost surgical precision, so coolly, in fact, that this material becomes fundamentally if idiosyncratically comic.

"Idiosyncratically comic" is the tamest description one could apply to Todd Solondz's taboo-smashing *Happiness*. Ironically titled like *Your Friends and Neighbors*, *Happiness* has been referred to as Solondz's second feature after *Welcome to the Dollhouse* (1995), although it is actually his third. (Solondz's first film was the little-distributed *Fear, Anxiety, and Depression* [1989], which brought misleading comparisons with the work of Woody Allen.) And, if Neil LaBute could be called the poet cinematic of Indiana (where much of *In the Company of Men* took place, and in the biggest city close to which, Chicago, *Your Friends and Neighbors* is rumored to have been shot), then Todd Solondz must be called the poet cinematic of his native New Jersey. Indeed, LaBute's smiling response to the question, "Where does all your negativity come from?" could just as well have come, with a change of state, from the writer-director Solondz: "I live in Indiana. We're brutally honest here. We realize we're in the middle of nowhere, and we're very sore about it."

In the comedy of desperation *Welcome to the Dollhouse*, Solondz was sore not only about the "excruciating torment," the cruel humiliations, of his seventh-grade experience at the hands of various bullies (including his parents, teachers, and siblings), but also about the general experience of growing up in the kitschy suburbia of the Garden State. His self-confessed alter ego in *Welcome to the Dollhouse* was eleven-year-old Dawn Wiener, an ugly duckling with stern, oversized glasses (like Solondz's own), an unrelenting array of unbecoming floral dresses, a gangly strut, a chirpy voice, and the sadly defeated frown of a middle-aged woman. God only knows, and only the Moral Majority cares, which character is this *auteur*'s alter ego in his latest picture.

What Solondz is sore about in *Happiness*, however, is clearer: the sexually-cum-romantically dysfunctional American landscape, a suburban world that is at once blandly familiar and almost surreal; a moral darkness or hellfire on the edge of town where, in the words of Wallace Stevens, "the pure products of America go crazy." (And of Europe, too, as Alain Berliner's *Ma vie en rose* [*My Life in Pink*, 1997] and Mike Leigh's *Life Is Sweet* [1991] have shown us.) The edge of town in this alternately dark comedy and pathetic tragedy of desire and despair is located, of course, in New Jersey, where the three thirtysomething Jordan sisters, Joy, Helen, and Trish, live. Not yet unhappy, perky Trish is a housewife with a husband, Bill, who's a psychiatrist, and three children, notably eleven-year-old Billy. Glamorous Helen, unmarried, is a melancholy, self-dramatizing writer who invents pornographic traumas in her past to feed her poetry, and who complains from her New Jersey apartment, "I hate Saturday nights. Everybody wants me. You have no idea." Also unmarried, but looking for life in all the wrong places, is more or less careerless (telemarketer, TOEFL teacher, singer-songwriter, etc.) Joy, the family dartboard, who resides in her parents Mona and Lenny's home while they spend retirement winters down in Florida where, at Lenny's instigation, he and his wife are in the process of separating.

Two of the three sisters, Helen and Joy, are integral to *Happiness*'s manifold narrative, whereas Trish fades into the background as husband Bill moves to the center of her story strand. The two opening scenes set the grimly amusing tone for, as well as introduce the most prominent players in, the rest of the film's action. The first of these begins with an immense close-up of the tremulous Joy in a tacky restaurant, where she is trying to break up with her overweight, nerdy boyfriend Andy. The meal is finished and, to top it off, he has even brought an expensive gift to give to Joy; instead he gets dumped in as kindly a manner imaginable. Then *Happiness* veers from sentimental romance to mordant satire when the tearful Andy plaintively asks, "Is it someone else?" and Joy matter-of-factly answers, "No, it's just you." Later, when this lonely, frustrated young woman attempts by telephone to get her celebrity sister to empathize with her in her plight – and, significantly, right *before* Joy learns of Andy's suicide – we get the following exchange as further evidence of Solondz's ability to cut to the quick of cliché-ridden, angst-obsessed, middle-class speech:

HELEN: Don't worry, I'm not laughing at you, I'm laughing *with* you.
JOY: But I'm not laughing.

The second scene occurs in the office of Trish's husband, psychiatrist Bill Maplewood, where Allen, a plump and miserable mouth-breather with ugly glasses as well as flat, greasy hair, describes in the terms of porno magazine fantasy his unrequited lust for a neighbor in his apartment building. That neighbor turns out to be Helen Jordan, whom he titillates (not plagues) with obscene phone calls by night as he boozes and masturbates. The joke here seems obvious because, just as Allen says he must be boring Dr Maplewood with his story, the bored doctor goes over in his mind, in voice-over, the laundry list of things he has to do after work. The real joke, however, is retrospective, for we learn that Bill Maplewood would have been very interested in Allen's story, indeed, had it been homosexually pedophilic in nature.

This is a man, you see, who masturbates to preteen boys' magazines in the backseat of his car, outside a convenience store; who asks his son

Billy, himself becoming sexually itchy, whether he knows how to masturbate and offers to instruct him (which the boy politely declines);
and who drugs his whole family and Billy's sleepover friend, the effem-
inate Johnny Grasso, so that he can sodomize the visiting youngster,
even as he will later sodomize another neighborhood boy left home
alone for the evening by his parents. So drugged was Bill's wife, Trish,
that the next morning, in yet another sick joke, she thinks (and he con-
firms) that she and her husband had sex the night before for the first
time in several years. When Dr Maplewood sees his own psychothera-
pist about his and Trish's "sexual incompatibility," as well as about the
homicidal fantasies he has been having, the scene is shot by the cinematographer Maryse Alberti (who shot Todd Haynes's differently per-
verse *Velvet Goldmine* [1998] in similarly fitting, lackluster color) with
an imaginative crane maneuver that pulls away from Bill's prosaic exterior until the camera reaches parts unknown, a visual metaphor for the
exact way in which this domestically satirical yet eerily frightening film
works. Tellingly, Bill doesn't discuss his pedophilic compulsions with
his psychiatrist, and by the end of *Happiness* his sodomy is discovered
by Johnny Grasso's physician, the police come calling, and the otherwise unrepentant father, in response to Billy's question "Would you
ever fuck me?" pensively tells his son, "No, I'd masturbate instead."

Allen may continue to masturbate as well, for his one meeting with
the sexually adventurous Helen, at her request and to the comic
accompaniment of *Così fan tutte* on the soundtrack, ended in his almost
instantaneous rejection. And Kristina, a homely, oversized woman
across the hall who is even more desperate than Allen and with whom
he had begun a tentative if felicitous affair, may continue her mastur-
batory ways in prison, as she has been arrested for murdering the widowed doorman who raped her, then cutting his body into pieces for
storage in her freezer. There might be Joy for Allen, however: after the
disaster with Andy and a one-night stand with a thieving Russian taxi
driver whose live-in Russian girlfriend assaults her, Joy agrees to be set
up by Helen with "some guy" in her building.

Their father, Lenny, is still with Mona at the movie's conclusion,
though this self-described "feelingless" sixty-five-year-old has already
had one dalliance with a sex-starved, middle-aged divorcée and
remains on the prowl. In *Happiness*'s concluding scene, Lenny sits at
the (Thanksgiving?) dinner table down in Florida with his wife and
daughters, including Trish, who has understandably left the soon-to-be-
jailed Bill and taken their three children with her. The oldest one, Billy,
standing on the balcony of his grandparents' condominium, sees a

shapely young woman in a bikini sunning herself below by the pool, masturbates, and, for the first time, achieves orgasm; thus, Solondz implies, he takes his first step toward joining the ranks of the sexually addicted. As he goes in to report his achievement proudly to the other Jordans (who have just drunk a toast "to happiness") with the picture's last line, "I came!," the family dog licks Billy's semen from the balcony rail, then goes inside and licks Trish's face. Up comes the parodically tepid "Happiness" theme, which has shared the soundtrack with the ironically deployed, sprightly classical music of Vivaldi and Mozart, on the one hand, and the equally contrapuntal, saccharine popular songs "Mandy" and "You Light Up My Life," on the other, and the film is over.

It's no accident that masturbation – with a minimum of two graphic ejaculations – is routinely practiced by three to four characters in *Happiness*, and by at least one in *Your Friends and Neighbors*. (The chief gag of *There's Something about Mary*, in which Ben Stiller gets his penis caught in his zipper, also derives from masturbation.) For onanism is the ultimate act of self-love as well as self-gratification, and the sexual self is what nearly every one of these characters seems to think about all the time, to the exclusion of virtually anything else. This naturally makes them figures of fun or objects of scorn, which is precisely the filmmakers' point, about them as well as about American society as a whole.

If it's argued that *Happiness* and *Your Friends and Neighbors* in reality reflect only a small portion of the U.S. population, it can be countered that this is the way in which our time *thinks of* itself, *visualizes* itself in the mass media (from the angle of sex as well as from the reverse angle of violence), or in any case is tacitly eager to be *shocked at* itself. The same argument has been made against Restoration comedy: that it did not truly represent Restoration society. Nonetheless, such was the theatre relished by the society of the period and that, like all good art, tells us by implication, contrast, or omission as much about other segments of the population – in this case the Puritans of late seventeenth-century England, with their Christian fundamentalist counterparts in late twentieth-century America – as about the upper class it depicts.

Perhaps the real question about *Happiness* and *Your Friends and Neighbors*, apart from their social representativeness, is whether they are "good" works of art or examples of what William K. Wimsatt once called "vile art": art that presents immoral acts irresponsibly, if not with approval and joy. In a reworking of Wimsatt's related term, the intentional fallacy, critics of Neil LaBute, for instance, have called him "acridly misanthropic," "cleverly malignant," and "cheaply titillating." But can he himself be so described, or are such pejorative adjectives better directed at his characters? In other words, are LaBute's critics confusing the messenger with the message of this "modern immorality tale" (the movie poster's subtitle for *Your Friends and Neighbors*) and thereby making the same mistake, toward the end of the twentieth century, that Chekhov's detractors made toward the end of the nineteenth? To wit, the Russian writer was accused of depicting a horse thief in one of his short stories ("Thieves," 1890) without condemning, and thus seeming to condone, his actions, to which the good doctor calmly responded, "I have to tell you that horse thievery is bad?" *Mutatis mutandis*, LaBute could ask the same question of his critics about his own moral intent vis à vis the rapacious sexuality or solipsistic vanity displayed by his characters in *Your Friends and Neighbors*.

Todd Solondz is another matter, because his chief predator preys on children, and Solondz appears to have fun with, or make light of, his character's pedophilia: Dr Maplewood's attempts to dope Johnny Grasso's late-night snack, for example, are played almost as farce, while his interactions with little Billy read like a prurient send-up of the father-son chats in *Leave It to Beaver*. ("You'll come one day, you'll see!" exclaims Bill to his disheartened pubescent.) At the same time, however, Bill Maplewood is portrayed as a loving family man who knows, and says, that he is sick yet can do nothing about it. We are clearly meant to sympathize, if not identify, with him, as we are with the heterosexual, perhaps bisexual pedophile in another sex-as-salvation piece, Paula Vogel's 1997 play *How I Learned to Drive*. There can be no more shocking view of such a doctor than an understanding one. Hence the sometimes unbearable tension between normality and deviance, comedy and tragedy, alien distance and fellow feeling, in the scenes that feature this character – scenes that are central to *Happiness* if only because, for all his faults, Bill is the kind of active, take charge-protagonist favored by the cinematic medium over insipid or ineffectual types like Joy and Allen.

I don't mean by this that the film lightly glosses over or omits entirely the grim consequences of Bill Maplewood's crimes of molestation, as some of Solondz's critics believe. Them I would advise to consider Chekhov's rhetorical question in the context of Bill's horrendous actions. What I do mean is that his homosexual, pedophilic obsession is put on the same satiric, pathetic level with the carnal obsessions of the other, heterosexual characters, and is thus made to seem more representative than aberrant. Indeed, this doctor's iniquitous behavior is placed on a *higher* level because, unlike the rest of the people in *Happiness*, he's consciously aware of his particular malady, and this awareness confers a certain measure of sad dignity on his tortured, doomed, destructive self. Bill Maplewood is courageously acted by Dylan Baker, who, without the safety net of repentance and reform, chillingly balances this man's grave, contemplative, medical mien against his unbalanced, benighted mental state.

In a movie whose acting could easily and ridiculously have gone "over the top," everyone else from Jane Adams (Joy), Lara Flynn Boyle (Helen), Cynthia Stevenson (Trish), Ben Gazzara (Lenny), Louise Lasser (Mona), and Elizabeth Ashley (Diane the Florida divorcée) to Philip Seymour Hoffman (Allen), Rufus Read (Billy), Camryn Manheim (Kristina), Jon Lovitz (Andy), Evan Silverberg (Johnny Grasso), and Jared Harris (Vlad the Russian cabbie) fills his or her role to the brim with a sense of both internal conviction and external connection, of individual commitment and ensemble integration. As in Dylan Baker's case, this took more effort than most cinematic characterizations on account of *Happiness*'s subject matter, particularly for the youngsters Read and Silverberg.

I don't know how Solondz got their parents' permission to use them in this savage comedy of manners (or the lack thereof) – as I write, I think of, or rather cannot imagine, my own eleven-year-old in either part – but the fact that he did may tell us more about the realism of *Happiness*'s world than we'd like to know. No one would want to live in such a world, yet somehow, I suspect, we all do (a suspicion that David Lynch tried but failed to give us in his merely bizarre, even revolting *Blue Velvet* [1986]). And Todd Solondz has been brazen enough to say so – sniggeringly to tell us, like his coeval Neil LaBute and unlike the merely narcissistic Woody Allen, who our friends and neighbors really are. Those boys and girls, alas, are us.

10

Getting Straight

On Lynch's *The Straight Story* (1999, USA)

In 1999, major writer-directors with reputations for treating *outré* subjects released movies to which we could all take our young children. That poetically profane critic of American materialism, David Mamet, turned out his stirring adaptation of Terence Rattigan's *The Winslow Boy* (1946), a verbally buttoned-up English period piece. Wim Wenders, known primarily for Teutonic puzzle-pictures of anxiety and alienation, came up with an uplifting concert movie called *Buena Vista Social Club*, about a group of forgotten Cuban folk musicians. The otherwise camp, even sadomasochistic sensibility of Spain's Pedro Almodóvar gave us the uncharacteristically gentle, soberly comedic *All About My Mother*. And David Lynch, best known for exploring the darker recesses of the human psyche as well as the darker corners of the American landscape in such cult films as *Eraserhead* (1977), *Blue Velvet* (1986), and *Twin Peaks* (1992, from the 1990–91 television series), created an eloquently simple, representatively American, straightforwardly emotional, and extraordinarily moving picture titled *The Straight Story* (G-rated and released by Disney, no less).

As for why he and other big-name directors turned to more "serene" material, Lynch's explanation rings as true as his latest film: "Sex, drugs, violence, and obscene language have been pushed to an absurd extreme, to the point where you don't feel anything anymore" (*The New York Times*, 22 May 1999, p. A25). In other words, less is more, or restraint can produce its own form of artistic freedom. But let's not be too quick to predict a shift from blunt literalism to imaginative suggestion in the prevailing cinematic wind, for contemporary audiences, conditioned not only by (action) films but also by cable television, video games, and even best-selling books, are used to having everything spilled as well as spelled out. (Moreover, teenagers make up the largest audience of moviegoers, and therefore they are the ones the studios most often aim to please, as well as the ones least likely to appreciate imaginative suggestion or restraint.) Ask Martin Scorsese, who, after the Buddhist idyll of *Kundun* (1997), returned to his physical senses with *Bringing Out the Dead*, a gritty tale concerning the life and work of big-city emergency medical technicians.

Even David Lynch wasn't sure that he would undertake another "experiment in purity" like *The Straight Story* (*The New York Times*, 10 October 1999, p. 16 of "Arts and Leisure" section). As he put it, "My sensibility was probably too warped at a young age for me to do more than dabble in the serene." Nonetheless, he did so dabble in this instance and in the process made not only his best film but also the best American film since *Sling Blade* (1996). The idea for the picture itself came from *The New York Times*, where Mary Sweeney (Lynch's professional as well as social partner, and the co-author of *The Straight Story*'s script along with John Roach) read a report in 1994 about a seventy-three-year-old resident of Laurens, Iowa, named Alvin Straight. It so happened that Alvin had traveled three hundred miles eastward to Mount Zion, Wisconsin, to visit his stroke-afflicted, dying brother Lyle, whom he had not seen for ten years on account of a terrible quarrel. Naturally, these facts in and of themselves would not have constituted a "story"; what made them one was Alvin's mode of transportation: a 1966 John Deere tractor-style lawn mower, with a trailer attached, which he used because his deteriorating eyesight had cost him his driver's license and he couldn't stand buses, and despite the fact that he could walk only with the support of two canes. It took Alvin all of September and a fair portion of October of 1994 to reach his older brother, camping along the way and occasionally receiving hospitality from people he met. But reconcile with Lyle he did before dying of emphysema in 1996. And it is to Alvin Straight that David Lynch dedicated his new film.

Aside from its "sereneness" (more on which later), what did Lynch see in this *Reader's Digest* material, the very kind that might once have inspired the cover art of a *Saturday Evening Post*? He saw, I think – especially as a result of Sweeney and Roach's verbally distilled yet veristically precise screenplay – that Alvin Straight's sentimental journey need not lapse into narrative sentimentality. He also sensed that the usual tempo of one of his pictures – in our era of the shrunken attention span, an unapologetic *adagio* that can accommodate this director's measured, attentive gaze – would unobtrusively serve Straight's simple, unadorned tale just as well as it self-consciously heightened the eccentricity-cum-grotesquerie of such Lynch movies as *The Elephant Man* (1980) and *Wild at Heart* (1990). The title of *The Straight Story* thus names not only the film's human subject but also its artistic style, as if that title were playfully attempting to tell us this will be a factual tale or journalistic account filtered through the consciousness of a cinematic Thomas Eakins rather than a moviemade Norman Rockwell.

Still, the David Lynch of old obtrudes teasingly into the rarefied, almost abstractly tender world of *The Straight Story*, like Edward Hopper trying to put his signature on an Eakins canvas, or Diane Arbus attempting to make a Walker Evans photograph in her own image. We see, or think we see, that Lynch at the start of the picture, where all the usual Lynchian elements seem to be in place: the mock-innocent, faux-resonant score by Angelo Badalamenti; a threateningly bland, overhead shot of Midwestern fields in early autumn, followed by an eerily sunny vista of one-story clapboard houses, neatly trimmed lawns, and a main street that is vacant save for its resident running dogs; the first human being in the form of a mildly grotesque, supinely plump woman sunning herself before her house with a reflector as she gobbles junk food, and as the camera swoops down on, then moves in toward, her; finally, the window of the house next door on the left, to which the same chillingly slow, predatory camera has traveled and where we hear a sudden thumping noise deep from within, after which this first sequence ends, without a word, on a fade-out.

In fact, there is nothing ominous, threatening, mocking, removed, eerie, bizarre, chilling, or predatory about the movie that follows; Alvin Straight's odyssey never intersects with the Twilight Zone, and the normal, wholesome façade of his hometown is no façade at all: it's the essence of Laurens, Iowa. To be sure, Alvin is something of a small-town eccentric, like many a figure in the Lynch gallery, but here the character's eccentricity or intense individualism is hitched to a genuine theme and not made a voyeuristic subject in its own right. That theme has to do not only with our national self-image or ideal personification – deliberately, almost perversely conveyed through the figure of the senescent Alvin – as a self-reliant, stubborn, taciturn, yet humane and courageous loner. It has also to do with transcendentalism, American-as well as cinematic-style.

For American transcendentalism, as sponsored by Ralph Waldo Emerson, emphasized the practice of self-trust and self-reliance at all times, at the same time as it preached the importance of spiritual, or spiritually expansive, living, by which it meant living close to nature – a nature where God's moral law could be intuited by divinely receptive man – rather than submitting to religious dogma. Transcendental style in the cinema, as sponsored by Paul Schrader, similarly unites the spiritual style of religious cinema with realism's redemption of the physical world. That is, transcendental style seeks to express the universal holiness or organic wholeness of reality itself – of people, nature, and things. It does this not only through a realistic shooting style consisting of (1) limited cutting within a scene or the frequent use of long takes; (2) the deployment of a camera that seeks out natural light while eschewing the heat of the close-up for the repose of the full shot indoors as well as the long shot outdoors; and (3) the repeated interjection of "dead time," or shots of the material world that are devoid of the film's human characters, for the purpose of calling attention to the mystery, inviolability, and primacy of that world. Transcendental style also attempts to fulfill its mission by reveling in the temporality or mundaneness of quotidian living – of working, eating, washing, drinking, talking, shopping, walking, sitting, traveling, playing, sleeping – at the expense of more dramatic activity such as murder, mayhem, rape, robbery, even simple altercation (or its opposite, jejune romance).

So we get almost none of the latter "action" in *The Straight Story*, which is the reason the film hasn't gotten – nor will it get – much attention from the press and consequently will not receive any awards. The very nature of Alvin's transportation (which moves at approximately five miles per hour) means that the pace of his journey, and thus of the picture, will be slow, unlike that of an action movie. Lynch is interested in this man's mental journey into his past via the people he meets on the road in the present; mental journeys take a long time, for they are arduous; and, although Alvin has chosen to travel by lawn mower for physical reasons, one senses the suitability of his choice to the purpose at hand – his own as well as David Lynch's. That purpose is not merely a brotherly visit, or else Alvin would not refuse proffered transportation along the way (which he does do). He *wants* to suffer the hardships of his inner as well as outer journey, since it is a penance for, or expiation of, past misdeeds, including years lost to drinking and nastiness (toward his wife, now deceased, and seven children) as well as to his falling out with Lyle (whom Alvin calls the Abel to his Cain). This journey, then, is a gift that he is fashioning both for his brother and his family, just as a craftsman might finish a fine object, and it is a gift that he presents by the very fact of his arrival in Mount Zion on the snail-paced lawn mower. Therefore Alvin must make this trip alone and in his own way – this trip that at first looks so ludicrous, even cranky, but that soon becomes a spiritual pilgrimage (not least because of the serendipitous name of his final destination).

So determined is Lynch to get us used to his cinematic pace, as opposed to the fast, factory kind we've become conditioned to expect, that he has Alvin's journey begin with a false start: the septuagenarian's first mower blows its engine a few miles from Laurens, so he must hitch-hike home to purchase another, used one at what is a considerable cost ($325) for this pensioner. (This part of the Straight story may be true, but that doesn't mean the filmmakers had to include it.) As for the old lawn mower, Alvin sets it on fire in his backyard with two rifle shots to the gas tank in the film's one ironic nod to the cinema of spectacle. Yet even this bizarrely comic moment resonates with unforced seriousness in a movie whose overarching seriousness of intent is an article of faith. For Alvin's adult daughter Rose, with whom he lives, witnesses with trepidation the incineration of the broken-down mower, and we only later learn why. This "slow," speech-impeded woman, you see, is the single mother of four children who have been removed from her custody forever on account of a house fire in which one of them was badly burned – a fire apparently caused by Rose's "incompetence" or neglect. Rose lives in mourning for, and memory of, those children who were once her family; and now her present family, consisting only of her elderly father, is about to embark on a perilous journey conceived, as it were, in flames yet dedicated to reuniting him with his familial past in the form of his estranged older brother.

Hardly by accident, Alvin's mower-breakdown occurs near a sign announcing that the Grotto of the Redemption (in West Bend, Iowa) is five miles away. And, once back on the road, Alvin duly passes by the Grotto on the road to his own redemption. Prior to his meeting with Lyle, that road consists of a series of stations (about seven to Christ's fourteen Stations of the Cross), each marked or punctuated by (aerial) traveling shots of corn crops and grain fields at harvest time; long takes on the sun as it rises, the rain as it falls, or a fire as it burns; by passing glimpses of woods, rivers, vehicles, and barns; and, above all, by crane shots that begin by catching Alvin's puttering progress from behind, rise into the sky with epic majesty, then gracefully sweep down to reveal the man and his mower-cum-trailer about ten feet farther down the highway. Some commentators have taken these crane shots to be an elaborate visual joke on Alvin and his pilgrim's progress, but nothing could be farther from the truth. Along with the other "travelogue" footage, as well as the recurrent, companionate shots of a starry night-

Richard Farnsworth, as Alvin Straight, makes his journey in *The Straight Story*.

time sky – the very first as well as the very last image in *The Straight Story* – they are sublimely designed to suggest the spiritual nature of the protagonist's quest, to serenely unite Alvin, as it were, with natural elements in space as a way of creating for him a supernal warp in time.

To be sure, the skyward or heavenly shots additionally suggest the benign oversight of a supreme being, but Lynch is far more concerned with Alvin's watchful gaze here on earth. Indeed, it is from his inspired point of view that the camera frequently looks up at the firmament, for such a vista reminds him of his boyhood in Moorhead, Minnesota, where he and Lyle spent summers sleeping outdoors under the stars. And it is from Alvin's point of view, or from the omniscient point of view of the camera as it also watches *him*, that we watch mundane occurrences like rainstorms and sunsets. He seems beatifically moved by such simple, natural events, and we are left to wonder why: to imagine, that is, the inner journey that Alvin takes, even as we witness his outward one; to have our own spirits thus awakened at the same time as we observe the material stages of Alvin's trek in the most material artistic medium yet known to man.

After his false start, those stages include an encounter with a pregnant, teenaged runaway, who spends the night by his campfire and with whom Alvin shares information about his family as well as wisdom about the concept of family in general. Although probably the scene in *The Straight Story* that comes closest to sentimentalism, this one works well because of the irony at its heart: the two conversationalists are a teenaged runaway who says her family hates her yet who is about to start a family of her own, and a wizened old fellow who is a latter-day version of Robert Warshow's archetypal Westerner. A melancholy, intensely individualistic loner, this figure is a man of repose and self-containment who seeks not to extend his dominion but only to assert his personal value as well as comport himself with honor, and who above all else resists the need for others upon which the modern world insists, which Europeans accept as a perennial fact of life, yet which Americans see as the lapse of Rousseau's natural man into the compromise and frustration of social life as we know it. Alvin Straight is the (mid)Westerner in contemporary, socialized form, if you will, the outsider who nonetheless dwells within the family circle. And David Lynch or his screenwriters suggest Alvin's ambivalence by means of his private symbol for the family unit: a bunch of sticks bound together so they won't break, or a wooden bundle that the Romans used to call a *fascia* and that, under Mussolini, became the Italian symbol for family of a thoroughly insidious kind.

Menaced on the highway the next day by enormous, rumbling eighteen-wheelers, lone Alvin is also lapped by a herd of bicycle marathoners, who invite him into their camping area when they retire for the evening. Why bicycle racers? Because each is the very image and essence of what Alvin is not or is no longer: a physically adept young man rushing headlong through life, obsessed with the finish line instead of being attentive to the road that will get him there, preoccupied with the ultimate destination rather than being mindful of the incremental journey to that end. One of these bicyclists asks Alvin, in a friendly but telling way, what the worst part is about getting old. Alvin thoughtfully replies that "The worst part is rememberin' when you was young" – an ambiguous statement that sentimentalists will take as an exaltation of youth in all its vitality or freshness but that a catholic realist like myself reads as a denigration of youthful impetuosity as well as immaturity.

We get an instance of such impetuosity in the very next scene, when Alvin comes upon a distraught driver who, in the process of her frantic daily commute to work, has just killed her thirteenth deer in seven weeks – deer that she tearfully says she loves. "Where do they come from?" she wails. Alvin can do little to comfort this woman, and at first we think she's just a sideshow exhibit from David Lynch's gallery of freaks. But then something almost magical happens: we watch, that evening, as Alvin eats a portion of the deer for supper (the last supper or food we will see him eat in *The Straight Story*), surrounded by twelve living (or resurrected) deer who observe him. And the following morning we find the buck's antlers attached to Alvin's trailer, right above the seat on his lawn mower (where they remain for the rest of the film), in a humble transfiguration of Christ's crown of thorns into Straight's crown of horns.

Like Christ and his human counterparts in the episodic mystery or morality plays of the Middle Ages, Alvin is traveling his own *via dolorosa*; and, like Christ, he stumbles three times along the way. The first "stumble" occurred when Alvin's first mower broke down; the second occurs when, sixty miles from Lyle's place in Wisconsin, the second mower picks up so much speed going down a hill that its drive belt snaps. Miraculously unhurt, Alvin is assisted by a group of volunteer firemen, who had been putting out a practice fire on a nearby barn. (Like the burning bush in Exodus 3, this flaming building is of no danger to anyone.) Just as miraculously, one of his helpers is a former John Deere salesman, Danny Riordan, who arranges to have the mower repaired (by identical-twin mechanics who, in their petty bickering, are comic foils to Lyle and Alvin) and allows Alvin to camp on his property in the meantime. Alvin *camps* in Danny and his wife Darla's backyard: he doesn't bother to ask if he can sleep on their sofa, he won't even enter their house to call Rose (he takes the Riordans' cordless phone outside, then leaves it on the doorstep – with three or four dollars for the long-distance charges – when he's finished), and he politely but stubbornly refuses the ride that the kind, tactful, and empathetic Danny offers him to Mount Zion. Again, this is a man on a mission, and part of that mission is self-mortification and self-excoriation as well as self-purgation, as we see in what may be *The Straight Story*'s most moving scene.

It occurs toward the end of Alvin's stay at the Riordans' when an elderly neighbor named Verlyn Heller stops by and invites him to a quiet bar for a drink. Alvin goes but, having long ago been cured of his alcoholism by a preacher, he drinks only milk while his companion sips a Miller Lite. Both Alvin and Verlyn are World War II veterans, so their conversation in alternating medium close-up naturally drifts to each man's anguished memory of combat – a conversation we feel so privileged to hear in part because Lynch had his cinematographer, Freddie Francis, discreetly photograph the men's initial meeting, on Danny Riordan's lawn, in a medium long shot with under-miked sound. A crack shot of a hunter before the war, Alvin was used as a sniper during his service in France, where most of the Germans he killed subsequent to the Normandy invasion were "moon-faced boys." But Alvin also killed one of his own men by accident; no one ever discovered this, nor has he ever admitted it to anyone; and now, with tears in his eyes, he admits it to Verlyn. We see no images of fighting, no flashbacks. We hear only some popular music from the 1940s in the background – a tune that slowly turns into the muffled sounds of heavy artillery. The focus here is obviously not on the Spielbergian saving of a Private Ryan, on spectacular action and heroic adventure, but on saving Alvin Straight's soul. For this we must hear his confession, we must see his face, and through his eyes we must look into his heart. Only then can we leave the scene in more or less the same way that we entered it: in medium long shot, with Alvin's and Verlyn's backs to us, and not a word to be heard as the two men sit on stools while the lone bartender nearly dozes as he stands off to their left.

Alvin moves on the next morning and becomes exultant as he approaches, then crosses the Mississippi River into Wisconsin – the Promised Land, as far as he's concerned, and, like the Biblical Canaan, a state bordered in both the east and the west by a body of water. That night, the one before his reunion with Lyle, Alvin camps in one of the oldest cemeteries in the Midwest – where the seventeenth-century Jesuit explorer and missionary Jacques (Père) Marquette lies buried, as Alvin happens to know – and there is visited by the priest whose rectory abuts the graveyard. No formal confession occurs here, since Alvin is a Baptist by birth, yet the facts that this scene occurs in a graveyard, that the priest had ministered to Alvin's equally Baptist (but nonetheless dying) brother in the hospital, and that Alvin refuses the priest's offer of bodily sustenance speak for themselves. Loneliness and longing are the subjects of the two men's conversation – not religions or their pre-scribed rituals – and brotherly love or communion is its object. The priest as celibate brother seems to need to talk to the widowed Alvin as much as the latter needs to talk to him, and the only "amen" this priestly father utters is in response to Alvin's earthly desire to swallow his pride and ask for Lyle's forgiveness.

Before he swallows that pride, Alvin first swallows a beer in a bar a few miles from Lyle's ramshackle wooden home. It's his first alcoholic drink in years; he stops after one Miller Lite, his thirst quenched; then, with directions to his brother's place provided by the bartender, he climbs back onto his load of a lawn mower in order to finish his jour-ney. But before he can, Alvin "stumbles" for the third time, when his mower appears to "die" just short of its final destination. Appearing lost, he simply sits there – for so long that Lynch must punctuate the passing time with fades, until another old man on a big tractor passes by and (in another reverentially inaudible medium long shot) reveals

exactly where, off the beaten path, Lyle's house sits. After this
encounter, Alvin wondrously restarts the inert mower and rides it to a
point where the road ends, so that he must hobble down to his
brother's porch-in-the-woods on his two trusty canes.

Once there, Alvin calls out Lyle's name, Lyle responds by calling out
Alvin's as he emerges with support from a walker (something his
younger brother has consistently refused to use), and the two men sit
down together in twilight on the porch, largely silent but deeply moved
by their long-deferred reunion. When Lyle asks his brother, "Did you
ride that thing all the way here to see me?" Alvin's response is the last,
reticently reaffirming line of the film: "I did, Lyle." As I've indicated,
The Straight Story's final shot is of the leitmotif-like starry night, into
which the camera continues majestically to travel as the credits roll.
Alvin had told the Catholic priest that this was all he wanted to do: sit
with his older brother in peace and look up at the stars, just as they did
as youngsters. And this is all we see them do – with sentiment but without sentimentality, with words yet without wordiness, with fraternal psychology but without paternalistic psychologization – as their point of
view merges with that of the celestial-bound camera. (Recall how
roughly analogous scenes between relatives were handled in maudlin
pictures like *Terms of Endearment* [1983], *Places in the Heart* [1984], and
Steel Magnolias [1989], and you'll appreciate the terse magnitude of
Lynch's achievement here.) *The Straight Story* ends, then, precisely
when it has fulfilled its artistic design – neither before nor after it has
done so – and such design is intimately connected to Alvin Straight's
place in his own mind, in his family, and in the family of man; in Laurens, Iowa, America, the natural world, the cosmic universe, and in the
mindful eyes of God. Alvin found his place in the end, and this film has
indelibly etched that noble place in human memory.

One of the reasons *The Straight Story* succeeds to such a degree is its
stellar acting. Let's begin with the small roles, each of which features
an actor (in some cases doubtless a non-professional one) who both
looks and sounds credible as a rural person from the Midwest – from
Everett McGill as the dealer who sells Alvin the (second) mower that he
uses on his trip, to Wiley Harker as the fellow oldtimer with whom he
exchanges grim war memories, to Russ Reed as the man who serves
Alvin a beer in Mount Zion. These people breathe authenticity, commitment, and understanding, down to the way their clothes fit and
their bodies move; they are never what they would be in standard Hollywood fare: condescending country caricatures, on the one hand, or
miscast as well as underdirected urbanites, on the other. The very best

of the "small" performances is delivered by James Cada as Danny Riordan, who may spend more on-screen time with Alvin than anyone else
in *The Straight Story*. Watch the concentrated Cada's restless eyes, and
you'll see an actor who fully comprehends his character's interest in
Alvin Straight. As an early retiree with too much free time on his hands
(so much that he attends the volunteer fire department's staged fire),
the cigarette-smoking Riordan is the type (like my late father) who's
always nervously looking forward to the next project, trip, event, visit,
or holiday, and who finds that, for a few days at least, he need look no
further than Alvin for the absorption of his attention.

Two other small parts feature well-known actors who have either
worked with David Lynch in the past (Harry Dean Stanton, in *Wild at
Heart* and *Twin Peaks: Fire Walk with Me*) or have enjoyed a longtime
friendship with him (Sissy Spacek). Stanton is on screen for perhaps
two minutes at the end as Lyle, yet his gratifying presence – consisting
of a halting voice, feeble walk, and tired look belied by a compassionate core – continues to haunt my memory. Spacek, as the "simple" Rose
with her speech impediment and habit of building birdhouses, initially
seems like a refugee from the Lynch carnival of grotesques, but she
gains in gravity with each scene in part because she undercuts her
secret scars with unaffected warmth. Spacek's excellence, like that of
everyone else associated with the making of this film, would come to little, however, without Richard Farnsworth in the titular role.

Born in the same year as Alvin Straight, Farnsworth has worked in
movies since 1937 and has been everything from a stunt man, in Westerns and Biblical epics, to a minor supporting player in *The Stalking
Moon* (1969) and *The Duchess and the Dirtwater Fox* (1976), to a prominent performer in *Comes a Horseman* (1978), *Resurrection* (1980), and
The Grey Fox (1982). Tall, skinny, white-bearded, and weak-hipped (like
Alvin), quiet yet dogged, Farnsworth ended a two-year retirement to act
in *The Straight Story*, and the result is a valedictory performance of the
highest order. This aged actor understands the part of Alvin as the one
toward which his whole career has been moving, and that is the primary reason he can lend such immense dignity to so otherwise unassuming an old man approaching the end of his days. Farnsworth also
understands that playing a character Alvin's (and his own) age is more
about *being* than *doing*, and therefore more about allowing the camera
to penetrate into the essence of that being than presenting to the camera a reality framed by architectonic language. (Think about how
much an overbusy actor like Jack Lemmon, a mawkish one like Walter
Matthau, or a performing self [seal?] like Wilford Brimley would do or

want to do in such a role, and you'll appreciate the minimalism of Farnsworth's creation.) *When* Farnsworth speaks, his gravelly voice lingers in the mind; as we look at his wizened face, we read beneath it layer upon layer of meaning, experience, consequence, and resolve.

He's helped – yet could have easily been hindered – by Badalamenti's music and Francis's cinematography. Alvin is in the autumn of his years, even as *The Straight Story* takes place in September and October, but Francis doesn't make the mistake of prettifying the autumnal Midwest, on the one hand, or of tarnishing it, on the other. He works here as he has in the past, in such a color picture as *Glory* (1989) and in a black-and-white film like *Sons and Lovers* (1960): by filling the world with color in its infinite variety (or, *mutatis mutandis*, black and white in their multiplicity of shades), yet with hues that are photographed in autumnal or otherwise diminished light and therefore appear understated. The result is the visual equivalent of combining poignance with exhilaration, pathos with wonder, passion with anguish – precisely the mixed emotional tone Lynch's movie is trying to sound. And we get a similar mixture in Badalamenti's plaintive yet lilting score, which is rooted in the spirited tradition of bluegrass but propelled by its elegiac incorporation of strings. Badalamenti, like Francis, has collaborated with David Lynch before, but his best previous work was for Paul Schrader in *The Comfort of Strangers* (1991), which itself mixed emotional tones by suggesting the Byzantine quality of Venice and the story taking place there at the same time as it acted as a momentary, melodic balm to viewers' troubled senses.

So masterful and unified is every aspect of *The Straight Story* that even so seemingly minor a detail as the protagonist's smoking habit fits into its master plan. Alvin is warned early in the film by his doctor to quit smoking, but he refuses to do so – even refusing to have his lungs X-rayed. He likes his "Swisher Sweets" and he continues to puff on them for the duration of the movie, even as his daughter (for one) smokes cigarettes. But Alvin never lights a cigarillo while he is doing something else, only when he is in a state of watchful repose. Consciously or not, Alvin uses smoking to slow down his already slow-paced life, for the purpose of taking in the fullness or richness of the peopled world around him. He seems to realize that smoking is paradoxically a delicious moment in time and, in its inutility, a savory moment out of time, a little artistic world unto itself in the magical insubstantiality of its delicate puffs. And this mystery that attaches to tobacco – the danger in its pleasure, the foulness in its beauty, the arrogance in its evanescence – only enhances a man's appreciation of the mystery, the sheer multitude

or denseness, that underlies life's dailiness, which is far more complicated and inspiriting than most films or other artworks could ever
make it out to be.

The Straight Story is one of the exceptions, of course, and I for one
thank God, man, and country for its transcendent union of human
redemption with the phenomenal redemption of physical reality. Not
even Bergman's celebrated *Wild Strawberries* (1957) – *The Straight Story*'s
closest cinematic relative in its archetypal portrayal of an old man
(played by Victor Sjöström in his own valedictory performance) taking
a long car trip that turns into a life's journey as well as the intimation
of his mortality – was able to achieve so organic a dual focus (partly
because the Swedish director's films prior to this one had led progressively to the rejection of religious belief). And this places David Lynch's
picture very high, indeed, on my list of the greatest movies ever made
– American or otherwise.

11

Stones and Roses

On the Dardennes' *Rosetta* (1999, Belgium) and Schrader's *Affliction* (1998, USA)

The Dardenne brothers' *Rosetta* won the *Palme d'Or* at the 1999 Cannes Film Festival over David Lynch's *The Straight Story*, and I suspect that the American entry lost not only because of the increasingly virulent anti-Americanism of the French but also because of this picture's unashamedly Christian overtones in an era unparalleled for its greedy secularism. But *Rosetta* has its Christian overtones as well, though they have been missed by every commentator I've read, probably on account of the movie's seemingly unrelieved bleakness of tone. Luc and Jean-Pierre Dardenne themselves have not helped their cause by comparing Rosetta to the modernist hero of Kafka's *The Castle* (1926), a land surveyor called "K" who tries in vain to be recognized by the very officials who supposedly have summoned him to their village (which is overlooked by a castle on a hill).

She has more in common, however, with Bresson's protagonists than with Kafka's "K" – in particular with the late, great French filmmaker's Mouchette and Balthasar. Their parables represent a departure from the Christian certitude to be found in such earlier works by Bresson as *Diary of a Country Priest* (1950), *A Man Escaped* (1956), *Pickpocket* (1959), and *The Trial of Joan of Arc* (1962); still, a principle of redemption or a promise of transfiguration operates in *Mouchette* (1966) and *Au hasard, Balthasar* (1966) as well, even if it may be found only in a humanity or an animality redeemed from this earth. Both these pictures are linked with *Rosetta* in their examination of the casual, gratuitous inhumanity to which the meek of this earth are subjected, a fourteen-year-old girl in the former case and a donkey in the latter.

Mouchette is the loveless, abused, humiliated daughter of an alcoholic father and a dying mother, living in a northern France made to seem unreal by the juxtaposition of village life from another century with the modernity of jazz and automobiles. So relentlessly oppressive is Mouchette's young existence that she finally drowns herself – to the accompaniment of Monteverdi's *Magnificat*, which is Bresson's way of indicating that death alone is victory over such a spiritually wasted life. Balthasar, by contrast, begins his life as a children's pet who is formally christened, virtually worshipped like a pagan idol, and generously adorned with flowers. But the world of hard labor brutally intrudes: Balthasar is beaten and broken in; becomes a circus attraction; gets worked almost to death grinding corn for an old miser; then is hailed as a saint and walks in a church procession after his rescue, only to be shot to death by a customs officer during a smuggling escapade. The donkey's only saving grace, in a bizarre world of leather-clad motorcyclists and roughhewn millers, is that he is allowed to die on a majestic mountainside amid a flock of peacefully grazing sheep.

I've summarized *Mouchette* and *Au hasard, Balthasar* in some detail because I believe that the Dardenne brothers know both these films as well as the religious tradition, or spiritual style, of which they partake – one dominated by French Catholics even subsequent to Bresson, in such pictures as Cavalier's *Thérèse* (1986), Pialat's *Under the Sun of Satan* (1987), Rohmer's *A Tale of Winter* (1992), and Doillon's *Ponette* (1996). Luc and Jean-Pierre Dardenne happen to be Belgian, not French, and prior to *Rosetta* they spent twenty years making sociopolitical documentaries for European television before turning to fiction film in the socially realistic *La Promesse* (1996). That fine and unforgettable work burrowed into a rough chunk of proletarian life in Liège today, an economically deterministic environment in which the struggle to survive leads, ravenously, to the exploitation of workers by other workers. Into this pit of money-grubbing vipers comes an African family that shows a morally degraded, teenaged Belgian boy – simply through their dignity and pride – that another kind of existence is possible, even in the muck. We are in the heavily industrialized city of Liège again in *Rosetta*, and again we are dealing with a Belgian teenager, this time a girl. But in their second feature film the Dardennes (who write their own screenplays) not only forsake this world of proletarian realism for the nether one of subproletarian naturalism; at the same time, paradoxically, they seem to invoke an otherworldly realm that, unbeknownst to Rosetta (or anyone else in the picture, for that matter), runs parallel to her own.

Living in a tiny, beat-up trailer (sans toilet or running water) with her alcoholic, irresponsible, utterly dispirited mother, who mends old clothes for peddling in second-hand shops when she is not turning tricks in exchange for drinks, eighteen-year-old Rosetta is a furiously sullen bundle of energy. This adolescent longs to have a "normal" life – which for her means having a "real" job – and become a productive member of society, but even this modest goal appears to be beyond her grasp. (Hence her identity as a member of the lumpenproletariat, or proles who haven't had mechanized or otherwise rote work long enough to be dehumanized by it.) At the film's outset, Rosetta must be bodily removed from a factory where she's just been fired, for reasons unspecified. Subsisting in existential angst, quietly terrified that she will slide into the abyss like her bedraggled mother, the fresh-faced daughter wages a desperate, purely instinctive battle to lift herself out of her wretched, nearly feral existence and achieve a material state of grace.

Like some form of brute life force, the barely socialized Rosetta will do anything but beg to survive; like a jackal (as opposed to Balthasar, a passive pack animal), she will nip at any chance to prolong her life – including poach fish with rudimentary tackle from a pond so dank and muddy that it could be called a swamp. Indeed, this movie makes a spectacle of Rosetta's repeated dodging across a highway and ducking into the woods that adjoin her trailer park: as quick and cunning as an animal, she scrambles for her life, then covers her tracks, hides her things, and hoards her food (sometimes outside, where she'd rather compete with the foxes for it than with her shiftless mother). Ever walking briskly when she is not actually running, Rosetta appears to compensate for the paralyzing, anomic dread of her implacable existence with a defiant, headlong tread.

Determined to find regular work after being fired from the factory job – and equally determined not to go on welfare – Rosetta applies for several menial vacancies without success before landing a position at a waffle stand. There she replaces a young woman whose sick baby caused her to miss ten days of work in one month, and there she meets Riquet, a young man from the countryside who ekes out his own pittance at the waffle stand while secretly skimming profits from his boss. (This taskmaster runs a number of such stands throughout Liège and is played by the voracious Olivier Gourmet, the father in *La Promesse*.) Delicately performed by Fabrizio Rongione, Riquet is the

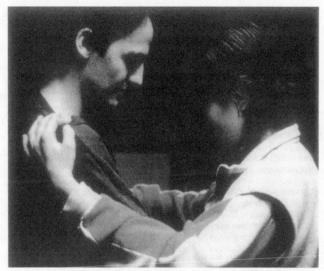

Émilie Dequenne, as Rosetta, and Fabrizio Rongione, as
Riquet, start to dance in his apartment in *Rosetta*.

only person in the film to show Rosetta any kind of sympathy, and the
two develop a tentative friendship – though his awkward attempts to
gain her romantic interest go completely unacknowledged by the preoccupied girl. During one such poignant try at Riquet's crude apartment (which appears to be carved out of a warehouse), he treats
Rosetta to a dinner of beer and fried bread, stands on his head, then
plays a tape of himself amateurishly banging on a set of drums (the
only "music" we hear during the movie, since, as in *La Promesse*, the
Dardennes wisely eschew the adornment of a musical soundtrack)
and tries to teach her to dance. She remains unresponsive, however,
especially because of an attack of stomach pain, one of several such
(unexplained) attacks that recur throughout the film. But she does
ask to sleep at Riquet's place, just to get away from her mother for a
night – which she does, in her own bedroll, untouched by her understanding host.

Before falling asleep, Rosetta utters in voice-over (even as we see
her on screen) the following mantra of reassurance, words that at the
same time painfully attest to the degree of her alienation from a self
that she has nearly objectified in an effort to steel her humanity
against the world's cruel indifference: "Your name is Rosetta. My
name is Rosetta. You've found a job. I've found a job. You have a
friend. I have a friend. You have a normal life. I have a normal life.

You won't fall into the rut. I won't fall into the rut." To indicate the relative normality that Rosetta has achieved, the Dardennes film most of this scene at Riquet's apartment in a static, becalming long take, with the camera in medium shot. Much of the rest of *Rosetta*, by contrast, is photographed with a handheld camera that remains disorientingly close to the heroine as she dashes about, with a twofold effect. On the one hand, the restless, uneven camerawork of Alain Marcoen (who was also the director of cinematography for *La Promesse*) creates the visual equivalent of the instability and uncertainty in Rosetta's life; on the other hand, the handheld camera seems to dog Rosetta with an angry intensity that matches her own, as it were her *doppelgänger*-cum-guardian angel or, antithetically, the devil of destiny in disguise.

The jagged, hurtling camera immediately resumes its ways in the scene following Rosetta's sleep-over at Riquet's, where she is fired from the waffle stand after being on the job for only three days. (She is replaced by the boss's son despite her efficiency, and despite the fact that this girl has never seemed happier – and therefore more personable – than when she's been serving up waffles.) So desperate is she not to "fall into the rut," which now gapes wide open before her, that, after she's terminated, the raging teenager pathetically clings to a heavy sack of flour as though it were simultaneously a life raft and the anchor preventing her forcible removal from a life-giving ocean of work. Rosetta possessed no such lifeline when, earlier, she and her estranged mother had become embroiled in a fight along the shore of the turbid, stagnant pond near the trailer camp (ironically named "Grand Canyon," by the way), at the end of which the older woman tossed her daughter into a moat so thick with mud that the youth could barely pull herself out of it. Down into the metaphorical abyss she went – appositely, at her mother's hands – and down there, in the hellishness of high water, she almost suffocated.

Riquet nearly succumbs to the pond as well when, subsequent to Rosetta's dismissal from the waffle stand, he finds her fishing, tries to help, and accidentally falls in. So intent is this girl on not going down with him – literally or figuratively – that she nearly lets her only friend drown. But she relents and saves him at the last minute, only to get Riquet's treasured job through another means: by blowing the whistle on his scam at the waffle stand (which she has long since detected and a share of which he had even offered to her, albeit unsuccessfully), after which the boss instantly installs Rosetta in the stunned boy's place.

Again, however, she doesn't remain on the job for long, except that this time the working girl terminates herself: in part because Riquet's physical and mental harassment in the wake of his own dismissal has awakened her moral conscience; in part because Rosetta is tired of fending for her drunken mother in addition to herself, and therefore has decided to quit not only work but also life. This she plans to do by turning on the propane gas in the house trailer she has made airtight – gas that will dispatch her passed-out mother along with her – but the canister runs out before the job is done. So Rosetta must go to buy another one from the seedy, opportunistic caretaker of the trailer court. As she struggles to carry the extremely heavy new canister back to the trailer – for this young woman, even committing suicide will be hard work – Riquet arrives on his scooter for one more episode of harassment. But he senses that something is terribly wrong when Rosetta drops to the ground in tears; he gets off his motorbike, goes over to the fallen girl, and compassionately lifts her up; they look silently into each other's eyes for a moment, after which the camera switches to a held shot of Rosetta's face in medium close-up; then the film abruptly ends with a quick cut to black.

That *Rosetta* has Christian overtones should be evident from this final scene, as well as from the titular character's one outfit of clothing, her recurrent stomach pain, and the food she eats. This pain, like the stomach cancer of Bresson's protagonist in *Diary of a Country Priest*, is meant to reflect not only the physical stress of Rosetta's impoverished life, but also its spiritual dilemma. That she can get relief from her pain only by turning a blow-dryer on her abdomen ought to tell us that human warmth, or fellow-feeling, is missing from her life as well. That human warmth comes to this latter-day Everywoman, as a miraculous godsend, in the form of Riquet, who in several scenes pursues her as inexorably with his scooter as the Dardennes do throughout with their camera, and who more than once wrestles with Rosetta as he were struggling, like a saintly figure from a medieval religious drama, for the possession or salvation of her soul.

Rosetta's habitual costume itself underscores her near-medieval existence, foraging for sustenance in the wilds of the postmodern Western European economy. Though her facial mask is expressionless, she dresses in a jumbled garb of red-and-black jacket, thick yellow tights, gray skirt, and rubber boots – in other words, in a kind of fool's motley that vividly stands out against the sparse and somber, cool and wet, winter landscape of Belgium. This is initially no wise fool, however, for all her survivalist cunning; Rosetta gets her (other)worldly wisdom, emotional lift, or spiritual resurrection from none other than the sad-eyed, drably dressed, otherwise corporeal Riquet, who, in a reversal of gender roles, plays the Columbine to her Harlequin (or who, as a former gymnast, represents the accomplished acrobat and dancer in Harlequin to Rosetta's wily if dense servant). And that resurrection, that uplift, comes at the end of Rosetta's own *via dolorosa*, during which, like Christ carrying his wooden cross, she stumbles three times with her canister of propane gas. She has finally exchanged her material state of grace, however minimal, for grace of another kind, and the implication is that Rosetta had to forego the body before she could bare her soul – a body that we have seen her nourish only with fish (the traditional symbol of Christ), bread, waffles (whose cognate term is the [Eucharistic] wafer), and, near the very end, a revivifying hard-boiled egg.

Those who have argued that *Rosetta*'s tone is unvaried in its grimness – that this girl is trapped throughout and the Dardenne brothers' film is merely a documentary-like chronicle of her depressing case – choose to ignore this work's spiritual element, in addition to the fact that, unlike Bresson's Mouchette or Balthasar, Rosetta is alive and in good company at the conclusion. Put another way, there's a mite of hope for this young heroine, and it comes from another person, from the human spirit of Riquet. That hope does not derive from the redemption of physical reality, from uniting Rosetta with natural elements in space, as it would if *Rosetta* had been shot in realistic-cum-transcendental style (like *The Straight Story*, to cite the most recent example). Rosetta's sphere is circumscribed, as the handheld camerawork (with almost no room for establishing shots, panoramic vistas, or "dead time" spent dwelling on the phenomenal world that surrounds her) reveals, and the only way to reach her is by force, as Riquet learns.

Oddly, the man who (as a critic) coined the term "transcendental style in the cinema," Paul Schrader, wrote and directed a 1998 movie completely bereft of the transcendent or the spiritual – one whose tone *is* unrelievedly grim. That would be *Affliction*, a high-fidelity adaptation of Russell Banks's semi-autobiographical novel of the same title from 1989, and one that returns Schrader to the directorial form he displayed in *The Comfort of Strangers* (1991) after two unsuccessful digressions into mongrel forms of comedy with *Witch Hunt* (1994) and *Touch* (1997). (Paul Sarossy, the cinematographer who also shot the 1997 film adaptation of Banks's *The Sweet Hereafter*, adds to *Affliction*'s grimness by making snow seem part of interiors, and thus making those otherwise warm rooms appear no more habitable than the cold expanses that surround them.) I'm not going to discuss this picture at much length, except to describe how it has some elements in common, and some in contrast, with *Rosetta*.

Affliction's central character, forty-one-year-old Wade Whitehouse, is the sheriff (and sole law-enforcement officer) of a small, snowbound, economically precarious New Hampshire town, on the outskirts of which he lives alone in the shambles of a trailer. But his uniform, gun, and relative stature do not make up for deep feelings of worthlessness – the product of childhood (and continuing) abuse at the hands of a soddenly alcoholic, relentlessly bullying father. (Rosetta, in contradistinction, may have no full-time job – certainly not one with stature – but she does have some sense of self-worth despite her own wretched upbringing by a hopelessly alcoholic mother.) Like his father, Wade is a big man, and he himself is given to spurts of violence; like Rosetta, he's frequently in excruciating pain, in his case the result of a rotten tooth. But this affliction of his remains only that: a physical affliction that he finally removes with a rusty pair of pliers, then disinfects with a shot of whiskey; unlike Rosetta's stomach pain, Wade's aching tooth is not used as a sign of the spiritual cavity in his life.

That spiritual emptiness remains in the end, despite the pathetic Wade's aspirations toward common decency in his dealings with his young daughter, his (remarried) ex-wife, his girlfriend (acted by the redoubtable Sissy Spacek), and his younger brother, Rolfe. A history professor in Boston who, for reasons unexplained, was untouched by his father's toxic rage – even though this man's physical abuse extended to his elder son as well as his servile wife – Rolfe is the first-person, retrospective narrator of Banks's novel. Though Rolfe gives us a scene-by-scene account of events he himself did not witness, he adopts the novelist's freedom to reconstruct these scenes down to the last detail and to enter into his older brother's every thought and feeling. Objectively, this is presumptuous, and we are mystified by Rolfe's nearly omniscient narration; such narration works much better in the naturally omniscient medium of film, where the unfettered or unrestricted camera is doing the telling, and where Rolfe need only occasionally be brought in, in voice-over (as he is in Schrader's *Affliction*), to remind us from whose point of view the story was originally told.

Affliction begins with the apparently accidental death of a wealthy weekend visitor on the first day of deer-hunting season; then, from this

Nick Nolte, James Coburn, Willem Dafoe, and Sissy Spacek at the cemetery in *Affliction*.

death (the mystery of which does not form this fiction's propulsion or core of interest, as it would in a whodunit), events lead to Wade's loss of his job; to his involvement, under pallid skies in the dead of winter, in more deaths – including his father's murder; and to his eventual disappearance from the town and from everybody's ken. This film, then, unlike *Rosetta, is* the case history of a subject (replete with flashbacks that replay the horrors of Wade's youth as fuzzy fragments from a pirated home movie) who is naturalistically afflicted, demonized, and driven in more ways than a social worker could count. But, like the Dardennes' picture, *Affliction* is also about a stratum of society trapped in a societal jet lag, marooned in a more complex world, except that here Rosetta's medieval, female foraging has been replaced by frontier brawling, or the manifest, masculine display of raw, undomesticated bodily strength both for its own inexorable sake and as a form of surrender to the implacable imperatives of misshapen character.

One can imagine Wade Whitehouse as a Travis Bickle (the protagonist of *Taxi Driver*, which Schrader wrote for Martin Scorsese in 1976) who stayed home in the country instead of going to the wicked city, married, had a child, got a good job, knocked himself out to be sane and normal – yet still ended up in middle age as a solitary brooder, inwardly howling for a savage act of redemption that never came. Or, if it did come, would only permit Wade to grow into Paul Newman's sixty-year-old character from *Nobody's Fool* (1995): an aging, unemployable, hard-drinking, solitary misfit from rural New York by the name of Donald "Sully" Sullivan, who walked out on his family years before, leads a dead-end existence playing cards in his rented room, and ends up in jail at the film's conclusion for punching out the town's lone police officer.

Nick Nolte's acting of the part of Wade Whitehouse is almost dismayingly accomplished in its piercing conviction. (He didn't get the 1999 Academy Award for which he was deservedly nominated, but James Coburn, as his father, won Best Supporting Actor in a far easier role.) I say "dismayingly" because, with hardly a single sympathetic or admirable action, Nolte makes his hulking, blustery brute of a character somewhat poignant. And it's Nolte the performer who does this – by continuing to find and reach into the bewildered Wade's deep recesses of feeling – not Banks the novelist or Schrader the screenwriter-director. The scenes, for example, in which this wrecked man refrains from releasing his fury on his abject, drunken, incoherent father after this man has allowed Wade's mother to freeze to death in her own bed, or where he tries to show some tenderness toward his daughter during their troubled visitations, are so remorselessly exact, so unerringly truthful, that they're difficult to watch without flinching. As Rosetta, Emilie Dequenne (Best Actress at Cannes), for her part, shows little tenderness toward anyone – including herself. Yet she is so thoroughly immersed in her otherwise unappealing (and most unglamorous) character's simmering fierceness – so free of the self-regard that can tinge even the best actors' work – that, by sheer force of will, she forces us to pay attention to Rosetta's appalling life in all its squalor.

Hence there was an extra-aesthetic pleasure in wondering what Dequenne herself is like and *was* like between takes during the shooting of *Rosetta*, so extreme is the role into which she plunged herself. There was another kind of pleasure, too – one as damning as it is astonishing. That is the pleasure we take in paying rapt attention to, and thinking a lot about, characters and subjects in film (in theatre and fiction as well, but especially in cinema, the most wide-reaching and therefore the most democratic of arts) to which we wouldn't normally give a large amount of consideration in real life. This, of course, is the special, intriguing power that all art holds over us: the power to engage merely by the act of isolating and framing. I bring it up in the context of *Rosetta* and *Affliction* only because it is more pronounced in the naturalistic mode than in any other. And because naturalism, when combined with a spiritual or a transcendental style, has the power to exalt like no other mode: to shift our concern, to elevate our solicitude, from self to other, from man to God and thus to other men. Outstanding among them must be counted the wretched of the earth, the Rosettas of this world who race through their time here because they mortally fear to wade.

12

Hot and Cold, or Seasons Change

On Rohmer's *Autumn Tale* (1998, France)
and Assayas's *Late August, Early September*
(1998, France)

There exists a large strand of Gallic cinema for which the refined and psychologically acute depiction of urban middle-class manners is a mainstay. At its most superficial, this strand produces movies like Martine Dugowson's *Portraits chinois* (1997), where the privileged milieux of fashion, art, and the media are the picture's flimsy substance rather than its pretext, and in which the characters' angst seems to be just another eye-catching item in a large display window. At its best, this type of French film has come to be identified with the work of Éric Rohmer. As Arnaud Desplechin said a few years ago when he introduced his own *My Sex Life, or How I Got Into an Argument* (1996) at the New York Film Festival, "For a French guy, this sort of movie" – with its anatomization of the emotions and deployment of well-articulated thought as a form of action – "is like a western for Americans." The latest examples of such Franco-filmic cuisine to reach America are the last of Rohmer's *Tales of the Four Seasons, Autumn Tale* (1998), and Olivier Assayas's seventh feature, but only his second (after the very different, slyly witty cult success called *Irma Vep* [1997]) to find commercial distribution in the United States: *Late August, Early September* (1999).

Let's begin with Rohmer, now eighty-four, who is one of the few surviving (and active) writer-directors of the French New Wave that so invigorated the film world in the 1950s and 1960s. Yet, except for a few early shorts made with Jean-Luc Godard, Rohmer's films have always seemed to share more with Bresson's spiritual austerity and Renoir's lyrical humanism than with the youthful flamboyance or iconoclasm of Truffaut, Rivette, Chabrol, and Godard. Here, for example, is Rohmer's Renoir-like description of his cinematic style:

I do not like long shots, because I like to place the characters in a setting where they can be identified, and at the same time I like to put them so that they can be identified with the backgrounds. Therefore, if I put them in a long shot you won't see the people, and if I go to a close shot you won't see the décor. Instead of using a long shot, I would rather use a panning shot which describes the milieu to the audience in the same way a long shot would ... I ... have the camera move ... to show where [the characters go] without changing the frame. ... The camera does not move on its own authority. ... [I] think that [my] characters are bound to their environment, and that the environment has an effect upon them.("Interview with Éric Rohmer," *Cinema* [Los Angeles], Fall 1971)

Rohmer described this style shortly after completing *Claire's Knee* (1970), the fifth of his *Six Moral Tales*, for which it was completely appropriate. In the best of the *Moral Tales – My Night at Maud's* (1969) and *Chloe in the Afternoon* (1972) as well as *Claire's Knee* – the main characters, men, are self-absorbed and absorbed in the surfaces of life: primarily, the surfaces of beautiful women; the environments of these films, kept carefully in view, serve as moral comments on their heroes. Jérôme, for example, says in *Claire's Knee* that for him "looks don't count, only intellect," but the young woman he chooses to pursue and the setting in which he immerses himself (the tediously, nearly oppressively beautiful Lac d'Annecy on the Franco-Swiss border) indicate the opposite. The moral of these delicate little tales is "know thyself," and the frightening implication is that knowing oneself in a modern world where superficial beauty is prized above all else may be undesirable, if not impossible: beneath one's own surface, one may find nothing.

Rohmer has further described the style of the *Moral Tales* as (French) neoclassical: a style, that is, of restrained camera technique, distilled emotion, taut construction, and pointed language instead of overt action. Rohmer's style, however, replaces Racine's Catholic Jansenism with the German Heinrich von Kleist's Kantian subjectivism, which, paradoxically coexisting with Kleist's own neoclassical impulse, postulated that character is destiny and that feeling rather than reason dictates character and determines "truth." Surely, then, it was no accident that Rohmer came to film Kleist's novella *The Marquise of O.* (1976) after completing *Chloe in the Afternoon*, the last of the *Moral Tales*. And perhaps just as surely it was no accident that, in attempting to repeat the success of the *Moral Tales* in another series of six films, *Comedies and*

Proverbs, he would parody himself, in part because his new subject would be, not the superficiality of men who do not realize they are in love with surfaces, but instead the interiority of women who are learning to fall in love with essences.

Rohmer would be the Marivaux or Musset of cinema in the *Comedies and Proverbs*, in which he dramatizes the psychology of incipient love, the actions and reactions of his lovers – primarily his heroines – as they respond less to the external intrigue of romance than to the inner promptings of the heart. The drama of such "proverbial comedies" as *The Perfect Marriage* (1982), *Pauline at the Beach* (1985), and *Boyfriends and Girlfriends* (1987) is thus largely internal and as such belongs closer to the camera and even indoors, if not onstage, where we can concentrate on the revelations of language and gesture. Instead, Rohmer places these works mostly outdoors, where the environment takes on a role far in excess of the one it should have – its surfaces' even calling attention to themselves as surfaces rather than to what lies underneath. If Rohmer can be accused in these pictures, as were Marivaux and especially his imitators in their plays, of betraying the spareness of the neoclassical aesthetic with a profusion of rococo ornamentation, then the ornament here is visual, not verbal as in the case of French drama in the first half of the eighteenth century, and it often distracts from and finally contradicts the delicacy of what occurs between and beneath the lines. (By the time we get to the theatre of Musset in the first half of the nineteenth century, Marivaux's rococo elaboration of language is newly understood as the Romantic pursuit of expressiveness or self-expression.)

The internal lives of women or, better, the fluctuations and even fibrillations of their love lives, continue to occupy this director in his third series of films, *Tales of the Four Seasons*, of which *Autumn Tale* is the last. One might expect environment or setting to play a big part in the *Tales*, since their focus seems to be on the seasons as motivating factors in human behavior. However, the visual punctiliousness for which Rohmer has become known – or notorious – is appositely absent from these movies. *A Tale of Winter* (1992), for example, is not concerned with depicting wintry landscapes, but rather with chronicling the time of year between Christmas and New Year's as it affects a couple's "rebirth" or reconciliation. Hence what we see in winter are Paris and Nevers shorn of their picture-postcard or movie-travelogue, winter-wonderland beauty. There are no superficially inviting colors or backdrops on the screen in this movie as there were in such "proverbial comedies" as *The Aviator's Wife* (1980) and *Full Moon in Paris* (1984).

Furthermore, because of the weather we are indoors much of the time – precisely where we should be for a film whose drama is largely an interior one and therefore requires our concentration on matters of the spirit rather than the spiritings of matter, on the experience of time or season instead of the influence of space or environment.

Autumn Tale, for its part, takes place mostly outdoors in the Rhône valley of southern France. Nevertheless, once again, landscape is enlisted not as calendar art but as temporal contributor to the largely internal narrative – an internality that is all the more notable for being (gingerly) juxtaposed against the external beauty of this wine country. (Diane Baratier's color cinematography consists mainly of crisp medium shots that avoid the two visual extremes of "autumnal" pictures: pretty, full and long shots suffused with the golden, heartening glow of the fall sun, or intense close-ups of melancholy faces in autumn rain, amidst falling leaves.) Harvest time has come to the vineyards of the Rhône valley, and it is in the mellowing effect of this time on his characters that Rohmer is interested, not in the lush harvest itself. Thus his film's title has a double meaning: not only have the valley's grapes ripened, but four of its inhabitants – the principal figures in *Autumn Tale* – have come to that mature age of forty-five or so when the reality of winter, or the fact of mortality, first comes into view.

The film revolves around two friends: the friskily dignified Isabelle, who owns a bookshop in Montélimar and lives in the countryside (with a husband who is irrelevant to the story as well as a daughter who is soon to be married), and Magali, her friend since childhood, a widowed mother of two grown children who runs a vineyard in the vicinity. A wiry, vital woman with snapping eyes, pouty mouth, and an unruly bush of hair, Magali is very much interested in remarrying but believes that it is too late – and too difficult (particularly out in the country) – to find a man. When Isabelle suggests placing a personal ad, her simultaneously proud and shy best friend is revolted by the idea. So Isabelle secretly places such an ad in the local newspaper, seeking a suitable suitor and presenting herself as her friend. When the courtly Gérald, a divorced businessman, responds, Isabelle interviews him extensively over several lunches before revealing to her dumbfounded date that she is merely acting as an unbidden liaison for someone else.

Complicating matters is the fact that the only other person to whom Magali feels close is Rosine, the girlfriend of her callow son, Léo. Magali feels that Rosine is too good for her own child, while Rosine says she loves Léo's mother more than she loves him. But the two women do not, as a result, unite in a trendy lesbian love relationship: instead, the

Marie Rivière, as Isabelle, and Alain Libolt, as Gérald, consider the romantic possibilities in *Autumn Tale*.

younger woman tries to fix the older one up with her ex-lover and former philosophy professor, the fortysomething Étienne. These two are no match, however, partly because Étienne is still smitten with Rosine in particular and younger ladies in general. He even heavily flirts with a new woman at the climactic wedding of Isabelle's daughter – which is where he meets Magali for the first time and she is introduced to Gérald.

They happen to be drawn to each other – and before they receive any formal introductions – though Magali is not at all pleased when she learns the manner in which Isabelle has brought them together, while Gérald for his part is still disappointed that Isabelle was just a surrogate for her best friend. So is she disappointed, it seems, for she not only flirts with Gérald at her daughter's wedding, she also gives him something more than a friendly kiss – a kiss interrupted by a startled Magali. At the very end of *Autumn Tale*, though Magali and Gérald have made a date for the feast to celebrate the end of harvest season, it is not this couple that we see, but rather a pensive Isabelle dancing with her oblivious husband to a sprightly, accordion-accompanied folk song. The final image fades to black on the sublimated face of this *femme d'un certain âge*, who earlier had revealingly told Gérald, "I want all men to love me, especially those that I don't love."

If the preceding plot summary sounds like the description of a French bedroom farce *à la* Feydeau, it well could be except for a few, signal ingredients. First, Rohmer is, of his own admission, a practicing if sometimes reluctant Catholic (like yours truly). Therefore, in *Autumn Tale* as in his other films (particularly *Chloe in the Afternoon*), he continually toys with temptation of a moral kind. Yet, unlike the farceur, he does not let his flirtation with temptation slide into the banality of carnality. For Rohmer the Catholic, as opposed to Feydeau the amoralist, that banality contains bane as well – hence the providential design of Rohmer's cinema as opposed to the mechanical one of farce. Design for him, because he is a Catholic, is not an independent, mathematically schematic truth. Design is not simply a question of intricate plotting, as it was for the nineteenth-century farceur whose plots (consisting of human parts) dramatically reconstituted the well-oiled machines of an era of rapid industrialization and technological advancement.

Design for Rohmer – the very power intelligently to conceive it – is a chief spiritual clarity, and chief manifestation of the Spirit, amidst the physical chaos of existence. (The very fact that he likes to work in clusters, as in his *Moral Tales, Comedies and Proverbs*, and *Tales of the Four Seasons*, is another warrant of design.) And this means that, together with the design, one must create sentient, articulate, inspired characters of a kind not seen in farce, where single-minded, one-dimensional figures are ultimately dehumanized by their object pursuit of sensual gratification. (Thus does Rohmer marry, in *Tales of the Four Seasons*, Jansenist determinism to Kantian subjectivism.) One way to approach the films of Éric Rohmer, in which assorted combinations of attractive, cultivated Europeans rearrange their lives amid much exquisitely verbalized soul-searching, is to see them (particularly if you are a non-believer) as sophisticated fairy tales in which, despite what setbacks characters may encounter, an overarching plan emerges in the end that replaces confusion and disappointment with order and acceptance. Along the way, rational decision-making is rewarded, just as is the trust of one's deepest intuitions. True love (never adulterated lust) – or the closest one can come to such romance in this life – is the ultimate reward, but it cannot be savored or even intimated until every moral quandary has been aired and somehow resolved. Hence the anti-climactic nature of

Rohmer's climaxes, which come at the end of stories whose telling, not their ultimate predictability, makes them such rich, emotionally satisfying experiences. And that telling consists of emotional as well as intellectual dissection along a continuum – of measuring the vacillations or vibrations of introspective love – rather than emotional and mental upheaval that moves toward a genuinely dramatic peak.

That telling also consists of verbal comedy, in contrast to the physical kind found in farce. *Autumn Tale* is, after all, a romantic, not a sex, comedy, although to the extent that Rohmer satirizes the modern French professional class, with its highly civilized code of behavior, advanced educational level, and leisure to indulge in amorous whim, the film is also a comedy of manners. Albeit a gentle one, and in this sense Rohmer's latest, perhaps last picture has something in common with both Verdi's light, feathery, and benevolent late masterpiece, *Falstaff* (1893), and Shakespeare's majestic, magical, ultimately mysterious final play, *The Tempest* (1611) – each of which signifies the sublime stage of (let us call it) distilled humanism at which its author had arrived.

Here's one example of such humane distillation in *Autumn Tale*: the sullen Léo, who doesn't seem to like his mother very much, is appalled by Rosine's "monstrous" attempt to match Magali and Étienne, which he views as a kind of Oedipal scenario in which his romantic rival would become his stepfather. "Kids shouldn't mess in their parents' lives," Léo explains, to which Rosine responds that Étienne is not her father. In age, however, he could be, and he could become her father-in-law if he were to marry Magali and Rosine were to marry Léo. What Magali's son fails to realize, though – and it is this piece of information that puts the humorous topping on this particular cake – is that his girlfriend has no intention of marrying him or even of being his girlfriend any longer. He's a bit obtuse, then; she's a trifle manipulative, like Isabelle; and Étienne is really in love with himself. But none do, or come to, any harm in the divineness of Rohmer's comedy, and, unbeknownst to her at this point, Magali will finally separate herself from her friends' machinations at the same time as she tastes the fruit of their wiles.

She's played with just the right amount of moodiness by Béatrice Romand, who made her film début, at age fifteen, in *Claire's Knee* and has since appeared in several other Rohmer pictures, including *The Green Ray* (1986). Marie Rivière, who brings far more than the requisite volatility to Isabelle, also acted in *The Green Ray*, having first collaborated with Rohmer on *Perceval* (1978). Together these two women show why *Autumn Tale* has been labeled a "women's picture" and

Rohmer a "women's director," for they act (and he directs them to act) less as if they are taking action (*à la* a men's action-adventure picture) than displaying the action that is within them; less as if action need ultimately be physical or corporeal than that it must fundamentally be mental. For Isabelle, Magali, and their *auteur*, then, cogent thought and articulate speech are the bases of humane action if not forms of action themselves.

As for the two principal men in *Autumn Tale*, Étienne and Gérald, they are performed with resource by Didier Sandre and Alain Libolt, respectively – a resource that, in their case, comes from considerable experience as stage actors. Libolt may be the more impressive in the mercurial play of his nimble mind and fretted emotions, but Sandre may have the more difficult role, not only because his character is out of his element here (the element of the *Six Moral Tales*), but also because he must play a student of philosophies whose personal philosophy appears not to probe any deeper than the nearest pretty female face and figure. It was the almost classical musicality of Sandre's and the other actors' language (the *French* language, let us not forget) – in its symmetrical order and rhythmic completeness – that makes me unable to say, even to this day, whether *Autumn Tale* has background music. Claude Marti gets credit for a musical score, but all that I can – or perhaps want to – remember is the music of spoken words.

I remember the actual music from Olivier Assayas's *Late August, Early September* (1999), partly because it consists chiefly of the haunting, elusive guitar work of Mali's legendary Ali Farka Touré, partly because the characters in this film don't stand still long enough to expound in the beautifully rounded sentences of Rohmer's people. Nor, unlike Rohmer's camera, does Assayas's (in Denis Lenoir's hands) remain stationary for any length of time: it is almost always on the move, shoulder-borne, and up close. Thus shot *vérité*-style in natural light as well as in Super-16, which desaturates the picture's turquoise-dominated color scheme, *Late August, Early September* could not look more different than *Autumn Tale*, or from such previous films by Assayas himself as *A New Life* (1993) and *Paris Awakes* (1991). In his latest feature this writer-director (and, like Rohmer, former member of the editorial board of *Cahiers du cinéma*) may return to the subject matter of these earlier movies, but the formal dexterity he revealed for the first time in *Irma Vep* remains on display.

And that dexterity is an appropriate match for the speed of the lives of Assayas's thirtysomething Parisians, who may reflect on career and mortality but who, unlike the characters in *Autumn Tale*, seem unable to resign themselves to the constrictions of either work or life as they move, hand-to-mouth, from one job and one domicile to another. Assayas follows his four main subjects from late August of one year to early September of *the next*, and his title is meant not only to suggest the rapidity with which time passes as one advances in age but also to refer to a time in life (late summer, which is not the same as Rohmer's mid-autumn) when the easy indolence of youth is ending and the hard work of adulthood – of figuring out who you really are and what you most want to do – is beginning. Calling his narrative perspective "kalei-doscopic" and even "Cubist," Assayas has pointed to David Hockney's Polaroid collages of fragmented landscapes as a model for his style. Despite its division into six titled episodes, however, *Late August, Early September* doesn't actually have a multifocal structure, let alone a con-sistently *Rashomon*-like, relativistic one in which the information we get from the protagonist in one episode is contextualized, questioned, and then offset in subsequent episodes by the perspectives of the other characters. (The only otherwise narrative picture in recent memory that I would call Cubist is Jim Jarmusch's *Mystery Train* [1989].) Nor need the film have such a structure, for its approach to character and human dealings is oblique or elliptical enough, as it centers on the effect of the illness and death of the oldest of its *dramatis personae*, the just-turned-forty Adrien Willer, on the group of friends who surround him.

Late August, Early September is thus more concerned with Adrien's social death than his physical one (we never learn, for example, the name of his terminal illness, nor do we witness his death throes), more interested in unraveling the tangles of dependence and indepen-dence that mark friendships inflected with artistic ambition than in investigating the nature of artistic creation itself. For Adrien Willer is a serious writer of (four) overlooked novels whose seriousness – and desire to be taken seriously by a wider public – infects all those who come into contact with him. Chief among them is Gabriel Deshayes, the protagonist, a would-be writer caught between his old relationship with an intelligent woman (Jenny) who romanticizes their past together and his new relationship with a gorgeous girlfriend (Anne) who lives in a continuous present of manic lust (for other men as well as for him). Clever but not necessarily smart, Gabriel seems to admire the fact that Adrien writes more than *what* Adrien writes; and although fascinated by the idea of creating imaginative literature, the most the younger man can bring himself to attempt – until late in the film – is ancillary or middleman work like editing, translating, and journalistic ghostwriting. (One of his projects is the making of a television documentary about his author-friend.)

Psychologically, the difficult and distracted – yet forceful and fatherly – Adrien looms over Gabriel in an obviously longstanding Oedipal relationship. And while it devastates Gabriel even to think of losing Adrien, there is also the promise of liberation in the prospect of his mentor's death. So much so that by the end of *Late August, Early September*, the "son" is not only working on his own novel, he is also eyeing the sixteen-year-old former lover (Véra) of his deceased elder, wearing some of the latter's clothing, and disparaging Adrien's well-received, posthumously published fiction before an audience of young Willer-aficionados. ("You die and you're a genius," Gabriel opines. "His best books were ahead of him.") Gabriel's ex-girlfriend Jenny – in whom Adrien had confided more than anyone else – for her part has moved on to a relationship with an Adrien-surrogate: his former literary agent, Jérémie.

Gabriel is played by the boyish, urchin-like, even slightly feral Mathieu Amalric, who performed a role not unlike this one in Desplechin's *My Sex Life, or How I Got Into an Argument*. With his darting eyes and rumpled look, he is not always easy to read, but that's because – paradoxically for a movie about individualistic overachievers – his character is defined less in and of itself than in relationship to the other, equally uncertain or insecure characters (for whom the same is true). Accordingly, the actors in *Late August, Early September* not only act as an ensemble, playing or glancing off one another, they, or their characters, take their very existence from it. This is true even of Jeanne Balibar, playing Jenny, who in any one scene "does" more or is theatrically "busier" than her fellow actors. Blessed with the uncanny ability to express three conflicting emotions at one time, Balibar gives Jenny a quirky, skittish presence – all nose, eyebrows, and gangling limbs – somehow focused by her offbeat beauty and crooked smile. She and Amalric, who are a couple off-screen as well, are becoming the contemporary face of the thirtyish urban-educated French couple, having appeared opposite each other over a three-year period in *Late August, Early September* and *My Sex Life, or How I Got Into an Argument* (where Balibar brought great intensity to the damaged young philosophy student), and in Jean-Claude Biette's *Three Bridges Over the River* (1999).

As for Adrien and Anne, they are played, respectively, by the Dustin Hoffmanish François Cluzet and by Virginie Ledoyen, that luminous presence last seen in Benoît Jacquot's *Single Girl* (1995). Cluzet is as grave and thoughtful as Assayas's screenplay makes him, though per-

Mathieu Amalric, as Gabriel, and Jeanne Balibar, as Jenny, in a light moment from *Late August, Early September*.

haps not as cruel and manipulative as reported by the bitter Lucie (a woman his own age with whom he had once lived for ten years). This is not necessarily to fault Cluzet: it may have been his and the director's intention, in so "kaleidoscopic" a narrative, to portray Adrien in one way but to have someone close to the man see him from a different angle. As the least "developed" of *Late August, Early September*'s principal characters, Ledoyen's Anne is viewed more or less only from the angle of her quasi-kinky sexuality, whose calibrated tics and twitches the actress handles well enough. An unmarried woman she continues to be, but one whose dependent and carnally defined, impulsive and nearly self-destructive character here is the opposite of lone Valérie Sergent's in *A Single Girl*.

Indeed, sex for Anne is a kind of compulsive (pre)occupation and, as such, has its place in *Late August, Early September*, which is less about love and relationships than work and ambition. *Late August, Early September* may not be about Rohmerian men who are totally absorbed in the surfaces of beautiful women, but neither is it about Rohmerian women who desperately yearn to fall in love with essences. Assayas's primary character is in fact a man, Gabriel – and, by extension, his alter ego Adrien – whose obsession with literary achievement rules his professional as well as his social existence. So much so that he no longer has time for romantic love of the kind articulated in Rohmer's cinema; animalistic lust is now his game, although even that he plays sporadically. (Not by accident, Gabriel does so with Anne, an "interior" designer of household surfaces and furnishings, and potentially with the teenaged Véra, who can know little of real love but much of passing infatuation.) On the one hand, Gabriel's desire for intellectual success in a materialistic world is commendable, and perhaps only in France could one encounter such a figure on the screen as well as in the movie audience. On the other hand, he would achieve that success of mind at the expense of close family ties (represented by his happily married, disapproving brother Thomas, who lives in the country with his wife and children) and lifelong or longtime friends (of whom we see none).

Maybe, Assayas is suggesting, Gabriel and others like him – perhaps including the filmmaker himself – have no choice but so to isolate themselves even in France, where increasingly, as in the rest of the West (the world?), people are judged according to how much money they make for the goods they produce. Maybe, for the Gabriels of this earth, the permanence and form of artistic work take the place of the instability, fleetingness, or amorphousness of their lives. Art, for these individuals, consequently becomes a species of life, while their actual lives take on the character of laborious work. (That the fifth of the six episodes in *Late August, Early September* is cryptically titled "The Joseph Beuys Drawing" is evidence Assayas had such a theme in mind. The German Beuys's "happenings," "actions," and "installations," products of his theory of "Social Sculpture" as well as his association with the avant-garde group Fluxus, were based on the related – but altered – premise that "life is art, and art is life.") And we leave Gabriel on the verge of such life-giving artistic achievement, which may seem like a slight payoff for the diffuse plot, with its trail of vignettes, that has preceded. But a "verge" is often a precarious place, and Assayas leaves us there, without tidy formal closure, precisely so that we can ponder the limits of art and aspiration – his own as well as Gabriel Deshayes's.

13

All about My, Your, Their Mother

On Zambrano's *Solas* (1999, Spain)
and Waddington's *Me, You, Them* (2000, Brazil)

Pedro Almodóvar continues to be the most overrated European director now at work. Perhaps this is because he's from Spain, which until
the death of Franco in 1975 censored film to such an extent that directors could express "subversive" ideas only in the form of elaborately
veiled metaphors. Their movies were thus made nearly impenetrable to
a wide foreign audience – that is, if they were lucky enough to reach
one. Well, there's nothing impenetrable, or even subtle, about Almodóvar's work: he's transparent, tasteless, *and* Spanish, and therefore a
quick sell to audiences who like their trash dressed up in European
artiness, in pseudo-daring, the more exotic the better. In his case, complete freedom of artistic expression has only revealed how little art he
has to express.

Almodóvar's films (all with screenplays by him) contain sex without
being about sex, let alone passion. They feature neurotic urbanites –
mainly women – without exploring their neuroses. And these movies
include comedy not because they spring from a comic vision, from
comic seriousness, but because they are the product of an impoverished imagination, which will always resort to the cheap or sensational
laugh rather than confront the artistic possibilities of its own creation.
Throw in gratuitous symbolism, lots of cinematic self-reference, a self-
consciously removed camera, and a designer color scheme that says
more about the art director's taste in fashion than it does about either
Almodóvar's characters or the world they inhabit, and you have – in
High Heels (1991), *Tie Me Up! Tie Me Down!* (1989), *Women on the Verge*

of a Nervous Breakdown (1988), *The Law of Desire* (1987), and *Dark Habits* (1983) – films only a postmodernist could love.

Almodóvar, who prefers to be known by the single surname even at this relatively early stage in his career, has already been compared to Luis Buñuel, but the comparison should stop at their country of origin. Working mainly in France and Mexico, Buñuel certainly made his share of bad films. But at his best, in such pictures as *L'Age d'Or* (1930), *Viridiana* (1961), and *That Obscure Object of Desire* (1977), he could do what Almodóvar cannot: combine surreal fantasy, religious irreverence, sexual commentary, and social criticism in meaningful, passionate ways. Almodóvar's is a camp sensibility out to do little more than express its own sense of homosexual disenfranchisement in a predominantly heterosexual world, and in this sense his movies are not-so-elaborately veiled metaphors that, unlike their metaphorical counterparts made during Franco's reign, are guilty of moral dishonesty. He has said that he speaks for all the disenfranchised of this world, especially women, but in reality he speaks only for himself and his camp followers. That is why his films have the flat, hysterical feel of all propaganda.

Finally, we get an antidote to the poison of Pedro Almodóvar in the best Spanish film to reach these shores since Carlos Saura's *Ay, Carmela!* (1990):[1] *Solas* (1999), the feature début of thirty-three-year-old Benito Zambrano, who wrote as well as directed. Tellingly, *Solas* is set in Seville, in the southern region (formerly province) of Andalusia (where it was shot on a mere $750,000 budget), not in Madrid or Barcelona, in the northern part of the country, where Spanish filmmaking – Almodóvar's in particular – is concentrated. Zambrano probably filmed in the south because, unlike Almodóvar, he is concerned with what is traditionally Spanish as well as with the new Spain that emerged with the advent of democracy in the mid-1970s. And nowhere in this country is the dichotomy between the old world and the new clearer than in Andalusia, with its major port city of Seville on the Guadalquivir River. That *Solas* may have been intended as a counteractive response to Almodóvar is also suggested by its dedication, "For my mother, for all mothers," which is the same dedication that accompanied Almodóvar's most recent movie, *All about My Mother* (1999).

---

1 Saura's latest picture is one more "down" in his up-and-down career: *Goya in Bordeaux* (2000), an unusually photographed but nonetheless sentiment-streaked, canonizing biopic about the final years of French exile of the eighty-two-year-old Spanish artist (born, like Saura, in the province of Aragon in northeastern Spain).

Typically, however, *All about My Mother* is more about sex (or "alter-native" sexuality), drugs, and the woman trapped inside Almodóvar than it is about mothers or motherhood. *Solas*, by contrast, is about a genuine mother and her daughter, who is a mother-to-be. Their lives have been spent in inner isolation, hence the picture's title – which translates as "alone" but has more to do with loneliness than with the literal fact of being alone. Those who speak English may also associate Zambrano's title with the word "solace," which is derived from the Mid-dle English word "solas" and, of course, means "comfort or consola-tion." As one might guess, the double nature of this film's title bespeaks the double nature of its narrative, its theme, and its major characters. But, with the possible exception of its ending or coda, *Solas* is no Span-ish *Stella Dallas* (1937), no tearjerker or soap opera content to indulge in bathos and banality for their own sordid sake. This quiet, quietly moving movie is a paean – or paella – to unconditional love, selfless renunciation, and human dignity in a cinematic world shorn of sex, violence, visual or verbal pyrotechnics, even the plottiness we've come to expect from conventional fiction films.

Solas immediately establishes one aspect of the title's meaning by iso-lating its key female figures in the opening scene. On the other side of a hospital window, Rosa, the mother, observes her husband, who has just undergone major surgery and must now breathe through a respi-rator. A rural inhabitant who had traveled to Seville only for her hus-band's operation, the sixtyish Rosa has been staying at the hospital, but the doctor suggests that she move in with her thirty-five-year-old daugh-ter, María, who lives by herself in the city. The two women are clearly estranged, however, from each other as well as from their husband-father. And we realize this when the camera quickly finds the daughter, not next to her mother (who is called only Mother throughout the film) or at her father's side, but in a waiting room impatiently smoking a cigarette. Without benefit of dialogue, Zambrano's camera has thus shown us three family members, each of them alone or apart – emo-tionally as well as physically or spatially.

The father, even while recovering in the hospital, is a mean-mouthed tyrant who grunts, growls, and glares at his eternally patient, long-suf-fering wife from his bed. (His daughter goes to his bedside only once during the picture, but they do not speak.) A sour, primitive, grasping old peasant, this is one of those hard men who mask dependency as dominance; over the years, that dominance has taken the form of phys-ical abuse of Rosa and María as well as drunkenness, womanizing, and gambling. His daughter is definitely her father's child – one of four, in fact, including two boys, who have since fled to northern Spain, and one girl, who married at a very young age. For she shares his bad temper, taste for alcohol, urge to gamble, and even his keen sense of smell (but not his promiscuity). Yet María hates her father not only for the violence he visited upon her but also for having refused to pay for any higher education for his only unmarried daughter. This otherwise attractive (if gaunt-faced) and intelligent but no-longer-young woman thus finds herself in a dead-end urban existence that consumes her with anxiety, rage, and bitterness.

At the start of *Solas* she has just moved into a once elegant but now faded apartment house in the dangerous, run-down neighborhood of San Bernardo in Seville, despite the fact that she doesn't have a job. And the only job we see María get – as a cleaning woman working the night shift in a luxe office building – we watch her quickly lose. She is dismissed because she loathes her bosses and co-workers in addition to the rich businessmen who pass her by in the corridors as if she doesn't exist. To make matters worse, María has managed to get involved with a man as cruelly insensitive as her father: the burly truck driver Juan, who uses her for sex, gets her pregnant because he refuses to wear a condom, then peremptorily declines to accompany his girlfriend to an (expense-free) abortion clinic. Small wonder, then, that María is a bundle of raw nerves, exposed, and that she can barely abide, let alone respect, the mother who for years has put up with a "john" of her own.

Mother – stolid yet solid, taciturn but comprehending, illiterate at the same time as she is wise – has spent her life kowtowing to a man who treats her like garbage, calls her stupid and ugly, and accuses her of being with other men. In Seville, moreover, she defers to a daughter who rails against the world and its injustices while never taking the time to realize that, if anyone has a right to curse her fate, it is her mother. Yet Mother understands both her daughter and her husband and selflessly lives with the two of them in the mode that is required for each. She knows that she is not really close to either, but closeness seems to matter less to her than faithfulness or devotion.

Plainly dressed and stockily built, thick-faced and weather-beaten, this lone maternal figure appears lost in the big city, whether she is slowly traversing the polished hallways of the hospital or haltingly navigating the mean streets of San Bernardo. (She manages to negotiate the neighborhood branch of Seville's bus line, but pay phones on the street present an insurmountable challenge.) Still, Mother knows her way around a home, and, despite an unenthusiastic reception from María, she gradually begins to make a difference in her daughter's existence by adding color and life to the latter's stark, drab, mildew-suffused apartment. Just a few flights up from a neighborhood tavern frequented (with the exception of María) exclusively by tough hombres, this place has only one window – and it opens up onto a brick wall.

Aside from bestowing her own luminous spirit on the dwelling, Mother's first act of kindness is to bring home one flowering plant, then another; next she adorns the place with a rocker that someone else has discarded; and, throughout her stay, she buys fresh food, cooks, and cleans. She also knits a sleeveless cardigan for her daughter (together with a pink outfit for the baby girl born to her husband's doctor). In each of these nurturing acts she is every mother who ever watched a grown-up child struggle through life, swallowed her sadness and disapproval, and silently did what she could to help. Help for this woman seems even to include "possessing" the apartment when María is not present. It is as if – merely by alternately sitting there and searching out its every corner – she were warding off evil spirits or filling a vacancy with an abiding humanity that for too long this space has done without.

That help does not include introducing María to religion, though Mother's grave profession that she has a clear conscience – together with four other distinctive acts – suggests both that Rosa Jiminez Peña is a devoutly religious woman and that Benito Zambrano is more than interested in his narrative's Christian overtones. Those acts are the tending of a bloody hand-wound her daughter has suffered at work (and suffers for much of the picture), three times requesting that María accept the invitation to be godmother to her cousin Isabelita's child (without the knowledge, which she never receives, that María herself is pregnant), twice giving money to a blind beggar on the street, and lighting the lights of a crèche (even though it is not Christmas) left behind by the previous tenant of María's apartment. Mother's most charitable act, however, is to introduce María to her own downstairs neighbor, a courtly old pensioner who lives alone with his loyal, well-behaved German shepherd, Achilles, and is desperate for the warmth of human companionship.

This elderly but handsome fellow (who, like María's father, remains unnamed throughout *Solas*) initiates contact with Mother by lending her some money at the grocery store. Through sharing food, gossip, and Achilles with him, Mother poignantly learns, over the course of only a matter of days, how life might have been had she married so kindly, dignified, and respectful a man. Indeed, their friendship begins to turn into a courtship – certainly as far as the widower is concerned.

This courtship is emphasized in the editing (by Fernando Pardo) through the juxtaposition of scenes at the hospital with Rosa's surly, vituperative husband against scenes at the apartment building with María's caring, gracious *vecino* (or "neighbor," as he's listed in the credits). But Mother is too traditional ever to have an affair, however much she may treat this old gentleman like a surrogate husband. At one point she even lovingly tends to him when he is stricken with diarrhea, calmly coping with the mess he has made, good-humoredly preserving his dignity as she showers him, and gently putting him to bed under the watchful eyes of the ever-loyal Achilles.

In perhaps the most overpowering of their several touching (but never sugary) scenes together, Mother and man exchange the following words at their parting:

NEIGHBOR: May I write to you?
ROSA: I can't read.
NEIGHBOR: May I call you?
ROSA: We have no telephone.
NEIGHBOR: May I leave a message with one of your neighbors?
ROSA: We have no neighbors.
NEIGHBOR: May I visit you?
ROSA: Stop. We're acting like children. If I return to Seville to visit my daughter, I'll come by to see you.

Alas, Rosa never returns, but her influence is felt in the budding friendship between María and the widower, who, prior to the mother's visit, had not yet spoken to each other and probably never would have done so in this anomie-driven, anonymous big city.

After eliciting from María the solemn promise that she will serve as godmother to Isabelita's baby, Mother leaves her daughter not only with the sleeveless cardigan she knitted. She also gives her some money, new as well as old photographs of the two of them together, and several balls of pink yarn. The old woman leaves the old neighbor with what seems like very little but in fact is much more: in addition to his memories of her, a fish he bought especially so that they could share it, but that she never had the time to prepare. That fish (a bass expertly selected by the pensioner, who says he's far better at choosing fish than beef in the marketplace) becomes the centerpiece of this gentleman's first meal with María, during which they also drink wine, play cards, and discuss their mutual sorrows. She says she had never eaten bass before but likes it immensely; and the metaphorical implication is that, by partaking of the fish, a traditional symbol of Christ, the aptly named María has for the first time begun to partake in a compassionate, mutually beneficial, spiritualized relationship with a man. For that is exactly what her first communion with this *vecino* will become.

After María reveals to him that she is pregnant by a man who has no intention of marrying her and that she is still considering getting an abortion, these two get into a pro-choice, pro-life argument. María wants the baby, she says, but fears not only that she will be unable to support it but also that she may repeat the sin of her father and physically abuse the child. The old neighbor counters by offering to pay child support out of his pension, in return for the rights of an adoptive grandfather. (His only child, a son, died at a young age before he could marry or father children.) She thinks he's mad or senile; he knows he's serious and thinks she is disrespectful. As the old man begins to weep and asks for a cup of tea, María says she'll think about his offer of a kind of platonic or custodial union – after which she addresses him as "Grandpa." They have talked late into the night, and, appositely, it is now dawn. "God has given us one more day," the widower declares, then the film cuts to a shot of Mother at home in the country, smiling as she lies in the sun and falls asleep (with the suggestion that it won't be long before the "big sleep" overtakes her).

This is where *Solas* should have ended, with a slow fade-out on Mother's image. Instead, we get a syrupy coda in which, as María and her *vecino* visit a cemetery with their (grand)child in tow, she tells her deceased mother the following in voice-over: the baby is named Rosa, in honor of her grandmother; María and "Grandpa" will soon move from Seville to the countryside, for the child's sake; and she still sees men her own age, one in particular, though she regrets that her pensioner isn't a bit younger. As this odd couple leaves the grave site of María's mother, as well as that of her father, and slowly walks off into the distance in long shot, the superfluous coda ends.

It's superfluous not only because we could have guessed or imagined all of this on our own. The coda is also superfluous because the first "ending" left open the realistic possibility that María would have rejected the widower's offer. But, touched by his generosity as well as by her mother's magnanimity, she would have had the baby anyway, would not have denied the old man access to her child, and wouldn't have terminated their mutually beneficial, neighborly relationship. And the reasons for her rejection of the pensioner's offer would be clear: his advanced age together with María's consequent need to provide for herself and her little girl in the long run. (This she could do either through rewarding work of her own or through marriage to a younger, equally companionable man – perhaps that "one in particular" she mentions in her voice-over.)

Solas's coda may be excessive, then, but nothing else is in this film (which, incidentally, was nominated for eleven Goya awards, the Spanish equivalent of the Oscars). Let's start with Antonio Meliveo's background music for piano and violin, which is discreetly melancholy or delicately plaintive. It is neither overscored nor overorchestrated (sometimes consisting of only a single, repeated note on the soundtrack) and, thank God, never resorts to a heavenly choir in order to push our emotional buttons. *Solas* hits all the right notes, paradoxically, by not hitting them, or by letting its images and acting speak for themselves. Let me give you one (additional) example from the *mise en scène* – whose camera, in Tote Trenas' hands, assiduously eschews the quick, misty-eyed close-up for the sober, lengthy medium-to-full shot, and judiciously opts for nuanced or shaded color over the eye-candy kind mass-produced by the movie industry everywhere in the world.

This instance occurs at about mid-point in the picture when, following her boyfriend Juan's declaration, "If you want a husband, look somewhere else," María departs his company for the last time. She's in a warehouse district, so in addition to the trucking garage where she meets Juan, there are railroad tracks full of freight cars. As María begins to cross those tracks on her way home, she hears a train coming and appears to think of throwing herself in front of it. Then the train inexorably speeds by, blotting out her image except for the six times or so we see her in millisecond frames in the gaps between the cars. After the train passes, we see the real reason for María's nervous hyperventilation: not the anticipation of her own suicide, but the fear that someone else, with a child, would accidentally be run down by the successive railroad cars. (In fact, no one gets hurt.) Thus, without a word of dialogue or a note of music, Zambrano has conveyed the change that this woman is about to undergo at the crossroads of her life, as a result of the benign intervention of her mother. That change is from hate-filled isolation and self-pity or self-justification to pregnant fellow-feeling and self-denial or self-sacrifice; from living death to life lived in emulation of her dead mother's nurturing model.

María is played by Ana Fernández, but "played" is probably the wrong word, since there seems to be nothing "acted" about this character's experience. In a role that could easily have devolved into one hysterical, histrionic fit after another, Fernández carefully balances her portrayal of María in such a way that this woman's angry, gray weariness is complemented by a persistent ray of slim hope. Fernández knows that depicting anger on screen is relatively easy – it's a shortcut to feeling. So, aided by Zambrano's script as well as his direction, she doesn't take the easy way out and makes her character all the more compelling as a result. No easy way out was available to María Galiana, the mother, whose difficult job was to portray watchful, unselfish, heartbreakingly noble devotion unaided even by very much dialogue. Her character's outward emotions limited to small gestures and seemingly involuntary looks, Galiana reveals once and for all, through the sheer intensity of her concentration and commitment, that neither psychologically revealing words nor externally imposing actions need be a component of great acting. (Galiana appears here in her first leading role, after playing small parts in twenty movies over the past decade, including that of the brothel owner in the 1994 Oscar-winner for best foreign language film, *Belle Époque*.)

I haven't seen nearly silent film acting as good as this since Chieko Higashiyama's rendition of the mother in Yasujiro Ozu's masterly *Tokyo Story* (1953). And about Carlos Alvarez-Novoa's performance as the old neighbor, I can say something similar: it reminded me of Carlo Battisti in a comparable role, as a pensioner with a dog as his closest companion, in Vittorio De Sica's own masterwork titled *Umberto D*. The professional Alvarez-Novoa is naturally a bit more polished, more studied, less raw, than the non-professional Battisti, but the Spanish actor manages nonetheless to vitalize his somewhat familiar part with warmth, charm, and geniality. The cast of *Solas* is superbly rounded out by Juan Fernandez as María's boyfriend, Paco De Osca as her father, and Antonio Dechent as his doctor. Each of them, in his own way, creates a multinote performance out of a one-note role.

The cast of the Brazilian *Me, You, Them* (2000) is equally excellent, if its subject is the opposite: not loneliness, isolation, or apartness, but togetherness, consolidation, and accommodation. This is thirty-one-year-old Andrucha Waddington's second picture (with a screenplay by Elena Soaréz) after a brief career making commercials and music videos. But a Brasil! tourist brochure – like *Woman on Top* (1999) and *Bossa Nova* (2000) – *Me, You, Them* decidedly is not. Nor, despite superficial similarities between the two works, is it a prurient piece of magic or fantastic realism like the Brazilian *Dona Flor and Her Two Husbands* (1978). Neither is *Me, You, Them* a travelogue of a romantic comedy-drama such as *Bye Bye Brazil* (1980) or a sentimental road picture akin to *Central Station* (1998). Unlike the latter product of Brazil, *Me, You, Them* did not receive an Oscar nomination for best foreign language film,[2] but, similar to *Central Station*, it does treat characters from the lower rungs of Brazilian society. This time, however, we're not even in the big, transport-rich city of Rio de Janeiro; instead, *Me, You, Them* is set in the state of Bahia in the remote northeastern interior – one of the most impoverished areas of the Americas, and therefore the perfect place, as I shall argue, for a folk tale of polyandry, as opposed to a patrician drama of polygyny (which you can find in the Chinese *Raise the Red Lantern* [1991]).

Me, You, Them is based on the true story of Marlene de Silva Saboia, who was in her early fifties in 1995 when a Brazilian television station broadcast a special, seen by Andrucha Waddington in Rio, about her unconventional domestic arrangement. In macho country, here she was living under the same roof at the same time with three husbands (only one of them being her legal spouse), each of whom had fathered children by her. "Wow, great story!" was Waddington's response. "But we saw that it would not work in truth. It was too flat. So Elena Soaréz and I retained the archetypes from the original report – the tough guy, the friendly one, and the handsome chap – and we also retained the character of the woman, a strapping, good-natured rustic. But, with my help, Soaréz constructed the plot so that it would be better." The result is an improbable mélange of rural neorealism, daytime soap opera, and late-night sex comedy, whose narrative of romantic complication is less a plot than simply a series of events that unfolds in as graceful, low-key, even relaxed a manner as could be imagined.

When we first meet the heroine, Darlene Lima, she is visibly pregnant and preparing to leave her mother's home in this dry, dusty, desolate corner of Brazil. Here the dazzlingly blue skies may be beautiful but very little else is, in what appears to be a perpetual autumn featuring leafless trees and arid waterholes. (The cinematographer Breno Silveira, however, makes the most of his palette of reds, browns, and

---

2 As usual where the Academy Awards are concerned, the more maternal, sentimental, *and* proletarian, the better: *Madame Rosa* (1977), the French prototype for *Central Station*, itself won the Oscar for best foreign-language film. This occurred mostly because Simone Signoret's maudlin performance as an aging madam, who earns her keep by sheltering prostitutes' children, makes that of Fernanda Montenegro (as a spinster-turned-foster mother) in *Central Station* look positively restrained by comparison. For the Czech rendition of such mawkishness, see *Kolya* (1996) – another Oscar-winner – with a middle-aged male in the central role.

ochres under varying kinds of light: the sunrises and sunsets, the blistering midday glare, the snug intimacies as well as deep shadows created by lamplight.) "God prevent your having a daughter," the weary mother says by way of farewell. We quickly realize how poor this region is when we next see Darlene, wearing a wedding dress, riding a donkey in long shot across a barren landscape dotted only by an occasional cactus. Left in the lurch when her groom never appears at the altar of the local Catholic church, she throws away her veil and hitches a ride on a truck full of men. But, figuratively speaking, we know that Darlene isn't going anywhere by the manner in which Silveira shoots this moment. He does so with a telephoto lens, which keeps distant objects relatively large while flattening depth between planes, and which therefore makes a character or a vehicle moving away from the camera hardly seem to move at all.

In the following scene, Darlene returns home – but it is three years later and she has a little boy with her named Dimas. Unbeknownst to Darlene, her mother has died and this is the day of her funeral. It will also become the day on which Osias Linhares, a wizened old bachelor, goat-farmer, and landholder, proposes marriage to the thirtyish Darlene. She doesn't think about her decision for long because she has no viable alternative: Darlene accepts what will amount to a relatively loveless union in return for food plus shelter for herself and her son. But she will have to work for that room and board, since Osias' chief occupation is to lie in his hammock and listen to his transistor radio. Not only must she cook Osias' meals, clean his adobe or mud-brick house, and tend the goats, but Darlene must also trudge off each day to a backbreaking job in the sugar-cane fields.

A man both dominant and supine, with buzzard-black eyes and a face that seems compressed by an undersized helmet, Osias knows a good deal when he sees one. So when Darlene bears a second, dark-skinned son by a provincial soldier, this grouch keeps his objections to a minimum. He even names the boy, calling him Edinardo, as he will name both of Darlene's subsequent sons (Ednaldo, then Edvaldi) by different men; and, ultimately, he will register himself as the father of all the boys at the regional clerk's office. But Osias' actions seem based more on pride of possession than pride of paternity. If the children are technically considered his, he is content – given what can only be termed his temperamental inertia – not to have had to rouse himself from his hammock in order to conceive them biologically. Moreover, he includes Dimas among his legal "possessions," even though, in an agonizing sacrifice, Darlene had earlier given the boy up for adoption

Regina Casé as the earthy Darlene in *Me, You, Them*.

in the hope that he might wind up with an urban family that could offer him an education.

If Osias provides Darlene and sons with economic security, Zezinho, the father of blue-eyed Ednaldo, provides her with emotional support, with deep affection and warm companionship. The middle-aged, up-to-now unmarried Zezinho is Osias' cousin, and had previously lived with their elderly aunt and Osias' homely, shrewish, widowed sister, Raquel. But after the aunt dies, Zezinho moves in with the Linhares family – to protect Raquel's reputation. And once there, this gentle, genial, nurturing soul assumes management of the household, cooking and cleaning in place of Darlene. (She didn't do either particularly well, and she enjoys the hot lunches that Zezinho takes to her by bicycle in the fields.) He even shaves Osias (who is more than happy to have an extra pair of hands to wait on him) and looks after Edinardo as well as his own, newly arrived little boy. Ednaldo arrives partly out of his mother's passion for dancing, which her legal husband is unable or unwilling to satisfy. She must consequently teach his cousin to dance at what passes for the area nightclub, while Osias sits and drinks, and what becomes Zezinho and Darlene's mutual passion for dancing quickly leads to passion of another kind.

That passion cannot be wholly satisfied by a timid homebody like Zezinho, however, for he is no more than a humble chicken trying to

play the part of a rooster. And this is where the third member of our
ménage à quatre, or romantic rectangle, enters the picture. He is the
young, good-looking, virile Ciro Antunes, an itinerant agricultural
worker whom Darlene spots at the club, meets at the sugar-cane harvest, and brings home for dinner. Zezinho is immediately jealous
because he realizes the threat that this phallic fantasy-figure, with
his curly hair and swarthy features, represents; but the ostentatiously
hospitable Osias invites the visitor to spend the night anyway. Yet it is
Zezinho, ironically, who will have to convince his cousin (at Darlene's
suggestion) to add a room onto the house for Ciro, for otherwise their
wife will leave with the stranger and they will both be sad and lonely. So
Ciro gets his room and hammock, and Darlene gets the torrid sex she
wants together with yet another son – which she tells Zezinho she
didn't want.

And her unwanted pregnancy gets us to the heart of this conjugal
matter, which in the end is more about economics than sex (or sexual
politics, for that matter). For Darlene has no means of birth control,
including abortion, at her disposal. Her men don't have a lot of
options, either – sexual, economic, or otherwise. The key to appreciat-
ing *Me, You, Them* is thus in understanding that these people simply live
or live simply on this land, dearly depend upon it for survival, and honestly don't have anywhere else to go. In a society like our own, where
mobility and choice are taken for granted, the Linhares menagerie
would lack what drives it here: social and financial *necessity*.

These characters surely have never heard of Karl Marx, but they intuitively find his formula useful: from each, according to his abilities; to
each, according to his needs. Darlene essentially needs three men to
give her one complete husband in this backwater of a Brazilian state,
and each man is given the opportunity to provide what is in his nature
and nothing more, for neither of these three really wants the role of
the other two. As Andrucha Waddington himself put the matter,
"Around this region I knew of twin sisters living with a guy, one guy with
three wives, and one woman who lived with two brothers. I think it's
such a difficult place to live that people need each other, and they try
to find a way to be together."

This is another way of saying that Brazilians might not find *Me, You,
Them* as incongruously funny, as oddly or unconventionally appealing,
as we Americans do. Still, they have responded well to the film, and
among the reasons, I think, is its non-judgmental tone. (The movie's
most judgmental line, "That woman [Darlene] knows no shame," is
placed in the mouth of the character with the least moral authority:

Osias.) Another reason is the consistent understatement of its scenes, which downplay material that could easily have turned into violent melodrama, bawdy farce, or pathetic tearjerker. Take the final scene, for example, after Osias returns from registering the births of his "sons." It consists solely of a long, slightly overhead take of Darlene, Zezinho, Ciro, and Osias standing outdoors, each of them at one of the four angles on an imaginary rectangle. But this is a rectangle tilted so that it looks like a baseball diamond, with earth-mother Darlene appropriately occupying home plate. Slowly she, Ciro, and Zezinho leave the frame, one after the other, as Osias remains alone to the far right. Then Darlene comes back. Osias sees her but doesn't move, and she just stands there about fifteen or twenty feet from him, staring pensively in his direction, as an abrupt cut to black ends the film.

Waddington's method, then, is unsensational and his tempo relaxed, as his picture enjoys its characters and their accommodation of stricture to circumstance – their adjustment to, rather than struggle with, situations that occur or events that transpire. He's helped by Gilberto Gil's insinuatingly seductive, subtly sinuous score, as he is by his non-clichéd casting of the chief role. Waddington knew that "to put a Julia Roberts or a Gwyneth Paltrow in the part would be ridiculous." So he chose the lantern-jawed, big-toothed, almost horse-faced Regina Casé, a popular television talk-show host (the South American Oprah Winfrey, she has been called) who has done some acting for the theatre. Casé combines the sex appeal of Sophia Loren with the elemental maternalism of Anna Magnani, in a peasant's body designed by Pablo Picasso. Add a funny, finally devastating smile, the sensuous Portuguese language, and what can only be called the ease of Casé's full-bodied womanliness, stir, let simmer for about an hour and forty minutes, and you'll have more than enough love to go around. Certainly enough for Osias, Zezinho, and Ciro, who are played by Lima Duarte, Stênio Garcia, and Luís Carlos Vasconcelos, respectively. All three are effective but the very best is Garcia, whose humorous mix of fussiness and suavity suggests a Brazilian Jerry Stiller.

Andrucha Waddington's original ending to *Me, You, Them* was to have included a brutal murder, possibly of Garcia's character but more likely of Ciro, the stranger or non-family member, by Osias. (When the latter gathers up the three boys early one morning, before anyone else is awake, we suspect kidnapping to be accompanied by violence, but Waddington had a change of heart. There is no violence, and the telephoto shot of Osias and his "sons," departing in a donkey-driven cart, tells us once again that theirs will be a circular journey [to a government records office, no less] that will reunite them in the end with Darlene, Zezinho, and Ciro.) And there would have been precedent for such a finale in Waddington's own work: namely, an acclaimed music video that he made in 1999. At its conclusion a polygamous wife – played by the director's spouse, Fernanda Torres – kills all three of her husbands, poisoning one, strangling another, and suffocating the last. But terminal bloodshed like this would have been untrue to the collective or communal spirit of *Me, You, Them*, even as Benito Zambrano's tacked-on (albeit pacific) ending was unfaithful to the spiritual requirements of *Solas'* plot.

Similarly, feminist polemics have no place in *Me, You, Them* – or any work of art, for that matter – and, happily, none are found here or in *Solas*. Feminist-minded critics prefer to look at the world in melodramatic terms, finding this woman strong, that one victimized, and portraying men either as weak, evil, or nondescript. But the world is more complex than such simple-minded, didactic commentators like to think, and its complexity is reflected in *Me, You, Them* as well as in *Solas*. Waddington's film isn't about superior Darlene's strength or power, cunning or manipulation, as opposed to the three, lesser men's lack thereof, just as Zambrano's picture doesn't claim as its subject the hatefulness and oppression perpetrated by men such as Juan and María's father.

Out of comparable ingredients – grinding poverty; pregnancies out of wedlock; dead or dying (grand)mothers; unconventional, non-traditional, or non-nuclear unions; and the want of educational opportunity – *Solas* and *Me, You, Them* have created gently insinuating, incisively humane dramas of contemporary womanhood. One may take place in a rural area and the other in an urban one, but they meet on the common ground of personal travail, self-denial, mutual compromise, and fellow-feeling. Be it in the fragmented, atomizing world of the big city or the integrated, extended one of the countryside, human beings never had it so bad ... or so good.

14

Of Virgin Suicide, Human Bondage, and Male Indulgence

On Coppola's *The Virgin Suicides* (2000, USA), Gitai's *Kadosh* (1999, Israel), and Doueiri's *West Beirut* (1998, Lebanon)

Once again, before getting to the real subject of this chronicle, I shall have to dispense with an American release that has been receiving far more attention than it deserves. I refer to *The Virgin Suicides* (2000), a first film adapted and directed by Sophia Coppola (yes, that Coppola) from a first novel of the same title (1993) by Jeffrey Eugenides. This picture is supposedly about generalized teenaged angst leading to multiple teenaged suicide – five suicides, in fact, committed by five sisters (ages thirteen to seventeen), who are the children of caring but over-protective parents in the affluent Michigan suburb of Grosse Pointe. I say "generalized" angst because Coppola's movie paradoxically wants to portray these girls' deaths as (1) mysterious and (2) symptomatic of something seriously amiss in society at large. Yet there is no real mystery, since the mother of this brood is harshly authoritarian, going so far as to take her daughters out of school and imprison them in their rooms just because one of them stays out all night (virginity unaltered?) with a boyfriend after a high school dance, while the father, a math instructor, is astigmatic, ineffectual, and nondescript. Moreover, the girls are all beautiful and therefore the (unattainable) objects of adolescent male desire. To top matters off, this family is strictly Roman Catholic and the sisters go to the Catholic school where their father teaches. Get the picture?

The real mystery of *The Virgin Suicides* may be the year in which it takes place, 1975. The clothes and cars and popular music fit the period, but it's not clear what relevance the time has to the action.

The Lisbon daughters (including Kirsten Dunst as Lux) pose in *The Virgin Suicides*.

Nothing essential about that action would be out of date today –
indeed, everything about it would be *more* believable today. As for
teenage suicide as a symptom of societal malaise, this film describes the
symptom but doesn't penetrate any cause outside the family circle.
Hence the deaths of the five sisters are equivalent to the destruction of
the elm trees that line their street: they are lovely and it's sad to lose
them, but since they (like their parents) have no inner life or spiritual
depth – at the same time as they are paradoxically self-absorbed – the
girls cannot have any emotional or intellectual connection to the external, wider world around them. (Not for nothing does Lux, the most
distinct of this otherwise indistinct group of girls, share her name with
a brand of dishwashing detergent.) They remain *obscure* objects of
desire who are removed from reality and whose existence is conferred
on them only by the male gaze – a gaze rendered gauzy if not dewy-eyed
by Edward Lachman's color cinematography.

  The Virgin Suicides could have been called *American Beauties*, so much
does its method, as well as some of its matter, have in common with
American Beauty (1999): the treatment of a symptom but the failure to
analyze its causes beyond the superficially psychological (in *American
Beauty*'s case, the symptom being the dehumanizing delimitation of the

Kevin Spacey undergoing a midlife crisis in
American Beauty, in the company of a teenager,
played by Mena Suvari.

human spirit within the purported confines of suburban America);
both the mythopoeic exaltation of youth and its prosaic delineation or
demarcation, as well as the fetishization of teenaged, female sexuality
(in *American Beauty*'s case, by an adult male); the inconsistent, if not mis-
guided, application of a darkly comic perspective to deadly serious
material (including, in *The Virgin Suicides*, a ludicrous, grotesque
sequence near the end in which a fashionable debutante party is celebrated with an asphyxiation theme); the use of portentous voice-over
(in *American Beauty*, from the deceased protagonist, speaking from God
knows where; in *The Virgin Suicides*, from one of the girls' admirers
grown into an adult, albeit one who still seems boyishly infatuated with
the five Lisbon sisters); and the deployment, in both pictures, of an original musical soundtrack whose ethereality – a generic cross between the
themes of *The Twilight Zone* and *The X Files* – attempts to create mystery
or eeriness where there is only deadening pedestrianism.

If you want to see a film in which a character's suicide is genuinely
mysterious, have a look at Hirokazu Kore-eda's profound and majestic
Maborosi (1995). If, by contrast, you'd like to watch a picture where a
woman's suicide is luminously explicable, turn to the Israeli director
Amos Gitai's exquisite, heartrending, and haunting *Kadosh* (1999). This

is the third fiction film in a trilogy by Gitai, who had previously made documentaries both for Israeli television and for theatrical release (among them *Yoman Sadeh* [*Field Diary*, 1982], about the Lebanon War). The three pictures together are meant to be, in their creator's words, "a portrait of contemporary Israel as seen through its largest cities." *Devarim* (*Things*, 1996), set in Tel Aviv, depicted the first generation of Israeli sons born to the pioneers of 1948, whereas *Yom Yom* (*Day after Day*, 1998) explored the cultural intermingling between Israelis and Palestinians in Haifa. Set in Mea Shearim, the ultra-Orthodox Jewish quarter of Jerusalem, *Kadosh* (which means "sacred" in Hebrew) investigates the constraints that orthodoxy places, or can place, on personal freedom – particularly the freedom of women – in a Hassidic community dedicated to preserving its eighteenth-century traditions and to isolating itself from the secularism of contemporary Israeli society.

Kadosh opens with a beautifully patient scene, shot (like many of the film's scenes) in one long take, of a Hassidic man's extensive waking ritual. As dawn's pale, blue light pushes its way into his modest bedroom, and while his wife still sleeps in a neighboring twin bed, the Hassid carefully washes, dresses, and recites a string of prayers in gratitude for every increment of the day's beginning – his first blink, his first breath, his first touch. Rocking back and forth with devotion, he punctuates his prayers with the following, oddly discordant benediction: "Blessed is the eternal God who has not made me a woman." Yet, upon awakening his wife, he declares, "I have such respect for you." Thus do Gitai and his co-scenarist, Eliette Abecassis, swiftly highlight *Kadosh*'s theme: the simultaneous worship and oppression of women within the patriarchal society of Orthodox Judaism. Not for nothing does Rivka, the wife, tell her husband, Meir, that "Women cry even in their sleep" after he has questioned the apparent tears in her eyes.

At the center of this film are two sisters, the aforementioned Rivka and the slightly younger Malka, whose stories are told contrapuntally. Rivka and Meir, for their part, have been married for ten years and share a profound love. But they have no children. Therefore, according to the Talmud (which Hassids like Meir study full-time, together with the Torah, while their wives work at secular jobs such as accounting), their marriage is illegitimate. And in a religious community that values women according to the number of children they bear, Rivka's presumed barrenness has made her a shunned outcast and her husband an object of ridicule. Meir's rabbi – who is also his father – tells him that, as a Jew ordered to propagate in order to fulfill Israel's future, he must divorce Rivka and marry a fertile woman. Meir demurs; his father

Yaël Abecassis as Rivka and Yoram Hattab as Meir in *Kadosh*.

the rabbi insists; and his wife secretly goes to a female obstetrician-gynecologist, who finds that she is not barren and thinks that Meir may be the sterile one, but who knows that a Hassid would never submit to a sperm count, let alone artificial insemination. (Rivka says nothing to her husband about her own fertility or the doctor's visit.) So the divorce proceeds, despite this couple's love. Rivka despairingly moves into a rented room, while Meir prepares to take a new wife named Haya – whom Rivka and Malka's own mother (against her will, though in fulfillment of her professional-cum-religious duties) must ritualistically bathe so as to purify this bride-to-be for the purpose of childbearing.

In a desperate attempt to conceive, Rivka had re-submitted to such a ritualistic bath (including twelve dunkings for the twelve tribes of Israel) at her mother's hands, and we watch Malka undergo one as well. For this sister is being forced to marry the devoutly religious, aggressively proselytizing, physically brutish Yossef, since the rabbi and her mother will not permit Malka to wed the man she loves. He is the studly Yaakov, and union with him is taboo for two reasons: he has rejected the Orthodox community to which he once belonged (although he still considers himself a good Jew), and he is a rock singer. But the fetching Malka is more rebellious than her older sister and, though she sacrifices her virginity to her husband, she makes adulterous love to Yaakov in a late-night rendezvous at the club where he works. This action effectively ends her marriage, as Yossef viciously beats Malka when she returns home and she must flee for her safety. Her last words to him are, "Men like you ruined my sister's life," and we see the culmination of Rivka's ruin after a final reunion between the two sisters.

Malka begs her sibling to escape Orthodox Judaism with her, but Rivka chooses suicide instead – and suicide of a most vengeful kind. To deliver herself from her plight, but also to pay Meir back for his aborted visit to her room – apparently in search of sex – on the holiday known as Purim, she first takes poison, then quickly goes to her former home to make love to her startled husband (who has not yet re-married, and whom she awakens from a deep sleep) for the last time. Afterwards, when Meir tries to rouse Rivka from what appears to be her own deep sleep, he realizes that she is dead. "Rivka, wake up," he tearfully implores her over and over, but the only "awakening" that occurs here is the camera's, as it leaves the couple's bed, travels to the left, and trains its gaze on Meir's religious library.

The last scene of *Kadosh* follows, in which Malka wanders through the parched hill-country outside Jerusalem, with the city in extreme long shot behind her. She walks alone, not with Yaakov, since her freedom to choose him has been the issue, not their romantic union itself. And after Malka walks out of the frame, the camera-eye remains fixed on the city of Jerusalem as it again travels to the left before coming to a final rest. The treasured, turbulent heart of Israel has, after all, been one of *Kadosh*'s subjects, or rather Gitai's choice of the Hassidic community as his subject is the perfect metaphor for Jerusalem itself: a capital marked, like the Hassidim, by its historical significance, religious piety, complicated allegiances, and questionable politics.

Although both of *Kadosh*'s stories end in ways that do not redound to the glory of Orthodox Judaism, orthodoxy itself is not vilified in this film, which is more tragic than melodramatic. Indeed, all the authority-wielding men, with the possible exception of Yossef, are sympathetic. It is easy, for example, to understand, if not agree with, the rabbi's point of view. He is not arbitrarily cruel; rather, he has his own obligations, and the point of them is not trivial.

Only in an American movie like *Keeping the Faith* (2000) could marrying within one's faith – here, Judaism broadly conceived – be trivialized. A moralizing romantic comedy starring Edward Norton (who also directed) and Ben Stiller, this picture – yet another American one to dispense with – cribs its premise from the classic bar joke about the rabbi, the priest, and the blonde. Norton (the priest, Father Brian Finn) and Stiller (the rabbi, Jacob Schram) are best friends from elementary school who meet up in New York. Each is struggling to introduce his Upper West Side congregation, dozing beneath heavy blankets of tradition, to the hipness of faith. And so they entertain as much as they minister: the rabbi recruits a Harlem gospel choir to burst through his synagogue's doors; the priest ambles around the pulpit with a mike like a stand-up comic.

But, as one might guess given this movie's national origin, *Keeping the Faith* is not concerned as much with the two men's clerical duties as with their love lives. The priest struggles nobly with his vow of celibacy in a city filled with beautiful, available women. The rabbi struggles to parry the relentless assaults on his datebook from Jewish mothers seeking to match him up with their daughters. Then matters get complicated when Anna, the blonde, arrives on the scene. A childhood pal of both the rabbi and the priest, she's now a high-powered businesswoman, not to mention a gentile or *shiksa* (a term, by the way, also used by Orthodox Jews to denote a Jewish girl who does not observe Jewish precepts). And, of course, both the rabbi and the priest fall in love with "Anna Banana." She favors the rabbi, and the two begin a scorching affair, which they keep secret from his as well as the priest's prying congregants. The rabbi, however, is torn – his mother (Anne Bancroft) has already disowned his brother for marrying a Catholic, while the congregation is keen for him to meet a nice Jewish girl – but eventually he succumbs and "follows his heart" like a true American sentimentalist. Near the film's emotional climax, he visits his mother in the hospital, expecting a reprimand. Instead, she tells him sweetly, "I was wrong. You are a good man." At that climax, the rabbi addresses his congregation on Yom Kippur, the holiest day of the Jewish year, and decides to come clean. After making a few lame jokes, he confesses his relationship with Anna – only to have the congregation nod approvingly, touched by his sincerity.

American movies like *Keeping the Faith* thus tend to celebrate romantic love only when it battles against, and defeats, the other commitments that define one's life. A disciplined dedication to tradition, of the kind we see displayed in *Kadosh*, is assumed by these films to be at odds with the preservation of a free and feeling heart. And I'll be the first to admit that there is something wacky about hinging a people's destiny on an individual's romantic inclinations. Men and women are much more than their religious identities, and the choice of a mate should be based on the satisfaction of many needs. Furthermore, religious commitments are sometimes used as a cover for genuine bigotry:

some Jewish, as well as Catholic, parents say they don't want their children to marry outside the faith, whereas what they really fear is that their son or daughter will marry someone non-white.

But, these qualifications notwithstanding, the desire to marry and raise a family with a person who shares one's religious heritage is not necessarily a manifestation of intolerance or even of love's surrender to the deadening forces of tradition. Why should romantic love have to be separated from the love of tradition and family and heritage? Love for another human being is no less noble when it enhances pre-existing identity – as in the case of Rivka's love for her Orthodox husband – than when it trumps that identity, as it does for the rabbi in *Keeping the Faith*. The choice to marry within one's religion should not be imposed, as it is for *Kadosh*'s Malka (and as the decision to divorce is imposed on Meir), but neither should it be a source of shame.

Amos Gitai recognizes the complexities of religious belief as well as romantic love, which is one of the reasons his two main characters find themselves in different dilemmas: Rivka, torn between the forbidden lure of modern medicine and the sacred demands of religious doctrine; Malka, in love with Yaakov yet trapped in a loveless union with Yossef. (Had the blonde fallen for him, the priest in *Keeping the Faith* could have found himself in an irresolvable dilemma, or in any event one not resolvable without suffering or embarrassment, but this Hollywood movie naturally took the path of least resistance – through the synagogue.) Moreover, Gitai fuses love and religion in a way almost unimaginable in any but a French Catholic film like Cavalier's *Thérèse* (1986) or Bresson's *Diary of a Country Priest* (1950). Everything Rivka and Meir do before their break-up, for example – particularly their tender lovemaking (before which he dons his yarmulke) – is so infused with a looming love for God that this couple's relationship seems charged with an intangible potency that should more than make up for their want of progeny.

One of the reasons for that potency is the tremendously concentrated acting of Yaël Abecassis, as Rivka, and Yoram Hattab, as Meir. They, like Meitel Barda (Malka), are helped by the Italian Renato Berta's camera, which has previously served the films of such luminaries as Fassbinder, Tanner, Rohmer, and Resnais. Here that camera understands the revelations possible in the human face and, accordingly, shoots a fair portion of the picture (much of which places the Hassids apart, not only in their own quarter of Jerusalem, but also indoors) in medium close-up. Such close camera-work, combined with the minimal cutting of which I have already spoken and Berta's muted palette of blacks, blues, browns, and grays, fixes the characters of

Kadosh movingly in their fates. The accompanying musical score, by Philippe Eidel for horns and accordion, is minimal, indigenous, implicative – which is all that it need be in a motion picture where script, performance, and image carry the day.

The Briton Stewart Copeland, who has composed the music for several films by Ken Loach, did the score for another picture out of the troubled Middle East: *West Beirut* (1998). And, even more so than Eidel's score, this one – mainly for guitar – is reticent, native to the region, and nimbly suggestive. This is as it should be for this first, "unfinished" film by Ziad Doueiri, born in Beirut in 1963, who had his professional education in the United States, worked here as an assistant cameraman for Quentin Tarantino, then went home to make this largely autobiographical feature (from his own script) about his memories of growing up during the civil war in his native city. The year is 1975, as in *The Virgin Suicides*, but here the year has relevance and resonance. (As it does in Randa Chahal Sabag's recent fiction film *A Civilized People* [1999], which is also about the Lebanese civil war.) Here, too, as in Sophia Coppola's movie, the principal characters are adolescents, but, instead of being a suicidal tale, this is a coming-of-age or rite-of-passage story, about young people who are full of life despite the death and destruction that surround them.

They live in a city as historically divided or quartered as the Jerusalem of *Kadosh*: East Beirut is controlled by Christian militias, West Beirut by Lebanese Muslims. (Lebanon became a state shortly after World War I when, on behalf of Lebanon's Maronite Catholics, the occupying French separated the country from Syria and its Arabic population.) And with the April 1975 massacre of a busload of civilians (thirty-one to be exact) – a slow-motion re-creation of which we see in *West Beirut* – the capital is well on its way to becoming a war zone. Doueiri is interested in the effects of the fighting, not its causes, though there is some reference to the presence in Lebanon of the Palestine Liberation Organization – the main reason for Israeli invasions of the country and for much of the subsequent civil strife between left-wing Muslims and conservative Christian groups (not to speak of the differences between pro-Iranian Shiites and Syrian-backed Druse Muslims). The effects of war for this director are calculated in specifically human terms rather than generalized political or economic ones, although, again, there is mention in the film of Beirut's loss of its roles as an international trade center and as the commercial and financial center of the Middle East, on account of the hostilities of 1975–76.

All that Doueiri really wants to show is that two Muslim boys and a Christian girl had their adolescence in this fractured, convulsive situation, and his narrowing of scope is one of the senses in which *West Beirut* is "unfinished." It begins *in medias res*, as a jittery camera trains its eye on the coarsely textured, black-and-white image of mugging teenagers in a schoolyard, then tilts upward to find warplanes fighting it out in the sky; and the movie ends obliquely – using the same, coarsely textured black-and-white cinematography – with no tidy resolution of the three (pre)teens' story despite the final freeze frame, and certainly with no conclusion to the Lebanese conflict (which began again in 1978 after the ceasefire of 1976 and has erupted sporadically ever since, though as of late May 2000 at least the Israeli occupation of a swath of southern Lebanon had ended).

West Beirut is also intentionally "unfinished" or unintegrated in a cinematic sense, since it uses three different types of color photography, all by Ricardo Jacques Gale (desaturated, lush, and grainy); the aforementioned, blown-up black-and-white footage from a Super-8 camera; documentary images of political leaders from the period as well as of the havoc their military forces have wrought; and a number of hand-held shots (as in the first sequence) in addition to those of the conventional, stationary kind. Chaotic form cleverly mirrors chaotic content, in other words, without ever crossing the line into artistic disarray or incoherence. One wry truth about art is that it needs a little arrangement in order to seem unarranged, and *West Beirut* has just enough not to leave us feeling dissatisfied with its incomplete or inorganic nature.

Some of the film's "arrangement" comes immediately from its juxtaposition, or rather uniting, of character: the two Muslim friends and the beautiful Christian girl who pals around with them. The point, clearly, is that children and teens can transcend the oppositions and tensions that divide the rest of Beirut, from the religious to the nationalistic to the regional (for example, a vulgar, shrewish, loud, unkempt, and finally comic southern Lebanese woman versus the educated, attractive, discreet, urbane but ultimately grave Beirut mother of one of the Muslim boys), from the domestic (between neighbors living on top of each other in one battered apartment building after another) to the generational (adolescents versus elders). Yet Doueiri wisely doesn't take the union of these adolescents too far: there is talk of romance between each of the boys and the girl, but no action (which you will find in *A Civilized People*, where a Christian girl, who has just come from the country to work as a maid in Beirut, patly falls in love with a young Muslim, to the peril of them both). That kind of action is reserved for a brothel, where Christians and Muslims alike (many of them soldiers) are welcomed by its feisty madam, who rhetorically asks, "Since when does religion matter in bed?" Sex here, naturally, has nothing to do with romance and everything to do with lust, which is the flip side of animalistic aggression. And it is with the contrast between such aggression – the killing, torture, maiming, and bombing, often of civilians – and the persistence of ordinary life that Doueiri is primarily concerned. Romance between religions, of the kind apotheosized in *Keeping the Faith*, would only get in the way of this director's mission.

Ordinary life for Tarek, Omar, and May, the three youngsters, consists of roaming the war-torn streets of Beirut in search of adventure. May craves it because she is new to this western seaport, having arrived with her family from Baalbek to the east. Tarek and Omar need to wander because their school (which is French, and thus provides yet another opposition in the film, between a colonialist-minded schoolmarm and her rebellious young charges) has been closed on account of the fighting, and staying at home means staying under an adult's thumb in addition to staying in one place – not the best strategy for escaping incoming mortar fire. Moreover, it is Omar who owns the Super-8 camera that periodically substitutes for Doueiri's 35mm one, and the only store that can develop his film (primarily voyeuristic footage of his middle-aged uncle's sexy young wife) is on the other side of town, in the Olive Quarter of forbidden East Beirut. Hence another, ostensibly compelling reason for the girl and boys' ultimate venture into no-man's land, with its bombed-out buildings, rubble-strewn streets, military checkpoints, frequent sniper fire, and one (protected) bordello. The kids get into some predictable mischief together (particularly at the brothel), tease, quarrel, idle, and snack like their counterparts everywhere, and take risks that even the most intrepid of peacetime schoolboys would have trouble imagining.

Even the most lyrical of Tarek, Omar, and May's moments together – their bicycle ride beginning along the Mediterranean shore, continuing through downtown West Beirut, then moving back to the seaside – contains intimations of mortality. For this sequence recalls a similar one from Truffaut's *Jules and Jim* (1961), in which two men and a woman joyously bicycle to the beach as the camera circles about them, and as they sometimes go round in circles themselves. The circles, of course, coupled with the most momentary of stop-action shots of the characters during the ride, are meant to suggest the inevitable dead-end of Jules, Jim, and Catherine's quest to preserve, not only the *joie de vivre* of La Belle Époque in the face of the Great War's harsh encroachment, but also their romantic dream of living in total freedom beyond the limits of social convention. Similarly, the circular path of *West Beirut*'s threesome is intended to indicate the short-lived nature of

Tarek, Omar, and May's idyll in a city once known as the Paris of the Middle East, but fast becoming a kind of multi-ethnic hell on earth.

We see another homage to François Truffaut at the very end of *West Beirut*, when Tarek and his mother, Hala, are caught in flight by Omar's Super-8 camera in the black-and-white freeze frame to which I referred earlier. They are on the beach, at water's edge, just as Antoine Doinel is at the end of Truffaut's semi-autobiographical *Four Hundred Blows* (1959). He is fleeing from reform school and the prison of his childhood, toward what he does not know. Antoine finally arrives at the edge of the sea and stops, for he can run no further. He turns back toward the land, in the direction from which he has been running, and suddenly the moving image freezes, stops, loses its motion – and turns into a still photograph (at the time a startling and rare visual effect, subsequently debased into the most obligatory of television and movie clichés). Where can he go? What can he do? What is to come? What will he become? What is there to become? Truffaut's first feature film ends with a question mark, for us and for himself. Doueiri's first feature film ends with a similar question mark, for us and for himself.

This is not the first time in *West Beirut* that Hala has attempted to flee the city with her son. A lawyer unable to work on account of the civil strife, she wants desperately to get out, whereas her beloved husband, the philosophical Riad, is determined to stay in the place of his birth and wait out the war. For this intellectual, there is nowhere else to go – particularly not to America – despite the mortal danger, the shortage of food, and the breakdown of communications. He remains behind at the end, accepting a life composed of equal parts of beauty and horror, which Doueiri shows us when his camera cuts to scenes of carnage and ruin after a scene where Riad has feelingly played his wife's favorite musical instrument. (This is the second such harsh juxtaposition in the film: the first occurred as May played classical piano in a practice room while Omar and Tarek listened attentively outside, only to be interrupted or replaced by shots of warfare, devastation, and suffering.) But, for their part, where can Tarek and his mother go? What can they do? As Doueiri's alter ego, Tarek went to America, we may presume. Doueiri himself is now back in Beirut, however. And what will come of him there? What kind of filmmaker will he become? What kind can he become in Lebanon as we know it?

We know, from a press note, that Mohammed Chamas, winsome as the physically slight Omar, was orphaned by the war, has not done any acting since this picture, and currently lives in a shack in a refugee camp on the outskirts of Beirut. Like Rola Al Amin, the quietly charming May, and Ziad Doueiri's younger brother, Rami, who plays the lanky Tarek as an engaging scamp, Chamas is a non-professional. Doueiri is following the example of Italian neorealist directors, who, as noted in previous chapters, frequently used non-professionals – children prominent among them – in order to give their movies an authenticity-cum-spontaneity not normally associated with the performances of stars or veteran character actors. (Notable exceptions are, as Tarek's parents, Joseph Bou Nassar and Carmen Loubbos, each of whom warmly shows that the right pro need not interfere with a director's search for the truth in ordinary people – indeed, he or she can illuminate it.)

When I see such small-scale yet far-reaching gems as *West Beirut* or *Kadosh* – each the product of a modest national cinema, if national cinema it can be called (*Kadosh*, for example, was the first Israeli entry at the Cannes Film Festival in twenty-five years) – I think of our own immodest cinema and all the money it spends each year on domesticated duds. (I mean artistic duds like *The Virgin Suicides* and *Keeping the Faith*, which more often than not turn out to be commercial successes.) Our cinema has always functioned in this way; that is why it properly calls itself "the industry"; and that is why most of its products are disposable or perishable. This situation isn't going to change, but it's nice to be reminded yet again, this time by the Middle East, of the large possibilities – some would say responsibilities – inherent in film art, particularly of the low-budgeted, independent-minded kind. (So independent was *Kadosh* that the so-called Quality Film Encouragement Fund of Israel refused to support this quality picture at any stage in its creation.)

One of those possibilities-become-responsibilities, exemplified by both *Kadosh* and *West Beirut*, is to unite us with exotic people, to show us the linkages under our common differences, and to render those differences comprehensible. It's true that Ozu didn't make his films as "explanations" of Japan, nor did Ray of India, nor does Kiarostami of Iran or Zhang Yimou of China; their pictures are artworks, not tracts or lectures. Still, anyone who has seen the work of these directors, or Amos Gitai's trilogy and Ziad Doueiri's first feature, must get the feeling that cinema particularizes the minutiae of everyday life, everywhere, in a way that political news, in its search for dominant aspects, does not do. Every art can do this, of course, but one of the special benefits of film is its immediate immediacy. The movies, in their one hundred years and in all their expansiveness, surely have made the globe smaller, if they have not created that most elusive of elusives: global harmony. Alas, even saint cinema has its limitations.

15

The Space of Time, the Sound of Silence

On Ozon's *Under the Sand* (2000, France) and Tsai's *What Time Is It There?* (2001, Taiwan)

"The soundtrack invented silence," wrote Robert Bresson, and some of the best directors in history, including Bresson, have fixed silence on film. For them, silence is both aural and visual – not merely the absence of talk but the presentation of persons who fill our imaginations with what they are *not* saying. Two such directors are the Malaysian-born Taiwanese Tsai Ming-liang and the Frenchman François Ozon, each of whom has made a movie not only encased in quiet but also occupied with love, yearning, or union. In Tsai's *What Time Is It There?* (2001) and Ozon's *Under the Sand* (2000), however, such a feeling or state is of the mysteriously paradoxical, not the lushly romantic, kind: deathless yet lifeless, present yet absent, palpable yet laconic.

Let's begin with the French picture, for it has some obvious cinematic precedents: the maudlin *Ghost* (1990) and, despite its title, the unsentimental *Truly, Madly, Deeply* (1991). *Under the Sand* has more in common with the latter, which is about a blissful London couple whose marriage is ended by the sudden death of the husband. His wife is simply unable to accept this fact, and he himself returns from time to time – not a ghost, the husband. No explanations are offered, but the two roles were so movingly played by Juliet Stevenson and Alan Rickman that the film had no trace of the egregiously spooky or the freakishly supernatural. *Truly, Madly, Deeply* seemed to be, calmly and credibly, straightforwardly and seriously, about a love stronger than – even synonymous with – death.

Now Ozon gives us *Under the Sand*, which he wrote along with Emmanuelle Bernheim, Marina de Van, and Marcia Romano, and which is about another wife who cannot accept the death of her husband. Thirty-five years old, Ozon had previously made more than a dozen shorts and three features, including *Truth or Dare* (1994), *A Summer Dress* (1995), *See the Sea* (1996), and *Criminal Lovers* (1998). All of these films are saturated with erotic longing and situated firmly outside the mainstream with their disturbing images and *outré* subjects (such as queer sexual politics in *Water Drops on Burning Rocks*, made in 1999 from a play by Rainer Werner Fassbinder). All of them are also somewhat mannered and, in the manner of cinema-school products, proud of their mannerisms. (Ozon studied directing at the famous French film academy known as *La fémis*.) The mannerisms disappear in *Under the Sand*, but not the current of sexual yearning and not the single quality that characterizes all the work to date of this young Frenchman: a desire to reveal the fragility and vulnerability that underlie seemingly secure or solid bourgeois appearances.

Marie and Jean Drillon are an upper-middle-class Parisian couple who have been married, without children, for twenty-five years. English-born Marie is somewhere in her late forties or early fifties yet is timelessly, strikingly beautiful; a one-time competitive swimmer who continues to work out regularly at a gym, she works as a university lecturer in English literature. Her somewhat older husband is a businessman with a bear-like physique, a homely yet quietly commanding masculine presence, and a distinctly melancholy air about him. At the start of the film Jean and his wife are driving to the Landes region of southwestern France, where they have a spacious summer home not far from a splendid beach. After they arrive and open the house, the two of them eat spaghetti and drink some wine, then go to bed.

This first sequence proceeds with a smoothness appropriate to a couple that has been happily married for so long. Warmth, ease, and consideration are evident in their every move or gesture; in fact, they are ostensibly so comfortable in their relationship that words – of which there are few in the opening scenes – are unnecessary. We hear none of the casual chatter that we might expect from a sophisticated, middle-aged Gallic husband and wife. Nonetheless, Jean seems a little too quiet for comfort – intellectually disengaged or emotionally aloof would be the best description – and there are other clues that all is not quite right or that calamity impends.

Under the Sand opens, for example, with the image of two boats traveling down the Seine, then immediately cuts to the same river bereft of boats altogether before panning to the right to find Marie and Jean leaving Paris by car. (They are listening to aptly chosen classical music,

selections from which we shall hear again later on the soundtrack –
salient among them Gustav Mahler's Symphony no. 2 in c minor, *Resurrection*.) Then after Jean and Marie reach the south of France, they
enter a house that has understandably been "dead" for some months,
with its covered furniture, shuttered windows, and dank air. And when
he goes out to get wood for a fire, the camera holds on what appears
to be a dying tree as we hear the overweight Jean breathing hard; when
he lifts a fallen branch from this tree, ants swarm beneath in fear for
their lives or in search of new cover and new prey. As Marie herself
looks into the bathroom mirror while she gets ready for bed, she sees,
and registers, yet another intimation of mortality: her aging face.

The next day at the beach, where Marie and Jean are more or less
alone, the camera lingers in medium close-up on him as he stares out
at the distant, crashing waves while she relaxes at his side. Eventually he
gets up to go down for a swim, but Marie declines to join him: instead
she naps in the sun. After a while, she awakens to discover that her husband has not yet returned; Marie then briefly diverts herself by reading
a book she has brought along before being forced to conclude, in a
panic, that Jean is missing. Lifeguards and the police search for him,
but they find nothing, and their only supposition is that he drowned.
Marie, however, is left with a host of unanswered questions. Was Jean's
death accidental or did he kill himself? Is he really dead or did he fake
his death and disappear? Is there anything Marie could have done to
prevent his drowning, or what did she do to cause his disappearance?

Without answers, Marie closes up the couple's summer place in
order to return to Paris, and with her return the first part of *Under the
Sand* – a little masterpiece of domestic-unease-become-mounting-ter-
ror – is over. The second section, set mostly in Paris (and shot by
Jeanne Lapoirie and Antoine Héberlé in a format that one might term
less glossy, except that the film's initial cinematographic format itself
was somewhat muted in its color range as well as in its light intensity),
shows Marie Drillon's life without Jean. Or, more precisely, the second
section of *Under the Sand* reveals her radical refusal to admit that a life
without Jean exists. Marie may be "in denial," but the appearance on
the soundtrack, twice, of Portishead's song "Undenied" suggests that
she will *not* be denied in her desire to be reunited with her husband.

Not only does Marie behave as if he were still alive, Jean himself
appears as a living, breathing, talking entity, a human being – not a
specter – at least five times in his wife's otherwise lonely apartment.
Naturally she sees him, and so do we. *Our* belief in what we see is irrelevant, however; the woman's belief is what matters, and Ozon boldly

chooses to make it tangible, not delusional. By doing so, this writer-
director begs some questions of his own – aimed at himself as well as
the audience of his film. To wit, who can actually accept, deep within
herself, the fact that her most loved one has vanished forever or is
dead? (Think here of George Sluizer's not unrelated thriller *The Vanishing* [1988, 1993], or especially of Hirokazu Kore-eda's sober rumi-
nation on spousal suicide titled *Maborosi* [1995].) And who wouldn't,
at least for a time, accept madness as the price of getting that person
back? Moreover, if love is all it's cracked up to be, can death kill it? If
so – as in cases where people have lost their loved spouses, learn to love
again, then re-marry – doesn't that make us wonder what love, in all
sentient beings, really *is*?

In any event, Jean's death or disappearance does not kill Marie's love
for him. Like an ostrich with its head in the sand – not like a woman in
mourning, dressed in sables (the film's French title, *Sous le sable*, cleverly puns on this masculine noun, which means both "sand" and
"sable") – she lives her private, social, and professional life as if her husband were still around. At home Marie acts as if Jean were lying next to
her in bed, sharing breakfast, chatting with her about the events of the
day. She even buys him a tie. To their friends, Marie speaks of Jean in
the present tense, as if he simply were away on a business trip. Her best
friend, Amanda (also British), while not aware of the full measure of
Marie's denial, advises therapy, only to be rebuffed.

Amanda's advice brings to mind Freud's likening of mourning to a
kind of madness that needs to be played out over time. But in contemporary society one is supposed to return to work and routine after only
a few days of bereavement, with the result that Marie's denial not only
makes her something of a social outcast, it also endangers her liveli-
hood. Amanda's husband, Gérard, who is also the Drillons' attorney,
warns Marie, for example, to curb her spending because Jean's assets,
should he not be found, will be frozen for ten years. She cannot escape
such reminders of her husband's absence, the most unsettling of which
occurs during a lecture Marie gives to her English literature class on
Virginia Woolf's *The Waves* (1931).

Reading aloud from the text, she stumbles as the loss of Jean suddenly becomes real to her – as it should in treating a novel introduced
as well as divided by sections of lyrical prose describing the rising and
sinking of the sun over a seascape of waves and shore; a novel, moreover, that features an absent character whose death becomes the focus
for the other characters' fear and defiance of mortality. Jean's death or
disappearance becomes real to Marie not only because of *The Waves* but

Charlotte Rampling, as Marie Drillon in *Under the Sand*, is massaged by the hands of Jacques Nolot, as Vincent.

also because one of her students was a lifeguard who assisted her in Landes in the search for her husband. When this young man approaches Marie in a sympathetic way after she cancels the class on *The Waves* in mid-lecture, she refuses to acknowledge that she remembers him.

Virginia Woolf recurs as a motif during Marie's relationship with a charming, handsome, single, accommodating, *and* middle-aged book publisher named Vincent, to whom she is introduced by Amanda. Over dinner with him, Marie recites from memory Woolf's suicide note ("I have the feeling that I am going mad ..."); she also remarks that the novelist, who heard voices even as Marie says she does, committed suicide by walking into the Ouse river and drowning herself. Vincent responds with a comment about British morbidity, but he nonetheless begins an affair with Marie. Once, when they are having sex, she glances up and sees Jean peering through the bedroom doorway. But this doesn't disturb Marie: she acts as if she expects her husband to understand what she calls her adultery, and he apparently does. So much so that, at another point in *Under the Sand*, Jean's hands massage Marie's body together with Vincent's while she masturbates. We see only the men's hands on either side of Marie's recumbent, partially nude figure as the camera photographs her from slightly overhead, in a stunning visual commentary on the interrelationship-bordering-on-indistinguishability not only between reality and fantasy, but also between life and death.

Yet Vincent can only be so accommodating of Marie's inability to separate herself from the memory – nay, what she thinks to be the reality
– of her husband. Vincent has known, or has believed, for some time
that Jean is dead, and he parts with Marie over her refusal to stop practicing what he calls her charade. For how long has she been "in
denial"? The film is unclear about this matter, but its temporal inspeci-
ficity is not a flaw, for Ozon wishes to suggest, I infer, that in a sense
time has stopped for Marie, that the present has become a kind of eternal past where Jean still exists. The present begins to catch up with
Marie, however, in the person of Jean's mother, who has her own reasons to think that her son is still alive. From the nursing home where
she resides, this old woman bitterly argues to her daughter-in-law that
there is no history of suicide in the Drillon family; that Jean was taking
medication for depression (the used-up prescription for which Marie
has already found), which was the product of boredom with Marie and
disappointment that she never bore him any children; and that he simply faked his death so he could begin his life anew, with another
woman, somewhere else.

So shockingly denying, if not delusional, is the senior Madame
Drillon that, for the first time, even Marie begins to admit that Jean
may be dead. She has been in touch with the authorities in Landes
since her return to Paris, and, she declares to her mother-in-law, the
police left a message on her answering machine saying they have
retrieved a body that matches Marie's description of her husband.
Marie never returned the officer's call, as requested, but now she takes
the train back to Landes for *Under the Sand*'s *scène à faire*. There she
meets with the lead investigator, who says that a strong undertow
caused Jean to drift out to sea, where he got caught in a fisherman's net
and drowned. Then the coroner, who is also present, reports that the
body has decomposed to such an extent that Marie would not be able
to identify her husband, but a DNA test, using tissue samples from the
corpse and Jean's mother (who therefore already knew of the body's
retrieval during her meeting with Marie?), has confirmed with ninety
per cent certainty that the body is Jean Drillon's.

Still, Marie wants to see the putrefied remains and does so, despite
the warnings of the detective and the coroner; *we* see nothing except
the dizzied, horrified expression on her face. When the coroner shows
Jean's blue swimming trunks to Marie, she says she thinks they
belonged to her husband. When he returns Jean's watch, though, she
claims that it isn't her husband's – despite the fact that this watch
matches the description she originally gave to the police. Whether the

watch actually belonged to Jean is less important, of course, than Marie's rejection of any device that would signify the cessation of her husband's biological clock and the concomitant continuation of her own. After that rejection, she understandably returns, in *Under the Sand*'s final scene, to the beach where Jean disappeared.

That beach is now cool, windy, and sunless, as the camera holds on Marie in close-up when she sits down and stares out, crying, moaning, and finally digging in the sand with her hands. Then Ozon cuts to another held shot: this time a long one in which Marie, in profile in the foreground, sees a man walking along the shore in the background. Sensing that he is Jean, she gets up and runs toward him – into the long shot, as it were, on which the camera remains fixed until the screen abruptly goes to black before Marie reaches the man. Is this in fact Jean? We do not know; we cannot tell. The mystery persists at the end, and the problem of identification is never "solved." Marie's love lives on, either in corporality or only in her own mind. That she may have been right all along in believing that Jean continued to live is less the film's clever conceit – its "Macguffin," to use Alfred Hitchcock's term – than its heartfelt reality. In any event, it's not important that we know whether Jean actually lives or lives only in Marie's imagination; in fact, Ozon may be suggesting that the one is as good as the other, or that the imagination has its own reality even as reality has its share of unbelievableness.

Ozon says he based *Under the Sand* on a personal experience he had at the beach when he was a child: "Every day we would meet a Dutch couple in their sixties. One day, the man went for a swim and never came back. It was a shock for me and my family." Such a traumatic event incites the action of *Under the Sand*'s ninety-five minutes, but, as should be clear by now, that action is largely static. A better word would be contemplative, and no actress could have better embodied this essential quality of the film than Charlotte Rampling (whose given name happens to be Marie Drillon and who, though English-born, is bilingual). I saw her for the first time in Liliana Cavani's *The Night Porter* (1974), in which she made a bit of a name for herself by playing a concentration camp survivor who resumes the sadomasochistic relationship she had with a former ss officer. This wasn't her first venture into the bizarre: that occurred in Luchino Visconti's *The Damned* (1969), which takes place in Germany during Hitler's rise to power; and the *bizarrerie* of Rampling's roles continued with *Stardust Memories* (1980), where she played the woman who helped Woody Allen to rape Federico Fellini. As a matter of fact, one could say that Rampling has done more to reinvent the fetishistic nature of love and death than any other screen actress.

So one can well understand the superficial reason why Ozon – himself no stranger to the exotically erotic – cast Rampling as Marie in *Under the Sand*. The deeper reason is that, since Ozon's minimalistic film can be reduced to the relationship between the camera and a character who for the most part doesn't talk about her feelings, he had to use an actress who could communicate subtle psychological states without words. And this Rampling can do, does do here, through gesture, look, and phrasing (when she actually speaks) – a Lauren Bacall without the mischief, I would call her. She first showed the ability to create inner torment combined with emotional nakedness in Sidney Lumet's *The Verdict* (1982), where she was taciturn and true as a schemer eventually devastated by her scheme. Now, older of course (fifty-seven, though she doesn't look her age) and never before as attractive, she creates a woman who is clearly intelligent, worldly-wise, even slightly stern or intimidating, yet who, without any awareness of abnormality, continues to live with a husband who is either dead or somewhere else.

That Rampling's character in *Under the Sand* is not a young woman is what makes this picture so different from *Truly, Madly, Deeply* as well as the artistically inferior *Ghost*. It is impossible to watch Ozon's movie and not be reminded that European actresses like Rampling and Catherine Deneuve continue to get mature parts in mature pictures that comparable American actresses like Meryl Streep and Jessica Lange could never hope to land in today's Hollywood – where there are no such roles for women and few such films for middle-aged men, for that matter. Indeed, Rampling followed up her fine work in *Under the Sand* with two performances opposite Stellan Skarsgård: first in *Aberdeen* (2000), where she plays his long-divorced wife who is dying of cancer, and next in *Signs and Wonders* (2001), in which Skarsgård and Rampling portray a happily married couple who begin to grow apart after seventeen years of marriage. (Michael Cacoyannis' *Cherry Orchard*, made in 1999 with Rampling in the role of Madame Lyubov opposite Alan Bates as her brother Gaev, arrived in the United States in the spring of 2002, just as I was sitting down to write this chronicle.) For their part, the middle-aged men playing opposite Rampling in *Under the Sand* are the dependable Bruno Cremer (Jean), a veteran actor well known for his portrayal of Georges Simenon's Inspector Maigret on French television, and the gruff-looking yet smooth-acting Jacques Nolot (Vincent), whose work may be familiar to those who have seen Claire Denis's *Nénette and Boni* (1996) or André Téchiné's *Wild Reeds* (1994).

A middle-aged man is the only character to appear in the long (four to six minutes) opening, virtually wordless scene of Tsai Ming-liang's *What Time Is It There?*, but we soon learn that he has died and he doesn't appear again until the end of the film [*sic*]. Like *Under the Sand*, this Taiwanese film took its origin from an event in the life of its director and co-author (with Yang Pi-ying): the death of his father in 1992. And, also like Ozon's picture, *What Time Is It There?* shares thematic as well as stylistic characteristics with its *auteur*'s previous work, at the same time as it adds existential depth and metaphysical anguish to what until now could be seen merely as offbeat or unconventional, rebellious or even flippant. In Tsai's case, I'm referring to the teenaged disaffection of *Rebels of the Neon God* (1992), the affected anomie of *Vive l'amour* (1994), the hermetic symbolism of *The River* (1996), and the deadpan comedy of *The Hole* (1998).

Tsai is one of three Taiwanese filmmakers whose films have begun to be distributed in America; the other two are Hou Hsiao-hsien, represented most recently here by *Flowers of Shanghai* (1998), and Edward Yang, whose *Yi Yi* (2000) won the Best Director award at the Cannes Festival before arriving in the United States. The new Taiwanese cinema seems to be as nimble as that of Hong Kong, without the commercial constraints, and as serious as Chinese film without being burdened so much by the dead weight of an often mythological past. As Tsai himself has observed,

Taiwanese film has begun to develop its own style without any political influences ... Now that it's come to us we feel strongly that movies must be personal and spring very much from one's own heart. I think we're searching for a narrative style that is different from Hollywood's ... and different from our predecessors in Taiwan cinema.

Those predecessors were faced chiefly with the political question of whether Taiwan would remain independent or reunify with mainland China. The Taiwanese New Wave, by contrast, sees itself confronted by an inescapable cultural question, particularly in an era when even the Beijing Communists are trying to capitalize on the Asian economic miracle: these writer-directors question the nature of their very existence in the culture-in-transition that is Taiwan, where brash Western values promise ever-increasing materialistic gain yet provide little moral direction and even less spiritual fulfillment to Eastern sensibilities.

In this quest – epitomized by the title of Yang's fifth film, *A Confucian Confusion* (1994) – the young Taiwanese moviemakers have something in common with the French New Wave, whose most famous member, François Truffaut, makes an appearance in *What Time Is It There?* via his film *The Four Hundred Blows* (1959) and his alter ego, Jean-Pierre Léaud. The French *nouvelle vague*, seemingly like the Taiwanese one, was at bottom less a wave than an epidemic of faith and of desperation – a desperate belief that film might prove to be an answer to much that was harassing French society and culture, which, to use the title of Jean-Luc Godard's first feature, was "out of breath." Among those "harassments": the political uncertainties of post-World War II France, the Vietnamese and Algerian debacles, the growth of ideological disillusion almost into an ideology, and a conviction of sterility and vacuum in the nation as well as in traditional art (particularly the old-fashioned, worn-out format of industry-financed, studio-crafted, finally impersonal filmmaking). Paradoxically, though there is nothing impersonal about the making of recent Taiwanese cinema, its own themes are urban impersonality, isolation, or alienation; social dissonance bordering on dysfunction; and psychological malaise glossed over by private obsession or compulsion – themes that are manifestly the products of an Asian nation in a limbo of the body as well as the soul.

What Time Is It There? begins, in a sense, with an elliptical meditation on body and soul. Sitting down to eat in the small dining area of his apartment, the father of a family smokes a cigarette, then goes to call his wife (who is apparently in a room off the kitchen) to the table. Returning, he sits down to his meal, but he does not eat and his wife does not come. The man then gets up and goes first to the kitchen, then to the back porch, where he fiddles with a potted plant, smokes another cigarette, and remains standing until the end of the scene. The main emotion here appears to be melancholy, the chief "drama" absence, not presence (the father exits the frame once, then retreats from the table in the foreground to the porch in the background, while the mother never appears or even speaks off-camera); and the abiding activity seems to be waiting or simply being, even wasting away instead of eating in order to sustain life. Indeed, what we don't realize in our MTV-impatience, even after we have finally cut to another scene, is that we have just witnessed the final minutes in the life of a man numb with illness and solitude. The very stasis of this opening scene – opening shot, really – should have told us as much, for it is filmed in a single long take at full-body distance, with no camera movement, no music, some "dead time," total ambient sound, and spare sidelighting.

This is to be the cinematic style for the remainder of *What Time Is It There?*, a minimalistic or reductivist one that is the natural distillation of Tsai's previous filmmaking, and which combines the seemingly disparate aesthetic principles of Ozu, Bresson, and Jacques Tati (or of Antonioni, Jim Jarmusch, and Andy Warhol, for that matter). Much of the film's action transpires indoors (apartments, hotel rooms, cars, subway trains, movie theatres), and the space of those interiors is confining, as characters move about in awkward silence or even a somnambulistic state of contemplation bordering on depression. Oddly, photographing these figures mostly in full shot – sometimes at medium range but almost never in close-up, and occasionally with a wide-angle lens that presents an image with a greater horizontal plane as well as greater depth of field – without editing exacerbates the sense of their being confined or entrapped by their environment. (Sometimes that environment itself becomes the sum of everything that "happens" or is revealed during a scene.)

I say "oddly" because such a shooting style is normally equated with freedom of movement, action, and association for the characters (not to speak of continuity of performance for the actors), freedom of choice (as to where to look and what to see) for the viewer, and respect for the divine mystery of reality in all its wholeness or sanctity. In *What Time Is It There?* this third element may come into play, but, as for the second one, there isn't so much happening in a scene like the first that the viewer must exercise any power of selection. And, where the initial element is concerned, the people of Taipei and Paris (the two cities where the film takes place) themselves may be "free"; however, their great physical proximity to each other in such densely populated places ironically only increases their emotional-psychological separation. And this in turn leads to self-isolation if not self-immobilization within the otherwise "uncut" confines of their homes, their automobiles, their workplaces, their recreation spots. Furthermore, the cinematographer, Benoît Delhomme (who has also worked with the Vietnamese director Tran Anh Hung, most notably on *The Scent of Green Papaya* [1993]), has photographed these inner spheres with fluorescent light sources, the effect of which is to give an anesthetizing reflective gloss to images dominated by the cool colors of blue, green, and gray.

Those images in the end don't amount to a drama so much as the weaving together of three interconnected stories or lives, along with the three concepts of time, space, and the time-space relationship as, at any one time, they affect two of the picture's three main characters. After the death of the film's patriarchal figure, one of those three main characters, his middle-aged widow, becomes obsessed with the notion that his spirit will be reincarnated and that she must ritualistically facilitate his or its arrival (shades here of Marie Drillon). This she does by always setting her husband's place at the table; burning incense and saying prayers (led by a Buddhist priest on at least one occasion); eliminating all light sources from without as well as within; and by preparing his supper at midnight, which she interprets as the time – 5 p.m. in his new "zone" – at which the evening meal would be served (hence one possible reason for the film's title). The widow gets this idea from her kitchen clock, which one day mysteriously appears re-set seven hours earlier than the time in Taipei. But it is her twentysomething son, Hsiao Kang, who has re-set the clock, even as he obsessively re-sets every watch and clock he has or sees to Parisian time.

One could argue that Hsiao does this because he's grieving for his father and wants to turn back the hands of time to when the old man was alive, or that such a repetitive activity is the perfect escape from his overbearing mother and claustrophobic home life, where in a sense time has stopped. (The only noisy scenes in *What Time Is It There?* are those between Hsiao and his mother as he tries to temper her compulsive effort to invite her dead husband's return.) But clearly Hsiao is also re-setting as many of Taipei's timepieces as possible because this is the only way he can re-connect himself to a young woman he met on the street (yet never sees again) in his job as a watch peddler, and separation from whom may reiterate or intensify his separation from his father. Her name is Shiang-chyi and, en route to France for a holiday of sorts, she convinces Hsiao Kang to sell her his own dual time-zone wristwatch. (Hsiao needs convincing because, as a Buddhist by birth, he believes it would be bad luck for a man in mourning, like himself, to sell his watch; as a Christian, Shiang-chyi says that she doesn't believe in bad luck.) Such a watch will allow her simultaneously to keep track of the time in Paris and Taipei – thus the other possible reason for the movie's title.

Not that Shiang becomes involved in a long-distance relationship with Hsiao or anyone else in Taipei; in fact, she never refers to him again after their initial encounter, nor is there any sense of love lorn in *him* despite his obsession with Parisian time. And the lightness of this young couple's encounter, the fact that it does not lead to any romantic or even mystical union, is essential to Tsai's design. For he wants to show, not that they yearn for each other, but rather that each yearns for a heightened awareness of the world she or he does not know, yet which to a substantial degree determines the nature of their lives. This seems to be the overarching reason why Shiang goes West to Paris, in space, and Hsiao goes there in time. But he goes there in virtual space

A pensive Chen Shiang-chyi, as Shiang, in *What Time Is It There?*

as well when he buys a videotape of *The Four Hundred Blows* (reportedly Tsai's favorite movie) because it will enable him to see images of Paris. (Significantly, the only other French film Hsiao could have purchased in this particular shop was Alain Resnais's *Hiroshima, mon amour* [1959], itself a kind of meditation on East-West relations through the persons of a French film actress and a Japanese architect and their respective "places," Nevers and Hiroshima.)

What Hsiao sees in *The Four Hundred Blows*, however, is less Paris than the existential crisis of a character caught between childhood and adolescence, on the one hand, and neglectful parents (one of them a stepfather) and a tyrannical public school system, on the other. Along with Hsiao in his darkened room, we watch two scenes in particular from Truffaut's first major film: the one in which the fourteen-year-old Jean-Pierre Léaud, as Antoine Doinel, drinks a stolen bottle of milk for breakfast after having spent the night alone on the street; and a second scene at an amusement park, where this boy flouts gravity by refusing to stick to the side of a rotowhirl ride as it spins around with greater and greater velocity. As someone who flouts time by setting even public clocks back seven hours throughout Taipei, and as a son who himself seeks refuge on the street from a mother more concerned with her dead husband's spirit than her son's life, Hsiao can identify with the protagonist of *The Four Hundred Blows* – even if he can see Antoine's Paris only by night or in the black and white of an overcast day.

What Shiang herself experiences in Paris, as an almost accidental tourist who doesn't speak French, is severe dislocation and even dissociation. This is not the candy-colored, landmark-dotted Paris of romantic movies; Shiang's relationship to the city is relatively loveless as she moves from her dreary little hotel to one café, small grocery, or cheap restaurant after another. When she isn't crowded into a subway car that must suddenly be vacated because of "a serious incident," she becomes the second-hand victim on the street of an angry Frenchman's pay-telephone tirade. When Shiang gazes shyly at an Asian man standing alone on the opposite platform down in the Metro, her face suggests a young woman desperate to shed her loneliness for a little native-culture connectivity, while his visage stares back at her as if she were an apparition.

So detached is this all-too-visible Asian outsider in a world of white Europeans that human contact for her becomes what would be a nuisance or disturbance to anyone else: the sound of loud noises and heavy footsteps in the hotel room above hers. Sensing Shiang's loneliness, Jean-Pierre Léaud himself (now fifty-eight) strikes up a terse yet friendly conversation with her, in English, as they sit at opposite ends of a bench outside a cemetery. Though not much is said, Léaud does scribble his phone number down on a piece of paper, hand it to Shiang, and introduce himself (as Jean-Pierre) before the scene – as well as their acquaintance – ends. (Léaud's last such cameo was in Aki Kaurismäki's *La vie de bohème* [1992], a melancholic yet darkly humorous meditation on the lives of artists, set, like *What Time Is It There?*, in a surprisingly bleak contemporary Paris.)

Shiang does finally meet a young woman from Hong Kong who has also come to Paris alone, as a tourist. But their friendship – the only one formed in *What Time Is It There?* – ends unexpectedly after an unconsummated lesbian encounter between the two women. This scene, set in the Hong Kong girl's hotel room, is cross-cut with two other sex scenes in what, for this film, is a burst of quickly edited action. We cut back and forth between Shiang and her would-be lover, Hsiao and a prostitute copulating in the backseat of his parked car, and Hsiao's mother masturbating on the floor of her home before a candle-lit photograph of her departed husband (autoerotism that makes Marie Drillon's self-stimulation in *Under the Sand* look mild by comparison). That none of these scenes takes place between two people who love each other, or concludes with tenderness of any kind, is telling. For Tsai, it appears, sex is no more sensual, personal, or intimate than any other mundane act to be performed in the urban landscape, be it Eastern *or* Western. In fact, the sexual act gets less screen time than Hsiao's urinating, which we watch him do twice in his room at night – from start to finish – into bottles or plastic bags, because he is afraid he will bump into his deceased father's spirit if he walks to the bathroom.

Hsiao is asleep in his car when we see him for the penultimate time in *What Time Is It There?*, as the aforementioned prostitute steals his suitcase full of watches and slithers off into the night. That suitcase, or one like it, then appears in the film's final scene, which is set in Paris. Shiang-chyi is sitting silently by a pond in the park-like area outside the Louvre, apparently collecting her thoughts the morning after her aborted affair with the woman from Hong Kong. Then a suitcase floats by – into and out of the frame – atop the pond. An older man farther along the edge of the water hooks the suitcase with his umbrella handle, brings it ashore, leaves it there, and moves on. Shiang is now asleep. *What Time Is It There?* ends with this older man – played by the same actor (Miao Tien) who played Hsiao's father in the opening scene – lighting a cigarette and walking away into an extreme long shot, in the background of which a large Ferris wheel begins ever-so-slowly to revolve. The father's spirit has returned to earth, Tsai would give us to believe, but why to Paris and not Taipei?

Perhaps this is where the old man is needed, as a guardian angel of sorts to the beleaguered Shiang in a godforsaken, consumptive West that should be regarded as the source of, rather than the answer to, the East's problems. His wife, after all, has an overgrown pet goldfish and her hothouse-like plant (both of them constrained by walls of glass within the already walled-in confines of the family's apartment) as well as her son. Indeed, Hsiao's last act in *What Time Is It There?* (after his evening with the prostitute) is to cover his sleeping mother with his jacket and lie down next to her for some rest. The film thus ends in quotidian serenity, a mood that has been broken throughout by cracked or dotty comedy, but also one that has allowed for the continual raising of larger, epistemological questions.

If the contrast between Tsai's large questions or subjects – time as an immutable, inexorable, incorporeal construct that humanity nonetheless seeks to control or manipulate; space itself as an infinite construct that, on earth at least, we have tried to render in convenient divisions such as East and West; and the relationship among time, space, and matter – and his film's structural spareness suggests the existential absurd, this seems to be the worldview that Tsai espouses. Such a reduced structure then becomes Tsai's realistic response to the diminished and disconnected lives he finds around him in today's "shrunken" world, lives such as Hsiao's and Shiang's as well as those of Hsiao's mother and father. Similarly, Tsai's emphasis, through long takes, full shots, and "dead time," on the space that surrounds those lives turns into a metaphorical attempt to privilege the integrity, inviolability, or permanence of the natural world over against the insignificance and evanescence of the people who inhabit it.

It's equally possible that the true subject of *What Time Is It There?*, as the culmination of Tsai's cinema, is less the droll Taiwanese landscape and the characters, in both senses of the word, who inhabit it, than filmmaking itself – the sheer fashioning of motion pictures out of celluloid snippets in time. Cubism was probably the first movement that made the person, setting, or object depicted a pretext for the artist's exploration of the geometry of space, to be joined by Futurism's investigation of the physics of time. And it wasn't long before painters and sculptors were creating truly abstract art, from which the recognizable world had been totally banished. But film, which can move and talk, seems inextricably bound up with the representation of physical reality in a way that painting or sculpture does not. Hence the divided impulse in a director like Tsai – and, most notably, in Jim Jarmusch before him as well as Godard before *him* – between abstraction and representation, formalism and realism, allocation in space and being in time.

That divided impulse carries over into Tsai's work with actors. On the one hand, like Jean-Pierre Léaud in Truffaut's series of five films featuring the character Antoine Doinel, Lee Kang-sheng (as Hsiao Kang) has been the protagonist of all five of Tsai Ming-liang's movies. Moreover, Lu Ti-ching (as the mother) and Miao Tien have played Lee's parents in each of Tsai's four previous pictures as well as in *What Time Is It There?* Others in the cast, like Chen Shiang-chyi (as Shiang) and even the goldfish "Fatty," have worked with Tsai before. (Sets also reappear in his films: Lee Kang-sheng's home provided the setting for *What Time Is It There?*, *Rebels of the Neon God*, and *The River*.) So there's the sense that these people (and that fish) are Tsai's artistic collaborators in addition to making up a familiar or recognizable family of actors, like the "repertory company" that Ingmar Bergman regularly used.

On the other hand, Tsai's actors are also his performative instruments in the Bressonian sense. That is, some of them are not professionals or were not before they began working for Tsai, and several have never worked for anyone else. Bresson called his mostly non-professional actors "models" and spoke of using them up in the creation of a sacred cinema that would rival any other art in its ability to invoke mystery, ineffability, or otherness. Tsai, who has praised the reticent "enacting" in Bresson's films (as opposed to the manufactured emoting of professionals to be found in movies everywhere), similarly uses otherwise human figures as inscrutable yet evocative chesspieces in the creation of his own finely formal, poetically transcendent, immanently cinematic design.

Possibly there is some danger in loading *What Time Is It There?* with more weight than it can bear. But unless we shed our reservations about this film's gravity or its director's courage in disregarding almost every convention that holds most pictures together, we reduce *What Time Is It There?* to a piece of avant-garde eccentricity, even concentricity, designed to keep us on the outside looking in. Similarly, unless we are stirred to deep questions about the nature of love, illusion, and being in *Under the Sand*, we reduce it to a piece of sentimental trickery designed to invite us in and close the door on the outside world behind us. Which fate neither of these extra-ordinary artworks deserves.

16

Aberdeen on the Adriatic

On Moland's *Aberdeen* (2000, Norway) and Moretti's *The Son's Room* (2001, Italy)

Even though the Academy Awards are several months away, it's time to bash the American cinema once again – indirectly, at least. For I refuse to waste much space on the mostly execrable and often juvenile products of the "entertainment industry" collectively known as Hollywood. That space, or this column, is reserved for films like *Aberdeen* (2000), a co-production of Norway and Scotland, and *The Son's Room* (2001), made in Italy but partly financed by the French. These two pictures are comparable not only because they are both domestic dramas whose drama is triggered by the recent or impending death of a family member. They are also connected because each features a stereotypical screen figure, stereotypical particularly in the United States, and treats him credibly, sympathetically, perceptively – without caricature, on the one hand, or romanticization, on the other. In *Aberdeen*, that figure is the acute alcoholic; in *The Son's Room*, he is the psychiatrist or psychoanalyst.

Let's start with the screen alcoholic prior to *Aberdeen*. Why have even the most high-minded American films, like *The Lost Weekend* (1945) and *Days of Wine and Roses* (1962), tended to romanticize acute alcoholism, usually in the figure of a man? Is it the very nature of movies to glamorize such extreme and repugnant behavior? Even the much-admired (by others, not by me) *Leaving Las Vegas*, whose central character drinks himself to death, invests its suicidal protagonist with the heroic aura of a sacrificial victim whose flame burns a little more brightly than everyone else's. That 1995 movie was only the latest Hollywood manifestation of what might be called the *Under the Volcano* syndrome (from Briton Malcolm Lowry's autobiographical novel published in 1947, but an American-financed and -directed picture released in 1984), in which marathon boozing assumes a Wagnerian grandiosity.

One of the strengths of Hans Petter Moland's small, beautifully acted *Aberdeen* is its refusal to give its characters' substance abuse (liquor *and* cocaine) even the faintest patina of hipness. Another strength is the heat with which it treats the range of emotional possibilities between a young woman and her father. I can't think of any American movie that comes close to *Aberdeen* in this department. In desperation, I could reach for *A Bill of Divorcement* (1932), in which Katharine Hepburn made her screen début as John Barrymore's daughter, or for *The Heiress* (1949), where Olivia de Havilland played a spinster dominated by Ralph Richardson in the role of her cruel, unloving father. But the father-daughter sentiments in these otherwise serious films (for Hollywood, in any event) were comfortably ensconced in social acceptances of the time. Hence they have no relation to the fierce ripping or acidic bathing of such sentiments in *Aberdeen*, which obviously is as much a product of its age as the aforementioned George Cukor and William Wyler movies.

The forty-six-year-old Moland happens to have been educated in America, though he was born in Norway. *Aberdeen*, which he co-wrote with Kristin Amundsen, is his third feature but only his first film in English. It begins in London, where Kaisa, a corporate lawyer on the rise, is having sex in her apartment. (It's very much to the point of her hard-edged, feisty, even ribald character that she's on top, that we never see the man or learn anything about him, and that he doesn't appear again in the picture.) The morning after, this young woman gets a telephone call from her mother, Helen, who lives in Aberdeen, Scotland. She wants Kaisa to go to Oslo and bring her father, Tomas Heller, a Norwegian, to Aberdeen. Helen and Tomas were never married and they ended their relationship fifteen years earlier (actually, she left him), but now she hopes for Tomas's rehabilitation, in Scotland, from the alcoholism that saddles him and prematurely ended his career as an offshore oil-rig worker. The real catalyst for mother as well as daughter, however, is Helen's disclosure that she has cancer in an advanced stage and yearns for a family reunion that will culminate in her legal marriage to Tomas.

Immediately after the opening credits but before the above-described bedroom scene, we see Kaisa, as a child of about ten sporting a red clown-nose, running to greet her returning father (who, whether off the Scottish or the Norwegian coast, worked for two weeks at a time in the North Sea, followed by two weeks at home), in his Italian sports car, in a rush of feeling. We shall watch this grainy, slow-motion, sunlight-suffused flashback again during *Aberdeen*, just as we shall see both the red clown-nose – attached, in the present, to Kaisa's key ring and at one juncture to her father's nose – and the now-vintage automobile, an Alfa Romeo that sits gathering dust in an Aberdeen garage but will be Helen's reward to her daughter for retrieving Tomas.

Yet any sentimentalism that might be attached to either object is undercut by the fact that a red clown-nose is also the sign of a severe drunk (whose nasal capillaries burst as a result of excessive alcohol consumption), and that Tomas Heller is anything but an Alpha personality or a Romeo type. Sentimentalism is also undercut by the irony of the song playing on the soundtrack during the aforementioned flashbacks, as well as during one scene in the present: "I'm Getting Along Just Fine Without You," written by Hoagy Carmichael but performed by another addict, the drug-user Chet Baker, whose music the adult Kaisa peevishly says she deplores solely on account of his heroin habit. (The rest of *Aberdeen*'s minimal, minimally orchestrated score by Zbigniew Preisner is subdued when it is not stately, refusing to behave like conventional movie music and milk the audience's emotions, cue its members' feelings, or kill their thoughts.)

Kaisa may once have been strongly attached to her father (though, like him, she dislikes her mother), but she hasn't seen Tomas for ten years. As a workaholic with a fear of intimacy, a vulnerability to substance abuse herself (she's the coke-snorter, which gives *her* a red nose in the form of nasal bleeding), and a love of life in the fast lane, Kaisa is a classic case of "like parent, like child." And those who are the children of alcoholics know that she is courting disaster in trying to deal with a father who not only is a drunk but also has not heard from his daughter for such a long time. At least Kaisa has his address in Oslo, whither she flies, dressed in a smart black business suit, and promptly rents a flashy new car with which to impress Tomas (claiming it as her own). She traces him to a pub, naturally, where he is truculent and sodden but somehow strong, with the special pathos and irritation of an intelligent, even well-read, man who is a hopeless boozer.

Kaisa has told herself that she can deliver her father to her mother in the space of a day, and she is sufficiently assertive that Tomas, who continually smokes as well as drinks, agrees reluctantly to accompany her. But he is so falling-down drunk that he is not allowed to board the plane to the United Kingdom, while chip-off-the-old-block Kaisa is so verbally abusive toward the flight attendant that she nearly lands herself in jail. Perversely, this airport fracas creates a sort of bonding between father and daughter. And in the automobile Kaisa has rented, she and Tomas proceed to drive to the port of Bergen, where they will board a ship to England. He has taken along a supply of beer and whiskey, which Kaisa constantly threatens to ration, and she has her stash of cocaine, a fix from which she decides to take at one point after she suddenly stops her car along the highway. Staggering out into the snowy desolation of the Norwegian countryside, whose frigid weather reflects the chilliness of this father-daughter relationship, Kaisa is startled by a pair of passing reindeer as she kneels down to snort her drug. Comically if somewhat grotesquely, she screams the following memorable line in response to the oblivious four-legged creatures: "There's too much fucking nature in this country!"

Significantly, this is the only time that Moland makes any direct use of the desolate landscape that Scots and Norwegians share, along with the oil industry, and which has sometimes been such an inspiration for northern European filmmakers (Ingmar Bergman outstanding among them). Nature in *Aberdeen* is largely absent, being present only in the relentless rain beating down on city streets or car windshields, and in the alternation of dank darkness with cold light on the windows of business offices, roadside restaurants, hotel bars, assorted sleeping quarters, or the hospital room where Helen waits alone for the union of her dysfunctional family. (The cinematographer Philip Øgaard increases the chill of *Aberdeen*'s images by dampening whatever color they may possess through the use of a bluish green filter, as well as by undercutting even the "softness" or warmth of interiors with as many sharp lines and hard angles as can fill the frame.) It thus becomes all too understandable why alcoholism – a defense against both personal failure and ghastly weather – should be so characteristic a curse of the otherwise hardy, rugged, and fiercely independent northern soul, from Aberdeen all the way to Archangelsk.

Alcoholic or not, Tomas is unimpressed by Kaisa's fancy car, designer clothes, and sharp tongue. He criticizes her for being "angry and predatory," like a man (though he says nothing about her cocaine habit after he learns of it), and wonders aloud what happened to the sweet little girl he remembers. Kaisa, in turn, is disgusted with this odious drunkard who tries to steal her money, vomits all over her business suit, urinates in public (as well as, occasionally, all over himself), and has no intention of entering any detoxification program once they get to Aberdeen. Still, to Aberdeen they go, via Harwich, London (where Kaisa quietly rents another car and checks in at work, only to be closely followed by her father, then mightily embarrassed by him when he identifies himself to the head of the law firm), Leeds, and Edinburgh, as *Aberdeen* turns into a road movie with a twist. For, unlike most road pictures, which are about escape, this one is about trying to reach a goal or destination – as its title indicates – rather than traveling away from it.

Yet it is the journey, not the arrival, that matters most, or, in any event, without which there could be no arrival. The real being of this film, in time and space as well as substance, lies in the journey, in the anatomy of tensions between a father who is a stranger to his daughter and a daughter who slowly discovers herself in the mirror of her unruly, besotted father. As in many road movies – which at their best are always about moral, spiritual, or emotional pilgrimages, not about literal journeys – these two protagonists undergo something of a role reversal as the trip progresses. For Tomas the development from sodden despair to qualified hope is comparatively straightforward. But for Kaisa the transformation from careerist callousness to timorous intimacy is more complex, as this young woman's brittle confidence gives way to reveal her own version of addiction, self-dissatisfaction, and a need so desperate that it will embrace even as flawed a paternal figure as Tomas.

Pivotal in helping Kaisa to let down her emotional defenses is Clive, a kindly, self-deprecating, sensible truck driver who stops to assist Tomas and his daughter after their car blows a tire on an English road. When the sexually freewheeling Kaisa later puts the moves on Clive in a motel room, he blithely warns her that if she wants bad sex, she has come to the right man. Of course, this blue-collar bloke turns out not to be bad at all at sex or at life, and, though he is stunned by the angry, even abusive relations between the strange pair of Kaisa and her father, he stays with them. His motivation may partly be Kaisa's nearly sculpted good looks (augmented by dark hair, cream-colored skin, and a lithe figure), but director Moland's motivation in keeping Clive around has less to do with exploiting this couple's unorthodox romance than with offering the audience conventional relief from, or perspective on, the strained and straining dealings between a *pater familias* and his only child.

We need it, as they need Clive when, in one town on the way to Aberdeen, some well-dressed louts reduce Tomas to a circus animal begging for a beer in the middle of the street, steal Kaisa's wallet, and beat up the both of them. Next stop: Edinburgh, where the destitute Kaisa must sell one of her packets of cocaine to finance the rest of the trip, as well as to buy smarter clothing for her father and lower-key dress for herself. It is at a gasoline station outside Edinburgh that Tomas feels so harassed, dominated, and manipulated by his daughter as to tell her he may not even really be her (biological) father. This revelation leads to *Aberdeen*'s most unsettling, nearly repulsive scene, in which, to avenge herself, the frazzled and coked-up Kaisa makes an aggressively teasing attempt to seduce the disconcerted Tomas in the back seat of the rental car as the powerless Clive drives. "We could be lovers," she mockingly declares as she kisses Tomas's neck and gyrates in his lap, "how about it?" Thus does the movie move its father-daughter relationship into the naked arena of potential or possibly long-suppressed incest. But, truly, physical intercourse here, however disgusting, would be anti-climactic after all the other kinds of degrading intercourse between these two we have witnessed over the course of their journey: the imbibing and inhaling, sneaking and snookering, cursing and caterwauling, befouling and bemoaning.

Moreover, this congress of theirs doesn't exactly end after Kaisa and Tomas reach the "promised land" of Aberdeen. Kaisa's first loud words in the intensive care unit of St Ruth's Infirmary are, "Is my mom dead yet?" and both she and her father are subsequently ejected from the hospital for disorderliness before they can visit Helen. Still, they act in concert, not onanistically, and *Aberdeen*'s strong suggestion is that such low-down teamwork is to be preferred over any solo act of the high-flying kind. But Clive, for his part, can't take this road show any longer, and bolts after leaving some money with which Kaisa and Tomas can purchase flowers for Helen. They do so, then go to see the terminal member of their family. And the meeting of this threesome is everything it should be in *Aberdeen* yet everything such a *scène à faire* would not be in the American cinema (or, God forbid, network television): brief, terse, unsentimental, at times funny. (Helen, for instance, greets her daughter and common-in-law husband with the question, "Did you have a nice trip?")

Tomas is sober and Kaisa is clean, it's true, but these two are clearly on edge as a result of the strenuous effort required to get to this point. There are no hugs, kisses, or tears, yet there is a revelation: because it was Helen who, years earlier, had said in anger that Tomas was not Kaisa's real father, she penitently recants before both of them on her deathbed. So what do her daughter and former mate do? Accept Helen's word, rejoice, embrace, and vow from this point forward to treat each other (as well as themselves) with love and respect? Not in this film. They go to get a DNA test. Shortly thereafter, Tomas decides to take the rap when, during a routine search, the police find cocaine in Kaisa's car; Helen dies and Kaisa retrieves her father's, now her, Alfa Romeo; and she leaves a tearful, supplicatory message on Clive's answering machine (to no avail).

Finally, Kaisa drives the Alfa to the prison where Tomas is being held, not only to disclose the result of the DNA test – which proves conclusively that he is *not* her biological father – but also to take his place in jail as the genuinely guilty drug-possessor *and* to bring a permanent end to their relationship. Tomas resists her with the words, "I'm the only father you ever had. You're my only daughter." Then he asks Kaisa to dance as they used to do when she was a little girl: with her feet atop his as he hums and trundles her about the room. But this isn't really a room: Kaisa may be teary-eyed in Tomas's embrace, but they're in a holding cage next to his cell, they're all alone as she weighs down on him, and the camera has moved from a long take in medium-close range to a shot from high overhead (not the first such "oppressive" camera placement in *Aberdeen*) as the image fades to black. The end.

A happy ending? Yes and no. This last scene is certainly a *move* toward personal rehabilitation, familial reconstruction, and human redemption, but it gives no guarantees; indeed, Moland and Øgaard's *mise en scène* here suggests that the road ahead for Kaisa and Tomas will be nothing less than arduous. Aberdeen may be more than simply the city to which their journey moves: it may be the site for father and daughter of a cleansing through pain. Nevertheless, Aberdeen is still the "Granite City," and it is the granite of their own fully petrified characters that Tomas and Kaisa will be up against for the rest of their lives. Together they have harrowed their way through a harrowing experience, and they both doubtless know what they have been through. What each has "learned," however, or how much either has "changed," is another matter. This pair's final scene in *Aberdeen*, then, may be less a completion or linking up for formality's sake (like a brief coda in music), even less a bouquet for the maudlin movie world, than a brief respite for Tomas as for Kaisa before a recurring storm of emotions, abrasions, buffetings, and repellents. No longer imprisoned by biology, they are now abutted only by circumstance.

Wondrously abutted in *Aberdeen* by the circumstances of the film world are the actors Stellan Skarsgård (Tomas), Lena Headey (Kaisa), Charlotte Rampling (Helen), and Ian Hart (Clive). This is Moland's second picture in which Skarsgård portrays a drunk, the first being *Zero Kelvin* (1996), in which he created the brutal, caustic portrait of a fur-trapper in 1920s Greenland who endures a terrible secret. In *Aberdeen* this actor is even better, for, despite his dreadful physical and social degradation, despite the fact that the camera in this film likes to get up close and personal, he never hams up his drunkenness. Clenched and brooding, churning with both rage and self-loathing, Skarsgård's Tomas is one of the most realistic lushes ever to reach the screen. Far from the lurching, wild-eyed maniac of movie cliché who asks simultaneously for your collusion and condemnation, he is a furtive, cunning animal who grows more sullen (not more sympathetic) and more infuriating (not more lovable) the more alcohol he consumes. Even as his journey to Aberdeen challenges Tomas Heller to rediscover his basic decency, intelligence, and responsibility, Skarsgård always retains the ambiguity of a man for whom sobriety is both a fond hope and a potentially unbearable torment. Indeed, when Tomas is sober in *Aberdeen*, one can almost smell the sour sweat of his rising panic and desperation.

Skarsgård reprises his role here not only from *Zero Kelvin* but also from Lars Van Trier's *Breaking the Waves* (1994), where he first played a Norwegian whose work on offshore oil rigs had gotten him involved with a Scottish woman. (That is where the comparison ends, however, since in *Breaking the Waves* his character, quite unlike the self-destructive Tomas, was a vigorous romantic struck down by cruel fate.) Charlotte Rampling, as Helen, herself performs a reprise of sorts as she is reunited with Skarsgård after having teamed up with him in *Signs and Wonders* (2001). Recently so finely reticent in *Under the Sand* (2000), Rampling must in *Aberdeen* again create a character that can communicate subtle psychological states without many words, here without much screen time and only from her hospital bed. She thoroughly succeeds in radiating quiet beauty in addition to turbulent depth, though I confess I don't know why, when Rampling does speak, she doesn't have the Scottish accent used by the actress who plays Kaisa.

She is Lena Headey, and she is fabulous. Last viewed in the undistinguished *Onegin* (1999) and soon to be seen in Neil LaBute's *Possession* (2002), Headey (like Rampling, English-born) gives a tour-de-force, star performance in a way that most starring performances avoid: she doesn't mind being made to seem ugly rather than pretty, and her lack of vanity means she also doesn't care whether we "like" her character. All that concerns this actress is the verity of the moment and the authenticity of every word and gesture on the part of her emotionally conflicted character, and the result is a controlled abandon that attracts, discomforts, estranges, and even amuses us – sometimes all at once, but never in sequential order. To watch Headey in the role of the headstrong Kaisa is to feel a war within oneself between wanting and fearing, between desiring and dreading the crystalline object of one's desire. In the role of Clive, Ian Hart correlatively and effortlessly captures this mixed emotion or divided impulse. Hart once played John Lennon (in *Backbeat* [1993]), and he has Lennon's warm, kind eyes, which he uses here, more than his alert disposition or his physical resourcefulness, to convey Clive's simultaneous disheartenment and delectation at encountering so denuded a piece of work as Kaisa.

The acting in *The Son's Room* is of an entirely different order from Lena Headey's or Stellan Skarsgård's in *Aberdeen*: low-key, or in a lower emotional register, given its main character's profession, the movie's subject, and especially its treatment of that subject. This is the third film (of ten features) by the Italian director Nanni Moretti to reach the United States. The first to arrive (and best, in the opinion of many) was *The Mass Is Ended* in 1988, though it was made in 1985; and its subject, the collision of a young priest (played by Moretti) with the crisis of faith in our day, is indirectly related to the subject of *The Son's Room*, whose protagonist, a psychoanalyst, could be called a secular priest of the contemporary world. The second Moretti film to be shown here was *Caro Diario* (1994), in which this writer-director actually appeared as himself, in a seriocomic collection of vignettes that dealt with his problems as a director and as a patient undergoing (an ultimately successful) treatment for lung cancer.

At one time in his career, Moretti was known as the "Italian Woody Allen" because he writes, directs, and stars in movies that frequently feature autobiographical threads in addition to mixing humor with pathos. But there is none of Allen's (rapidly vanishing) physical comedy in Moretti's work; there is no physical resemblance between the two men (the forty-nine-year-old Italian is tall, slim, bearded, and good-looking); and, for all its comic touches, Moretti's cinema is predominantly, uniquely serious in modes much deeper than Allen could ever hope to explore. Moreover, the central position of psychoanalysis in Allen's life and films is replaced, in Moretti's, with politics. His *Palombella Rossa* (1989), for example, was about the problems of a politically radical water-polo player – which the leftist Moretti himself once was, on the Italian national team – while *Ecce Bombo* (1978) concerned a disillusioned student's struggle to recover the fervor of his erstwhile political militancy.

The Son's Room (which Moretti co-authored with Linda Ferri and Heidrun Schleef) clearly marks a departure in his career in several ways. It is more straightforward than his other pictures, with none of the long-windedness and tendentiousness (not to mention the political topical-

ity) that mar his lesser work; it was not filmed in his native Rome; and
Moretti's character lacks the numerous (untreated) neuroses, as well as
the absurdist vigor, for which his cinematic alter ego, Michele Apicella,
has become known. In *The Son's Room*, those neuroses can be found in
his character's patients, for here he plays Giovanni Sermonti, a middle-
aged psychoanalyst who doesn't have a hint of Allenesque ridiculous-
ness, but who does have a highly successful practice (conducted in a
consulting room at the back of his house) in Ancona on the Adriatic,
a nice-looking wife named Paola, who runs a small art gallery-cum-pub-
lishing house, and two well-adjusted teenaged children, Irene and
Andrea. This family is close, balanced, and loving without being cloy-
ing – something one cannot say about Nicola Piovanni's tinkly, italiciz-
ing score, which gives new meaning to the term familial harmony – so
much so that they can actually sing together while driving with no trace
of irony or goofiness. For well over half an hour, it turns out, we simply
follow the Sermontis' lives in all their dailiness, and we are interested
because *they* are interested in one another.

It's an unspoken rule, of course, that dramatic or cinematic stasis,
especially when there is a state of unadulterated bliss, cannot last. Yet
even this family's bliss has some small taints to it, for Moretti has no
heavy-handed Hollywood desire to set up one cozy goody after another,
only patently to knock them all down in one fell swoop. As a professional, for example, Dr Sermonti presides with creeping, mid-life ennui
over a querulous clientele to whom he gives little more than amused
compassion, much of it arising from his own seeming lack of problems.
To all these patients (only one of which, a kind of sex monster, appears
to be seriously ill), he dispenses a variant of the calming advice that will
ultimately come back to haunt him: "We can't control our lives completely. We do what we can. Just take a more relaxed approach to life
and the world."

This is just the approach Irene's pot-smoking boyfriend takes, as
does Andrea in his refusal to become a competitive tennis player
despite superior athletic ability – and both young men earn the disapproval of Giovanni, who holds up the model of the aggressive basket-
baller Irene to each of them. (Giovanni is pointedly introduced, on the
street at the end of his morning run, gazing in smiling disbelief at a
group of dancing, chanting Hare Krishnas, whose ability to live unencumbered in the moment turns out to be the opposite of the careful,
deliberate manner in which he conducts his life and work.) Andrea's
"relaxed approach" includes stealing a fossil from his school's science
lab, as a prank, and then lying about it. Still, this rent, together with the

other ones in the Sermonti family fabric, is relatively minor and hardly elicits any overreaction from the *pater familias*, who, for the most part, is a model of paternal grace and spousal solicitude as well as professional concern (for his patients *and* for his own detachment from, or boredom with, their problems). The essential happiness of Giovanni and his family's bourgeois existence, then, is the happiness that in the Russian phrase writes white on the page, its unassuming contentment being all but invisible.

It is into this scenario that a horrible destiny, or a random disaster, intrudes itself, the kind that most of us know too well (especially in light of the events of September 11) can strike out of nowhere, leaving surviving family members stunned, grief-stricken, angry, and desperate both to find a reassuring answer and to regain some measure of stability. One Sunday Giovanni decides, in compensation for his growing conviction that he is not doing his patients much good, to make an unprecedented house call to an analysand who has telephoned in panic to reveal that he has just been diagnosed with lung cancer – despite the fact that he has never smoked. In order to serve his patient (who lives some distance outside Ancona), Giovanni must cancel a proposed jogging session with his son, thus freeing the boy to go scuba diving in the Adriatic with several friends. Andrea subsequently drowns in an offscreen, underwater accident that is never fully explained.

Before he does so, in what at first seems to be a curiously, even clumsily edited piece of montage (by Esmeralda Calabria), Paola has a collision at an outdoor flea market with someone apparently running away from the scene of a theft, Irene nearly collides with another biker during a road race, and Giovanni himself narrowly misses being hit by an oncoming vehicle as he drives to see the man precipitously diagnosed with cancer, while all the while the blissfully unaware Andrea heads out to sea in an inflatable dinghy. Fate or chance can suddenly strike down any of us, the conjunction of these shots makes clear, but in this case it is Andrea who gets hit, leaving the Sermontis bereaved and Giovanni consumed by guilt. The dead son's room itself is left untouched, almost as a means of maintaining his presence – a presence suggested by the title of the film in its original language, *La Stanza del figlio*. A "stanza" in Italian is both a room and a unit of verse, part of a poem or part of a family unit left to stand forever.

Andrea's "personal space" may remain untouched, but his tragedy lays waste to everything it touches, and there's nothing connected with the Sermontis that it doesn't affect. However, unlike the family in Todd Field's typically American *In the Bedroom* (2001), which also concerns

Nanni Moretti, as Giovanni, deals with feelings of grief and guilt in *The Son's Room*.

the death of a beloved son and makes effective use of a parent's halting venture into the dead child's inner sanctum, the surviving family members in *The Son's Room* simply have to endure their paralyzing pain, almost in a vacuum. Field's movie externalizes grief and loss by turning the father into a handgun-wielding tough guy who exacts revenge on his son's murderer. Moretti's film, by contrast, has Paola, Irene, and Giovanni retreat into themselves, without knowledge of the exact circumstances of Andrea's death, let alone the consolation of a revenge fantasy. (*The Son's Room* stands out for its simplicity and restraint not only with *In the Bedroom* but also with at least two other films that have dealt with the corrosive effects of grief and the irrational feelings of guilt that often go with it: Kenneth Lonergan's *You Can Count on Me* [2000], also from the United States, and Shinji Aoyama's *Eureka* [2000], from Japan.) You tell me which scenario is more convincing and therefore more moving, if less "thrilling."

The Sermontis' retreat into themselves is effectively underlined by the camera's frequent isolation of each family member in his or her own frame. That withdrawal is also highlighted, ironically, both by the cinematographer Giuseppe Lanci's shooting of this picture in almost continuous, ordinary daylight, and by the production designer Giancarlo Basili's creation of a series of unobtrusive, unassuming, pastel-colored interiors furnished with muted good taste. (Giovanni's one venture alone into the night, shortly after his son's death, lands him in an opposing environment: a garishly colored amusement park where the noise is loud and the rides are rough.) *The Son's Room* is a drama of *internal* darkness and disquiet, and these elements are all the more apparent for being juxtaposed – in something approaching real time for much of the picture – with interiors (not to speak of daylit exteriors) that are themselves visibly unadorned or indifferent. I'm thinking of Paola's art gallery, for instance, to which she stops going after Andrea's death, preferring instead to howl her pain unnervingly from her bed; or of Irene's basketball court, from which she is banished for fighting during a game in what can only be a displacement of anger at her brother's untimely, if not senseless, demise.

Giovanni, for his part, turns into a more aloof version of his former self as he begins to confront the biggest practical question posed by Moretti's narrative: how can a well-meaning psychoanalyst simultaneously analyze his patients with empathy and cope with a devastating personal loss of his own? Particularly when one such patient celebrates his aliveness, oblivious to his doctor's deadness, and another mentions his distaste for children despite the recent death of Giovanni's son. During one session, this therapist goes so far as to lose his composure and sob when an older woman expresses her regret at never having been able to conceive a child. Eventually Giovanni answers the above question by suspending his practice, but he may also be rejecting psychoanalysis itself with its ceaseless, self-indulgent amplification and dramatization of ordinary anxieties or mild disorders. (The doctor himself has a mild case of obsessive-compulsive disorder.)

And Giovanni's apparent repudiation of psychoanalysis or psychotherapy points to the larger, spiritual question posed by *The Son's Room*. Moretti's analyst embodies so many of the qualities admired by the culture of secular humanism – intellect, empathy, humor, and irony – only to discover that no amount of reason or feeling or knowledge is enough in the face of death (particularly of the sudden, unexpected, familial kind), even for the most scientifically objective among us. By making his protagonist a psychoanalyst *and* a non-believer (like the rest of Giovanni's family), Moretti thus puts on the line a distinctly contemporary way of life that premises itself on the promise of earthly fulfillment in what can only be termed a post-religious age. Irene may ask that a mass be said in Andrea's memory, but for her and her parents this is a farewell ritual, not an act of religious devotion; neither of the three receives communion at the church, and Giovanni bitterly complains afterward that the priest who gave the sermon was "full of shit." For the Sermontis, Andrea's life unquestionably ends with the sealing of his coffin, which they and we watch in an overwhelmingly powerful scene. These people cannot or will not allow themselves the comfort, the balm, that the boy's soul lives eternally.

But they get a surprise when a letter arrives from a girl named Arianna, whom Andrea had met the previous summer on a camping trip, whose existence his parents knew nothing about, and who writes in the hope that she can meet her friend again. Desperate for even indirect contact with their dead son, Giovanni starts to write a return letter (which he never completes) to Arianna and Paola telephones the girl (who is unreceptive). Then a few months later, in a kind of ephiphanous coda, she visits the Sermontis unannounced, not disconsolately but in the company of another boy with whom she is hitchhiking to France, and bearing photos Andrea had sent her of himself in various happy poses in his room. Giovanni, Paola, and Irene offer to drive Arianna and her new friend to a highway rest-stop, where they can continue hitchhiking west to France. But when they get to the rest-stop, the hitchhikers are both asleep in the backseat and Giovanni does not want to wake them. So they all drive the entire night to the west coast, where the traveling pair can catch a bus at the border between Italy and France.

After the bus leaves at dawn, the analyst and his wife suddenly begin to smile and even laugh. Their daughter, puzzled, asks them why they are laughing, but they do not reply: they just keep on laughing. We know why, however. They have learned, through the instrument of Arianna (who is no angel of reconciliation, as she would have been in a Hollywoodized version of this story), that life is irresistibly, almost brutally, continuous. This girl has recovered from her attraction to Andrea and found another boy; Irene worries about how the long drive back to Ancona may cause her to miss basketball practice; while Giovanni and his wife have found, through their unintended, all-night drive to the Ligurian Sea, that they are still able to respond to each other with affection and hope. Their lives – as husband and wife and father and mother, if not doctor and curator – will move forward despite Andrea's drowning. (Quite literally they have crossed or come to a border at the conclusion of this film; the past is another country.) Similarly, in W.H. Auden's great poem "Musée des Beaux Arts" (1938), Icarus may fall into the sea but farmers still plough their fields, "dogs go on with their doggy life," and ships sail ever on to their appointed destinations.

Yet *has* the death of their son begun to become a fact of their lives that Giovanni and Paola will carry with them, instead of staying in one place with *it?* As this couple and Irene stand near the sea (a sea of life as well as death) in the final scene of *The Son's Room*, we simultaneously observe and move away from them in a tracking shot from the bus that carries Arianna and her companion into France. As we do so, we hear a plangent, nearly morbid soft-rock number called "By the River," by Brian Eno, from his compact disk *Before and After Science* (1976), which is playing on the soundtrack but which Giovanni had earlier purchased for himself in Andrea's memory. The words and music of this song contradict the final behavior of the Sermontis, or at least their laughter, and, along with the concluding tracking shot that leaves this family on the beach, they render the ending of Moretti's film highly ambiguous, indeed.

These are the lyrics of "By the River" in their entirety:

Here we are
Stuck by this river,
You and I
Underneath a sky that's ever falling down, down, down
Ever falling down.

Through the day
As if on an ocean
Waiting here,
Always failing to remember why we came, came, came:
I wonder why we came.

You talk to me
as if from a distance
And I reply
With impressions chosen from another time, time, time,
From another time.

Are these tuneful words that give *The Son's Room*, as well as its audience, what the therapists call closure? Or are they thoughtful lyrics in a world "before science," where the sky is falling, memory and life are short, and time or history is synchronous ("another time, time, time ..."), and Catholic or at least Christian religiosity rules? If the latter, then Moretti, himself a non-believer whose own real first name, like the doctor's, happens to be Giovanni, is boldly suggesting at the end of his latest picture not only that the Sermontis could be fooling themselves with their smiles and laughter. He is also suggesting that their spiritual healing in the wake of Andrea's drowning cannot, will not, take place without the ministrations of the Holy Spirit – and therefore may not take place at all. *La stanza del figlio*, then, may remain just that: an earthly shrine to an idolatrous attachment.

One of the reasons this deceptively simple movie succeeds is Moretti's own reluctance to become, via Method acting, idolatrously attached to his cinematic character. He is quite credibly Giovanni Sermonti, but, as he has been before, he is also Nanni Moretti, acting or narrating this character at one remove – in the third person, as it were. (Woody Allen tries to do this, too, but he can't act.) And this presents on screen the kind of duality of which Brecht was so fond on the stage. Compare Moretti's performance with Robin Williams's as the psychologist Sean McGuire in *Good Will Hunting* (1997), and you'll see the difference between acting that triggers thought as well as feeling, and acting that wants to do nothing more than tug at your heartstrings. This is a pity in Williams's case, since he has the uncanny comic or objective ability, but not the directorial authority, to do with a "serious" character like McGuire exactly what Moretti does with Dr Sermonti. (Such an ability is not shared by numerous other actors who have tried to portray therapists in American movies, from Ingrid Bergman in *Spellbound* [1945] and Lee. J. Cobb in *The Three Faces of Eve* [1957] to Judd Hirsch in *Ordinary People* [1980] and Barbra Streisand in *The Prince of Tides* [1991].)

The other featured actors in *The Son's Room*, Laura Morante as Paola, Giuseppe Sanfelice as Andrea, and Jasmine Trinca as Irene, don't "split" their characters in the same way as Moretti because, again in Brechtian terminology, too much such division would be too "alienating." But their performances are sufficiently modulated (particularly Morante's) to be entirely in keeping, ensemble-style, with Moretti's. The reasons should be obvious why such modulation is absent from the performances in *Aberdeen*, about which there is nothing low-key except perhaps the brief appearance of Charlotte Rampling as Helen. And the high-wire nature of this acting naturally has a lot to do with the screaming dysfunction of the family in Hans Petter Moland's picture, in contrast with the extreme unison or togetherness of the Italian Sermontis.

For Moland completely conceived of his *Aberdeen* as an unsparing, even Strindbergian descent into two affinitive yet warring psyches, and, with an authoritative directorial talent, he has not flinched. (Moreover, Moland himself grew up with an alcoholic father like Tomas, though his film is not autobiographical as such, even as Moretti's picture isn't, despite the fact that he got the idea for *The Son's Room* when he learned that his wife was expecting a son.) Just as clearly, Moretti conceived of *The Son's Room* as a different kind of descent, into the otherwise attuned hearts and minds of a family in emotional free-fall, and, with an actor's authority, he does indeed flinch or pull back – at the same time that he moves forward.

PART THREE

Form, Genre, Oeuvre, and Other Arts

17

Wooden Allen, or Artificial Exteriors

On the Film Career of Woody Allen

I am frequently asked why I don't write about the films of Woody Allen. Here's my answer.

Woody Allen used to be a funny guy. Then he became a serious artist, or thought he did at any rate. His first screen "drama," *Interiors* (1978), is an embarrassing episode in Woody Allen's career, to be followed by such others as *September* (1987), *Another Woman* (1988), and *Alice* (1990). *Interiors* represented a feeble struggle to escape from his more authentic self, an incredible concession to the snobbish misgiving that comedy is an inferior art – something that doubtless would be news to figures as diverse as Aristophanes and Molière, Charlie Chaplin and Billy Wilder. Prior to this film, Allen had exercised a welcome talent for parody and a shrewd recognition of the clichés by which many American urbanites live, even though he never allowed his comedic talent to develop much beyond the gag-and-skit stage of *Take the Money and Run* (1969), *Bananas* (1971), *Everything You Always Wanted to Know about Sex ... But Were Afraid to Ask* (1972), *Sleeper* (1973), and *Love and Death* (1975).

As a *showman*, Allen has developed a professional eye when choosing a cinematographer, a lively ear for the musical score, and a refined taste in actresses (such as Barbara Hershey). Not in actors, however: witness his casting of himself in the leading roles of his comic and semi-comic movies, which a better actor (like Dustin Hoffman) would make even wittier, along with his exclusion of himself from his utterly serious films, where he could perhaps do some humorous good. As for the oft-made, desperate-seeming remark about what a competent *director*

Allen has become, all that I can say is, with his bankroll and artistic sup-
port-system, I too could become a competent director after so many
pictures. To echo André Bazin on *auteurs*, competent director, yes, but
of what?

He certainly didn't help his cause with such a narcissistic meditation
on the filmmaking experience as *Stardust Memories* (1980), itself a rip-
off of Fellini's *8 ½* (1963), even as the comic fantasy of the vastly overrated *Purple Rose of Cairo* (1985) is lifted in reverse form from Buster
Keaton's *Sherlock, Jr.* (1924). And to say that he has resolved his artistic
dilemma by striking a balance between the solemn and the funny in
movies like *Annie Hall* (1977), *Manhattan* (1979), *Hannah and Her Sisters* (1986), even *Crimes and Misdemeanors* (1989) and *Husbands and
Wives* (1992), is to miss the extent to which such pictures fail as genuine tragicomedy. Rather than combining the serious and the comic
into a unique new form, they just irresolutely lay the two elements side
by side, or overemphasize one at the expense of the other, against the
backdrop of culturally rich, culturally hip, psychically neurotic New
York, which these films expect to do the real work of "meaning" for
them. In movies like these, Allen is continually sending love letters to
himself and to that province of provinces, Manhattan, and I for one
don't enjoy reading other people's mail. A woman once told me that I
should see *Hannah and Her Sisters* with someone I love. I don't know
what she could have meant by this exhortation, given the film's solipsism, and I'm glad I didn't see it with her.

But, some people will say, those artsy Europeans, especially the
French, love Woody Allen. Yes, well, they loved Samuel Fuller and Don
Siegel not so long ago, and look where that got us. Europeans think
that Americans (read: New Yorkers) are fabulously nutty at the same
time that they believe America (read: New York) is wonderfully glamorous. That's why they love Woody Allen, Manhattan diarist. New Yorkers and all who aspire to be New Yorkers like *Annie Hall, Manhattan,*
and *Hannah and Her Sisters* (among other Woody vehicles) because
these films congratulate them on their choice of city in which to live,
and because these people think that Allen is the cinema's answer to
drama's Chekhov: serious, comic, and deliciously melancholy, all
wrapped up in the same tidy little package.

One, just one, difference between Allen and Chekhov (it's difficult
to join their names in the same sentence) is that the latter had some
distance on himself and life, to put it mildly. Irony played a large part
in his art, as did his knowledge of the theatrical tradition that had
immediately preceded him. Allen loves himself and New York so much,

he's nostalgic about both before the fact, to the point of making it and his own person the real subject of his films. And the very first time he thought about tradition, he tried to imitate Ingmar Bergman, the result being the disastrous *Interiors*, whose genesis and execution I would now like to consider at length. For this picture reveals not only a comedian's betrayal of his comic self but also a filmmaker's mistaken assumption that one can create great art by consciously setting out to do so, according to this or that recipe, instead of intuitively using artistic means to capture for all eternity an image or idea of humanity.

According to the biography of Allen by Lee Guthrie (which, significantly, was withdrawn from distribution shortly after the opening of *Interiors*), the comedian once admitted that, although he admired the films of Bergman, they could only be a bad influence on his work, "because they're so antithetical to comedy."[1] He went on to explain that Bergman interested him more than any other filmmaker, owing to "the consummate marriage of technique, theatricality and themes that are both personally important to me and that have gigantic size – death, the meaning of life, the question of religious faith" (75). In other words, Allen was impressed by the austerity of Bergman's style and by what he reads as the master's tragic view of life. So impressed was he that, in a later declaration, he was prepared to throw previous caution to the wind and reach for just those "gigantic" themes, which he was now translating as "more personal" than those of his contemporaries. From the same source, we get the following statement: "I'm not sure any American film maker makes the kind of movie I want to make. I don't want to do films like *Bonnie and Clyde* or *Mean Streets* or *Badlands* ... To me, serious American movies always have one foot in entertainment – and I like more personal drama, though there may not be a market for it. The drama I like is what you see in the plays of O'Neill and Strindberg and Ibsen – and in foreign films" (173).

God forbid that a "serious" movie should have one foot in the swamp of entertainment! And as if *Annie Hall* and *Crimes and Misdemeanors*, to name only two of Allen's seriocomic films, don't try to entertain at the same time as they confront – however lamely or indecisively – significant themes. But there you have it: the puritanical hunger for the High Serious, the discontent with authentic veins of American subject matter. Such material may not be shot through with the subtle values of living to be found in European movies – you know, all that wisdom,

1 Lee Guthrie, *Woody Allen: A Biography*. (New York: Drake, 1978), p. 75. Hereafter cited by page number.

refinement, and *tendresse* – but it is nonetheless vital in its consideration of the harsh characteristics of so much of American life: baseness, greed, and brutality.

Incidentally, this coupling of O'Neill and Strindberg on the part of Allen is meaningful. Strindberg was the artistic stepfather of Eugene O'Neill, who successfully transplanted the Swede's suffocating (Lutheran) ethos into Irish-American (Catholic) settings, and who, for his part, managed to write only one comedy (*Ah, Wilderness!* [1932]) among his many works for the theatre. The Swedes flattered O'Neill and his solemn sensibility back by staging all his plays at Stockholm's Dramaten in addition to awarding him the Nobel Prize in 1932 (before he had written his great naturalistic dramas, I might add). Strindberg is also, of course, the single most influential figure behind all Bergman's work, although the filmmaker seems to substitute excessive love for women for the dramatist's extreme antipathy toward them. Both men, however, share an aversion to comedy, though Bergman did master it for once in *Smiles of a Summer Night* (1955) – a movie more or less remade by a spent Woody Allen in 1982 as *A Midsummer Night's Sex Comedy.*

The sympathetic link between these Swedes and the Americans is the fundamental puritanism they culturally share. It has been said that the smothering family atmosphere (if not the religious pall) in certain Bergman films, even as in Strindberg's naturalistic *The Father* (1887) and O'Neill's *Long Day's Journey into Night* (1941), appealed to Allen by reason of his special Jewish vulnerability to comparably oppressive parents in his own environment. I would not wish to pronounce on this probability, if probability it is, but I suspect that the driving force behind Allen's wistful Bergman-worship is rather an aspiring intellectual's love of conceptual perfection and a confusion of it with the less-is-more aesthetic of Scandinavian reductionism, together with the snobbish misgiving that comedy is an inferior art and an obsessive love for women that Allen confuses with a desperate need to validate his narcissistic love for himself.

Be that as it may, the truth is that it takes more independent imagination, greater cinematic scope, and a richer sense of life's poetry to make *Bonnie and Clyde* (1967), *Mean Streets* (1973), or *Badlands* (1973), *Midnight Cowboy* (1969), *The Wild Bunch* (1969), or *Chinatown* (1974), *Raging Bull* (1980), *House of Games* (1987), or *Tender Mercies* (1983), than it does to make *Interiors*. Unlike a host of American movies in which the citizenry's blindest self-satisfactions with the status quo are upheld, or in which the most immoral and fantastic projections of callow romanticism, spurious religiosity, or miserable sentimentality are indulged, these films insist on writing down contemporary American society as they see it: a society alarmingly animated by powerful minority factions that are debased and selfish when they are not downright criminal; that is grotesquely peopled by a fringe of parasites surrendered to listless perversions or violent exploitations, or alternatively populated by a growing number of decent yet subsocial creatures who lead unexamined if not unworthy lives; that is forever encumbered by a floating majority, pitifully bewildered, vulgarized, and juvenile, which is sadomasochistic at its core, hence wanting in all resolution, guidance, and dignity except perhaps in time of war. If this is not the whole truth about the American experience, it is that part of the truth most commonly suppressed for public consumption.

What, by contrast, is Woody Allen's *Interiors* centrally about? Certainly not "the meaning of life" – a silly predication for a work of art, in any case. And though the rejected wife and mother kills herself, *Interiors* is in no awesome way about death. The people involved are not tragic, although some of them would like to be; they tend instead to be hysterical, obtuse, or pathetically abusive. Their behavior more closely resembles that of the pseudo-intellectual New Yorkers of Paul Mazursky's films, who simultaneously know too much about one another and bitch all the time at their own limitations. Is this quality what makes the movie, for Allen, "more personal"? Is this the quality that he admires in *Scenes From a Mall* (1980), Mazursky's absurd take, starring Allen himself, on Bergman's *Scenes From a Marriage* (1973)?

Interiors should have been the tragedy (or even the comedy) of a man's attempt, alternately assisted or opposed by his three daughters, to win his own soul by ridding himself of their mother, his wife. I say "should have been" because Allen's conception of that man is so feeble (in the Bergman tradition of the ineffectual male), and the performance of E.G. Marshall is so uninflected, that he emerges as a far less sympathetic character than the compulsively meticulous wife played with twitchy naturalism by Geraldine Page. Arthur, as he's called, persists in his bid for freedom – he wants to go to the Mediterranean, presumably to be reborn – against the warnings of his plaintive wife, who threatens suicide before actually attempting it, and against the querulous protests of his daughter Joey, more closely identified with her mother than her sisters are, probably because her own identity is insecure (as yours might be, too, if you were burdened with a name normally reserved for the opposite sex). The father-husband returns from Greece uttering the same banalities as before – nothing about him has

Bracing themselves for what lies ahead, Renata (Diane Keaton) and Frederick (Richard Jordan) share a quiet moment in *Interiors*.

changed, not even his ties – together with a personable if clownish woman whom Joey indignantly and correctly describes as vulgar. When Arthur marries the creature, mother, sure enough, walks into the sea. Loyal Joey is all but drowned in a vain attempt to save her, and she in turn is resuscitated by the unrefined stepmother: which proves that this name-flashing tourist may be an ox in the drawing room, but when it comes to fundamentals she is the pragmatist who saves the day.

Implicitly, Eve the mother deserves her fate, for in the explanation given her (too late) by Joey, she felt herself too good for this world and so created another, of interiors – of décor and decorum – which had demanded, from those around her, responses too strict for any of them to meet. Yet it is difficult to imagine that everyone around Eve is as derailed as they all seem to be by an excess of good taste; the calamities represented are in excess of the cause alleged. (No one suggests, incidentally, that an exquisitely dictatorial mother might have been the answer to a visibly bland father.) The articulated miseries of the daughters and their men are strenuously reached for, and hence appear contrived. They are phony excavations of the interior – of interior life – whereas Allen's specialty has always been the humorously

Renata (Diane Keaton) and Flyn (Kristin Griffith)
take to the beach for an intimate conversation in
Interiors.

objective observation of exteriors, the coolly comic send-up of surfaces.
Diane Keaton plays intelligently an unintelligent poet whose self-con-
tempt is fairly inexplicable, since her ignorance should be her bliss.
Similarly, her husband, a churlish literary genius who's fearful that he
is not as good as the critics say, decides to assert his misgivings by trying to rape his sister-in-law, a television actress given to drug addiction.

   The whole embroilment is distorted by Allen's insistence on telling
his story in a style alien to the milieu he provides, a style that transposes
the tenor of an American metropolitan setting into the hushed and
claustrophobic atmosphere of Bergman's Baltic. He opens *Interiors* with
unornamented credits, no simultaneous visuals behind then, no music.

Each alone with her thoughts, three sisters – Renata (Diane Keaton), Flyn (Kristin Griffith), and Joey (Marybeth Hurt) – gaze out the window of their beachhouse in *Interiors*.

The exposition features single-shot close-ups of two sisters, each looking out a different window, followed by a medium shot of a male who, gazing at an urban panorama, commences a narration to himself and to the audience – a familiar Bergman beginning. Allen's man has his back to the camera, perhaps to alleviate the shock of our eventual recognition that he is none other than the tepid Marshall, informing us, in an unlikely outburst of rhetoric, that suddenly in the course of his contented marriage he "found an enormous abyss opening at [his] feet." Too much of the dialogue thereafter is like this, the sort of talk that, in earlier Woody Allen vehicles, would have speedily led to a verbal pratfall, but here only makes for tragicomedy of the unintentional kind.

Allen tries hard – perhaps too hard – to keep his settings from becoming as cluttered or static as his language, staging crucial scenes at the dining table and in the bedroom, then in an empty church and at a beach house in an attempt to exile the everyday domestic world. Self-consciously he employs a camera at rest, passively framing close-ups of faces or middle-distance shots of a stationary group, except for moments when he is recalling other Bergman strategies. The most conspicuous of these is the tracking shot of two sisters conversing as they walk along the beach, which sententiously evokes the world of *Persona*. With every sequence Allen thus appears to have asked himself not "How can I best shoot this?" but "How would Bergman shoot it?" Moreover, he ends his film with a strict reversion to the Bergman format that, at the same time, summons a whole repertory of understated curtain tableaux from post-Ibsenian drama. After church and the business with the white roses and the coffin, the three sisters are aligned in profile (a reminder of the opening shots, as well as of Chekhov's greatest play), staring at the sea. One says, "The water is calm," and another solemnly replies, "Yes, it's very peaceful." That Allen should have been trapped by so obvious an error as to believe that you can depict tragedy by imitating the surface of it from someone else's (already superficial) version – this, I must say, is truly amazing. But it is perhaps no more amazing than his belief that you can create tragicomedy or tragifarce by spicing up a vaguely serious story with Woodyisms and casting a ridiculous man (himself) in the role of the leaden leading character.

This director-screenwriter has said that such relatively recent films of his as *Manhattan Murder Myster* (1993) and *Mighty Aphrodite* (1995) – itself a parody of the original murder mystery, *Oedipus the King* (430 BC) – mark a return to his "earlier, funnier" brand of filmmaking, to which I can only respond, "too little, too late." So desperate is he to return to previous form or prior success that his 1996 movie *Everyone Says I Love You* nearly abandons reality altogether for the childish world of musical comedy, a world toward which Allen's Gershwin-and-Porter-driven soundtracks have been moving for some time. Except that "real" New York, in the form of carefully selected views of Manhattan's loveliness, is still on hand in this movie to be adored and to provide the action with a backdrop – ironically, the best word to describe the direction Woody Allen's career has taken since he went "deep" twenty-years ago and made the fateful *Interiors*.

I happen to be happy that Woody Allen plays the clarinet and has played professionally at Michael's Pub in New York. I wish he'd stick to clarinet.

18

Latter-Day Bergman

Autumn Sonata as paradigm

Ingmar Bergman began his film career with a paranoid invention salvaged by Alf Sjöberg, who, from the sketch submitted by Bergman, put the Swedish cinema on the map in 1944 with the film known in the United States as *Torment*. The germ of this movie was Bergman's fear that he would be flunked on his university entrance examination; his revenge in advance was his creation of a tyrannical schoolmaster whom he aptly named Caligula. (Sjöberg added a political implication by having the actor made up to resemble Himmler, chief of the Reichsführer ss.) Over the years, Bergman's compulsion to nourish every slight, every adverse criticism, grew into his now familiar, never subdued war against Father, who once punished him by locking him into a closet. We are at liberty to wonder if this ever happened and simply to credit Bergman with singular tenacity for inventing an image that gratified him, and for extrapolating from it one of his twin obsessions (the other being the fatality of the couple): the despotism of the Father and hence the fallibility of God. (If there has always been something shopworn about Bergman's conception, it's because Dostoyevsky got there first, with the most.)

Among the many other obsessions of Ingmar Bergman that American critics have failed to note, or failed to question closely, is his pervasive resentment in his art of the achieved man and occasionally the career woman – doctor, lawyer, professor, business executive. From the evidence of his numerous films, Bergman hates every professional except the artist. Predictably, since he is a puritan, his defense of the artist as somehow sacrosanct has engendered a feedback of guilt: periodically, having enshrined the creative personality in one context or another, he seems driven to follow up with a thumping self-accusation of the artist as charlatan or as detached and inhuman being, as in 1968's *Shame* and *Hour of the Wolf.* You may be sure that Bergman in his heart does not believe this, but he needs to hear an answering echo from time to time that absolves him of his own accusation.

Thus *Autumn Sonata* (1978) is characterized by the same kind of ambivalence that undermined the artistic veracity of *Wild Strawberries* in 1957. In the earlier film, Bergman's portrait of an old professor, whose egoistic frigidity lost him an idyllic sweetheart and produced an impotent son, was at odds with the visibly sympathetic performance of Victor Sjöström. Just as Bergman was reluctant in *Wild Strawberries* to follow the implications of his own scenario by destroying the professor-figure entirely, so in *Autumn Sonata* he sets up Ingrid Bergman (in her final theatrical film) as a concert pianist-cum-mother who is supposed to have crippled her two daughters (one child being insufficient for the force of his accusation); then the *auteur* becomes so enamored of the personality he has given his character that he is hard put to convince us she could possibly be either as indifferent or as ruthless as her articulate daughter maintains.

To synopsize this picture accurately for anyone who has not seen it is almost impossible, since what takes place in *Autumn Sonata* beyond the severely limited action is completely a matter of individual interpretation. Every statement made by the characters is open to question, and the whole moral issue on which the film hinges is never depicted. The damaging relationship of which this mother-daughter confrontation is supposed to be the climax is not visualized in flashbacks, so that the viewer can judge for himself; it is, rather, wholly summarized in verbal terms through the daughter Eva's accusatory retrospect.

At the beginning, reading her diary while she awaits the visit of her celebrated mother, Liv Ullmann-as-Eva seems pretty clearly, in her spinsterish appearance and manner, to be a manic-depressive type, melancholy and retentive but prone to fitfulness as well. We glimpse her husband hovering in the background, from which he scarcely emerges during the subsequent encounter, and we learn that since her son, aged fourteen, drowned some years ago, Eva has kept his room as it was when he died and moons over photographs of him. This morbid devotion to the irretrievable contradicts the leading statement she reads from her diary: "One must learn how to live. I work at it every day." We further discover that, before her marriage, Eva had lived with a doctor, and that she had once had tuberculosis. Not until later in the film do we become aware that she is looking after her bedridden sister, who suffers from a degenerative disease that has affected her speech and movement, and whom her mother believes to be in a nursing home.

When mother arrives at this outpost of Ibsenism (Bergman's setting, during this period of his self-exile from Sweden, is among the Norwegian fjords), it is not too surprising that, after the first affectionate exchanges are over, as Eva listens obediently to her parent's necessarily self-absorbed chatter (she has come, after all, from the world of professional music as practiced in European capitals), the daughter all the while regards the mother with mingled amusement and suspicion. In no time at all, suspicion has become hostility, and step by step Eva rebukes her mother's self-secured authority in a crescendo of bitter reproaches that mounts steadily into the realm of hysteria. The younger woman makes the distressed elder responsible for all the ills of her life and blames her, besides, for the condition of the drooling sister upstairs, whose presence in the house is an unwelcome shock to the fastidious visitor.

Following a long sequence of passionate denunciation by her daughter, which she stems only at momentary intervals, the mother, inwardly shaken but outwardly collected, leaves to fulfill another musical engagement. Then after a few solicitous suggestions from her husband – who, again, has passively remained on the sidelines of this internecine struggle being waged under his roof – Eva writes a letter to the departed woman in which she retracts the burden of the accusation she had hurled and makes a pathetic bid for love. This letter is in part read over the image of the mother, traveling south for her next concert.

Critics have generally received this film as if it were indeed a straightforward indictment by the neglected daughter of a selfish parent, which means that they accept at face value the allegations of the girl and pay no attention either to the personality or the remonstrance of the mother. In fact we have only the daughter's word that her mother's inattention drove her into a messy relationship with that "doctor" who is briefly mentioned. What part any of this played in her contracting of tuberculosis is never clarified. How satisfactory or unsatisfactory her present marriage is, one is left to infer. Whether her mother had an affair with someone named Marten without telling her husband, Josef, depends on which of the two women you believe, and what bearing this has on anything else is never made clear. One is also left to decide whether or not the mother's absence at a crucial hour was the impelling cause of the sister's disabling condition.

Liv Ullmann and Ingrid Bergman at the piano in *Autumn Sonata.*

It is possible to take the other view, that Bergman intended the Liv Ullmann character to reveal herself unmistakably as a self-pitying neurotic, whose charges are patently cancelled by the clearly delineated superiority of the mother. (One of the most telling moments in the film would then be Ingrid Bergman's correction, at the piano, of her daughter's playing of a Chopin sonata: if the girl is to give the piece an authentic interpretation, declares the mother, she must avoid sentimentality and understand that the music should express "pain, not reverie.") However, even this view of Bergman's strategy may be ingenuous; it is much more in his line to establish an impeccably distinguished persona, poised against an unattractive spinster who is nonetheless married, in order to make the latter's accusations appear at first unlikely, then the more convincing, precisely because the accused has the more sovereign air. (This mechanism was invented by Strindberg in his play *The Stronger,* from 1889.)

In truth, near the end of *Autumn Sonata,* Bergman loses confidence in his own gambit. He cuts, in the most excruciatingly obvious way, from the sick daughter writhing helplessly on the floor, to the entrained mother coolly informing her agent that her visit home had been "most unpleasant": in other words, she shrugs it off. Unless we are to suppose she is acting, this is outrageously unbelievable; it totally contradicts the character of the woman we have witnessed, in merciless close-up, for the preceding hour. Evasive or hesitant she may have been when justifying a given response or action recounted by the vindictive Eva, but never for a moment did one feel that she was radically false. Equally unacceptable, as the film ends, is the abrupt change of heart that dictates Eva's remorse for the vehemence with which she has been arraigning her mother – thereby canceling, at the last minute, the substance of the movie's unrelenting inquisition.

There is small point in trying to weigh truth in the antithesis Bergman has contrived for *Autumn Sonata*. At any latter-day movie of his, including the slightly earlier *Serpent's Egg* (1977) and the subsequent, appositely titled *From the Life of the Marionettes* (1980), one cannot be sure whether this director-screenwriter is unaware of the dramatic incongruities that he creates through poor motivation or whether he doesn't really care. He seems indifferent to plot because a plot is action consistent with the revealed nature of its characters, and Bergman seems unable to perceive consistency; his characters say what he wants them to say, to an end he alone has chosen, as opposed to what they would say if allowed to speak for themselves.

He was, once, a master of comedy, as in his gloss on Renoir's *Rules of the Game* (1939), *Smiles of a Summer Night* (1955), for in secular, and even more so divine, comedy you can give full rein to the improbable. You can also do so in a religious allegory like Bergman's *Seventh Seal* (1957), if not in existential meditations of the kind exemplified by his "faith" trilogy of *Through a Glass Darkly* (1961), *Winter Light* (1962), and *The Silence* (1963), which, along with the earlier *Naked Night* (1953) and *The Magician* (1958) and the subsequent *Persona* (1966), justly secured the reputation of Ingmar Bergman in America. Even he seems to agree, however, that the enigmas of *Autumn Sonata* represent a parody of his earlier, better work: "Has Bergman begun to make Bergman films? I find that, yes, *Autumn Sonata* is an annoying example ... of creative exhaustion" (334–5 of his *Images: My Life in Film*, 1990).

It may be worth remarking here that while *Autumn Sonata* postulates the destructive consequences of perfectionism in life as in art, Bergman the recreant preacher has, in his own way, been aesthetically pursuing the absolute or the ideal like mad: by not-so-coincidentally choosing a central character with the primal name of Eva; and, most importantly, by creating immaculate cinematic compositions that achieve their immaculateness at the expense of worldly or natural con-

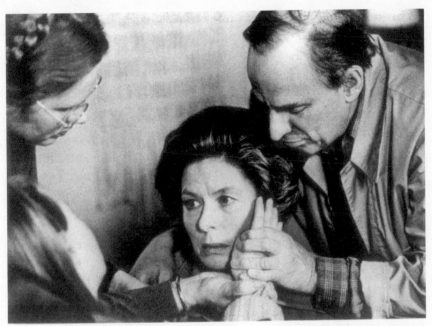

Ingmar Bergman directing Liv Ullmann and Ingrid Bergman in *Autumn Sonata*.

ception. (Almost all of this film was shot inside a studio.) With this in mind, we should not expect the mundane inventions of *Autumn Sonata* to have objective credibility; the characters' motives are flimsily explored, the actualities of their lives not dramatized but reported after the fact. If Eva knew so much about her mother's devices of evasion, for example, as well as about her own victimization at her parent's hands, she would long since have ceased to be a victim – or at the very least she would have remedied those absurd outer signs of her condition thrust upon her by Bergman via his wardrobe department: I mean the old-maid's provincial hair bun and the disfiguring eyeglasses. Women's faces, preferably under stress, are what Ingmar Bergman likes to photograph; objective coherence he no longer cares to cultivate. Like many other films in his canon, *Autumn Sonata* is a private tribunal. Bergman himself is the confessor, prosecutor, plaintiff, and as neutral or uncommitted a judge as he can risk being.

Critics in America consistently underrate this Swedish inability of Bergman to commit himself to the terms of a moral choice he has ostensibly initiated – unless, that is, he knows for certain he has a target to which absolutely no one will object. The sympathetic link between this Swede and Americans is the fundamental puritanism we culturally share; Bergman's Nordic damnations, like Strindberg's, are taken far less seriously, for example, by the Italians, the French, or even the English. Indeed, Strindberg is perhaps the only authentic father to whose authority Bergman has consented.

The "rehearsal" in *After the Rehearsal* (1984), for example, is of one of Strindberg's plays (*A Dream Play*, 1902), a number of which Bergman himself has directed for the theatre. And *Autumn Sonata* may derive its inspiration from that mad master's chamber drama-cum-dream play titled *The Ghost Sonata* (1907), not least because Bergman says he initially conceived his film like a dream in three acts, with "no cumbersome sets, two faces, and three kinds of lighting: one evening light, one night light, and one morning light" (*Images*, 335). For all its avant-garde theatrical devices, this early twentieth-century theatrical work is not unrelated in theme to its Bergmanian namesake, for Strindberg attempts in his autumnal *Ghost Sonata* to penetrate the naturally deceptive or mediating façade of verbal language, as well as of bourgeois exteriors – not only through the visual eloquence of scenic design, but also through the abstract purity of musical form.

Moreover, Strindberg composed *The Ghost Sonata* not long after the five psychotic episodes of his "inferno crisis," even as Bergman wrote *Autumn Sonata* immediately upon recovering from a nervous breakdown that resulted from his arrest in Sweden on charges of tax evasion. A major difference between these two artists, however, is that Strindberg's psychiatric crisis restored his religious faith, and that faith gave much of his post-inferno work a mystical cast in which benevolent or judicious transcendental powers were operative – expressing themselves even during the most everyday of occurrences. Bergman's breakdown, by contrast, had no such effect either on the director or his films, which from *The Seventh Seal* to *The Virgin Spring* (1960) to *The Silence* had led progressively not only to the rejection of all religious belief, but also to the conviction that human life is haunted by a virulent, active evil.

If without knowing anything whatsoever about the work of either director, one had seen Bergman's *Autumn Sonata* right after Woody Allen's *Interiors* (1978), one might easily have concluded, however, that the Swedish filmmaker had attempted to imitate the American rather than his own Swedish forebear. For these works share the same cinematographic and editing style, the same concentration on a handful of overwrought characters, and the very same subject – namely, maternal domination. Of course, the reverse sequence is the correct one: since

1971, if no farther back, the otherwise comedic Woody Allen had yearned to make what he thought of as a serious or tragic "European" film, preferably in the monastic style of Ingmar Bergman yet in an urban American setting. Finally, with *Interiors*, he made it, and fortuitously if not felicitously it resembles (at least in outline) the particular Bergman number that happened to be released in America at almost the same time. (In 1992, Allen managed to make two films derivative, not so much of Bergman, as of Godard and Kafka, respectively: *Husbands and Wives* and *Shadows and Fog*.) Would that each man, in this instance, in the coincidental year of 1978, had opted instead to remake the "merely" entertaining Hollywood love story known as *Intermezzo* (1939), itself remade from the Swedish *Intermezzo* of 1936 – with none other than Ingrid Bergman starring in both pictures as a young pianist in love with a renowned, but married, violinist.

As for the Bergmanian cultural puritanism or hunger for the High Serious that Eugene O'Neill himself shares in such plays as *Desire Under the Elms* (1924), *Strange Interlude* (1928), *Long Day's Journey into Night* (1941), and *A Moon for the Misbegotten* (1943), and of which Allen unsuccessfully attempts to partake in films like *September* (1987), *Another Woman* (1988), and *Alice* (1990) in addition to *Interiors*, such aspirations toward spiritual austerity and moral rigor are not particularly evident in the American cinema. (One possible exception that comes to mind is *Five Easy Pieces* [1970], but even this work – about a promising pianist who turns his back on classical music and the concert-cum-recording world – has more in common with movies like *Bonnie and Clyde* [1967], *Mean Streets* [1973], and *Badlands* [1973] than with *Autumn Sonata*.) In American movies, more than in our other arts, popular entertainment is the major enterprise, and it is rarely austere, seldom rigorous, and insufficiently moral – except, that is, insofar as it is at the same time sentimental. We may have our puritanical strain, then, but apparently we prefer to indulge it through the avenue of European cinema – in other words, by going back to its source.

19

Notes on Film Genre

On *Stagecoach* (1939, USA), *The Organizer* (1963, Italy), *The Cameraman* (1928, USA), *Psycho* (1960, USA), and *In Which We Serve* (1942, UK)

ALONE IN *STAGECOACH*

The Western appeals to Americans in part because it reflects a myth endemic to our society: that of the loner, the individual, the completely self-reliant man. Brewing at the back of American minds is a resentment against the need for others that the modern world insists on, which Europeans accept as a perennial fact of life, and which Americans see as a version of the Fall – the lapse of Rousseau's natural man into the compromise and frustration of social life as we know it. The resentment against the need for others stems from America's geographical isolation as well as from its founding by European refugees. This resentment was fueled by the industry and resolve of those who settled the frontier, as well as by the bravery and might of our armies in two world wars. It has also been reinforced by countless Western movies.

The only form of life that matters to us in Westerns is the lonely, unsettled, embattled career of the outlaw, the sheriff, or the range-hand – roles and jobs that guarantee movement, peril, and a radical separation from one's fellow men. The outlaw, unlike the gangster, need not be part of a gang; if he acts with others, it is as much because they provide him with male comradeship in place of family and community as because they aid him in his exploits. Although himself an outsider and an individualist, the gangster needs his gang in order to survive; he must never make himself vulnerable to the attacks of rival

John Wayne as the Ringo Kid in *Stagecoach*.

gangs by being alone. The gangster is dependent – on the city and the human services it provides, on money and possessions, on the newspapers that feed his delusions of grandeur. The outlaw, by contrast, is independent. For all the money he may steal, he cannot stay in the same place for long with it – he must leave the little town whose bank he has robbed for the desolate safety of the plains or the mountains. He must be content more with having money than with spending it, more with having enough to eat and drink than with acquiring the trappings of success.

The Ringo Kid appears to be an outlaw in John Ford's *Stagecoach* (1939). He has just broken out of prison, and he stops the stagecoach by firing his rifle into the air. We learn that he has escaped in order to avenge the murder of his father and brother by the Plummer boys; that he has been in jail because the Plummers framed him; and that he owns a ranch in Mexico to which he some day hopes to return (though we never learn how he acquired this property). Ringo is outside the law in the sense that he is taking it into his own hands to kill the Plummers. He is the archetypal Westerner: self-reliant, quiet, contained, and alone. (We never hear of any siblings of his besides the murdered brother, and there is no mention of his mother.) To emphasize Ringo's separation from society, Ford isolates him the first time that he is on screen: the camera singles him out, then quickly tracks in to him; Ringo grows larger and larger the closer the camera gets, until finally he looms over the surrounding plain. It is as if he has appeared out of nowhere, as if this stagecoach has invaded his private domain, to which he has retreated in order to enjoy a life without others, a life with no one, a pacified life in which even your own ego scarcely lifts its voice above a whisper.

Ringo gets aboard the coach, which is going to Lordsburg, where the Plummer brothers are. Once on it, he is immediately attracted to an outsider like himself, the prostitute Dallas (an orphan at birth as opposed to the orphan of sorts that Ringo has become), who has been thrown out of the last town in which she lived; both are shunned by the "respectable" passengers. In Western movies, the important character-istic of a prostitute is her quasi-masculine independence: nobody owns her, nothing has to be explained to her, and she is not, like a virtuous woman, a "value" that demands to be protected. Before he discovers Dallas's past, Ringo treats her like a lady, a value to be protected, at the same time as he admires her toughness and common sense; after he learns that she has been a prostitute, he continues to treat her like a lady and reiterates his marriage proposal. As far as he is concerned, her life began on the coach in the wilderness and is untainted by town life – by a life, that is, of social compromise.

After he kills the three Plummers, Ringo is permitted by Sheriff Wilcox to ride off with Dallas to his ranch across the border, where, it is implied, they will marry and raise a family. No matter how far from "civilization" Ringo's ranch in Mexico is, however, and no matter how individualistic he and Dallas have been, their lives will no longer be rootless: they will even create a small society with the birth of their chil-dren. So, in order to preserve the image of Ringo as the Westerner and Dallas as a prostitute, Ford does not depict the wedding ceremony and its aftermath. When the man in the movies goes home to his wife, his life is over. *The marriage must not be seen,* and the walk into the sunset is into a dying star: the couple live happily ever after – as long as they keep walking. Ringo and Dallas ride their wagon into the night; then we see shots not of their future home, but of Monument Valley, shots of which opened *Stagecoach* as well.

Ringo is not the only man in the film who is a loner. The alcoholic Doc Boone, who is kicked out of town along with Dallas, is unmarried, as are Sheriff Wilcox and the uprooted former Confederate-soldier-

John Carradine as Hatfield and Louise Platt as Lucy Mallory in *Stagecoach.*

become-gambler, Hatfield. All three ride the coach to Lordsburg: Hatfield as the pregnant Mrs Mallory's escort (he had served under her father's command during the Civil War), and the sheriff so that he can forestall a showdown between Ringo and the Plummers. Mrs Mallory goes in search of her husband, who is a cavalry officer; she was supposed to find him at the first stop but does not locate him until the coach arrives in Lordsburg, where he has been taken after suffering a wound in battle with the Apaches. By this time she has had a baby girl. Her husband, of course, missed the birth, and we miss him: he never appears on screen. The implication is that he leads the life of a loner, or at least of a man in a group – the army – that represents a temporary, wished-for exemption from the grim destiny of wife, children, and home.

Buck, the stagecoach driver; Chris, an innkeeper on the road to Lordsburg; Peacock, the whiskey drummer on his way back home to Kansas; and Gatewood, the banker, are all married but are still loners of a sort. Buck is married to a Mexican woman about whose cooking he complains and who, much to his dismay, keeps bringing her relatives from across the border to live with them; one may assume that he is happy to be away from such a home during his long hours as a stagecoach driver. Chris is a Mexican who is married to an Apache; he speaks to his wife only to order her about, and he describes her behavior as "savage." When she deserts him, she steals his horse, whose loss he laments more than losing her. Peacock and his spouse have five children, but, as a liquor salesman who travels great distances, he can't see much of them. Doc Boone befriends him only to get his whiskey samples; the doctor's heavy drinking, juxtaposed against the sobriety of everyone else, serves only to confirm him in his isolation. Gatewood embezzles $50,000 from his bank and takes the coach to Lordsburg, leaving his dour and officious wife behind; at the end of the trip he is arrested and led away to spend time alone in jail.

Women in the movies are the privileged representatives of society and civilized life, and marriage is the emblem of many entangling alliances. In one way or another, all the men described above have rejected marriage and the family. All are decompositions of or variations on Ringo, and they are interesting more for this than for their individual characterizations. Ringo moves through a landscape peopled more or less by men like himself. This takes away from his uniqueness and raises him to the level of the mythic, where, consciously or unconsciously, all who surround him, including the film audience, would imitate his behavior.

TOGETHER IN *THE ORGANIZER*

The world of *The Organizer* (1963; more accurately entitled *The Comrades* in Italian) is serious: Turin, Italy, at the turn of the century, where working conditions in the textile industry are terrible. A "professor" (Marcello Mastroianni), disenchanted with high school teaching, comes to town to organize a strike. He has some success until one of the workers, the teenager Omero, is shot by soldiers defending the textile plant and its owners against violence. The workers then return to the job, apparently without any improvement in their lot. The point, however, is that the first shot has been fired: not only literally, in the case of Omero's death, but also figuratively, in labor's struggle against management. (This is the first time that these workers have gone on strike.) Such a struggle, of course, will continue into the twentieth century and beyond with increasing success in many Western countries.

Marcello Mastroianni in *The Organizer*.

While the world of *The Organizer* is serious, many of its characters are somewhat comic. The professor is slightly ridiculous from the moment we see him peering from a small window in the train that has taken him to Turin. His dress and manner are odd, he seems to be as concerned about finding his next meal as he is about organizing the strike, and his sexual appetite is almost as strong as his appetite for food. Yet he is absolutely sincere and persistent in his efforts on behalf of the workers. His comic and serious sides are shown together best when he awakens in a hall in Turin to realize that a union meeting is taking place right in front of him. No one has seen him, since he is behind a curtain. Unfazed by the interruption of his sleep, he walks into the midst of the leaders onstage and immediately begins to advise the workers.

The biggest and toughest worker (Folco Lulli) is also the funniest, in the vulnerability or sensitivity we sense beneath his gruffness and in the difficulty with which he unleashes his strength, since his chest is so

Marcello Mastroianni in *The Organizer.*

large that he can barely get his arms around it to throw punches. We laugh at him in the fight at the train station between the Turin workers and the scabs from another city; we pity him when, slightly disoriented after the fight and still on the tracks, he is run down by a racing train. Even the managers of the factory have their comic side: they don't seem to know how to handle this first strike by their workers, and the owner never lets his managers forget it, insulting and hectoring them at every turn.

Furthermore, there is sexual tension between several couples. One worker (Renato Salvatori) pursues Folco Lulli's daughter (Gabriella Giorgelli) throughout the film; she comically rebuffs his advances, only to reveal her deep love for him by the end of the film. The daughter of a Sicilian worker slowly becomes attached to Omero, only to lose him to a soldier's bullet; she then mourns him as if he were her husband. The professor and a prostitute, the daughter of one of the workers, fall for each other; it is from her bed that he is called to lead the workers' assault on the factory, just as he had been "called" from his bed to address them during their first meeting. The one female leader among the strikers, Cesarina, enjoys a playfully sexual relationship with her colleagues despite her age; the old factory owner himself is not above attraction to women, as he indicates when he raps a lovely young woman on the behind as he passes her in his wheelchair during a party at his home. My point is not that sexual tension, or simply romance, is indigenous to comedy, but that in this film it is unrelated to the serious element. To be sure, the relationship between the Sicilian girl and Omero is ended when he is killed; but their love has not led to his death, as it would, say, in a tragedy about an affair between them doomed by the strong regional differences between their families.

One could say that the comic behaviors in *The Organizer* are leftovers from the director Mario Monicelli's previous films, many of which were comedies (a form to which he subsequently returned), and that these leftovers are not properly "digested" by the new film. Some critics believe that *The Organizer* is a tragicomedy, that Monicelli does in fact blend moments of comic relief with great tragedy in his film, but they offer no evidence of this blending. They seem to think that the mere existence side by side of humorous and serious elements is proof of tragic comedy bordering on the grotesque. My own feeling is that the comedy in *The Organizer* is jarring but that it is intentionally so. It does not exist in any real union with the serious elements, as it would if the film were a genuine tragicomedy or instance of the grotesque.

The Organizer's characters seem to be comic figures who find themselves in tragic circumstances, yet are not subsumed by them. It is almost as if these characters exist in suspension in the realm of tragedy, ready to return to their native realm at the first chance. (This tension is mirrored by the visual style of the film, in which images that suggest nineteenth-century photography exist nearly in suspension in a moving, talking picture.) Their comic natures seem to protect many of these characters in the face of privation and physical pain; they are not the same as characters who, in another film, would suffer bravely. The figures in *The Organizer* don't want to suffer, find it silly that they have suffered for so long without acting against the management, and do what they can to make their lives better. They seem conscious less that they are suffering than that suffering is not appropriate to their natures.

The Organizer is Mario Monicelli's act of defiance against poverty and exploitation at one moment in the industrialization of Italy. His characters triumph in art, through maintaining their comic integrity, whereas workers in real life had recourse to no such integrity in their struggle against the factory owners. Their work was their life. The opposite is true for Monicelli's characters: their life is their work, their labor of love.

Buster Keaton as *The Cameraman.*

CONTAINED IN *THE CAMERAMAN*

Buster Keaton's image has always suggested containment to me: the deadpan face, which reveals emotion only furtively, and the rigid acrobat's body, which subjugates feeling to form in its performance of feats. Keaton suppresses his personality as much as he can, given that it fits nowhere in a set scheme of things, yet Keaton's governing drive is to participate, to fit into the world's scheme. To this end, rarely does Keaton the director shoot Keaton the actor in an environment of containment; his physical presence suggested this idea sufficiently. We usually find him trying to make a place for himself in the wide world. But in *The Cameraman* (1928) there is a scene that combines restricted acrobatics with a restricted environment, and which thus becomes the fullest expression of Keaton's existential dilemma. Never in his films have his surroundings conspired to defeat him in the way that they do in the dressing booth at the pool, where he has come on a date with the girl he is trying to win.

The booth is made for only one person, but it is filled with two: Keaton and another, very big man. Each is attempting to change into his swimming trunks. We witness a prolonged struggle between them for space in which to move. The camera remains stationary for the entire shot, increasing the sense of confinement or claustrophobia. Himself the image of containment, Keaton is literally contained in the booth. He wants to put on his bathing suit so that he can join his date in the pool – acceptance by her means acceptance by the world – but the booth and its other user detain him. The big man acknowledges Keaton's physical presence – he cannot help but do so – but does not treat him like a person, like an individual with a right to privacy. He barges in on Keaton in the dressing room, then does not excuse himself and leave. That neither man leaves the booth for another (which would be the easiest thing to do) gives the encounter an air of fatedness and nearly imparts to the space the role of a character. It is as if the booth itself is keeping them there, in order to exert dominion over Keaton. He finally escapes, but it is no escape at all, since he has put on the big man's suit by accident.

Paradoxically, out at the pool, in an open space, Keaton will continue to be confined: the booth will still control him in a sense. The bathing suit is so large that he can barely keep it on, and his movement becomes restricted in his attempts to do so. Entering the pool for the first time, he begins to swim, only to find himself in just a few inches of water, on what amounts to a concrete sand bar. Since he is going nowhere, his arm and leg motions appear as wild and futile as they did in the dressing room. Keaton loses his suit when he jumps from the diving board, so that, naked in the pool, he is as confined, as unable to move freely (for fear of being noticed), as he was while changing. In order to have something to wear outside the pool, he steals the pants that a woman is wearing underneath her bathing suit. They obviously look odd on him and they make him feel uneasy, restricted in his movements, as he hurries back to the dressing room to change into his street clothes.

Keaton has been put through hell at the swimming pool, and he just does get his girl out of there before some admirers get to her. He finally wins her when he saves her from drowning at the beach. The atmosphere here, of course, is not one of containment, so that the contained Keaton has a chance to fit into the world's scheme somewhere. There are no dressing booths, no sand bars, no diving boards. He rushes into the water fully clothed and skillfully swims back to shore with the girl. A rival intervenes to take credit for the heroics, but so contained is Keaton that he does not pursue his love to tell her the truth. His newsreel camera – operated by his pet monkey – filmed the rescue, however; and the rival, himself trapped or confined at a screening of

Keaton's dailies with the girl (they all work for the same company), is exposed as a liar. She decides that Keaton is her man, not only for saving her, but also for obtaining valuable footage of a Chinatown gang war, and he finally finds his place in society.

Keaton is still contained enough, though, to question what appears to be a big parade for him at the end of the film. His hesitation is justified – the parade is in fact for Charles Lindbergh, yet Keaton has somehow arrived at the front of it. He may have won the girl, but he is still essentially a sensitive outsider in an indifferent universe, and he knows it.

SANE IN *PSYCHO*

Whereas *Psycho* (1960) manipulates the audience into identification with the thief and fornicator Marion and the psychopathic murderer Norman, through point-of-view shots as well as through their somewhat sympathetic characters, the film allows the policeman a cold, dispassionate view of Marion. We never see his eyes, since he wears sunglasses. Yet when he stares into the car parked on the side of a desert highway with her asleep inside it; when he follows her in his patrol car; when he stares at her in a used-car lot from his cruiser across the street (we see him in the background of a long shot); and when he stands with the salesman, California Charley, watching her drive out of the lot in her "new" car, the policeman observes Marion in a way in which we are never permitted to do.

We do see her in long shot once, or rather we see her *car*, parked along the side of the road, just before the officer pulls up. Significantly, she is asleep; once she awakens, we're in the car with her looking up at the policeman. The only other "long shots" we get in *Psycho*, aside from this one of the highway and an establishing shot of Phoenix, Arizona, at the start, are of two paintings in the real estate office where Marion works and of a photograph of a motorcycle officer in police headquarters at the end of the film (when the psychiatrist is "explaining" Norman). Those two paintings, which depict desert vistas, look forward to the vista in which we see Marion's car parked, with her sleeping on the back seat; the photograph of the officer looks back to the policeman who woke Marion from her sleep alongside the desert highway. We may stare at both the paintings and the photograph dispassionately if we will, but we would have to ignore the foreground action in order to do so. And Hitchcock discourages that – the foreground swallows us up; it makes us assume its inhabitants' point of view or otherwise identify with them.

Janet Leigh gets pulled over by the police in *Psycho*.

Paintings and photography may call for a dispassionate audience, but a Hitchcock film does not. There is a dispassionate observer *in* the film – the policeman – but we never see him again after the used-car-lot scene. And the suggestion is, had he followed his impulse that Marion was suspicious instead of coming to the dispassionate conclusion that he had no evidence of wrongdoing on her part, he might have inadvertently saved her life. When Marion followed her impulse by pulling over to the side of the road to sleep, she remained alive and safe. When she follows the trooper's rational advice that she spend the night in a motel, "just to be safe" in his words, she is knifed to death by Norman Bates. So Hitchcock appears to be mocking, through the policeman, the sober, considered response to life. Marion's interaction with him may be seen as the turning point of *Psycho*, for her next stop, made on his advice, is the Bates Motel.

It may seem curious that Hitchcock mocks the officer's attitude, since Marion's impulsive theft of $40,000 set her in flight in the first place. The director is not implying, however, that reason is "wrong" and impulse or emotion "right." Rather he is suggesting, I believe, the incompleteness of both responses taken alone. The policeman reasonably suggested that Marion spend the night in a motel, not parked on the side of the road; he should also have "unreasonably" pursued his feeling that she had committed a crime. Marion unreasonably stole $40,000 from one of her boss's customers; she should also have reasonably concluded before reaching the Bates Motel (only fifteen miles from her destination) that she could never get away with such a crime, since she would be the only suspect and could easily be traced to Fairvale, California, where she intended to live with her boyfriend, Sam, after they were married. Once she is at the motel, Norman's unreason becomes "married" in a macabre way to her own.

For cautionary reasons Hitchcock makes us identify throughout the film with Marion's and Norman's points of view rather than the policeman's. Most of us like to believe that we are rational people who can control our emotions, but the director makes us root for Marion to escape the policeman and later for Norman's murder of her to go undetected, against our better judgment. He shows us, that is, that our emotions can easily be swayed under the right circumstances.

SERVICE IN *IN WHICH WE SERVE*

Several critcs have objected to the interwoven flashbacks in *In Which We Serve* (1942) as a major inconsistency. According to this argument, the purpose of the interwoven flashbacks is ostensibly to allow each character remembering the events to tell his own story, from his point of view. A number of perspectives of one incident may thus be given. But although a flashback begins in the context of one person's memories, it often ends in the middle of another's; events in which the character who is "remembering" was not involved are somehow conjured up. (For example, all three Christmas dinners are in Captain Kinross's flashback, although he was present at only one of them.) Or, since the personal stories are somewhat interrelated, occurrences leading up to climactic moments (e.g., Blake telling Hardy of his wife's death) may be divided between two flashbacks regardless of who was actually privy to them.

Rather than being a major inconsistency, the interwoven flashbacks underline the film's theme: in general, the unity of all England in the face of the Nazi threat during World War II, and in particular the teaming up of all the men aboard the destroyer HMS *Torrin* to defeat the enemy. The flashbacks work to unite the three main characters – Captain "D" Kinross, Chief Petty Officer Walter Hardy, and Ordinary Seaman "Shorty" Blake – in their memories as these men cling to a raft in the Mediterranean Sea after their ship has been sunk by German bombers. Indeed, Kinross does flash back to Christmas dinner with his wife and two children, and this scene is immediately followed by similar ones at Blake's home and then at Hardy's. But the purpose is not to

Kinross (Noel Coward), Blake (John Mills), Hardy (Bernard Miles), and
other men from the sunken HMS *Torrin* in *In Which We Serve*.

make us think that the captain is recalling two dinners at which he was-
n't present; rather, the point is to show that *the three men are more or less
simultaneously having similar memories* as they await possible death by
drowning or gunfire. (German planes regularly strafe the raft.) The
same is true of Hardy's memory, or reconstruction, of his wife's and
mother-in-law's deaths in an air raid on London. He reconstructs the
event in his mind, Blake remembers reading in his wife's letter of the
two women's deaths as well as his son's birth, then each man comes to
the moment in his memory when Blake delivers the bad news to Hardy.

Throughout *In Which We Serve* the flashbacks, long takes, traveling
shots, and what critics have called the "weak contrivances" of the film's
plot, serve to join together the three main characters as well as the
other officers and sailors aboard the *Torrin* – men otherwise strongly
divided by class. (The men are *physically* divided on the ship, with the
officers on the bridge and the crew below, with a separate mess for the
officers; but the three main characters are physically *united* around the
life raft.) About the supposedly contrived interworking of the individual histories of Kinross, Hardy, and Blake, one could make the argument that the manner of Blake's chance meeting with Freda on the

John Mills as Shorty Blake (with the coffee cup) and Bernard
Miles as Walter Hardy in *In Which We Serve.*

train and the fact that she is related to his petty officer by marriage are
initial coincidences, which are augmented by Shorty's remark that his
parents met in a similar fashion. Further, that on their trip to Torquay
after their wedding, the Blakes just happen to encounter Kinross and
his wife, who in turn muse over their own honeymoon voyage taken
years before to the same destination. But the interworking of these
three men's lives is not a sentimental contrivance; it's an effective
device. Separated by class, Blake and Hardy become somewhat joined
through their relationship with Freda, who goes to live in Hardy's
home with his wife and mother-in-law once she becomes pregnant.
Even further separated by class, Blake and Kinross will at least have
shared the same town during their honeymoons.

Among the several traveling shots in this film, the one that stands out
in my mind takes place during an assembly of the crew and the officers
on the deck of the *Torrin.* The camera slowly tracks across the men until
it lights upon Kinross, then it tracks back over the entire company. The
director, David Lean, could just as easily have cut from one face to the
next, as directors often do before battle scenes in order to isolate each
man in his fear or anticipation. He chose instead, through the traveling action of the camera, to connect the men to one another and to

their leader, to unite them in their common enterprise: search out and destroy enemy ships. Lean also does this in three of a number of long takes during *In Which We Serve*.

The first occurs at the start of the film, with a group different from Kinross and his men. In this opening sequence or shot, we see HMS *Torrin* being constructed. In one long take we see a close-up of a red hot bolt in a furnace being taken out by a young worker. He carefully passes the molten bolt from his prongs to those of another worker, who does the same, etc. The bolt finally reaches its destination, where it is drilled into form. Thus we see in this shot the interdependence of individuals on one another, their cooperation in working together toward a common goal, and, finally, through the integrity inherent in the single shot, the concrete manifestation of man's shaping of the elements for his own purposes.

Another long take occurs when Blake tells Hardy of the death of the latter's wife: rather than go to a shelter, she stayed with her home, her "ship," and went down with it. This scene would normally be filmed in the classic Hollywood manner with a shot of Blake, then a reaction shot of Hardy, and so forth. But Lean preserves the integrity of the single shot, and the result is that we see Blake and Hardy united, communicating in joy and grief: the grief of *both* men at the deaths of Hardy's wife and mother-in-law, the joy of *both* men at the survival of Freda and the birth of her and Blake's son shortly after the air raid. Blake is not separated in a single shot, powerless to comfort Hardy and guilty because of his own good fortune, and Hardy is not isolated in a single frame, torn by grief and incapable of sharing in Blake's happiness.

There is one more long take at the end of *In Which We Serve*, after the survivors of the *Torrin* have been rescued: Captain Kinross is saying goodbye to his remaining men, who have been assigned to other ships to replace sailors killed in action, and the camera stays on him for some time as he shakes hands and exchanges a few words with every man. Again, there is no shot-reaction-shot pattern here; we see both the captain and, by turn, each sailor in the frame. They are united by the image – united in shaking hands, in grieving over the loss of the *Torrin*, and in their joy at the opportunity to fight on for England. So joined to his men seems Kinross that, after they have left the hall, he follows them, turning only to nod to the remaining four officers before he exits.

20

Notes on Film Form

On *General della Rovere* (1959, Italy), *Just Before Nightfall* (1971, France), and *Clare's Knee* (1970, France)

THE ENDING OF *GENERAL DELLA ROVERE*

Rossellini's *General della Rovere* (1959) contains a startling final sequence. In it, Bardone refuses to reveal the identity of the partisan leader Fabrizio to the Nazi colonel Mueller, choosing instead to go to his death in the guise of General della Rovere with ten Italian political prisoners, among whom are some Jews. He stumbles into the prison courtyard and takes his place before a firing squad. The other prisoners are strapped to posts; he is not. It is dawn. The camera is in long shot. At the far right of the screen, Bardone can barely be seen through the fog. The soldiers fire. Bardone falls, while the others jerk forward. The camera, still in long shot, tracks to the left, stopping on the four or five prisoners who were out of frame when the soldiers fired. Bardone is now out of frame as well. And presently the film ends.

Everything that has preceded this sequence, in the body of conventional dramatic film as well as in *this* film, might lead us to believe that Bardone would be the subject of the camera's interest rather than *all* the men who are executed. Up to this point, the camera has told the story of this charming embezzler and gambler who, caught in one of his schemes, agrees to impersonate the dead partisan General della Rovere in return for his freedom. As General della Rovere, he is imprisoned and appreciates for the first time the courage and commitment of the partisans. He sees a man tortured for refusing to reveal Fabrizio's identity; the man commits suicide rather than face torture again. Bardone himself is then tortured for bungling the plot to flush out Fabrizio.

Vittorio De Sica as Bardone in *General della Rovere.*

Lying in bed recovering from his injuries, he has someone read a brave, touching letter from della Rovere's wife and show him the photograph of her and her two young sons that comes with it. Waiting with the men to be executed, he witnesses their excoriation of a prisoner who complains that he has done nothing to hurt the Nazis and therefore should not be shot: this man is told by his comrades that his crime, indeed, is never having done anything to hurt the Nazis. Finally, rather than gain safe passage to Switzerland, together with a million *lire*, by informing on Fabrizio, whom he has finally met and been touched by, Bardone faces the firing squad. He has been converted from a criminal out for himself into a member of the Resistance who would rather die than betray a comrade.

Instead of singling out Bardone as a hero at the end and emphasizing that he has in a sense become the General della Rovere he has been impersonating, the camera stresses the sacrifice of all the political prisoners, including "della Rovere." It stresses that Bardone now belongs to the community of partisans and no longer walks alone, as he did when the camera first located him in the streets of Genoa (also at dawn). By tracking to the left, away from Bardone, the camera identifies him all the more as a partisan, neither more nor less important than any other. Bardone has not been melodramatically transformed into General della Rovere; he has been believably transformed into a partisan.

The credibility of Bardone's conversion is enhanced by the natural setting of his and the other prisoners' execution. Prior to it, Rossellini had filmed claustrophobic studio interiors and sound-stage street scenes, adding newsreel footage and even matte shots. To be sure, the prison is an actual one (or a building that was converted into a prison, probably during the war); and one or two buildings in the film may be real (as opposed to cardboard or flimsy reconstructions). But the scene of the execution is the only natural outdoor one. Even as the truth of Bardone's conversion supersedes the falseness or error of his erstwhile criminality, the authenticity of his execution site replaces the artificiality of his previous surroundings.

Our belief in Bardone's conversion is further enhanced by the realism in Colonel Mueller's characterization. The colonel is a sympathetic figure, hardly the stereotypical Nazi officer. He seems to sense the desperation of the German war effort in Italy, as it is 1943 and the Nazis are losing ground rapidly. He rightly tells his superior officer that executing ten partisans in reprisal for the murder of a Fascist leader will achieve the opposite of what is intended: it will only incite the remaining partisans to fight harder. Colonel Mueller actually likes Bardone (who himself is known as "Colonel" among his associates); as a favor to him, for example, he pardons the son of a man named Borghesio. The colonel has a soldier's respect for the actual General della Rovere's courage and leadership, and he treats the general's widow with kindness and discretion. He is a soldier first, a political man – a Nazi – second.

At the end of the film, Colonel Mueller is in the foreground of the long shot in the prison courtyard and off to the right. He says, "I've made a mistake," to a junior officer in charge of the execution who notices that eleven men are being shot instead of ten as ordered. The colonel says this to put the officer at ease, to relieve him of responsibility for the death of the eleventh man. But one senses that Mueller realizes that he has made a mistake in two other ways: he has underestimated the contagiousness of the partisans' conviction, as well as the character of Bardone, who was a thief but never an informer; and he has erred in allowing "General della Rovere" to be shot. In death, as a martyr to the partisan cause (the real della Rovere died less spectacularly in an ambush), Bardone will do for Italy what he failed to do in life. Colonel Mueller has his moment of recognition at the end of *General della Rovere*, then, just as Bardone has had his.

THE VISUAL TURNING POINT OF *JUST BEFORE NIGHTFALL*

Claude Chabrol's *Just Before Nightfall* (1971) contains two narrative surprises. First, it tells the story of a murder committed not by a hardened criminal or psychotic, but by an essentially good bourgeois family man. Second, when Charles Masson admits killing his mistress (an act that was, as he explains it, partly accidental, partly intentional) to his wife, Hélène, and his best friend, François, the husband of the woman whom he has murdered, they both forgive him immediately and urge him not to turn himself in. Charles is tortured by guilt, however, and insists on punishment. Instead of letting him confess to the police and disturb the tranquility of her and her children's bourgeois life, Hélène gives him a fatal dose of laudanum in a glass of water.

Through much of *Just Before Nightfall* the tranquility of his family life and the opulent comfort of his home (ironically, designed by François) have contained or smoothed over Charles's crime. Chabrol visually suggests that containment or smoothing over by placing the house below ground level and filling it with horizontals, including a dining room table that calls attention to its horizontality by being only a few feet off the floor. The horizontal lines of the house – a split-level whose second floor, of bedrooms, looks down on the living and dining rooms – are emphasized because they are not opposed by strong verticals. The unorthodox framework of marble, concrete, and steel is constructed around walls of glass – Charles and Hélène's bedroom wall, facing out on the areas below, is itself made of glass.

The only strong verticals exist outside the house in the cold of winter, and are associated, not with containment or concealment, but with the expulsion of Charles from the warmth of his home and the exposure of his crime. The first vertical in the film is the high-rise apartment building where he meets Laura, his mistress. It appears in one of the first frames, and its height is emphasized in a low-angle shot that has Charles looking up at it. Another vertical is the tall iron gate to François's house; Charles is framed behind its bars several times. Traveling home from work, he looks out the window of his train to a vertical from which many people have jumped to their deaths over the years: the Eiffel Tower, looming over Paris in long shot.

I would like to suggest that *Just Before Nightfall* contains a visual turning point, a cinematic as opposed to a dramatic crisis, at which soothing horizontals and harsh verticals meet and Charles's doom becomes certain. The turning point occurs at the beach (where Charles's mother owns a bungalow), to which Charles and Hélène have gone for a rest when it

appears that he is on the verge of a nervous breakdown. His guilt is getting the best of him, but his wife suspects only that the pressure of his
work as the head of an advertising agency has exhausted him physically
and mentally. At the moment Charles finally confesses the murder of his
mistress to Hélène, she is standing in front of him, slightly to his right:
they form in the foreground a vertical line more or less, and look out
from a sandy plateau onto the beach below. A woman pushing a baby carriage on the beach moves horizontally across the screen in the background, from left to right. The vertical of adultery and murder thus meets
the horizontal of domesticity and motherhood. Put another way, the
serenity of Charles's bourgeois life has been invaded, and his guilt must
surface. After he admits it to Hélène, he will tell François; then he will
want to go to the police. Hélène's own murder of Charles is foreshadowed
here, since she is the continuation of the vertical line begun by him.

The turning point of *Just Before Nightfall* has actually been prepared
for visually, just as turning points in plays are prepared for dramatically.
In the film's first sequence, after he has killed Laura, Charles sits down
next to her on the bed. She is nude and lies across it, her head and
arms almost touching the floor on one side while her feet graze the
wall on the other. The vertical of her body meets the horizontal of the
bed, and a cross is formed as a result. Although sitting down, Charles is
also a vertical that crosses a horizontal, since he sits on the side of the
bed, facing the camera. Charles and Laura are not in a hotel, but in the
cozy, tidy apartment of Laura's business partner, where they have gone
for all their encounters. In this way the idea of domestic peace shattered by sexual violence is underlined. (Charles strangles Laura in an
act of sadomasochistic love.) Chabrol surrounds the visual cross that
Laura's body makes on the bed with two allusions to Christianity:
Charles sits on the bed with his hands joined, as if in prayer, and above
the bed hangs a painting of a scene from the Bible.

Just before he strangled Laura, furthermore, Charles tore a crucifix
from her neck. At Laura's funeral a crucifix will reappear in the hands
of the priest. And at the train station, after the funeral, Laura's business
partner will cross the tracks to speak with Charles: she had seen him
once with Laura, and thinks that he may be the murderer. He rides the
train to work fearing that she will expose him. She does, to François,
but he does not find it unusual that Charles and Laura were seen
together, since they were friends, just as he does not find it unusual that
he met Charles in a bar near the scene of the crime, and far from the
latter's office, shortly before Laura's body was found.

The rising action, with its images of crosses, has led up to the turning point, and the falling action leads down from it. By the time Hélène gives Charles the fatal dose of laudanum, the conflict between horizontals and verticals has disappeared. The murderer will himself be murdered, and Hélène will live with her murder of him without conflict, well-provided for by his will. Their beds are shot standing vertically next to each other (the foot of each faces the camera); after Charles drinks the laudanum, he lies down in his bed, and Hélène lies down in hers. They join hands across the beds as if in agreement over the action that Hélène has taken: i.e., the two verticals are *joined* horizontally.

The final shot of *Just Before Nightfall* finds Hélène and her mother-in-law sitting on the beach, with Charles and Hélène's two children playing beside them. This is the same beach that Chabrol shot at the turning point. Now there is no vertical in conflict with a horizontal: we get only the horizontal of domestic life of mothers and children, resting on the long strip of beach. More precisely, we get the vertical of sorts that Hélène (herself now a murderer) forms with her mother-in-law, submerged or housed in the horizontal of the beach. Charles' vertical of adultery and murder has been expunged – so much so that his mother can say the children are already forgetting their father.

Chabrol places Hélène's and her mother-in-law's chairs in positions on the beach that are the opposite of those in which Charles and Hélène stood on the sandy plateau at the turning point. Hélène's chair is in front of her mother-in-law's and slightly to the left. It is as if Chabrol is complementing the line of rising action, which he suggested through the placement of Charles and Hélène at the turning point, with a line of falling action, and in so doing providing us with yet another visual clue to a reading of his film:

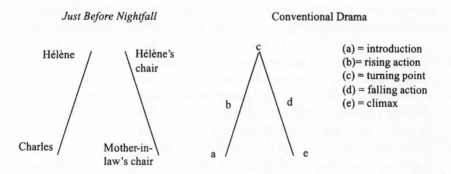

| *Just Before Nightfall* | Conventional Drama |

	(a) = introduction
Hélène / Hélène's chair	c	(b) = rising action
	(c) = turning point
	b d	(d) = falling action
	(e) = climax
Charles / Mother-in-law's chair	a e

THE CINEMATOGRAPHIC TEXTURE OF *CLAIRE'S KNEE*

Éric Rohmer's *Moral Tales* examine the withering away of genuine sentiment in the life of contemporary man. People, for Rohmer, use ideas as substitutes for feelings, and often to deny them. Thus the intellect works against man's deepest interest and desires, hiding from him his true self as well as the means by which he could satisfy the needs of that self. This dissociation of mind and body has resulted in frustrated, bored, dissatisfied people. Jérôme in *Claire's Knee* (1970), number five of the *Moral Tales*, believes that in his relations with women "looks don't count, only intellect." Yet during a revealing summer at Annecy, he chooses a woman, Claire, who is incapable of formulating a single idea. Why men become this way, burying their feelings, deceiving themselves with chimerical ideas, is the implied question buried in Rohmer's films. He leaves it unanswered.

I would like to suggest that the quality or texture of the cinematography in *Claire's Knee* underlines the film's theme and method. Rohmer used a 40mm lens throughout *Claire's Knee*, whereas some of his colleagues systematically use a 50mm lens, which corresponds more closely to normal eyesight. One of the reasons Rohmer shot *Claire's Knee* in 40mm was to compress the geography of his location, in order that, more so than in any of the other *Moral Tales*, he could through middle shots place the characters in a setting where they can be identified, and at the same time put them where they can be identified with the backgrounds. If he had put them in a long shot you wouldn't have seen the people, and if he had gone to a close-up you wouldn't have seen the décor. It is important to Rohmer to include characters and setting in middle shots, because the beautiful but monotonous landscape of blue sky, blue lake, mountains, and smooth green lawns provides a judgment on the empty, idle existence of the haute-bourgeoisie personified by Jérôme.

Another reason Rohmer used a 40mm lens in *Claire's Knee* was, I believe, to create an effect of subdued color and slight indistinctness, even haziness, in the image. Bodies and objects are not as sharply defined as they are in 50mm cinematography. One of the results of this, of course, is a near blending of human form and environment, for purposes described above. But a further result is the creation of a visual analogue for Jérôme's state of mind. If he buries his feelings or deceives himself with chimerical ideas, then Rohmer gives us near chimeras, nearly deceptive images in muted colors on the screen. If the character cannot see himself clearly, then we will not be able to see him clearly, either.

We feel vaguely discomforted by these images; we feel that we are not seeing as clearly as we might, that we are not seeing *everything*. The quality of the images serves the film's ultimate intentions: even as they are slightly indistinct, the film is indistinct about Jérôme's past – how he has become the way he is – and his future – what will become of him. (Will he, for example, really marry his fiancée, Lucinde, who has intellect but not the looks of a Claire?) *Claire's Knee* is indistinct as well about what Rohmer prescribes so that men like Jérôme can change. We know only that he is in a profession, diplomacy, that requires its own brand of cool deception; that he has returned to his boyhood home, Annecy, for vacation (not insignificantly, he grew up in a town associated with idleness and vapidity, but this alone is not enough to explain his character, nor is it intended to be); and that he will have to leave at the end of the summer.

Claire's Knee is told through Jérôme, the single main character. If he is not in a scene, he stands on its edges, observing, or he is the topic of conversation. The film is told directly through him, then, and indirectly through his friend Aurora. She is a writer who wants to see how susceptible Jérôme is to girls, and who therefore urges him to keep company with Laura, Claire's younger sister (who has a crush on him), subsequently encouraging him in his pursuit of Claire herself. Aurora thinks that his encounter with a girl will provide her with the idea for a story. Periodically throughout the film, Jérôme reports back to her on his experiences with one sister or the other. Thus he becomes a character in the story that Aurora will write. And the texture of Rohmer's images will become the nature of Aurora's prose: she will not be an omniscient narrator, but will write in the third person, from Jérôme's point of view – the partial, cloudy, or even distorted one.

One clue to Aurora's role as Jérôme's "creator" comes at the start of *Claire's Knee.* He pilots his motorboat through a waterway, but we do not know who he is yet. He passes under a small bridge and Aurora, standing on it looking out over the water, recognizes this man (whom she has not seen for some time) and calls out his name. The moment Jérôme hears her, his narrative begins.

21

Theatre and Fiction into Film: Notes on Two Paradigmatic Scenes, One Metaphoric Fiction, and An Omnibus Adaptation

On *The Little Foxes* (1941, USA), *Housekeeping* (1987, USA), *Trainspotting* (1996, UK), and *Dangerous Liaisons* (1998, UK)

I thought I'd say something about the adaptation of both drama and fiction into film, mainly because so little is understood about the process of adaptation by even the educated filmgoer. Many people still cling to the naïve belief that drama and film, for example, are two aspects of the same art, except that drama is "live" while movies are "recorded." Certainly there are undeniable similarities between the two forms. Most obviously, both employ action as a principal means of communication: that is, what people *do* is a major source of meaning. Live theatre and movies are also collaborative enterprises, involving the coordination of writers, directors, actors, designers, and technicians. Drama and film are both social arts in that they are exhibited before groups of people and are therefore experienced publicly as well as individually. But films are not mere recordings of plays. The language systems of these two art forms are fundamentally different, and movies have a far broader range of techniques at their disposal.

Actually, as many commentators have noted, film is closer in form to fiction than to theatre. Like fiction, film can move easily through time and space, and, like fiction, film employs narration – sometimes in the first person, through subjective camera and voice-over; rarely in the third person, through the anonymous commentaries that accompany certain documentaries; and most often and most naturally in the omniscient mode, which enables a filmmaker to cut from a subjective point-of-view shot to a variety of objective shots, from a single reaction in close-up to the simultaneous reactions of several characters in medium or full shot. Unlike fiction, or I should say in a more powerful way than fiction, film can go inside human beings to explore interiority. It does this through the voice and the voice-over, through the close-up, and through the ability to present multiple states of consciousness, as Federico Fellini does in *8 ½* (1963): present awareness, memory, dream, and daydream. A novel could do all this, of course, but its words wouldn't have the immediacy and effect of film, the power of the image and its accompanying sound. To be fair to the novel, the Russian filmmaker and theorist Sergei Eisenstein has shown how such cinematic innovations as fades, dissolves, and parallel editing were in fact taken directly from the pages of Charles Dickens. And to praise the novel, it has learned from film, as has poetry: a number of critics have remarked upon the cinematic qualities of much twentieth-century fiction and poetry, including Joyce's *Ulysses* (1922) and Eliot's "Love Song of J. Alfred Prufrock" (1915).

To talk now about the adaptation of drama into film, the surest sign of the clichéd mind in filmmaking is a feeling of obligation to "open up" plays when they become films and a conviction that this process proves superiority, that a play really comes into its own when it is filmed. We can really go to Italy in Franco Zeffirelli's film of *Romeo and Juliet* (1968), so the film, for all its cutting of Shakespeare's poetry, supersedes stagebound theatre productions. We can dissolve and cross-fade more easily in the movie of *Death of a Salesman* (1951), therefore the theatre proves yet again just a tryout place for later perfect consummation on screen – despite, in this case, the theatre's superior ability to suggest the childishness of Willy's sons (by having the adult actors of Biff and Happy play their boyhood selves) and the momentousness of Willy's adultery (by having it occur, not on location in Boston, but on the forestage – right in the Lomans' living room, as it were). And we can go outside in Mike Nichols' film of *Who's Afraid of Virginia Woolf?* (1966), so once more the theatre is shown up as cribbed or confined, if not superficially realistic, even though the claustrophobic nature of George and Martha's single-set living room on the stage is part of the point of this long night's journey into day.

The trouble here is a confusion in aesthetic logic, an assumption that we are comparing apples and apples when we are really comparing apples and pears. Fundamentally, film takes the audience to the event, shifting the audience continually; theatre takes the event to the audience, shifting it never. Just as the beauty of poetry often lies in tensions between the free flight of language and the molding capacity of form, so the beauty of drama often lies in tensions between imagination and theatrical exigency. To assume that the cinema's extension of a play's action is automatically an improvement is to change the subject: from the way theatre builds upwards, folding one event upon another in almost perceptible vertical form, to the way film progresses horizontally. Theatre works predominantly by building higher and higher in one place. Film, despite the literally vertical progress of planes in the image, works predominantly in a lateral series of places. By its very form, it can then be said, film reflects for spectators in the twenty-first century the belief that the world is a place in which a person can leave the past behind and create his or her own future (hence one of the reasons the cinema took such a foothold, so early, in the early history of the United States).

"Opening up" a play can be successful when the filmmaker knows clearly what he is doing and treats his film as a new work from a common source, as Richard Lester does in his admirable film of Ann Jellicoe's *The Knack* (1965). But most adaptors seem to think that any banal set of film gimmicks constitutes a liberation for which the poor cramped play ought to be grateful. One film that respects its dramatic source almost completely and is nevertheless cinematic is William Wyler's *The Little Foxes* (1941). Lillian Hellman's play from 1939 has undergone nearly no adaptation: for instance, there are no exterior scenes of dramatic action in the film – precisely the kind of scene, I have been arguing, that most directors would have deemed necessary in order to introduce a little "cinema" into this intractable theatrical mass.

The majority of the action in Wyler's film takes place on the same, totally neutral set, the ground-floor living room of a huge colonial house. At the back, a staircase leads to the second-floor bedrooms of Regina and Horace Giddens, which adjoin each other. (Regina and Horace are played by Bette Davis and Herbert Marshall respectively, and I shall use the actors' names in my discussion of the film version.) Nothing picturesque adds to the realism of this somber place, which is as impersonal as the setting of classical tragedy. The characters have a credible, if conventional, reason for confronting one another in the living room, whether they come from the outdoors or from their bedrooms; they can also plausibly linger in the living room. The staircase at the back plays a role similar to the one it would in the theatre: it is purely an element of dramatic architecture, which in this case will be used to set off the characters in the vertical space of the frame. Let's look at the central scene of the film, the death of Herbert Marshall, which happens to take place both in the living room and on the staircase. An analysis of this scene will reveal that to be cinematic a film adaptation not only doesn't have to go outdoors, it also doesn't have to feature either a mobile camera or lots of cutting.

First let me summarize the action of *The Little Foxes* up to and just beyond this point, which occurs toward the end. We are in the South at the turn of the century, where and when middle-class capitalism-cum-materialism has more than begun to eclipse aristocratic feudalism-cum-agrarianism. Two brothers, Ben and Oscar Hubbard, believe they can make a fortune by establishing the first mill in their town, which is surrounded by cotton plantations. Lacking the $75,000 needed for the venture, they seek the partnership of their sister, Regina Giddens, who, eager to share in the profits, promises to get the money from her wealthy husband, Horace, who is president of the local bank. Having just been brought home from the hospital in Baltimore by his devoted daughter, Alexandra, Horace has only a short time to live and refuses to become involved. Therefore, to help his father, Oscar's son, Lee, a clerk in Horace's bank, steals $80,000 in bonds from Horace's safe-deposit box, on the assumption that his uncle will not check the box for six months; and Ben and Oscar complete their business deal. Horace discovers the theft but tells Regina that he will not prosecute her brothers. On the contrary, he will call the theft a loan and make a new will in which Regina will receive only $80,000 in bonds, the exact amount of the theft. Thus Regina will share neither in her husband's fortune nor in the fortune the mill will make. While the two quarrel, Horace suffers a heart attack, but Regina refuses to administer a reviving drug and coldbloodedly stands by as he dies. With her knowledge of the theft, she then blackmails her brothers into assigning her a 75 per cent interest in the mill, lest she prosecute them. Our scene is the quarrel between Regina and Horace, or, to switch back to the actors' names, between Bette Davis and Herbert Marshall, who has revealed to her the theft of his bonds.

Bette Davis is sitting in the middle ground facing the viewer, her head at the center of the screen; the lighting enhances the brightness of her heavily made-up face. In the foreground Herbert Marshall sits in three-quarter profile. The ruthless exchanges between husband and wife take place without any cutting from one character to the other, since the very positions of Davis and Marshall emphasize their separation and antagonism. Then comes the husband's heart attack, during

Bette Davis, as Regina, gloats in the foreground as
her husband collapses on the stairs in the background in *The Little Foxes.*

which he begs his wife to get him his medicine from upstairs. From this
instant all the drama in this scene derives from the immobility of both
Bette Davis and the camera. Marshall is forced to stand up and go get
the medicine himself, and this effort will kill him as he climbs the first
few steps of the staircase.

In the theatre, this scene would most likely have been staged in the
same manner. A spotlight could have been focused on Bette Davis, and
the spectator would have felt the same horror at her criminal inaction,
the same anguish at the sight of her staggering victim. Yet, despite
appearances, William Wyler's directing makes as extensive use as possible of the means offered him by the camera and the frame. Bette
Davis's position at the center of the screen endows her with privilege
and power in the geometry of the dramatic space. The whole scene
revolves around her, but her frightening immobility takes its full
impact only from Marshall's double exit from the frame, first in the

foreground on the right, then in the mid-background on the left. Instead of following him in this lateral movement, as any less intelligent director would have done, Wyler's camera remains imperturbably immobile. When Marshall finally enters the frame for a second time and begins to climb the stairs, the cinematographer, Gregg Toland, acting at Wyler's request, is careful not to bring into focus the full depth of the image, so that Marshall's fall on the staircase and his death will not be clearly visible to the viewer. This artificial blurring augments our feeling of anxiety: as if over the shoulder of the dominant Bette Davis, who faces us and has her back toward her husband, we have to discern in the distance the outcome of a drama whose protagonist is nearly escaping us.

This analysis of Marshall's death in *The Little Foxes* clearly reveals how Wyler can make a whole scene revolve around one actor. Bette Davis at the center of the screen is paralyzed, like a hoot owl by a spotlight, and around her the staggering Marshall weaves as a second – this time mobile – pole, whose shift first out of the frame and then into the background, draws with it all the dramatic attention. In addition, this shift creates tremendous suspense because it consists of a double disappearance from the frame, and because the focus on the staircase at the back is imperfect. One can see here how Wyler uses depth of field: as I've indicated, the director elected to have Toland envelop the character of the dying Marshall in a certain haziness, to have his cinematographer, as it were, befog the back of the frame. This was done to create so much anxiety in the viewer that he would almost want to push the immobile Bette Davis aside to have a better look. The dramatic development of this scene does indeed follow that of the dialogue and of the action itself, but the scene's cinematic expression superimposes its own evolution upon the dramatic development: a second action, as it were, which is the very story of the scene from the moment Marshall gets up from his chair to his collapse on the staircase.

We can see here everything that the cinema adds to the means of the theatre, and we can also see here that, paradoxically, the highest level of cinematic art coincides with the lowest level of *mise en scène*. Nothing could better heighten the dramatic power of this scene than the absolute *immobility* of the camera. Its slightest movement, which a less skillful director would have deemed the right "cinematic" element to introduce, would have decreased the dramatic tension. Furthermore, the camera does not follow the path of the average viewer's eyes by cutting from Bette Davis to the frantic Marshall; instead, it obstructs our vision merely by recording, without full depth of field, the same scene in one continuous take. It is the stationary camera itself, in other words, that organizes the action in terms of the frame and the ideal coordinates of its two-dimensional geometric space. By means of the cinema, William Wyler has mined the artistic depths of this scene at the same time that he has respected its theatrical appearances.

To the real looks the actors would direct at one another on stage, one must add the virtual "look" of the camera with which our own identifies. And Wyler excels in making us sensitive to his camera's gaze. In *Jezebel* (1938), for example, there is the low-angle shot that clearly points the lens directly at Bette Davis's eyes looking down at the white cane that Henry Fonda holds in his hand with the intention of using it. We thus follow the dramatic line between the character and the object much better than we would have if, by the rules of conventional cutting, the camera had shown us the cane from the point of view of Bette Davis herself.

A variation on the same principle: in *The Little Foxes*, in order to make us understand the thoughts of the character who notices the small steel box in which the stolen bonds were locked and whose absence from the box is going to indicate theft, Wyler placed it in the foreground with the camera being this time at eye level and at the same distance from the box as the eyes of the character. Our eyes no longer meet the character's eyes directly through the beheld object, as in the above-mentioned scene from *Jezebel*, but as if through a mirror. The angle of incidence of our own view of the object is, as it were, equal to the angle of reflection of the character's view, which angle takes us to this person's eyes. In any case, Wyler commands our mental vision according to the rigorous laws of an invisible dramatic optics.

Paradoxically, insofar as Wyler never attempted to hide the novelistic or theatrical nature of most of his scripts, he made all the more apparent the cinematic phenomenon in its utmost purity. Not once did the *auteur* of *The Best Years of Our Lives* (1946), *Jezebel*, or *The Little Foxes* say to himself *a priori* that he had to have a "cinematic look"; still, nobody can tell a story in cinematic terms better than he. For him, the action is expressed first by the actor. Like a director in the theatre, Wyler conceived of his job of enhancing the action as beginning with the actor. The set and the camera are there only to permit the actor to focus upon himself the maximum dramatic intensity; they are not there to create a meaning unto themselves. Even though Wyler's approach is also that of the theatre director, the latter has at his disposal only the very limited means of the stage. He can manipulate his means, but no matter what he does, the text and the actor constitute the essence of theatrical production.

Film, then, is not at all magnified theatre on screen, the stage viewed constantly through opera glasses. The size of the image or unity of time has nothing to do with it. Cinema begins when the frame of the screen and the placement of the camera are used to enhance the action and the actor. In *The Little Foxes*, Wyler has changed almost nothing of the dramatic text or even of the set: one could say that he limited himself to directing the play in the way that a theatre director would have directed it; and, furthermore, that he used the frame of the screen to *conceal* certain parts of the set and used the camera to bring the viewer closer to the action. What actor would not dream of being able to play a scene, immobile on a chair, in front of 5,000 viewers who don't miss the slightest movement of an eye? What theatre director would not want the spectator in the worst seat at the back of the house to be able to see clearly the movements of his actors, and to read with ease his intentions at any moment in the action? Wyler didn't choose to do anything other than realize on film the essence of a theatrical *mise en scène* that would not use the lights and the set merely to ornament the actor and the text. Nevertheless, there is probably not a single shot in *The Little Foxes* that isn't pure cinema. Indeed, there is a hundred times more cinema, and better cinema at that, in one fixed shot of *The Little Foxes* than in all the exterior traveling shots, in all the natural settings, in all the geographical exoticism, in all the shots of the reverse side of the set, by means of which up to now the screen has ingeniously attempted to make us forget the stage.

All things considered, it's possible to imagine that we are moving toward a reign of the adaptation in which the notion of the unity of the work of art, if not the very notion of the author himself, will be destroyed. If the film that was made of Steinbeck's *Of Mice and Men* (1940; dir. Lewis Milestone) had been successful (it could have been so, and far more easily than the adaptation of the same author's *Grapes of Wrath* [1940; dir. John Ford]), the (literary?) critic of the year 2050 would find not a novel out of which a play and a film had been "made," but rather a single work reflected through three art forms, an artistic pyramid with three sides, all equal in the eyes of the critic. The "work" would then be only an ideal point at the top of this figure, which itself is an ideal construct. The chronological precedence of one part over another would not be an aesthetic criterion any more than the chronological precedence of one twin over the other is a genealogical one.

Even more so in the case of *Cabaret*, which began as fiction in 1946, then was transformed into a "straight" play (titled, of all things, *I Am a Camera*), a musical one, and finally a film version; or in the case of *Miss Julie* (1888), which was first a play, then a television movie and a wide-screen film, as well as finally a ballet, an opera, *and* a modern-dance piece.

To talk next about the adaptation of fiction into film, the chief problem for the adaptor is that of narration, and I'd like to discuss first the adaptation of novels written in the first person. As I suggested earlier, omniscient narration is almost inevitable in film: each time the director moves his camera – either within a shot or between shots – we are offered a new point of view from which to evaluate the action. Many films employ first-person narrative techniques, but only sporadically, because in order to produce continuous first-person narration on film, the camera would have to record all the action "subjectively," through the eyes of the narrator. The problem with such a subjective point of view is that it tends to create frustration in the viewer, who wants to *see* the hero. In fiction, we get to know the first-person narrator through his words, through the judgments and values he expresses in those words. But in movies, we get to know a character by seeing how he reacts to people and events, and unless the director breaks the first-person camera convention, we can never see the hero – we can only see what he sees. So the solution for the adaptor of a first-person novel is to include just enough first-person narration – usually in the form of voice-over – to remind us from whose point of view the story was originally told. But the adaptor must also solve the problem of tone, which is, of course, far more difficult to do: he must, if he is a faithful adaptor, capture in images the tone of the original narrator's words. How Bill Forsyth does this in his film of Marilynne Robinson's novel *Housekeeping* (1980) is the subject of the second quarter of this essay.

Housekeeping (1987) is the story of Ruth's and her sister Lucille's lives as teenagers in the care of their aunt Sylvie, a hobo who has come to Fingerbone, Washington, in 1955 to assume the guardianship of her two nieces after the death of their grandmother (who has left her life savings to the three of them); the girls' mother and Sylvie's sister, Helen, had killed herself seven years before. As we might expect of an itinerant confined to domestic life, Sylvie behaves eccentrically. She arrives tentatively – sidling up to the family home and standing outside awhile in the snow before knocking. She keeps old newspapers and fills the house with mounds of them; she washes used tin cans and carefully

Andrea Burchill, as Lucille, and Sara Walker, as Ruth, enjoy a smoke in *Housekeeping.*

stores them – hundreds of them; she never answers the phone; she wanders around Fingerbone and its environs for hours at a time, sleeping on park benches, listening for trains in the distance, looking into store windows. Sylvie barely supervises the activities of her nieces, although she genuinely likes them both. In time Lucille, who craves supervision, orthodoxy, and direction in her life, falls out with both her aunt Sylvie and sister Ruth and goes to live with her home economics teacher, who eventually adopts her. Ruth is Lucille's opposite in every respect and early reveals her affinity with Sylvie. Soon these two learn, however, that a court hearing is scheduled to decide whether custody of Ruth should be taken from the "unfit" Sylvie. Rather than be separated, they set fire to their house (where Sylvie and Helen as well as Ruth and Lucille grew up) and flee into the night to hop a freight train.

The director and screenwriter Forsyth wants to make a serious point in *Housekeeping* at the same time that he doesn't want us to psychologize a character like Sylvie, to explain her away as an oddball who has good reasons in her past for being odd. Inhabiting less her own mind than the world around her, beginning with her own clothing (which she rarely changes) and extending out to lakes, forests, and hills, Sylvie is not a freak or a mental case, but rather a warm and intelligent woman who has chosen her way to live and is unyielding in her commitment to that choice. Forsyth uses comedy to keep us blithely removed from and uncritical of her, so as to make us view the behavior of Sylvie and her acolyte Ruth more as a legitimate, spontaneous response to the world than as the result of longstanding, internal causes. In the second sequence, Forsyth sets the serious but comically distant tone for the rest of the film by making us amusedly accept Helen the mother's suicide as the act of someone who no longer wishes to live in such a world, rather than soberly ask what events have led up to this woman's decision to kill herself. Here's how he does it.

Helen puts her children, Ruth and Lucille, in the back seat of a borrowed Ford for a trip from Seattle to Fingerbone "to see Grandma." For some reason, she's in a hurry: we see her stop, in long shot, at a red light and then, after some pause, deliberately ignore the light and drive through the intersection. She drops her daughters off at their grandmother's house, gives them a bag of cookies, tells them not to fight and to wait for Grandma, then promptly leaves. We next see her impatiently sitting atop the Ford in a meadow. The car is stuck in mud, and three boys who have been fishing come along to help Helen out. To their puzzlement, she gives them her nice coat to put under one of the rear wheels for traction; mud sprays all over them, even over one boy's glasses, as Helen starts the engine and they finally push her car onto drier ground. She stops and, with the engine running, shoves her entire purse out the righthand window with the words, "Take it." The boys demur but she insists, dangling the purse in the air. Finally the oldest boy reluctantly takes it and all three watch in surprise as Helen drives the car across the meadow, off a cliff, and into a lake, which doesn't become visible until just before she plunges into it. The boys chase after her and stand at the edge of the cliff looking out as the car disappears under the water. All of this has occurred in full or long shot – there have been no close-ups of an anguished Helen during her ride down, nor of boys aghast at what they've witnessed.

This sequence occurs in Marilynne Robinson's novel, but it's not nearly as funny in the book. For one thing, Helen's plunge into the lake is a surprise in the film; in the book, Ruth tells us that Helen drove the Ford off a cliff, and then she reports the three boys' description of the event. Ruth's retrospective narration in the novel is dry and droll; we know that we're in the presence of a person as unusual as her aunt Sylvie, so we tend to accept the fact that she doesn't offer reasons for her mother's suicide and Sylvie's peripatetic life. Forsyth can't overwhelm us in the film with Ruth's voice-over narration in every scene, therefore he immediately establishes her as the narrator, reminds us of her role by bringing her in, in voice-over, sporadically throughout, and relies on whimsical comedy for the rest to create the effect that Ruth creates through her narration in the novel: one of detachment and amusement.

Anyone familiar with Bill Forsyth's other films – among them *Gregory's Girl* (1981) and *Comfort and Joy* (1984) – knows that he is adept at whimsical comedy. The difference in *Housekeeping* is that the comedy isn't whimsical for whimsicality's sake, however enjoyable that might be: it's linked to the idea, also present in Robinson's novel, that Sylvie and Ruth's whimsicality may be a legitimate and sustainable response to a world obsessed with *practicality*, with doing instead of being, with driving forward instead of floating along. We laugh when Sylvie and Ruth stop walking at one point to watch TV briefly through the window of someone's house (a moment invented by Forsyth), but at the same time we know that it wouldn't occur to either of these two to earn enough money to buy a television. They prefer to subsist in the natural world, to move through, remain in, and embrace it – a preference declared by the opening shot of *Housekeeping* (also invented by Forsyth) of the American plains, over which the camera tracks from left to right before it travels up to the mountains of Washington state.

Next I'd like to consider the adaptation of a novel written in the third person: Irvine Welsh's *Trainspotting* (1993). Let's start with Welsh's novel, whose title refers to the compulsive British hobby of collecting locomotive engine numbers from the national railway system. In its ultimate pointlessness despite its imparting of some structure or regularity to daily life, this activity is intended to be a metaphor for shooting heroin and the obsessional, senseless nature of the addict's life. Unlike the film, the book takes the trainspotting metaphor no farther than this. Equally unlike the film, its story is told not only by the main character, Mark Renton, but also by his friends, so that its narrative voices are several; otherwise Welsh writes in the third person so that he can stay close enough to his characters to get into their heads, yet far enough away to reveal their self-delusion. The movie of *Trainspotting* (1996), as you can well guess, economically gives us only Renton's first-person narration in an intermittent voice-over that is circumscribed by the natural omniscience of film form. The film sacrifices the "psychic distance" of Welsh's third-person narration because, given its different thematic intent, it doesn't require such distancing.

Welsh's novel is a coming-of-age story in the tradition, *mutatis mutandis*, of J.D. Salinger's *Catcher in the Rye* (1951). It is neither a glorification of heroin use, an anarchist's call for the destruction of society, nor, at the opposite end of the spectrum, a moralistic condemnation of drug addiction. Instead, the book makes the characters' desire for chemically induced oblivion comprehensible, given the sordid, disaffecting environment in which they live: Leith, a working-class area of housing projects on Edinburgh's old dockside. At the same time, Welsh questions the feasibility or merit of such a dangerous if pleasurable form of escape, and this questioning lends sporadic narrative drive to his episodic tale, for throughout we wonder above all else whether Renton will be able to "betray" his mates by kicking his heroin habit, moving on, and finally becoming his own man.

By the end of the novel he has *begun* to change, he has begun to see the tragic consequences of drug addiction; his transformation is thus not dramatic, but it isn't sentimental, either. In the first instance, the question of his going straight is left up in the air rather than decisively or dramatically answered: "But was he a junky? True, he had just used again, but the gaps between his using were growing. However, he couldn't really answer this question now. Only time could do that." In the second instance, the nature of Renton's break from his fellow users rules out the possibility that benign sentiment or virtuous feeling played any role in it: he steals all the money they have just made on a big drug deal (for which he served as the tester of the heroin's quality), then flees to the Netherlands. Welsh concludes the novel of *Trainspotting* with the following, guardedly optimistic passage:

[Renton] had done what he wanted to do. He could now never go back to Leith, to Edinburgh, even to Scotland, ever again. There, he could not be anything other than he was. Now, free from them all, for good, he could be what he wanted to be. He'd stand or fall alone. This thought both terrified and excited him as he contemplated life in Amsterdam.

The film of *Trainspotting* ends with the same thieving action on the part of Renton, but it is followed by a voice-over from him that is quite different in content from that of the above, third-person excerpt. I quote from the screenplay by John Hodge, which has recently been published in standard English – a language that is not to be heard in the movie, and that is limited to Welsh's narration in the book:

So why did I do it? I could offer a million answers, all false. The truth is that I'm a bad person, but that's going to change, I'm going to change. This is the

last of this sort of thing. I'm cleaning up and I'm moving on, going straight
and choosing life. I'm looking forward to it already. I'm going to be just like
you: the job, the family, the fucking big television, the washing machine, the
car, the compact disc and electrical tin opener, good health, low cholesterol,
dental insurance, mortgage, starter home, leisurewear, luggage, three-piece
suite, DIY, game shows, junk food, children, walks in the park, nine to five,
good at golf, washing the car, choice of sweaters, family Christmas, indexed
pension, tax exemption, clearing the gutters, getting by, looking ahead, to the
day you die.

Now compare this final monologue by Renton with his opening
voice-over rant in the film, which occurs in similar form in the book as
well but more than halfway through Welsh's narrative, so that its thematic impact is diluted:

Choose life. Choose a job. Choose a career. Choose a family. Choose a fucking
big television, choose washing machines, cars, compact disc players and electrical tin openers. Choose good health, low cholesterol and dental insurance.
Choose fixed-interest mortgage repayments. Choose a starter home. Choose
your friends. Choose leisurewear and matching luggage. Choose a three-piece
suite on hire purchase in a range of fucking fabrics. Choose DIY and wondering who the fuck you are on a Sunday morning. Choose sitting on that couch
watching mind-numbing, spirit-crushing game shows, stuffing fucking junk
food into your mouth. Choose rotting away at the end of it all, pishing your last
in a miserable home, nothing more than an embarrassment to the selfish,
fucked-up brats you have spawned to replace yourself. Choose your future.
Choose life. But why would I want to do a thing like that? I chose not to choose
life. I chose somethin' else. And the reasons? There are no reasons. Who needs
reasons when you've got heroin?

It is the relationship between these framing soliloquies, as it were – as
well as between them and their novelistic counterparts – that provides
the key to interpreting Danny Boyle's film and accounts for the difference in meaning between it and Irvine Welsh's original fiction.

Trainspotting begins with a literal rush as Mark Renton jumps over
the camera and hurtles down the street while store detectives chase
after him and his fellow shoplifter, Spud. Simultaneously, on the soundtrack, the thieving Renton is quietly reciting the aforementioned litany
of choices he has *not* made. He is one of an odd assortment of young
men (sensibly cut down to five from the book's larger cast of characters), including the hapless, gawky, goggle-eyed Spud and the

bleached-blond, narcissistic, self-styled intellectual affectionately known as Sick Boy, for almost all of whom heroin addiction is a "full-time business." The "business," of course, is robbery to support their habit, be it in the form of shoplifting, mugging, pinching money from relatives, or swiping drugs, prescription pads, and televisions from old-age homes – drug-dealing for this gang being the business of last resort on account of the constant risk, steady planning, and virtual abstinence required to be successful. Almost all these episodes of thieving are presented comically, as are some incidents of violence. This might lead one to believe that *Trainspotting* is as morally vacant or anarchic as a slew of movies from the French *Going Places* (1974) to the American *Pulp Fiction* (1994), both of which also use humor to grease their characters' murderous or exploitative acts. But the comedy in Boyle's film (as opposed to Welsh's novel, which, in keeping with its desire to gain a critical perspective on events, more often employs irony) serves an additional, higher purpose.

For one thing, it is a relief from the horrors of drug addiction, among them AIDS, which is contracted by the once clean, athletic, soccer-loving Tommy after Renton turns his friend on to heroin as a way of forgetting Liz, the girl who rejected him. The virus, in tandem with the narcotic, eventuates in Tommy's gruesome death on the floor of a dimly lit, ill-furnished apartment littered with cat feces. A ten-month-old baby dies in this film, too. He's the son of Sick Boy and his girlfriend, Allison – a son whose father never acknowledges him as his own until the baby suddenly dies of a combination of neglect and SIDS amid the discarded needles and scattered debris of the addicts' favorite shooting gallery. It is there, early in the novel as well as the movie, that Renton comforts the wailing, disconsolate, now childless Allison by giving her a shot of heroin – *after* he gives one to himself, tellingly. This is the most painful, jolting scene we see, even more so than the sequences devoted to Renton's accidental overdose and later, forced withdrawal.

So *Trainspotting* provides us with comic relief from moments like these, but its comedy is also designed to satirize bourgeois society and shock bourgeois sensibility – that is, to repudiate human life as we know it, or think we know it, in this age of global consumer culture. In the film, we see Renton and his pals' drug-taking as a reaction to the absurd banality of such life, whereas in the novel heroin use seems more to be a proletarian escape from the alienation and depression induced by capitalist-colonialist oppression. Hence Renton's diatribe against British rule merely rings poignant in the book, as it is spoken in a bar and directed more than anything else at Edinburgh Castle,

Ewan McGregor as Renton in *Trainspotting*.

which in its place high above the city is a symbol of everything the protagonist hates:

Ah don't hate the English. They're just wankers. We are colonised by wankers. We can't even pick a decent, vibrant, healthy culture to be colonised by. No. We're ruled by effete arseholes. What does that make us? The lowest of the fuckin low, the scum of the earth. The most wretched, servile, miserable, pathetic trash that was ever shat intae creation. Ah don't hate the English. They just git oan wi the shite thuv goat. Ah hate the Scots.

The same speech in the movie is delivered during a railway outing, arranged by Tommy (*before* he succumbs to drugs), to the Scottish countryside, whose picture-postcard beauty, fresh air, and open space comically inspire loathing in Renton, Sick Boy, and Spud. For this is the Scotland beloved by tourists – by the idle middle class, in other words – and it is the very Scotland that drives the boys back to heroin after their first try at kicking the habit.

At least one other scene is so designed to shock the bourgeoisie, and it is a species of bathroom humor. It comes quickly in the movie, so as to prepare us for (or send us packing from) what is to follow, and involves Renton as he dives into the "Worst Toilet in Scotland" to retrieve drug suppositories he has lost. He uses them to relieve the constipation that comes with heroin addiction, and he thriftily wants to use these two – the ones he has just shat into the bowl – again. This scene also occurs in Welsh's novel, but there it is merely stomach-turning or, if you will, excremental, and there Renton makes no such hallucinatory descent into the fecal underworld. Boyle's film slyly delivers what could be called the Martha Stewart version, in that in the process of getting back his suppositories, our hero also takes a cleansing swim in deep, sea-green water to the tune of sprightly yet sweet-sounding music on the track. We still get the bloody disgusting excrement both before and after Renton's plunge (as he climbs back up and out of the toilet), but the point is that in between we get a child's or bourgeois matron's fanciful view of the plumbing depths – as filtered through or equated with the vision of a drug-crazed mind.

Up to now, I've omitted any discussion of Renton's fourth mate, Francis Begbie, because unlike the others he is an alcoholic. That is, he abuses the *bourgeoisie's* drug of choice, and to Renton he himself is like an addiction. This sociopathic foil doesn't do drugs, he "does people," which is to say that he tyrannizes and brutalizes them. The film implicitly as well as shrewdly poses the easy question: as between choices, whom would you rather take, or who would you prefer to be, the viciously sadistic Begbie or the smartly sensitive Renton? To this end, naturally, *Trainspotting* depicts Begbie's violence, destructiveness, and intimidation without the farce that would make these traits digestible. By contrast, comedy *does* make palatable the crimes and misdemeanors, the mischief and mistakes, of the drug users in the film, even as satire momentarily renders harmless the pretensions and vices of the middle class. Moreover, Begbie's swaggering machismo pathetically if justly lands him in bed with a transvestite, whereas Renton, Sick Boy, and even Spud all have girlfriends who pursue them for their bodies – sometimes humorously so.

In the film of *Trainspotting*, in fact, Renton's desire to kick his drug habit is linked more to a desire to regain his sexual potency than to any wish of reforming or rehabilitating himself. He seems to want merely to exchange one pleasure for another, since the two don't go together and since promiscuous sex is less dangerous than heroin use (although not by much in this, the age of AIDS). The moral or ethical stigma attached to drug use is largely missing from the movie, then, as it is not from the novel, the only real choice for the cinematic Renton being between a speedy if euphoric death from heroin overdose and a slow death – punctuated by bouts of sexual stimulation – from bourgeois stupefaction. For in his mind the two lives are equally meaningless, equally cut off from religious, metaphysical, or transcendental causation or provenance. Philosophically speaking, life without drugs is just as absurd, just as pointless in the end, as life *on* drugs; in this view, each is its own kind of inane trainspotting, and the sole issue becomes how much you can, or want to, take of either.

Renton simply wants to postpone his own senseless death in favor of a minimally sentient life, so he swears off heroin three times in the film, only to fall back into the habit in each instance. The last time he is in London, where he has gone as much to escape the manipulative hypocrisy of Sick Boy and the indiscriminate bullying of Begbie as to clean up his act. There he gets a job with a fly-by-night rental agency showing overpriced apartments to overreaching yuppies in a gentrified London turned tawdry by Brian Tufano's slightly overexposed cinematography (which uses the reverse technique to exacerbate the squalor of the drug den). There also he is rejoined in his small flat by the sponging Begbie and Sick Boy, as well as later by the ne'er-do-well Spud, for the lucky sale of two kilos of heroin at a profit of £12,000. This is the point of his third relapse, where, as chief sampler of the smack, he shoots up again at least twice; and this is the loot he steals in the film as in the novel.

Except that the film of *Trainspotting* ends on a monetary or marketing note, not a metamorphosing one, with Renton's previously quoted voice-over monologue. Significantly, as Renton talks on the soundtrack, he grinningly walks straight at the camera, which remains stationary and therefore quickly turns his image into one big blur. Metaphorically, he is gliding into bourgeois-induced, rather than drug-initiated, oblivion. He says he has chosen life, but the ironic comments "I'm going to be just like you" and "looking ahead, to the day you die," along with the catalogue of bourgeois diversions from life's ultimate purposelessness, indicate that what he has really done is to choose one poison over another, the slow-acting rather than the fast, the pecuniary material high instead of the bankrupt mental one. Finally, Renton remains "bad" and unchanged in the movie. His moving on signifies, not the clear-eyed, bourgeois defeat of drug-supported idealism, but rather the moral equation of mind-numbing, spirit-crushing philistinism with narcotizing, soporific drug addiction in a world bereft of God and soul.

Finally, I'd like to treat what I call an omnibus adaptation – of fiction to drama to film – and the case in point is *Dangerous Liaisons*: a novel by Choderlos de Laclos (1782), from which Christopher Hampton took his play of the same title (1985), and from which Hampton then derived his screenplay for Stephen Frears' motion picture called, appropriately enough, *Dangerous Liaisons* (1988). Laclos's novel *Les Liaisons dangereuses*, for its part, is a product of its age in two senses: it is in epistolary form, a dominant narrative mode of the eighteenth century, and it embodies the conflicting philosophical and political impulses of this, the so-called age of reason. On the one hand, the French *comédie larmoyante* and *drame bourgeois*, as well as the English sentimental comedy, sentimental tragedy, and sentimental novel, were arguing along with Rousseau that man was by nature good and could remain so by following his instincts – that is, the promptings of his heart; evil persons, on their side, might be reclaimed (at the same time they might be punished) if their hearts could be touched, if the callus of their vice could be penetrated to reveal beneath the soft skin of their virtue. On the other hand, the Marquis de Sade was arguing that the "promptings of the heart" were in fact the product of reason, of teaching and socialization, not of instinct, which modeled itself after the chaos of the world and obeyed the laws of desire.

Sentimental literature was designed, of course, to appeal to the growing middle-class audience, to assist that audience in developing its own, self-congratualtory moral code and social ethic. Anti-sentimental literature – in the form of the libertine novel of eighteenth-century France and the British Restoration comedy before it – was designed, by contrast, to confirm the shrinking upper classes in their unsentimental self-knowledge as well as in their ability to use their superior intelligence to outwit others and *liberate* themselves: from repressive moral codes, from political domination, from social subserviance of any kind. Sexual intrigue and indulgence play such a great role in this literature partly because, for the idle and wealthy, gaming is the natural pastime, and sexual gaming is the most natural pastime of all.

Christopher Hampton's screenplay for *Dangerous Liaisons* happens, happily, to be faithful to the time period as well as the setting of the original. There are seven major correspondents in Laclos's *Les Liaisons dangereuses*, moreover, and all of them appear as characters in Frears' *Dangerous Liaisons* as well – characters who remind us of their origins in epistolary, or multiple first-person, fiction by periodically exchanging letters with one another during the film. (The very first shot is of someone's hands holding a letter, which itself bears the title of the film.) They are the Marquise de Merteuil, a young widow and arch manipulator of men; the Vicomte de Valmont, her former lover and an inveterate womanizer; the Présidente de Tourvel, the young and pious wife of a magistrate (a Présidente, or presiding judge) away on business in Burgundy, and the closest we shall come to a bourgeoise; Cécile de Volanges, the young and innocent daughter of Madame de Volanges, who has recently arranged the girl's marriage to the Comte de Gercourt, a former lover of Merteuil's; Madame de Volanges, confidante to Merteuil (her cousin), the Présidente de Tourvel, and Rosemonde, and one of Valmont's many previous sexual conquests; the Chevalier Danceny, a young music tutor and suitor for Cécile's hand as well as the eventual lover of Merteuil; and Madame de Rosemonde, Valmont's eighty-year-old aunt, who is the Présidente de Tourvel's close friend and the owner of a country estate between which location and Paris the action alternates.

The plot – and what a plot, given its seven "narrators" – hinges on Merteuil's desire for revenge against Gercourt for his engagement to Cécile, and on Valmont's desire for yet another night in bed with Merteuil. As part of her plan, Valmont agrees to seduce the fifteen-year-old, convent-bred Cécile, but regards this as such an easy task that he won't accept Merteuil's renewed favors unless he is also able to bed Tourvel, whose religion and virtue present him with a real challenge. Valmont succeeds easily with the young virgin, as he predicted, but must work so assiduously at seducing Tourvel that after he finally does, he realizes that he is as passionately in love with her as she is with him. Merteuil realizes this, too, and refuses Valmont his night in bed on the ground that he has breached the rules of their game: to achieve purely sexual consummations that are then rapidly and dispassionately severed.

Valmont severs his relationship with Tourvel but Merteuil still refuses him his prize, so jealous is she of his love; Valmont counters by arranging the first sexual liaison between Cécile and Danceny, Merteuil's own most recent conquest; and Merteuil retaliates by telling Danceny of Valmont's affair with Cécile. Danceny kills Valmont in a duel, but before dying the vicomte hands over his letters from Merteuil and Tourvel to the young man, thereby exposing the marquise's machinations and causing her public humiliation. Tourvel has retired to a convent, where she lapses into madness and dies; Cécile, who miscarried Valmont's child, will eventually enter a nunnery as a postulant; and the remorseful Danceny will opt for a life of celibacy as well by joining the Knights of Malta.

In Laclos's novel, Merteuil soon contracts smallpox, becomes so disfigured that she loses an eye, then loses a lawsuit and with it her fortune, whereupon she flees Paris for Holland. In Hampton's dramatic

Glenn Close, as the Marquise de Merteuil, and John Malkovich,
as the Vicomte de Valmont, are captured "in the clinch" in
Dangerous Liaisons.

adaptation as in the film version, we see none of this. We last view Merteuil on stage playing a game of cards (just as we saw her at the start of
the drama) as the shadow of a guillotine falls on the rear wall of the
theatre – a somewhat heavy premonition of the French Revolution and
the beginning of the end of the aristocratic class. Hampton's film ending is lighter in touch than both his stage ending and the ending of the
novel, and it fills in the "sentiments" that Laclos had only outlined.

The last shot of *Dangerous Liaisons* is a close-up of Merteuil in front
of her dressing-table mirror, removing her make-up after her humiliation at the opera, where her former friends booed her as she stood
alone in her box; the film had begun with a shot of her face in that
same mirror as she was preparing to make herself up. The implication
is that there are two Merteuils: the heartless, egotistical one "made up"
in the mirror, and the real woman beneath with a heart and with love
to give rather than desire to slake. After Merteuil removes the last of
the make-up from her pale face, she stares blankly – at herself – and
tears begin to fall as the screen slowly fades to black. She cries at her
own ruin, her own folly, but also at the death of Valmont, for whom she
had begun to have genuine feelings.

Valmont, for his part, tearfully declares before his death both his
love for Tourvel and his sorrow for the licentious life he has led: "Her

love is the only real happiness I have ever known"; "[Danceny] had good cause [to slay me]; I don't think that is anything anyone has ever been able to say about me." Ironically, it is Valmont's love for Tourvel that gets him killed in Hampton and Frears' interpretation. As he duels with Danceny, Valmont flashes back to his lovemaking with Tourvel even as the film cross-cuts to the scene of her being bled with leeches in the convent; their deaths thus become visually intertwined with their love, or their love becomes a kind of death. Tourvel dies of her love, and Valmont dies of his: clearly the superior swordsman, he lets his guard down at one point as his memories of Tourvel overtake him, and Danceny takes the opportunity to run him through. Our final look at Valmont is from on high, along with, by implication, a judgmental God: in a stunning high-angle shot, we see him lying on his back in pure white snow, his servant and Danceny hanging over him and a long, thick trail of blood leading randomly away from his body.

Like sexual gangsters, Merteuil and Valmont have had their way, up to a point, and like dutiful spectators, we have thrilled to their exploits, up to a point – the one where moral duty intervenes and we assent, with God, to their penitence and punishment. Religion triumphs at the end of the filmic *Dangerous Liaisons* more than revolution, sentiment more than slaughter, conversion more than conquest. The greater truth of Hampton's movie ending, as opposed to his stage ending, is that the bourgeoisie assimilated, rather than assassinated, the aristocracy (even as the twentieth-century cinema did to the nineteenth-century theatre, and that theatre itself did to the eighteenth-century novel); that the sentimental view of life outflanked, rather than outmatched, the anti-sentimental one. Sentimentalism acknowledged that good souls like Tourvel could be tempted to commit evil precisely because they were so good and trusting; and that even souls as evil as Merteuil could be made to see the error of their ways, precisely because their evil had finally consumed them together with their victims. If Sade's "instinct" obeyed the dictates of universal chaos, then sentimentalism's "heart" obeyed the dictates of providential design, and that design is adumbrated more by the omniscience of film form than by the discontinuous first-person narration of the epistolary novel, let alone the absence of narration in the drama.

In *Dangerous Liaisons*, we see events as they happen from the point of view of an omniscient camera/narrator not bound by time, space, or self-interest; we get Laclos's fragmented and disordered fiction, told by several people who don't know the whole story, converted into a complete and ordered film, told by someone who knows all. At the same time, Stephen Frears does his best to preserve the immediacy, intimacy, and secrecy, even solipsism, of the letter-form by shooting much of *Dangerous Liaisons* in close-up, going so far as to rack focus – to alter the plane within a shot – in order to isolate a character in medium close-up in the foreground of the image while turning the background (of which Frears has given us a compensatory glimpse) into a blur. The "epistolary" close-up alternates with Frears's omniscient, and highly skillful, cutting among scenes to give us what Laclos's novel really cannot – as no other novel could, either – and what Hampton's stage adaptation could only awkwardly attempt to convey (particularly without resort to simultaneous staging): the paradoxical sense that we share in the immediacy of confidences exchanged at the same time as we are in the hands of a silent divinity who overhears, and oversees, everything. *We* put together the pieces Laclos gives us when we read the 175 letters of the novel, or as we watch the eighteen scenes of Hampton's theatrical version; as we see the film, someone else is putting the pieces together, for us as well as for the characters.

I'd like to close not by arguing for the overall superiority of film as an art form – it is superior in some ways, inferior in others, which I have been careful to leave out of this discussion. What I would like to say, however, reiterates my statement from the introduction: film was certainly *the* art form of the twentieth century and promises to dominate the twenty-first as well, and that's because it's the one technology that is – or at least can be – absolutely humanistic in its outcome. It can put many of the technological impulses, cravings, and interests of our age at the service, not merely of the machinery of sensation, diversion, and profit, but of the mystery of the human spirit as well. I'm speaking about film at its best, of course. Why it often isn't at its best is a subject complicated by the commerce of the world, and one better left for another day.

22

The Preemptive Image

If the age turns away from the theater, in which it is no longer interested, that is because the theater has ceased to represent it. It no longer hopes to be provided by the theater with myths on which it can sustain itself.

– Antonin Artaud

These words of Artaud, written more than sixty years ago, continue to hold true today: the theatre does not represent our age, or doesn't represent our age nearly as fully and centrally as it might. It does not provide the age with sustaining myths, by which I think Artaud surely didn't mean "lies," the way we speak of political or social myths today. He meant accounts, wrought in the imagination and then enacted, or (to accord with one of Artaud's visions) fashioned directly on the stage – accounts of how it feels and what it means to be alive. And to be alive in that mysterious double way that art offers to us, the life of this moment together with the life of the long line of existence of which our time is both an instant and an instance.

Put another way, the crucial difference between the theatre and its upstager, film, is this: theatre began as a sacred event and eventually included the profane, by which it has since been overwhelmed; film began as a profane event and eventually included the sacred, by which (at its best) it is now dominated. It was Artaud, again, who spoke of the movies' having taken over what he called the "distribution" of modern myths, and if we take the meaning of "myths" here to be *tales told in images* – and images that are literally larger than life – *enactments of what life is like, and what it embodies, at its highest pitch*, then I think this is true also.

It has often been said that representationalism (realism or naturalism) has been usurped by film, because the cinema is able to go to actual places and capture truthful behavior in authentic environments to an extent impossible in the theatre. Yet film's representationalism, even in a well-made, neatly compressed, climactic adaptation, never precludes a mythical or allegorical component. To wit, a film such as *The Piano Teacher* (2001) reminds us, more evocatively than any (literal-minded) documentary on the subject of the Holocaust, of the physical horror implicit in the inspirited artistry of the past; reminds us not only that Vienna, that archetypal European cultural capital, was the site of the welcomed Nazi *Anschluss* in 1938, but also that arty Austria is the home today of the fascist political leader Jörg Haider. And *Our Lady of the Assassins* (2000), with its graphic depiction of brutal violence, pervasive drug use, rampant materialism (even among the poor), and sexual abandon alongside fervent religiosity in contemporary Medellín, Colombia, becomes something of a metaphor for the decline of the West – particularly when one considers that this Latin American city has massive fireworks displays each time one of its cocaine shipments arrives safely in the United States.

Film isn't flourishing just now the way it did from the late 1950s for a decade or more, when Antonioni, Fellini, Bergman, Ray, and the French New Wave created their marvelous series of works, and when, with the publication of *Agee on Film* in 1958, there was the beginning of a change in general attitudes toward serious film criticism in America. Yet Susan Sontag's proclamation not long ago that cinephilia is dead seems premature – it would seem especially so to the Iranians and the Chinese – and, professors aside, film still interests most intelligent people more than theatre does. (Indeed, if anything has helped to shrink the audience for serious movies, it is the academicization or compartmentalization of film – in courses, departments, "majors," colleges, advanced degrees, and universities – throughout Euro-America.) Why people group these two art forms together in the first place is a matter for some consideration, especially to someone like me – married to the theatre as I am, yet long ago seduced by the cinema.

The ability of film, for example, to select and isolate factors in a work instantaneously gives the medium a power that the theatre does not have. (Moreover, pictures like *Run Lola Run* [1998] have extended this "fluidity" to include alternative streams or chronologies of action, dependent upon which character's perspective is being adopted at any given moment.) Let me give an example, a negative one. I once saw a production of John Ford's *'Tis Pity She's a Whore* – a striking and even shocking play by the Jacobean dramatist who died in 1639, not a racy Western by the late American movie director of the same name. In the last scene the incestuous brother, Giovanni, comes in with his sister's heart impaled on a dagger and stands there with it almost until the end of the play. Now such an action is simply impossible to carry out these days. There's no way that this character can stand on stage with his sister's heart on the end of a dagger and play a long speaking scene with a host of other people.

Everyone in the audience was tittering. First, they knew that the heart was fake, and, second, even had it been a real heart, the scene couldn't have held the stage because obviously the distraction (to put the matter mildly) would have been too great. We're conditioned by film now to want what's important to be singled out and shown apart. A film director could have cut away from that damned heart-on-a-dagger so that you wouldn't have had to see it through the whole scene; you would have seen only the face of the brother or the faces of the other characters, or both in alternation. That's more than a mere convenience: it's in the nature of the filmic medium so to allow you, effortlessly, to arrange space and assign prominence.

Is this particular ability what accounts for the continuing ascendancy of film over theatre? That's a large question for which I don't intend to offer a single explanation or solution, but I will offer a few more thoughts. I think that the very abstraction of film – the fact that on it there are no *real*, physical bodies or objects, but only their images before our eyes – is another source of its power and freedom. I believe that the theatre's very confinement to place, the fact that it occurs here, now, on this stage, with these performers and those objects – conditions usually thought to be the source of its own power relative to film – may be a source of its present weakness.

It's true that experimental groups such as the Living Theater, the Open Theater, and the Performance Group created environmental theatre to try to overcome conventional drama's spatial limitations. They did this by using an existing environment that was as close to reality as possible, or by designing such an environment so that it enveloped the audience and thereby not only erased any distinction between viewing space and playing area but also freed the spectators from static positioning or a single point of vision. The cinema, for its part, responded to the same challenge to "get real" by experimenting with three dimensions through the use of special multicolored, seemingly multilayered eyeglasses, as well as by inventing such wide-screen processes as CinemaScope, Cinerama, and Panavision along with audio systems like Sensurround.

This may be a paradox, but in the age of technical miracles, of the annihilation of time and space, of technologized existence, if you will, an existence in which immediacy no longer has the simple meaning it once had and in which the line between a thing or a being and its image or reproduction has been nearly obliterated – in such an age the theatre's very "live-ness" may be what so often makes it seem to be less fully alive. Moreover, although theatre is inherently more life-like because it occurs live and in three dimensions, the presence of three-dimensional actors in a theatre – a non-real or artificial space – may actually undercut a production's resemblance to life at the same time that the actors increase its live-ness. (Indeed, theatre performance, by virtue of its live-ness, disappears as soon as it is said and done, while film performance, by nature of its preservation on celluloid and now on videotape or DVD, is kept "alive" in its original format in a way that even the best-taped theatrical productions – as opposed to their sources or blueprints, dramatic scripts – cannot be.)

How many times have you noticed, for example, that when in a play a film strip is suddenly employed, everyone's eyes instantly turn to whatever is shown on the screen, be it a face or something else? This has very little to do with the nature of what's being shown and everything to do with the way we are fascinated by the sheer presence of film, by its still mysterious, nearly ineffable, nature. Maybe our fascination has something to do not only with the framing of the motion-picture image and the manner in which that framing commands our voyeuristic gaze (as it certainly does, on a smaller scale, in painting), but also with film's god-like ability either to replicate our own world or to create out of the dark an alternative, imaginative universe of its own. Then there is the cinema's capacity to transcend the laws of physics (also biology, chemistry, you name it) and take us along for the ride; to make us think that we are dreaming though we are wide awake, and to wake us from our waking sleep by itself fading back into the black of an unfathomable void; even to make us believe that, at one time in the past, people lived their lives in black and white.

Whatever the case, I can remember watching a play during which a film sequence featuring the protagonist was shown – a dull sequence, by the way – while the actor himself was still on stage doing lively things, and finding myself looking at the film to the exclusion of the actual man, as almost the entire audience was doing. In a somewhat different vein, I recall that in a production by Mabou Mines of *Dead End Kids* from the early 1980s, by far the most effective sequence in this anti-bomb theatrical work was the showing of a short film made by the Atomic Energy Commission to extol the benefits of nuclear weaponry as a means of keeping the peace. "We turned the archives against themselves," the director, JoAnne Akalaitis, later said. Indeed they did, but how much less effective *Dead End Kids* would have been had Mabou Mines tried to enact on stage what the film was saying. Ironically, not only was Akalaitis' title itself taken from the series of films Warner Brothers made with the "Dead End Kids"(who, for their part, started out on Broadway in Sidney Kingsley's play *Dead End*) in the thirties and forties, but her Off-Broadway production itself was turned into a film in 1986 – also directed by Akalaitis – on the history of nuclear power, where it comes from, and what it does.

Speaking of explosive power, the abstract filmic medium's special effects have become so life-like that (in a reversal of what purportedly occurred at the initial screening of the Lumières' *Arrival of the Paris Express* [1896]), when the first footage of the attack on the World Trade Center was shown on television – captured from a myriad of angles by any number of personal video cameras, then aired by the news media again and again – it was virtually indistinguishable from what Hollywood studios could have manufactured for a picture such as *Armageddon* (1998). When film becomes this close to life, is it therefore life-like, or has reality started to resemble film? When video games of mass annihilation are found in the bedrooms of young people who have donned ski masks and shot their schoolmates, as two teenagers did at Colorado's Columbine High School, do we experience an uncomfortable moment at which we realize that some of our children can no longer tell the difference between created or fabricated images and ineluctable, irreversible reality?

We know that when movies began, for a long time they mostly imitated *theater*, something clearly implied in the term "photo-play," which remained in use well into the 1930s and was one of the reasons André Bazin unrhetorically titled his collected criticism *What Is Cinema?* Over thirty years ago, Jerzy Grotowski came to this country to tell us in lectures and in his book *Towards a Poor Theater* (1968), and to show us in productions like *Apocalypsis cum Figuris*, that what practitioners in the theatre must find out is just this: what is theatre? Grotowski's theatrical mission was thus to strip away the trappings of the theatre, to tread a *via negativa* in order to discover what it is quintessentially the theatre can do that no other art form can accomplish, and of course he was thinking specifically of film as the opponent or antagonist. The one thing the theatre shouldn't do, he said, was try to be like the cinema, since movies can manipulate time and space to a much greater extent. No matter how swift a revolving stage you have, how computerized your light board is, or how full of alacrity your stagehands are, how can they compete with the blinding, effortless speed of film editing?

What can theatre do that film can't? To the easy answer that the stage gives us "live" people (ultimately in communion with an equally live audience), I can only reply that I'm not at all satisfied by such an explanation. What sort of live people? What are they doing? What are they saying? And how are they different from, and more compelling than, live people on the street? Why, as I said before, does their very live-ness often strike us as peculiarly, very peculiarly, a source of boredom? Questions like these could hardly have been asked, of course, before the dawn of the modern industrial and technological age, but they have to be asked now.

What *can* theatre do that film and the other arts can't? – theatre the impure art, the so often-arrested and even incestuous form, the "sick man" of the arts, as Edgar Allan Poe called it. One of the ways to address this question – oddly enough, given the fact that theatre, like cinema, is already a composite or amalgam of all the other arts – is to listen to representatives from those other arts and other intellectual disciplines, and think along with them about how communication is made. It is through such dialogue that we are likely to learn more about how the theatre best communicates, and what its inimitable voice might be.

One of the reasons, by the way, that Poe described the theatre as "sick" is that the attitude toward it on the part of American writers is very different from the attitude in Europe. In other words, there is little dialogue across the literary arts in this country, whereas that dialogue is inherent in such artistic creation on the other side of the Atlantic. Namely, most European plays, unlike American ones, are written by men and women who are more than playwrights; very few of the greatest Western dramas have been authored by people who wrote only plays. Theatre was part, and only part, of the instrumentality of their culture. The theatre has always seemed, for the superior European writer, to be an open avenue for one kind of poem, a dramatic poem rather than a lyrical or narrative one. Not so in the United States, which is why earlier I applied the term "incestuous" to our theatre, and why we have had such difficulty in defining what its inimitable voice might be: lacking perspective, distance, or points of comparison, we cannot see our dramatic forest for its histrionic trees. (The example of our greatest playwright, Eugene O'Neill, comes readily to mind.)

Film may offer greater visual possibilities, not to speak of experiential ones, but that still doesn't prevent some of the most exciting and popular theatre in New York from being highly visual as a way of curing its own sickness. What about Bill Irwin's "new vaudeville" pieces,

Largely New York (1989) and *Fool Moon* (1993), productions that are virtually silent? What of similarly non-verbal productions such as Blue Man Group's *Tubes* (1991) and De La Guarda's *Villa Villa* (1998)? And, as early as 1971, how about Robert Wilson's three-hour speechless epic *Deafman Glance*, which created a combination Theatre of Silence-and-Images not unlike that of silent experimental film? It is precisely by choosing to overcome the limitations of their chosen medium that these artists have achieved success, for what greater thrill can there be than to see an art form transcend the boundaries that we have become accustomed to assigning to it?

Or to see an artist do so, for that matter. Think only of Julie Taymor's predominantly visual theatrical productions, *The Lion King* (1997) and *The Green Bird* (2000), and of her highly literate films *Titus* (1999) and *Frida* (2002). And consider that Neil LaBute makes predominantly verbal films like *In the Company of Men* (1997) and *Your Friends and Neighbors* (1998) at the same time as he fills the stage with arresting, even aggressive physical images in such plays as *Bash* (1995) and *The Shape of Things* (2001). The list of such artists could be extended as far back as Ingmar Bergman and forward to David Mamet, who continues to write and direct for the screen as well as the stage. And I nearly omitted the "rehearsal" films, or "filmed theater," made by people like Louis Malle (*Vanya on 42nd Street*, 1994), Denys Arcand (*Jesus of Montreal*, 1989), and Jacques Rivette (*Paris Belongs to Us*, 1957; *L'Amour Fou*, 1968; plus two others). But you get the picture by now.

Getting back to Artaud and the struggle of the imagination with reality, here is something Wallace Stevens once wrote: "One of the peculiarities of the imagination is that it is always at the end of an era. What happens is that it is always attaching itself to a new reality and adhering to it. It is not that there is a new imagination but that there is a new reality." For drama and theatre the task is to determine what that reality is, what has changed in it, and what hasn't; the imagination will take care of itself, on stage as well as on screen. For drama, all I can say is that such a reality does not consist of any one of these terms in isolation or combination: revival, musical, reverse adaptation (from film), or Disneyfication; discrimination, patriarchy, hegemony, or homosexuality (collectively making up the Theatre of Guilt, in Robert Brustein's words). And for film, that reality consists of one word for the time being: technology.

That is to say, when I look to the future and envision hundreds of thousands (if not millions) of homes with large, wide-screen televisions and surround-sound theatres, I wonder who will go to the multiplexes of today, which themselves made obsolete the movie palaces and drive-ins of yesteryear. I believe that in a short time most films will be viewed at home (with a movie title like *Home Alone* [1990] thereby taking on new meaning), or in museums by solitary film scholars, and that the multiplex will become the nearly exclusive province of teenagers trying to get out of the house – a trend, of course, that has already begun.

If I am right, and films become an overwhelmingly private experience, shared by small groups in living rooms, what might then become of theatre? Will the experimental theatre groups of the future perform in our living rooms, or will the desire for human contact and communality, together with a concern for the social fabric, drive us back to more traditional theatres? Alternatively, will 3-D IMAX be replaced by holographic film, creating three-dimensional worlds into which we can walk, until we eventually "holographize" old movies (just as we colorize them now) and offer audience members a chance to sit down with Rick in *Casablanca* (1942), have a drink, and then say, "Play it again, Sam"?

Whatever the case, the invention of the cinema, at its lowest or common level, answered a growing cultural desire to see the world in precise detail, to locate the viewer as closely as possible to both the spectacular and the everyday. For, despite all the advances of the nineteenth-century stage – seen most clearly in the melodramatic spectacles produced by Steele MacKaye, Henry Irving, and David Belasco – only movies could democratically take audiences to places they could not travel and position them closer to calamitous events than might otherwise be safe, in addition to valorizing the quotidian nature of their domestic lives. In a sense, the popular cinema had to be invented (as assertion confirmed by the fact that its invention occurred more or less simultaneously in three different countries): to save the theatre from itself, as more than one wag has put it, as well as to accommodate the entertainment needs of the exponentially growing number of underclass citizens throughout the world.

It is at their highest level, however – a level amply illustrated by this book, I trust – that the movies preempt so much of my time, and why I have been compulsively scribbling about them now for well over fifteen years. No longer in search of theatre as Eric Bentley was for so many years, I remain in search of cinema: *Saint* Cinema of the high arts even as it is a secular searchlight on the material world.

Further Reading

GENERAL

Adler, Renata. *A Year in the Dark: Journal of a Film Critic, 1968–1969*. New York: Random House, 1969.

Agee, James. *Agee on Film: Volume 1, Reviews and Comments*. New York: McDowell, 1958.

Arnheim, Rudolf. *Film as Art*. Berkeley: University of California Press, 1957.

Bawer, Bruce. *The Screenplay's the Thing: Movie Criticism, 1986–1990*. Hamden, Conn.: Archon Books, 1992.

Braudy, Leo. *The World in a Frame*. Garden City, New York: Doubleday, 1976.

Cardullo, Bert, ed. *The Film Criticism of Vernon Young*. Lanham, Md.: University Press of America, 1990.

Casty, Alan. *The Dramatic Art of the Film*. New York: Harper & Row, 1971.

Cavell, Stanley. *The World Viewed*. Cambridge: Harvard University Press, 1971.

Denby, David, ed. *Awake in the Dark: An Anthology of American Film Criticism, 1915 to the Present*. New York: Vintage Books, 1977.

DeNitto, Dennis, and William Herman. *Film and the Critical Eye*. New York: Macmillan, 1975.

Dick, Bernard F. *Anatomy of Film*. 4th ed. New York: St Martin's Press, 2002.

Durgnat, Raymond. *Films and Feelings*. Cambridge: MIT Press, 1967.

Eidsvik, Charles. *Cineliterarcy: Film Among the Arts*. New York: Random House, 1978.

Farber, Manny. *Negative Space: Manny Farber on the Movies*. Expanded ed. New York: Da Capo, 1998.

Ferguson, Otis. *The Film Criticism of Otis Ferguson.* Ed. Robert Wilson. Philadelphia: Temple University Press, 1971.

Gilliatt, Penelope. *Three-Quarter Face: Reports and Reflections.* New York: Coward, McCann & Geoghegan, 1980.

Greene, Graham. *Graham Greene on Film: Collected Film Criticism, 1935–1940.* Ed. John Russell Taylor. New York: Simon and Schuster, 1972.

Harrington, John, ed. *Film and/as Literature.* Englewood Cliffs, N.J.: Prentice-Hall, 1977.

Hoberman, J. *Vulgar Modernism: Writing on Movies and Other Media.* Philadelphia: Temple University Press, 1991.

Huss, Roy, and Norman Silverstein. *The Film Experience: Elements of Motion Picture Art.* New York: Harper, 1968.

Kael, Pauline. *5001 Nights at the Movies: A Guide From A to Z.* New York: Henry Holt, 1991.

– *Deeper into Movies.* Boston: Little, Brown, 1973.

– *For Keeps.* New York: Dutton, 1994.

– *Going Steady.* Boston: Little, Brown, 1970.

– *Hooked.* New York: Dutton, 1989.

– *I Lost It at the Movies.* Boston: Little, Brown, 1965.

– *Kiss Kiss Bang Bang.* Boston: Little, Brown, 1968.

– *Movie Love.* New York: Dutton, 1991.

– *Reeling.* Boston: Little, Brown, 1976.

– *State of the Art.* New York: Dutton, 1985.

– *Taking It All In.* New York: Holt, Rinehart, and Winston, 1984.

– *When the Lights Go Down.* New York: Holt, Rinehart, and Winston, 1980.

Kauffmann, Stanley, ed. *American Film Criticism, From the Beginnings to "Citizen Kane": Reviews of Significant Films at the Time They First Appeared.* New York: Liveright, 1972.

Kauffmann, Stanley. *Before My Eyes.* Harper & Row, 1980.

– *Distinguishing Features.* Baltimore: Johns Hopkins University Press, 1994.

– *Field of View.* New York: PAJ Publications, 1986.

– *Figures of Light.* New York: Harper & Row, 1971.

– *Living Images.* New York: Harper & Row, 1975.

– *Regarding Film.* Baltimore: Johns Hopkins University Press, 2001.

Knight, Arthur. *The Liveliest Art.* New York: Mentor, 1957.

Lane, Anthony. *Nobody's Perfect: Writings from "The New Yorker."* New York: Vintage, 2003.

Linden, George W. *Reflections on the Screen.* Belmont, Calif.: Wadsworth, 1970.

Lindgren, Ernest. *The Art of the Film.* London: Allen & Unwin, 1949.

Lorentz, Pare. *Lorentz on Film: Movies, 1927 to 1941.* New York: Hopkinson and Blake, 1975.

Macdonald, Dwight. *Dwight Macdonald on Movies*. Englewood Cliffs, N.J.: Prentice-Hall, 1969.

Mast, Gerald. *Film/Cinema/Movie: A Theory of Experience*. New York: Harper, 1977.

Murray, Edward. *Nine American Film Critics*. New York: Ungar, 1975.

Pechter, William S. *Movies Plus One: Seven Years of Film Reviewing*. New York: Horizon Press, 1982.

Perkins, V.F. *Film as Film*. Baltimore: Penguin, 1986.

Rafferty, Terrence. *The Thing Happens: Ten Years of Writing about the Movies*. New York: Grove Press, 1993.

Richardson, Robert. *Literature and Film*. Bloomington: Indiana University Press, 1969.

Robinson, W.R., ed. *Man and the Movies*. Baltimore: Penguin, 1969.

Rosenbaum, Jonathan. *Placing Movies: The Practice of Film Criticism*. Berkeley: University of California Press, 1995.

Ross, T.J., ed. *Film and the Liberal Arts*. New York: Holt, 1970.

Samuels, Charles Thomas. *Mastering the Film and Other Essays*. Knoxville: University of Tennessee Press, 1977.

Sarris, Andrew. *Confessions of a Cultist: On the Cinema, 1955–1969*. New York: Simon and Schuster, 1970.

– *The Primal Screen: Essays on Film and Related Subjects*. New York: Simon and Schuster, 1973.

Schickel, Richard. *Second Sight: Notes on Some Movies, 1965–1970*. New York: Simon and Schuster, 1972.

Simon, John. *Movies into Film: Film Criticism, 1967–1970*. New York: Dial Press, 1971.

– *Private Screenings*. New York: Macmillan, 1967.

– *Reverse Angle: A Decade of American Films*. New York: C. N. Potter/Crown, 1982.

Sklar, Robert. *Movie-Made America: A Cultural History of American Movies*. New York: Random House, 1975.

Sontag, Susan. *Against Interpretation*. New York: Dell, 1966.

Stephenson, Ralph, and J. R. Debrix. *The Cinema as Art*. Baltimore: Penguin, 1965.

Talbot, Daniel. *Film: An Anthology*. Berkeley: University of California Press, 1966.

Warshow, Robert. *The Immediate Experience*. New York: Atheneum, 1970.

Weinberg, Herman G. *Saint Cinema: Writings on the Film, 1929–1970*. New York: Dover, 1973.

Wood, Michael. *America at the Movies*. New York: Basic Books, 1975.

Young, Vernon. *On Film: Unpopular Essays on a Popular Art*. Chicago: Quadrangle Books, 1972.

NATIONAL CINEMAS

Canadian cinema

Beard, William, and Jerry White, eds. *North Of Everything: English-Canadian Cinema since 1980*. Edmonton: University of Alberta Press, 2002.

Canada's Film Century: Traditions, Transitions, Transcendence. Montreal, Quebec: Lonergan University College, 2000.

Dortland, Michael. *So Close to the States: The Emergence of Canadian Feature Film Policy*. Toronto: University of Toronto Press, 1998.

Evans, Gary. *In the National Interest: A Chronicle of the National Film Board of Canada from 1949–1989*. Toronto: University of Toronto Press, 1991.

Gasher, Mike. *Hollywood North: The Feature Film Industry in British Columbia*. Vancouver: University of British Columbia, 2002.

Gittings, Christopher E. *Canadian National Cinema: Ideology, Difference, and Representation*. New York: Routledge, 2002.

Harcourt, Peter. *Movies and Mythologies: Towards a National Cinema*. Toronto: Canadian Broadcasting Corporation, 1977.

Magder, Ted. *Canada's Hollywood: The Canadian State and Feature Films*. Toronto: University of Toronto Press, 1993.

JOURNALS, print or online: *Canadian Journal of Film Studies, Take One, Ciné-Tracts, Cinema Canada*.

Euro-American Cinema

Ellwood, David W., and Rob Kroes. *Hollywood in Europe: Experiences of a Cultural Hegemony*. Amsterdam: VU University, 1994.

Everett, Wendy. *European Identity in Cinema*. Exeter: Intellect, 1996.

Finney, Angus. *Developing Feature Films in Europe*. London: Routledge, 1996.

– *The State of European Cinema*. London: Cassell, 1996.

Higson, Andrew, and Richard Maltby. *"Film Europe" and "Film America": Cinema, Commerce, and Cultural Exchange, 1920–1939*. Exeter: Exeter University Press, 1999.

Hjort, Mette, and Scott MacKenzie, eds. *Cinema and Nation*. London: Routledge, 2000.

Kindem, Gorham. *The International Movie Industry*. Carbondale: Southern Illinois University Press, 2000.

Lev, Peter. *The Euro-American Cinema*. Austin: University of Texas Press, 1993.

Nowell-Smith, Geoffrey, and Steven Ricci. *Hollywood and Europe: Economics, Culture, and National Identity, 1945–95*. London: BFI, 1998.

Petrie, Duncan. *Screening Europe: Image and Identity in Contemporary European Cinema.* London: BFI, 1992.
Puttnam, David. *Movies and Money.* New York: Knopf, 1998.

Iranian cinema

Dabashi, Hamid. *Close Up: Iranian Cinema, Past, Present, and Future.* London: Verso, 2001.
Iranian New Cinema. Tehran: Farabi Cinema Foundation, 1998.
Issa, Rose, and Sheila Whitaker, eds. *Life and Art: The New Iranian Cinema.* London: National Film Theatre, 1999.
Issari, Mohammad Ali. *Cinema in Iran, 1900–1979.* Metuchen, NJ: Scarecrow Press, 1989.
Maghsoudlou, Bahman. *Iranian Cinema.* New York: Hagop Kevorkian Center for Near Eastern Studies, New York University, 1987.
Tapper, Richard, ed. *New Iranian Cinema: Politics, Representation, and Identity.* New York: Palgrave/I.B. Tauris Publishers, 2002.

JOURNALS, print or online: *Cinema Iran, Iran Media.*

Scottish cinema

Bruce, David. *Scotland the Movie.* Edinburgh: Polygon, 1996.
Dick, Eddie, ed. *From Limelight to Satellite: A Scottish Film Book.* London: British Film Institute, Scottish Film Council, 1990.
Fifty Years of Scottish Cinema, 1896–1946. Educational Film Bulletin, 1946.
Petrie, Duncan J. *Screening Scotland.* London: BFI, 2000.

JOURNALS, print or online: *Inside Out Film, Scottish Screen.*

Belgian cinema

Mosley, Philip. *Split Screen: Belgian Cinema and Cultural Identity.* Albany: State University of New York Press, 2001.

JOURNALS, print or online: *Cinopsis, Linkline: Cinema.*

Spanish cinema

Deveny, Thomas G. *Cain on Screen: Contemporary Spanish Cinema.* Metuchen, NJ: Scarecrow Press, 1993.

D'Lugo, Marvin. *Guide to the Cinema of Spain.* Westport, CT: Greenwood, 1997.

Evans, Peter William, ed. *Spanish Cinema: The Auteurist Tradition.* Oxford, England: Oxford University Press, 1999.

Jordan, Barry, and Rikki Morgan-Tamosunas. *Contemporary Spanish Cinema.* New York: Manchester University Press, 1998.

Kinder, Marsha. *Refiguring Spain: Cinema, Media, Representation.* Durham, NC: Duke University Press, 1997.

Stone, Rob. *Spanish Cinema.* Harlow: Longman, 2001.

Talens, Jenaro, and Santos Zunzunegui, eds. *Modes of Representation in Spanish Cinema.* Minneapolis: University of Minnesota Press, 1998.

JOURNALS, print or online: *El Amante, Otrocampo.*

Brazilian cinema

Johnson, Randal, and Robert Stam, eds. *Brazilian Cinema.* New York: Columbia University Press, 1995.

King, John. *Magical Reels: A History of Cinema in Latin America.* London: Verso, 1990.

Martin, Michael T. *New Latin American Cinema.* Detroit: Wayne State University Press, 1997.

Pick, Zuzana M. *The New Latin American Cinema.* Austin: University of Texas Press, 1993.

Vieira, Jono Luiz, ed. *Cinema Novo and Beyond.* New York: Museum of Modern Art, 1998.

JOURNALS, print or online: *Cinema Brazil.*

Norwegian cinema

Cowie, Peter. *Scandinavian Cinema.* London: Tantivy Press, 1992.

– *Straight from the Heart: Modern Norwegian Cinema, 1971–1999.* Kristiansund: Kom Forlag, 1999.

JOURNALS, print or online: *Norwegian Filmlexicon, Journal of Norwegian Media Research.*

Israeli cinema

Kronish, Amy. *World Cinema: Israel.* Madison, NJ: Fairleigh Dickinson University Press, 1996.

Kronish, Amy, and Costel Safirman. *Israeli Film: A Reference Guide.* Westport, Conn.: Praeger, 2003.

Loshitzky, Yosefa. *Identity Politics on the Israeli Screen.* Austin: University of Texas Press, 2002.

JOURNALS, print or online: *Israeli Film DataBase.*

Taiwanese cinema

Berry, Chris. *Perspectives on Chinese Cinema.* 2nd ed. London: BFI, 1991.

Browne, Nick, Paul G. Pickowicz, Vivian Sobchack, and Esther Yau, eds. *New Chinese Cinemas: Forms, Identities, Politics.* New York: Cambridge University Press, 1996.

Lu, Sheldon Hsiao-peng. *Traditional Chinese Cinemas.* Honolulu: University of Hawaii Press, 1997.

Lu, Tonglin. *Confronting Modernity in the Cinema of Taiwan and Mainland China.* New York: Cambridge University Press, 2001.

Semsel, George S., Chen Xihe, and Xia Hong. *Film in Contemporary China.* Westport, CT: Praeger, 1993.

Silbertgeld, Jerome. *China into Film: Frames of Reference in Contemporary Chinese Cinema.* London: Reaktion Books, 1999.

Tam, Kwok-kan, and Wimal Dissanayake. *New Chinese Cinema.* New York: Oxford University Press, 1998.

Zhang, Yingjin, and Zhiwei Xiao. *Encyclopedia of Chinese Film.* New York: Routledge, 1998.

JOURNALS, print or online: *Asian Film Connections, Cinemaya, China's Screen.*

DIRECTORS

Vittorio De Sica

Curle, Howard, and Stephen Snyder, eds. *Vittorio De Sica: Contemporary Perspectives.* Toronto: University of Toronto Press, 2000.

Darretta, John. *Vittorio De Sica: A Guide to References and Resources.* Boston: G.K. Hall, 1983.

Atom Egoyan

Desbarats, Carole, Jacinto Lageira, Danielle Rivière, Paul Virilio, Jacqueline Liechenstein, and Patrick De Haas, eds. *Atom Egoyan.* Trans. Brian Holmes. Paris: Editions Dis Voir, 1993.

Abbas Kiarostami

Saeed-Vafa, Mehrnaz, and Jonathan Rosenbaum. *Abbas Kiarostami.* Urbana: University of Illinois Press, 2003.

Zhang Yimou

Zhang, Yimou. *Zhang Yimou: Interviews.* Ed. Frances Gateward. Jackson: University Press of Mississippi, 2001.

Roberto Rossellini

Bondanella, Peter E. *The Films of Roberto Rossellini.* New York: Cambridge University Press, 1993.
Brunette, Peter. *Roberto Rossellini.* Berkeley: University of California Press, 1996.
Rossi, Patrizio. *Roberto Rossellini: A Guide to References and Resources.* Boston: G.K. Hall, 1988.

David Lynch

Alexander, John. *The Films of David Lynch.* London: Letts, 1993.

Eric Rohmer

Crisp, C.G. *Eric Rohmer, Realist and Moralist.* Bloomington: Indiana University Press, 1988.

Paul Schrader

Schrader, Paul. *Schrader on Schrader.* Ed. Kevin Jackson. London: Faber, 1992.

Claude Chabrol

Austin, Guy. *Claude Chabrol.* New York: St Martin's Press, 1999.

Mario Monicelli

Caldiron, Orio. *Mario Monicelli.* Filmography by Franco Mariotti. Rome: Under the Auspices of the Ministry of Tourism and Entertainment, 1981.

Selected Directorial Filmographies

1   JAFAR PANAHI, born 1960 in Iran
    Dayereh [*The Circle*] (2000)
    Ayneh [*The Mirror*] (1997)
    Badkonak-E Sefid [*The White Balloon*] (1995)

2   MARTINE DUGOWSON, born 8 May 1958 in France
    Les Fantômes de Louba (2001)
    Portraits chinois [*Shadow Play*] (1996)
    Mina Tannenbaum (1994)

3   ATOM EGOYAN, born 1960 in Cairo, Egypt; raised in Armenia and Canada
    Ararat (2002)
    Felicia's Journey (1999)
    The Sweet Hereafter (1997)
    Exotica (1994)
    Calendar (1993)
    The Adjuster (1991)
    Speaking Parts (1989)
    Family Viewing (1988)
    Next Of Kin (1984)

4   ABBAS KIAROSTAMI, born 1940 in Tehran, Iran
    Ten (2002)
    ABC Africa (2001)
    Bad ma ra khabad bord [*The Wind Will Carry Us*] (1999)

Ta'm e Guilass [*A Taste of Cherry*] (1997)
Zire Darakhtan Zeyton [*Through the Olive Trees*] (1994)
Zendegi Va Digar Hich ... [*And Life Goes On ...*] (1992)
Nema-ye Nazdik [*Close-Up*] (1990)
Khaneh-Je Doost Kojast? [*Where Is the Friend's House?*] (1987)

5 SAMIRA MAKHMALBAF, born 1979 in Tehran, Iran
Blackboards (2000)
De appel [*The Apple*] (1998)

6 MAJID MAJIDI, born 1959 in Tehran, Iran
Baran [*Rain*] (2002)
Rang e Khoda [*The Color Of Paradise*] (1999)
Bacheha ye aseman [*The Children of Heaven*] (1997)
Pedar [*Father*] (1996)
Baduk (1992)

7 ERICK ZONCA, born 1956 in Orléans, France
The Little Thief (2000)
The Dreamlife of Angels (1998)

8 LYNNE RAMSAY, born 1969 in Glasgow, Scotland
Morvern Callar (2002)
Ratcatcher (1999)

9 ZHANG YIMOU, born 1950 in the city of Xi'an in mainland China
Xingfu Shiguang [*Happy Times*] (2000)
Wo de Fuqin Muqin [*The Road Home*] (2000)
Yi Ge Dou Buneng Shao [*Not One Less*] (1998)
You Hua Haohao Shuo [*Keep Cool*] (1997)
Yao a yao dao wai po qiao [*Shanghai Triad*] (1995)
Huozhe [*To Live*] (1994)
Qiu Ju da guansi [*The Story of Qiu Ju*] (1992)
Da Hongdeng Long Gaogao Gua [*Raise the Red Lantern*] (1991)
Ju Dou (1990)
Meizhou Bao Xingdong [*Operation Cougar*] (1989)
Hong Gaoliang [*Red Sorghum*] (1987)

10 NEIL LABUTE, born 19 March 1963 in Detroit, Michigan
The Shape of Things (2003)
Possession (2002)

A Summer Dress (1995)
Truth or Dare (1994)

21 TSAI MING-LIANG, born 1957 in Kuching, Malaysia
Ni Neibian Jidian [*What Time Is It There?*] (2001)
Dong [*The Hole*] (1998)
Last Dance (1998)
Heliu [*The River*] (1996)
Wo Xin Renshi de Pengyou [*My New Friends*] (1995)
Aiqing Wansui [*Vive l'amour*] (1994)
Ching Shao Nien Na Cha [*Rebels of the Neon God*] (1992)

22 STEPHEN FREARS, born 1941 in England
Liam (2001)
High Fidelity (2000)
The Hi-Lo Country (1998)
Mary Reilly (1996)
The Van (1996)
The Snapper (1993)
Hero (1992)
The Grifters (1990)
Dangerous Liaisons (1988)
Prick Up Your Ears (1987)
Sammy and Rosie Get Laid (1987)
The Hit (1985)
My Beautiful Laundrette (1985)
Gumshoe (1972)

23 BILL FORSYTH, born 1946 in Scotland
Being Human (1994)
Breaking In (1989)
Housekeeping (1987)
Comfort and Joy (1984)
Local Hero (1983)
Gregory's Girl (1981)
That Sinking Feeling (1979)

24 HANS PETTER MOLAND, born 1956 in Oslo, Norway
Aberdeen (2000)
Zero Kelvin (1996)
The Last Lieutenant (1994)

25 NANNI MORETTI, born 1953 in Brunico, Bolzano, Italy
   Stanza del figlio [*The Son's Room*] (2001)
   Aprile [*April*] (1998)
   Il Giorno della prima di Close Up [*Opening Day of Close-Up*] (1996)
   Caro Diario [*Dear Diary*] (1994)
   La Cosa [*The Thing*] (1990)
   Palombella Rossa [*Red Wood Pigeon*] (1989)
   La Messa è finita [*The Mass Is Ended*] (1985)
   Bianca [*Sweet Body of Bianca*] (1983)
   Sogni d'oro [*Sweet Dreams*] (1981)
   Ecce Bombo (1978)
   Io sono un autarchico [*I Am Self-Sufficient*] (1976)
   Cime parli, frate? (1974)
   Paté de bourgeois (1973)
   La Sconfitta (1973)

26 DANNY BOYLE, born 20 October 1956 in Manchester, England
   28 Days Later (2002)
   The Beach (2000)
   A Life Less Ordinary (1997)
   Trainspotting (1996)
   Shallow Grave (1995)

Index

Index

Eckhart, Aaron, 144
Eggeling, Viking, 5
Egoyan, Atom, xii, 40–1, 43–5, 48, 49, 106, 331
Eidel, Philippe, 210
8 ½, 252, 293
Eisenstein, Sergei, 293
Elephant Man, The, 153
Eliot, T.S., 293
Emerson, Ralph Waldo, 153
Emma, 104
Encore, 77
England: Caroline, 141; Commonwealth, 140; Restoration, 140
Eno, Brian, 246
Eraserhead, 151
Ershadi, Homayoun, 53, 60
Eugenides, Jeffrey, 202
Eureka, 243
Europe '51, 6, 132–5
Evans, Walker, 153
Everyone Says I Love You, 259
Everything You Always Wanted to Know about Sex . . . But Were Afraid to Ask, 251
Exotica, 40, 50

Falstaff (opera), 181
Family Viewing, 40
Farnsworth, Richard, xiv, 156, 161, 162
Farrokhzad, Forough, 127, 128
Fascism (Italian), 88
Fassbinder, Rainer Werner, 209, 216
Father, The, 73
Father, The (play), 254

Fear, Anxiety, and Depression, 145
Feizi, Salimeh, 92, 95
Fellini, Federico, 10, 221, 252, 293, 316
feminism, 201
fémis, La, 216
femme douce, Une, 56–7
Ferguson, Otis, 9
Fernández, Ana, 194, 195
Fernandez, Juan, 195
Ferri, Linda, 240
Feydeau, Georges, 180
Field, Todd, 242
Fifth Generation (Chinese filmmakers), 113
film: abstract, 5; acting, 67, 76, 83–4; adaptation, 292–314; and tragedy, 5; *auteurist* critics of, 13, 14; blindness in, 89–90; children in, 6, 22, 26, 27–8, 62, 83–4, 90; criticism, ix–x, xvii, 9–14; departures from traditional notions of character and empathy in, 6; Iranian, xii, xiv, 17, 21–6, 50; myth in, 7; nature in, 50; *noir*, 17; public nature of, 16, 90; qualities of, 6–7, 15; self-reflexivity in, 62; societies, 10; space as a character in, 5; surrealistic and expressionistic, 6;Western, 268–72; "white telephone," 88

Film Heritage (magazine), 11
Film International (magazine), 23
Filth and the Fury, 105
First Graders, 51
Five Easy Pieces, 267
Flanagan, Tommy, 111
Flavor of Green Tea over Rice, The, 57
Flirting with Disaster, 144
Flowers of Shanghai, 223
Fluxus, 186
Fonda, Henry, 298
Fool Moon (play), 321
Ford, John (playwright), 316
Ford, John, 13, 269, 270, 299
formalism (Soviet), 76, 84
Forsyth, Bill, 104, 110, 300, 301, 302, 303, 335
Foruzesh, Ebrahim, 27, 62
Four Hundred Blows, The, 10, 87, 105, 213, 224, 227
Four Steps in the Clouds, 85
Four Weddings and a Funeral, 104
Franciolini, Gianni, 85, 88
Francis, Freddie, 158, 162
Franco, Francisco, 187, 188
Frankie and Johnny, 76
Frears, Stephen, 310, 313, 314, 335
French, Brandon, 13
French Revolution, 312

348   Index